CITIZEN'S MANUAL

OF

Government and Law.

THE

CITIZEN'S MANUAL

OF

GOVERNMENT AND LAW:

COMPRISING

THE ELEMENTARY PRINCIPLES OF CIVIL GOVERNMENT; A PRACTICAL VIEW OF THE STATE GOVERNMENTS, AND OF THE GOVERNMENT OF THE UNITED STATES; A DIGEST OF COMMON AND STATUTORY LAW, AND OF THE LAW OF NATIONS; AND A SUMMARY OF PARLIAMENTARY RULES FOR THE PRACTICE OF DELIBERATIVE ASSEMBLIES.

BY ANDREW W. YOUNG,

AUTHOR OF "SCIENCE OF GOVERNMENT," "FIRST LESSONS IN CIVIL GOVERNMENT," "AMERICAN STATESMAN," ETC.

NEW EDITION REVISED AND ENLARGED.

NEW-YORK:
J. C. DERBY & N. C. MILLER,
5 SPRUCE STREET, TRIBUNE BUILDINGS,
1864.

PREFACE.

To preserve and transmit the blessings of civil and religious freedom, is the declared object of the people of the United States, in establishing their present form of government. The question, Will our liberties endure? has ever been one of deep solicitude to every true American patriot; a question to which different answers have been formed by different minds.

It is generally conceded, that no other system of government ever devised, is so well adapted to secure the objects for which all just governments are instituted, as our own. Its excellence alone, however, can not insure its duration. The grand element of its strength, is the public virtue and intelligence. Hence, the only well-founded hope of permanent political prosperity, lies in a general and an efficient system of education.

Education is an interest of high importance to the people under any form of government; but it is more especially so in this country, where the people are not only in theory the source of power, but in practice are actually called upon to take an efficient part in constituting and administering the government. The exercise of political power ought to be directed by an enlightened judgment. The right of suffrage can scarcely be esteemed a privilege to him who is incapable of exercising it with discretion. While the constitution gives as much weight to the vote of the uninformed and ignorant, as to that of the well-instructed and intelligent citizen, the sources of information should be as numerous and as widely extended as possible.

In accordance with this sentiment, much has been done in this country to diffuse the benefits of useful knowledge. Improved systems of education have been established, and provision has been made, in every state, to instruct the people at the public expense. And to increase the efficiency of the schools, many useful sciences, not formerly taught, have been introduced.

It is admitted, however, that the course of instruction is still materially defective. It does not sufficiently contemplate our youth as soon to become invested with the powers and privileges of freemen. To qualify them expressly for the discharge of their political duties, is not, to any considerable extent, made a special object of school instruction. Even in most of our seminaries, the science of civil government either finds no place in the course of study, or is regarded only as of secondary importance. The study of the Grecian and Roman antiquities, in many academies, supersedes the study of the principles of our own government. The constitutions, laws, manners and customs of Greece and Rome, are made subjects of regular study, while the study of the practical subjects of our own constitutional law, and the principles of our civil jurisprudence, which are applicable to the common concerns of life, is not admitted as a part of the academic course !

A similar defect exists in our common schools. To gratify a pride of learning, or a taste for philosophical inquiry, some of the more abstruse and speculative sciences are introduced, to the exclusion of those which subserve the practical purposes of life. For the same reasons, or from a wrong estimate of its relative importance, the study of government is kept out of the primary schools, in which nineteen-twentieths of our citizens receive all their education. Some portions of arithmetic, the higher mathematics, and certain other branches, are of far less practical benefit to the citizen, and can be better dispensed with, than a knowledge of his political rights and duties.

For some years past, however, this subject has received the attention of the friends of education ; and considerable progress has been made in this department of educational improvement, by the preparation and introduction of elementary treatises on civil government. To this object, the writer has devoted several years of arduous labor. Yet, a long time must necessarily elapse before the study of political science shall occupy its proper place in the educational course.

It has occurred to the author, that, while this study is thus gradually making its way into the schools, much may be done in another direction for the general diffusion of political knowledge. The young men who have completed their school education, and commenced, or are about to commence the business of life, constitute a large and interesting class of American citizens. Upon the manner in which they shall discharge their political duties, depends, in a great measure, the future destiny of this great and growing republic. A work especially adapted to their wants appears to be a desideratum ; to supply which, is the primary design of this volume.

Surely, every young man inspired with a just degree of patriotic pride, must desire to qualify himself for the intelligent discharge of his duties and responsibilities, whether as an elector or private citizen only, or as one called to take a more direct part in the administration of the government. It is certainly to be lamented, that so many should have become invested with the rights of freemen without an adequate knowledge of their political duties. Questions of public policy of vital interest, perhaps involving constitutional principles, and even liberty itself, are not unfrequently decided at the ballot-box, by those who have never given the constitution the slightest examination.

The exercise of the elective franchise is not merely a right; it is a duty. The theory of free government is, that the people are associated for the common good. Hence every citizen is bound to every other citizen, to exercise his political power, and to do it in such a manner as to promote the best good of the whole. He should therefore act intelligently. No citizen has a moral right to jeopard the interests of a whole community by a random vote. It is his duty to make up his own mind on all the great questions that arise in administering the government, and to bring to the settlement of these questions the aid of an enlightened judgment.

Although this work is especially commended to the attention of young men, adults also will find it adapted to their use. It contains much information on the various subjects of which it treats, to which the mass of our adult citizens have not hitherto had ready access. In the selection and preparation of the matter, the object has been to condense, within a suitable compass, the greatest possible amount of information on the subject of the rights and duties of citizens; and to make the work emphatically what its title imports, a "Manual of Government and Law." It is doubted whether any other book of equal size contains as much matter to which the citizen has occasion to refer in the common concerns of life

The study of this work is also commended to females. It has long been considered a striking defect in our system of education, that females are not more generally instructed in matters of business. Although they do not take an active part in public affairs, they would, if rightly educated, exert a far more powerful and salutary influence upon our national character and destiny. And the question is submitted, whether this knowledge would not prove a far more valuable acquirement than some of those accomplishments which form so large a part of a modern female education, and which are usually lost amidst the cares of married life. As mothers, guardians, and teachers, they could apply the knowledge here recommended to valuable purposes

This work presents several features which do not appear in any of the author's former works. For the better illustration of the principles of civil government, and to show, by contrast, the superiority of our own government, an outline is given of the forms of government of the principal countries of Europe, and some of the ancient republics. To young persons generally, and to adults of limited historical reading, this part of the work will be read with interest.

The Law of Nations, also, is a subject with which few of our citizens are familiar, owing, chiefly, to their not having ready access to treatises on international law. The principal laws which regulate the intercourse of nations being deemed interesting and useful, as well as appropriate in a work of this kind, a digest of the same is given.

Another addition is the summary of Parliamentary Rules for the government of deliberative assemblies. As almost every citizen participates in the deliberations of public meetings, this part of the work can scarcely fail to meet with general favor.

A prominent feature of the present edition is its historical reference to the national constitution. A history has been given of the principal causes and the successive steps which led to its formation, with sketches of the debates of the convention of framers, presenting the various and conflicting views entertained in that body on some of the more important provisions, especially those known as the "great compromises" of the constitution.

Appended to the body of the work are copious Notes, supplementary to the several chapters referred to. These

Notes consist, chiefly, of the special enactments of the several states on the various subjects to which they relate; and, together with the Synopsis of the constitutions of the several states, and other portions of the work, present an intelligible view of all the state governments.

The sketch of Political Parties, will especially interest young readers and others who are not familiar with the political history of this country.

The body of the work is divided into chapters and sections of suitable length, to increase its convenience for reference. These divisions also adapt it for use in schools. Although not designed as a class-book, it may be studied in academies and high schools generally, to advantage.

In the compilation of this volume, the leading object has been UTILITY. That it is free from errors, is hardly to be presumed; it is believed, however, that they are few and unimportant. If any shall be discovered, they will be corrected in future editions.

CONTENTS.

PRINCIPLES OF CIVIL GOVERNMENT.

STATE GOVERNMENTS.

CHAPTER XXVI.

CHAPTER XXVII.

CHAPTER XXVIII.

GOVERNMENT OF THE UNITED STATES.

CHAPTER XXIX.

CHAPTER XXX.

CHAPTER XXXI.

CHAPTER XXXII.

CHAPTER XXXIII.

CHAPTER XXXIV.

CHAPTER XXXV.

CHAPTER XXXVI.

CHAPTER XXXVII.

CHAPTER XXXVIII.

CHAPTER XXXIX.

COMMON AND STATUTORY LAW.

LAW OF NATIONS.

PARLIAMENTARY RULES.

CHAPTER LXIV.

CHAPTER LXV.

CHAPTER LXVI.

CHAPTER LXVII.

CHAPTER LXVIII.

CHAPTER LXIX.

CHAPTER LXX.

CHAPTER LXXI.

CITIZEN'S MANUAL.

PRINCIPLES OF CIVIL GOVERNMENT.

CHAPTER I.

CIVIL GOVERNMENT; MANKIND FITTED BY NATURE FOR CIVIL GOVERNMENT AND LAWS.

§ 1. By *civil government* is meant that form of rules by which the conduct of men in civil society is to be regulated; or it is the authority exercised in controlling or regulating the social actions of men according to certain established rules. A *society* is a number of persons united for some purpose; as a Bible society, a temperance society, an agricultural society. But the term *civil society* is applied to the inhabitants of a state or nation in their associate capacity.

§ 2. A *nation* or *state* is a large society of men united for the purpose of promoting their mutual safety and happiness. And in order the more effectually to carry out their purpose, they agree to be governed by certain rules. This agreement between the people of a state, is sometimes called the *civil compact*; the word *compact* signifying contract or agreement. The nature of this agreement is, that each individual of the society shall do for the others everything which their necessities require, and which he can perform without neglecting the duties he owes to himself.

§ 3. Although the term civil society, in its most comprehensive sense, may apply to any people whose conduct toward each other is regulated by customs, usages, or rules of any kind ; civil society is generally considered to exist only where the people are in a *civilized* state, or state of social improvement, and are governed by established written rules and regulations. By civilization and social improvement is meant refinement of manners and advancement in knowledge. Wherever the people enjoy the benefits of learning, and other means of improving their social condition, or of making themselves more comfortable and happy, they are called civilized ; and the system or form of rules by which such people are governed, or the authority exercised in making and enforcing these rules, is called *civil government.*

§ 4. The rules by which the conduct of men in civil society is to be regulated, are called *laws;* as the commands of a parent or householder are the laws of the family, or as the rules of a teacher are the laws of the school. A law is therefore a rule prescribing what men are to do, or forbidding what they are not to do ; and implies the right and authority of those who govern to make the law, and the duty of the governed to obey the law.

§ 5. The necessity of civil government arises from the nature and condition of mankind. Man is a social being ; that is, he is fitted by nature for society. The Creator has given to all men a disposition to associate with each other, and made their happiness depend, in a great measure, upon such association. They derive from the social state a degree of pleasure which they could not enjoy if each one lived by himself.

§ 6. But man is so formed as to need the assistance of creatures like himself to preserve his own being. We can hardly imagine how a person could procure the necessaries of life without such assistance. But men have the gifts of reason and speech. By conversation with their fellow-beings, they are enabled to improve their reason and extend their knowledge, and to find out the means of satisfying their wants, and of improving their social condition.

§ 7. But although men need the assistance of each other, they are so formed that each must have the care of himself. By this arrangement in society, which obliges each one to provide for his own wants, a greater amount of labor is performed, a greater number cared for, and the general welfare better secured, than would be done if each were required to labor for the common benefit. From this arrangement comes the right of property. If the avails of each man's labor should go into a common stock for the use and benefit of all, there would be nothing that any one could call his own. But if each is to provide for himself, he must have a right to appropriate the fruits of his labor to his own use.

§ 8. Again, all men in society have wants; but these wants can be rightfully gratified only so far as it can be done consistently with the rights of others; for it is a fundamental principle in civil society, that the rights of all are entitled to equal respect. Hence we see the necessity of some established rules by which every man may be protected in the free enjoyment of whatsoever justly belongs to him.

§ 9. We see also that men are fitted for civil government and laws. They have power to discern their own wants, and the wants of their fellow-men; to perceive what is right and what is wrong; and to know that they ought to do what is right, and forbear to do what is wrong. Their reason enables them to understand the meaning of laws, and to discover what laws are necessary to regulate the actions of men.

§ 10. It is the opinion of some, that if all men in their social intercourse were actuated only by feelings of pure good will, and a sincere regard for each other's rights and welfare, laws for their government would be unnecessary. But with the aid of all the powers of reason and judgment which the Creator has bestowed upon men, they are incapable, in their present imperfect state, of determining in all cases what is right or wrong. Hence we conclude, that, with the best intentions of men to do right, laws would be necessary to declare what shall be considered just between man and man, and to enforce obedience to those laws.

§ 11. To give force to a law, it must have a penalty. *Penalty* is the pain or suffering inflicted upon a person for breaking a law; as, imprisonment or a fine is the penalty for stealing; hanging is the penalty for murder. If no penalties were annexed to laws, men could not be compelled to obey them; bad men would commit the worst crimes without fear; life and property would be unsafe; and general disorder would prevail in society.

CHAPTER II.

RIGHTS AND LIBERTY, AND LAWS, DEFINED.

§ 1 The object of civil government, as has been observed, is to secure to the members of a community the free enjoyment of their rights. A *right* is the just claim or lawful title which we have to anything. Hence we say, a person has a right to what he has earned by his labor, or bought with his money. Having thus acquired it, it is lawfully and justly his own, and no other person has a right to it. We have also a right to do as we please, and to go where we please, if in so doing we do not trespass upon the rights of others: for all men in society have the same rights; and no one has a right to disturb others in the enjoyment of their rights.

§ 2. The being free to enjoy what belongs to us, or to do as we please, is called *liberty*. The words *right* and *liberty*, however, have not the same meaning. We may have a right to a thing when we have not the liberty of enjoying or using it. John has a pencil which is justly his own; but James takes it from him by force. John's liberty to enjoy the use of his pencil is lost, but his right to it remains.—James has no right to the pencil, though he enjoys the use of it.

§ 3. All laws ought to be so made as to secure to men the liberty to enjoy and exercise their natural rights. *Natural rights* are those to which we are entitled by nature, rights with which we are born. Every person is born with a right to live, and freely to enjoy the fruits of his labor, and whatsoever is justly his own. Hence liberty itself is a natural right; that is, it is ours by nature, or by birth, and can not be rightfully taken from us.

§ 4. Some rights are also called *inalienable*. This term is often applied to natural rights in general. But in its strict and proper sense, it means only rights which a person can not lawfully or justly alienate and transfer to another; that is, rights which can not be parted with and passed over to another, by one's *own act*. But natural and inalienable rights may be forfeited by crime. By stealing, a man loses his right to liberty, and is justly imprisoned. If he commits murder, he forfeits his right to life, and lawfully suffers death.

§ 5. Rights and liberty are sometimes called *civil rights* and *civil liberty.* It may be asked, Wherein do these differ from *natural* rights and liberty? Rights and liberty may, at the same time, be both natural and civil. Speaking of them as being ours by nature, or by birth, we call them natural; when they are spoken of as being secured to us by civil government and laws, they are called civil. John's right to his pencil, being secured to him by the laws of civil society, is a *civil* right. It is at the same time a *natural* right, because, by the law of nature, he is born with a right to the free use of his property.

§ 6. Some consider natural liberty to consist in the freedom to do in all things as we please, without regard to the interests of our fellow-men; and that, on entering into civil society, we agree to give up a portion of our natural rights to secure the remainder, and for the good of other members of the society. But if mankind are by nature fitted and designed for the social state, and are all entitled to equal rights, then natural liberty does not consist in being free to say or to do whatever our evil passions may prompt us to do. To rob and to plunder may be the natural right of the tiger; but it is not the natural right of men. Natural rights and natural liberty are such only as are conferred by the law of nature, which forbids our doing whatever is inconsistent with the rights of others.

§ 7. The law of nature is the will of the Creator. It is called the law of nature, because it is a perfect rule of conduct for all moral and social beings; a rule which is right in itself, right in the nature of things, and which would be right and ought to be obeyed, if no other law or positive command had ever been given. It is right in itself that all men should have the liberty of enjoying the use of what is their own; and it would be right that we should give to every one his due, if we had never been commanded to do so.

§ 8. The law of nature is the rule of conduct which we are bound to observe toward our Maker and our fellow-men, by reason of our *natural relations* to them. Mankind being dependent upon their Creator, they owe him duties which they ought to perform, though he had never positively enjoined these duties. To serve our Creator is a duty which arises out of the relation we sustain to him. So the relation between parent and child renders it fit and proper that children obey their parents, on whom they are dependent for protection and support. And from our relations to our fellow-men, on whom also we are in a measure dependent, and who have the same rights as ourselves, it is our duty to promote their happiness as well as our own, by doing to them as we would that they should do to us. This is required by the law of nature.

§ 9. But if the law of nature is the rule by which mankind ought to regulate their conduct, it may be asked, Of what use are written laws? Mankind are not capable of discovering, in all cases, what the law of nature requires. It has therefore pleased Divine Providence to reveal his will to mankind, to instruct them in their duties to himself and to each other. This will is revealed in the Holy Scriptures, and is called the *law of revelation*, or the *Divine law*.

§ 10. But although men have the Divine law for their guide, human laws also are necessary. The Divine law is broad, and comprehends rules to teach men their whole duty; but it does not specify every particular act of duty; much of it consists of general principles to which particular acts must be made to conform. God has commanded men to do right, and to deal justly with each other; but men do not always agree as to what is right: human laws are therefore necessary to regulate the conduct of men. And these laws are written that it may always be known what they are.

§ 11. Again, it may be asked, What must be done when a human law does not agree with the Divine law? Must the human law be obeyed? A law clearly contrary to the law of God, we are not bound to obey. We may not, however, disobey a law simply because it does not require what is strictly just between men. A law may be very imperfect, as many human laws are, and yet we ought to obey it, and may do sc without breaking the Divine law. It is sometimes difficult to determine whether human laws and the Divine law agree. Hence the importance of having the laws made by wise and good men.

CHAPTER III.

DIFFERENT FORMS OF GOVERNMENT.—MONARCHY; ARISTOCRACY; DEMOCRACY; REPUBLIC.

§ 1. The people of all civilized countries live under government and laws; but their several modes and forms of government are very unlike; that is, the power or authority to govern is not in all countries placed in the same class of persons, nor exercised in the same manner.

§ 2. The governing power of a state or kingdom is usually called the *sovereign* or *supreme power*. Hence, where kings rule, they are called sovereign; and where the power is in the hands of the people, the people are sovereign. In the strict sense of the term, however, entire sovereignty, or supreme power, exists only where power is exercised by one man, or a single body of men, uncontrolled or unrestrained by laws, or by any other power. But in a more general sense, it is that power in a state which is superior to all other powers within the same.

§ 3. A form of government in which the supreme power is in the hands of one person, is called a *monarchy*. The word *monarch* is from two Greek words, *monos*, sole or only, and *arkos*, a chief; and is a general name for a single ruler, whether he is called king, emperor, or prince. A government in which all power resides in or proceeds from one person, is an *absolute monarchy*. If the power of the monarch is restrained by laws, or by some other power, it is called a *limited monarchy*.

§ 4. A *monarchy* is called *hereditary* in which the throne passes from father to son, or from the monarch to his successor, by inheritance. On the death of the sovereign, the eldest son is usually heir to the crown; or if there is no son, it falls to the daughter, or some other relative. A monarchy is *elective*, where, on the death of the ruler, his successor is appointed by an election. A few such monarchies have existed.

§ 5. Absolute monarchies are sometimes called *despotisms*. The word *despot* is from the Greek language, and means *master* or *lord*. It has nearly the same meaning as *tyrant*, which also is from the Greek, and signifies *king*. Originally these words meant simply a single ruler. But as unlimited power in the hands of one man has been so generally abused, these words have come to be used in an odious sense. They are now applied, for the most part, to rulers who exercise authority over their subjects with severity; and any government so administered as to oppress the people, is said to be despotic, or tyrannical. In an absolute despotism, the monarch has entire control over his subjects. They have no law but the will of the ruler, who has at command a large force of armed men to keep his people in subjection. The governments of many of the nations of Europe and Asia have always been of this description. Changes in some of them have occasionally taken place, but without any material improvement in the condition of the people.

§ 6. Governments called *aristocracies* have also existed; though no government, properly so called, is believed to exist at the present time. The word *aristocracy* is from the Greek words, *aristos*, best, and *kratos*, power, or *krateo*, to govern; and means a *government of the best.* Hence it has been used to designate a government in which the supreme power is in the hands of a few persons of rank and wealth. The word aristocracy is also used for the nobility of a country under a monarchical government. *Nobles* are persons of rank above the common people, and bear some title of honor. The titles of the English nobility are those of duke, marquis, earl, viscount, and baron. These titles are hereditary, being derived from birth. In some cases they are conferred upon persons by the king.

§ 7. Another form of government is a *democracy*. This word also is from the Greek: *demos*, the people, and *krateo*, to govern, or *kratos*, power; and signifies a *government of the people.* In a government purely democratic, the great body of freemen meet in one assembly to make laws, and to transact the public business. In ancient Greece there were a few governments of this kind; but they necessarily comprised small territories, scarcely more than a single town. All the citizens of a large community could not meet in a single assembly.

§ 8. The form of government in this country is different from all those which have been described. It is republican. A *republic* is a government in which the people enjoy common rights and privileges. Hence the name of *commonwealth* is sometimes applied to a republic ; as a thing is said to be *common* when it is enjoyed by persons in general. Sometimes this name is given to a state of this Union, as, the "commonwealth of Massachusetts ;" the "commonwealth of Pennsylvania." Every state in the Union is a republic.

§ 9. In a republic, the political power is with the people, as in a democracy. The words republic and democracy have, therefore, nearly the same meaning. Our government, though democratic, is not such a democracy as has been described. In a republic like ours, the laws, instead of being made by the people in a body, as in a pure democracy, are made by a small number of men called representatives, who are chosen by the people for that purpose.

§ 10. The government of this country is therefore a *representative government*, or a *representative democracy;* or it may with propriety be called a *democratic republic.* A representative is a person chosen or employed by others to make known their wishes, and to transact their business. He is therefore an agent. The word *agent,* however, more frequently denotes a person intrusted with the private business of another ; the term *representative* is generally used to designate one who is chosen to assist in enacting laws.

§ 11. Although most of the powers of government in this country are exercised by representatives, instead of the people in person, as in a simple democracy, our government is equally free, because the power to govern is derived from the people, and the government is such as they have chosen for themselves.

CHAPTER IV.

GOVERNMENTS OF RUSSIA, TURKEY, SPAIN, DENMARK.

§ 1. Having defined the different forms of government, as distinguished by the general names of monarchy, aristocracy, democracy, and republic, we proceed to give a description of the governments of some of the principal nations of

Europe and America, in which these several principles are illustrated. From this description it will appear, that very few of these governments are either wholly monarchical, aristocratical, or democratic; but that, in most of them, some or all of these several principles are combined.

§ 2. Of the class of monarchies called absolute or despotic, the government of Russia is one. The power of the emperor, or czar, is hereditary. The people have no part in the government, but are subject to the will of the sovereign. The monarch can make laws and repeal them at pleasure. He can make war or peace; raise armies and levy taxes; and he confers privileges and titles of honor upon whomsoever he pleases. He commands the nobles, and has their property directly or indirectly at his disposal. He is restrained, however, in the severity of his rule, by the fear of forfeiting his life, as was the case of one of his predecessors. The autocrat, (as he is sometimes called,) also has control of ecclesiastical matters. He must be of the Greek religion.

§ 3. In the government of an empire so extensive, there must be, as in other governments, several departments, and a large number of officers intrusted with some powers; but as they receive their appointment, directly or indirectly, from the emperor himself, and hold their offices at his pleasure, they have no material check upon his power. He has, for example, a directing senate, of sixty-two members, divided into departments; but the members being nominated by the monarch, and subject to his will, they serve little other purpose than that of promulgating his *ukases*, or decrees. The laws of an absolute ruler are usually called edicts, decrees, or ordinances.

§ 4. The great body of the nation is divided into the two extreme classes of nobles and slaves; the middle classes being less numerous. Many of the Russian nobles boast of high birth. The fortunes of some of them are enormous Their estates are estimated, not so much by the amount of their lands and rents, as by the number of slaves. The head of a certain family, reckoned the richest, is said to have owned 125,000! The slaves form the great mass of the people. They have no political rights. They are subject to the will of their masters, and may be scourged at pleasure by their masters, who are not brought to justice for excessive severity, unless death be produced within twenty-four hours. All the profits earned by the slave belong to the master; though it is not uncommon for the master to allow the slave a proportion.

§ 5. There are courts of justice in Russia; but they are too liable to be corrupted to administer justice at all times impartially. As a punishment, the knout is administered even to nobles of the highest rank who may have displeased their sovereign. The *knout* is a leather strap, with which stripes are inflicted upon the bare back! The sovereign power, however, is said to be exercised at present with considerable mildness; and the condition of the people is improving.

§ 6. The Turkish monarchy is still more despotic than that of Russia. All departments of the government, civil, military, and religious, are under the control of one man, called *sultan*, or *grand seignior*. The powers of government, however, instead of being exercised by the monarch himself, are devolved upon the *vizier*, the chief magistrate of state, assisted by a council of men called the *divan*. The vizier appoints all civil and military officers; and he may put to death all who oppose his measures. In war he commands the army in person, leaving at court in his absence a pacha, (pashaw.)

§ 7. The subjects of the sultan are taught to believe that their sovereign reigns by divine commission; that is, that he derives his right to rule from the Supreme Ruler of the world; and that nothing which he can do is morally wrong. Hence, they regard submission to their master as a religious duty. They consider him to be the proprietor of all the lands in his dominions, except such as are dedicated to pious uses. The *koran* is the fundamental law of the empire. The *koran* or *alcoran* is the Mohammedan book of faith written by Mohammed, or Mahomet.

§ 8. Of the absolute governments of Europe, the two which have been described are the most despotic, and have perhaps undergone the least change. Property and life, however, though not protected by written constitutions and laws in which the people have a voice, are tolerably secure; the ruler being restrained in the exercise of his power through fear of provoking his subjects to rebellion. Still, we can account for the abject submission of the people, only by supposing them to be under the influence of religious fear or superstition, and too ignorant to know that they can be in a better condition.

§ 9. The kingdom of Spain is a hereditary monarchy, and is usually called a despotism. Its government, *in form*, somewhat resembles a limited monarchy, there being a legislature to assist in making the laws ; but it is, in effect, perhaps, the most despotic of any in Europe, except those of Russia and Turkey.

§ 10. The legislature, called the *cortes*, consists of two houses, the peers and the deputies. The house of peers is an aristocratic body, composed in part of hereditary members, and in part of members named by the king for life ; thus being wholly independent of the people. The deputies are elected by a college of electors, who are chosen by the principal citizens ; the great body of the people having no voice in the election, and consequently no representation in the legislature. A legislature thus constituted, must be presumed to have a stronger sympathy with the sovereign than with the people. As every measure proposed by the cortes must receive the monarch's sanction before it can become a law ; and as the principal officers derive their authority from him, and are under his direction ; there can be little restraint upon absolute power.

§ 11. The kingdom of Denmark is an absolute monarchy, and the crown is hereditary. The Danish kings, though invested with supreme power, have exercised their authority with mildness. The nobles are not numerous, consisting only of one duke, nineteen counts, and twelve barons. The king himself presides at the supreme national tribunal. The great body of the people were not long since in a state of personal slavery. Their condition, though still poor and depressed, is improving.

CHAPTER V.

GOVERNMENT OF GREAT BRITAIN.

§ 1. Although a monarchy is literally a government of one man, some governments are called monarchies in which the authority of the prince is restrained by laws, and a part of the supreme power is in other hands, or in which the people have some voice. These, as has been observed, are *limited monarchies*, or *mixed governments*, partaking of the nature of both a monarchy and a free government.

§ 2. The kingdom of Great Britain is a limited monarchy, and the crown is hereditary. Its government is perhaps more liberal than any other government of the kind, and its people are more enlightened and better governed. It is the country of our ancestors, by whom many of the fundamental principles of civil liberty were introduced and established here.

§ 3. The manner in which the powers of government are divided and distributed among the different classes of officers, as well as the manner in which these powers are exercised, is much the same under the British constitution as under our own. One of the principal defects of that government consists in the limitation of political rights. The people have not the right of forming and adopting a constitution or form of government for themselves ; and they have but a limited voice in the election of any upon whom the administration of the government devolves.

§ 4. The legislative or law-making power is vested in the parliament, consisting of the house of lords and the house of commons. Proposed laws, or *bills*, as they are called, are framed and completed in the two houses ; the king taking no part in the enactment of laws other than that of signing them. No bill can become a law if the king refuses to sign it. When the king refuses to sanction a proposed law, he is said to *negative* the bill. The power thus to prevent the enactment of a law, is called the *veto* power ; *veto* being a Latin word, signifying *I forbid.* This is a very dangerous power in the hands of one who is disposed to abuse it. No king of Great Britain, however, has exercised this power for more than a hundred years. The veto power, in a qualified form, exists to some extent in the United States. (See Chap. XV, § 13, 14.)

§ 5. The house of lords is composed of the lords spiritual and temporal of England ; sixteen temporal peers of Scotland ; one archbishop, three bishops, and twenty-eight temporal peers of Ireland. *Peer,* literally, means an equal. The house of peers was so called because noblemen and barons were originally considered equal companions of the king. In England, persons belonging to the five degrees of nobility, dukes, marquises, earls, viscounts, and barons, are all peers. The lords spiritual are, for England, two archbishops and twenty-four bishops ; and for Ireland, one archbishop and three bishops. The lords temporal are not limited in number; the king having the right to appoint to the peerage any persons whom he thinks deserving. In 1833, the house of lords included 426 members.

§ 6. The house of commons is composed of representatives of the people. The right to the office is not enjoyed to the same extent as it is in this country. A person to be eligible as a member, must be the owner of a freehold estate of considerable amcunt. A *freehold,* or real estate, is property in lands, which a person may hold in his own right, and transmit to his heirs. Also the right of voting for representatives is restricted. To be a qualified voter, a man must occupy a house rated at £10, (nearly $50,) a year. Hence, a large portion of the citizens have no voice in the election of representatives.

§ 7. The duration of a parliament is seven years. It has the sole right of making, altering, or amending all the laws ; and by its authority alone can taxes be imposed or levied. Parliament meets annually. It usually commences its sessions in January or February, and continues them about six months.

§ 8. The powers of the king of Great Britain are large and numerous. Although he alone can not make laws as an absolute ruler, he can, as has been observed, defeat the passage of all laws. A parliament can not be held, unless it is convoked by him ; nor can it, except by him, be dissolved or prorogued. *Prorogue* means to prolong, also to delay ; hence, to delay the business of parliament by continuing the parliament from one session to another, as by adjournment. To prorogue parliament, therefore, is the same as to stop or put off its action by dismissing the body. This the king can do at any time. He has the power to create officers of state, ministers, judges, and other officers, and, in certain cases, to pardon persons convicted of crimes. He has also power to make war and peace.

§ 9. These powers, however, find a check in the control which the representatives of the people hold over the public purse. The money to maintain armies and fleets, to carry on war, and to pay the salaries of his officers, can not be obtained without the consent of parliament. He has the sole right to assemble parliaments; but he is required by law to assemble a parliament as often as once in three years. And though he is the head of the church, he can not alter the established religion, nor can he call persons to account for their religious opinions.

§ 10. The king has a privy council, appointed by himself, who are bound by oath to advise him to the best of their judgment, and with secrecy. This council inquires into all offenses against the government, and has power to put the offenders in safe keeping for trial in some of the courts of law. The privy council itself acts as a court in certain cases.

§ 11. The king has also a large number of officers of state, (about thirty,) appointed by himself, to conduct the business of state. Of these ministers he selects a number, (twelve, it is believed,) to constitute what is called a *cabinet council.* This council usually consists of those officers of state who are intrusted with the most important executive business, and are his responsible advisers. The duties of these executive officers are similar to those of the heads of departments in the government of the United States, who are called the president's cabinet. *Cabinet* is a select number of confidential counselors, who advise with the executive in matters of government.

§ 12. The courts of justice in Great Britain, and the manner in which justice is administered by them, are nearly the same as in the United States. The judgment of British courts has always been considered high authority in this country.

CHAPTER VI.

GOVERNMENTS OF FRANCE, GERMANY, AUSTRIA, HUNGARY, PRUSSIA, NETHERLANDS, SWEDEN, GREECE, SWITZERLAND, SOUTH AMERICAN STATES.

§ 1. The government of France, formerly almost purely despotic, was, by the revolution of 1830, changed into a limited monarchy, similar to that of Great Britain. Another revolution took place in 1848, which resulted in the establishment of a republic. Again, in 1851, the government was changed into one highly monarchical; but with no strong probability of its being permanent. The constitution, though adopted by the people, was dictated by the president of the republic himself, who, while he retained to himself the title of president, and to the government that of republic, was invested with the powers of a dictator rather than the limited powers of a republican president.

§ 2. The president was elected for the term of ten years. But not satisfied with a limited term of office, he, the next year, by some public announcement, declared himself emperor for life, subject, however, to the will of the people, which he succeeded in obtaining. The crown is hereditary in the male line only, and by right of primogeniture; that is, by right of being the first born son.

§ 3. The division and distribution of the powers of government, it is believed, were not essentially altered at the time of this change of the tenure of the executive office.—The emperor governs by means of the ministers, a council of state, a senate, and a legislative body. The ministers and the council of state are both dependent on the emperor for their offices. The ministerial departments amount to nine; namely, the minister of state and of the household of the emperor; the ministers of justice; of foreign affairs; of finance; of the interior; of war; of marine and the colonies; of agriculture and the public works; and of religion and public instruction. They, as well as persons employed by the state, take an oath of obedience to the constitution and of fidelity to the emperor.

§ 4. The legislative power is exercised by the president, the senate, and the legislative body. The senate is composed of cardinals, marshals, and admirals, and of such other citizens as the president deems fit to elevate to the dignity of senator. Senators may not be removed from office; and they hold their offices for life. The number of senators may not exceed 150.

§ 5. The legislative body, (if the constitution of the same has not been altered,) consists of deputies elected by the people, one deputy being allowed to every 35,000 electors. They are chosen for the term of six years. Neither the deputies nor the senators receive a salary. The president, however, may make the senators a discretionary personal donation, not exceeding 30,000 francs yearly. The privilege of voting in the election of members of the legislative body is not limited, as in Great Britain; but it extends to all male citizens.

§ 6. The laws, instead of being proposed by the legislative body, as in republics and in limited monarchies generally, originate with the emperor; who sends projects of laws to the legislative body for discussion. The president and vice-president of the senate, taken from the senators, and the president and vice-president of the legislative body or house of deputies, chosen from this house, are named by the emperor; and he also, by decree, fixes the salaries of these presiding officers. When he thinks fit, he himself presides over the senate and council of state. He may also, at pleasure, convoke and prorogue the senate; and convoke, prorogue, and dissolve the legislative body; but if he shall dissolve this body, he is bound to convoke a new one within six months.

§ 7. Besides the powers already mentioned, the emperor has power to pardon and grant amnesties; to command the land and sea forces; declare war, and make treaties of peace; to order works of public utility; and to make the rules and decrees for executing the laws. Hence it appears, that few monarchs possess more ample and more numerous powers than the emperor of France.

§ 8. The system of provincial government throughout France is simple and effective. The kingdom is at present divided into 86 departments, with their capital towns. These departments are sub-divided into 363 arrondissements, or districts, 2847 cantons, 36,835 communes. In each department the prefect is the chief magistrate, and, as well as the sub-prefect, is paid by government in proportion to the population and the extent of his jurisdiction; the salary varying from 40,000 to 10,000 francs a year, whilst that of the sub-prefect is 4000 francs.

§ 9. The government of Germany is not easily described. It is particularly complicated, chiefly on account of the great number and variety of the states of which it consists. It comprises about forty states, two of which are parts of the Austrian empire and the kingdom of Prussia. These two comprise a greater portion of the territory and population than all the rest. All the states have distinct and separate governments of their own. Of the smaller states, the leading ones are limited monarchies; some of which partake strongly of the monarchical and aristocratic features.

§ 10. The Germanic states are united in a confederation somewhat similar to the union of our American states. The confederacy has a kind of legislature called *diet*, consisting of deputies from each particular state. The office of the diet is to preserve the security of Germany, and to regulate the relations of the empire with foreign nations. Its object is also to preserve the independence and safety of its particular states, and to settle the disputes which may arise between one state and another; but it does not interfere with the internal regulations of any.

§ 11. Austria is a hereditary monarchy, almost absolute. The title of the sovereign is *emperor*. In most of the countries subject to Austria, there are legislative assemblies, called *states*. These assemblies consist of four orders or houses: clergy, nobles, knights, and representatives of the free cities. But the states impose no material check upon the monarch; their assembling being mainly for the sake of form, and for giving some assistance in the administration.

§ 12. Hungary is a member of the Austrian empire, and is a hereditary kingdom. The crown is held in the house of Austria. The Hungarian diet consists of four orders: the bishops and abbots; the magistrates or great nobles; the knights; and the representatives of the free cities. The diet assembles every three years, and sits during the king's pleasure. If three of the orders agree to any proposition, the fourth must give its consent. Without the consent of the diet, the king can not make or change the laws, impose taxes, or levy troops. The great body of the people, however, have but little share in the administration of the government, and are heavily burdened with taxation. An attempt was made some years since to revolutionize the government, but without success.

§ 13. The government of Prussia, though not an absolute monarchy, is not so far removed from it as are some other limited monarchies. Each of the several provinces of the kingdom has a legislative assembly. The power of these assemblies, however, is very limited. They can not originate any project of a law: they merely deliberate upon those proposed by the king. But no change in the laws can be made, nor a new tax imposed, without their sanction.

§ 14. The kingdom of the Netherlands, comprising the two former separate kingdoms of Holland and Belgium, is a limited monarchy. The legislative power of Holland is vested in two houses, or chambers, called the *states-general.* The upper house does not consist of hereditary nobles, as in Great Britain and some other limited monarchies, but in a council of from forty to sixty members, named by the king for life. The other house is a representative body elected for three years, one-third of their number being elected every year. The Belgian chambers are both elective; the senate, or upper house, for eight years, and the representative chamber for four years.

§ 15. Sweden is a limited monarchy. The legislature, called the diet, consists of four orders or houses: the nobles, the clergy, the peasants, and the burghers. The house of nobles consists of 1200 members; the head of each noble family being, by inheritance, its lawful representative. The house of clergy consists of the archbishop and all the bishops. The house of peasants is composed of the representatives of the numerous little proprietors of land who cultivate their own ground. The burghers are chosen by the towns; every freeman who pays taxes having a vote.

§ 16. The king has ample powers. He appoints all officers, civil and military. His assent is necessary to all laws proposed by the diet. He is not obliged to convoke the diet oftener than once in five years, or to continue its sittings longer than three months; but he may make the meetings more frequent and longer. No tax can be levied, or loan obtained, without the consent of the diet.

§ 17. Norway is united with Sweden in the same kingdom. The legislature of Norway, called the *storthing*, has greater privileges than the Swedish diet. The length and frequency of its meetings are not controlled by the king.—His consent to a proposed law is not necessary after it has been three times presented by the storthing. The number and influence of the nobles in Norway is not great, and a republican spirit prevails among the people.

§ 18. Greece is a constitutional monarchy. At an early period, the different little states of Greece threw off the yoke of their tyrants, as they then called them, and erected themselves into independent republics. The conquest by Rome terminated their political existence. The conquest by the Ottomans (Turks) finally extinguished in Greece all that remained of her ancient greatness. Since then she has made several attempts to regain her independence. In 1820, a grand insurrection against the Ottoman government took place; and after a severe struggle, the Turkish sovereign was expelled, and the Porte (the Turkish government) was obliged to consent to the independence of those portions of Greece which were the most Grecian.

§ 19. Switzerland is an independent state, and its government is probably the most democratic in Europe. It is divided into twenty-two cantons, each of which has a particular constitution of its own, though all are united by a federal government. This Union is sometimes called the *Helvetic confederacy*, from Helvetia, the former name of the country. The Helvetic diet consists of deputies from the different cantons, who meet once a year. Extra meetings may also be called on the demand of any five cantons. This assembly does not interfere with the internal affairs of the cantons; its action is confined to what concerns the foreign relations and general defense of the country.

§ 20. There are numerous other countries in Europe, whose governments we shall pass over without notice. Those which have been described embrace almost every shade of monarchy, from the most absolute to that which approximates most nearly to a republic; and present a sufficiently full view of the political institutions of that portion of the world to answer the purpose for which they have been described.

§ 21. The South American states and Mexico, were formerly subject to Spain. At an early period in the present century, a general revolution took place in these Spanish provinces, by which their independence was established.—The form of government adopted by them is, in its general features, similar to that of the United States.

CHAPTER VII.

THE NATURE AND OBJECTS OF A CONSTITUTION, AND THE MANNER IN WHICH IT IS MADE.

§ 1. From the foregoing view of the different forms of government, we conclude that those of the monarchical form, and those in which the principles of monarchy and aristocracy prevail, are not best adapted to promote the general welfare of a nation. Under a wise and virtuous ruler, the rights of person and property may be fully enjoyed, and the condition of the people may be in a good degree prosperous. But the requisite virtue and wisdom have seldom been found in any one man, or a few men. The prosperity of a people depends as much upon a good form of government as upon its being administered by good men; and experience has proved, that the objects of civil government may be best secured by a written constitution, founded upon the will or consent of the people.

§ 2. The form of government in the United States is expressed in a written constitution. A *constitution* is a form of rules by which the members of a society agree to be governed. The persons forming an association, draft a set of rules setting forth the objects of the association, declaring what officers it shall have, and prescribing the powers and duties of each, and the manner of conducting its operations. So the rules adopted by the people of a state or nation for their government, are called the constitution. They are in the nature of articles of agreement by which the people mutually agree to be governed.

§ 3. A constitution is a kind of law. It is, however, materially different from the laws made from year to year by the representatives of the people assembled in the capacity of a legislature: it is drafted by a body of men chosen by the people for that particular purpose, and adopted by the people themselves. It describes the nature and form of the government, declares what officers are to be elected, and prescribes their respective powers and duties.

§ 4. A constitution is sometimes called the *fundamental law* of a state, being the foundation of all other laws, which must agree with this fundamental law. Hence, it is also called a *frame* of government. As the frame fixes the form and dimensions of the building, and as the materials required to finish the building must be fitted to the frame; so the constitution is the frame-work of the government of a state; and every law made by the legislature, and every other act performed in the administration of the government, must conform to the constitution.

§ 5. The constitution is also called the *political law*, from its being the law of the great political body, or body politic. By the term *body politic* is here meant the people of a state incorporated into one body for purposes of government. It is also applied to small bodies of men associated for other purposes. (See Chapter XIX.) The constitution, being ordained by the act of the people in their political capacity, is properly the *political law*, as distinguished from the laws made from time to time by the people's representatives, and called the *civil* or *municipal laws*.

§ 6. Hence, the first and highest act of a free people, is the choice of a constitution or form of government. No people can be said to enjoy perfect freedom, whose political and civil rights are not secured by a constitution of their own choice. In no country, therefore, do the people enjoy greater political privileges than in the United States. In most of the governments described in preceding chapters, there is either no constitution at all, or none that has been adopted by the votes of the people. There are, even in absolute monarchies, some established forms or rules according to which the government is to be administered; but these rules are not binding on the sovereign, who can make or alter them without the consent of his subjects.

§ 7. Under no government called monarchical, do the people enjoy a greater degree of civil liberty than under the limited monarchy of Great Britain; and we hear of the British constitution; but it is not a written instrument like ours, adopted by the votes of the people. What is there called the constitution, consists of the aggregate or sum of laws, principles, and customs, which have been formed in the course of centuries. There being no established constitution limiting the power of parliament, no law which parliament may enact is unconstitutional. And any change in the laws of the kingdom, is virtually a change in the constitution, and goes to form a part of it. Not having a constitution to restrain the law-making power, the people are liable to suffer from the enactment of unjust laws.

§ 8. The object of a constitution is two-fold. It is intended, first, to guard the rights and liberties of the people against infringement by those intrusted with the powers of government. It points out the rights and privileges of the people, and prescribes the powers and duties of the principal officers of the government; so that it may be known when they transcend their powers, or neglect their duties: and, by limiting their terms of office, it secures to the people the right of displacing, at stated periods, those who are unfaithful to their trust, by electing others in their stead.

§ 9. But while a constitution is designed to restrict the powers of those who administer the government, it is intended also to place some restraints upon the people. The framers of our American constitutions, believing that an unrestrained democracy affords no greater security to public liberty than a monarchy, have provided safeguards against the abuse of liberty by the people, as well as against the abuse of power by their agents: and the people, in adopting their constitutions, have consented to these restraints.

§ 10. These constitutional restraints upon the people, however, do not abridge their natural rights and liberties. All men in society have equal rights; and mutually agree to be thus restrained, in order to secure to all the free enjoyment of their rights. Being voluntarily consented to by all, these restraints can not be said to infringe the natural liberty of any. Besides this, all political power being inherent in the people, they have the right to alter their constitution, increasing or lessening these restraints at pleasure. They are however bound by its provisions, while they exist, whatever they may be; nor can they alter it, except in such manner as the constitution itself prescribes.

§ 11. A state constitution is framed by a convention of delegates or representatives, chosen by the freemen of the state for that purpose. *Delegate* and *representative* are words of similar meaning. Members of representative assemblies other than legislative bodies, are usually called delegates, and, when assembled for business, are called a *convention*.

§ 12. The number of delegates composing a convention to frame a constitution, is usually the same as the number of representatives in the most numerous branch of the legislature, commonly called the house of representatives ; and the number elected in each county is the same as the number of representatives from such county in this branch of the legislature. In the New England states, representatives are apportioned among the towns instead of the counties.

§ 13. A convention to make or amend a constitution, is authorized by a law of the legislature. But the desired changes in a constitution, or the necessity of a new one, may not, by a majority of the people of the state, be deemed sufficient to compensate for the labor and expense of a convention ; the law therefore provides for submitting to the people, at an election, the question whether a convention shall be called. The law also designates the day for the election of delegates in case a majority of the votes at such election shall have been given in favor of a convention.

§ 14. The delegates meet on the day appointed by law, at the seat of government of the state, and continue in session until they have agreed upon a form of a constitution, which is then submitted to the people for their adoption, at an election on a day fixed by the law. If, at such election, a greater number of votes shall be given in favor of the proposed constitution than against it, it becomes the constitution of the state.

§ 15. As constitutions may need amendment when the necessary alterations are not of so great importance as to render a convention necessary or expedient, it is usual to insert in constitutions an article providing some other mode of amendment. Different constitutions provide different modes. In some states, perhaps the greater number, amendments are proposed by one legislature ; and, if they are agreed to by the next legislature, they are submitted to the people for adoption. In a few states, the concurrence of two successive legislatures is sufficient, without the sanction of the people. In others, amendments are made only by conventions, called by a majority of the voters voting therefor at an election.

CHAPTER VIII.

A JUST GOVERNMENT FOUNDED UPON THE CONSENT OF THE PEOPLE.

§ 1. It was in ancient times generally believed, that the power to govern was derived immediately from God; and that, when a throne became vacant, the right of sovereignty returned to the original source, to be again conferred on the immediate successor. By what means soever the throne was obtained, these were believed to be the occasions on which the Supreme Ruler bestowed power on the prince A later opinion, and one that still prevails to some extent, is, that the right is hereditary; and that, on the death of a sovereign, the right to rule passes to his lawful heir.

§ 2. States and nations have been compared to families; monarchs being in the place of fathers. As the father has a divine right to govern his family, and provide for his children, according to his discretion; so is a monarch, by the same right, the ruler and protector of his subjects. And as an argument against constitutions, it was held, that the people of a state governed by a written constitution, would be as unfortunate as a family in which the father, to prevent quarrels and discontent, should be obliged to refer to a written instrument, in which the duties of every member of the household were laid down.

§ 3. To this it has been replied, that families and states are governed by different principles. A family is composed of parents and children, bound together by the ties of natural affection. The ruling principle in the father's government is love and kindness. His affectionate regard for his children prompts him to render them the protection and support which their dependent condition claims at his hands, and to treat them with forbearance. A state is composed of men less closely connected and less dependent, and who are governed by stern justice and strict adherence to law.

§ 4. An attempt to govern a family by a code of laws prescribing, with precision, all the rights and duties of its members, and fixing a specific penalty for every transgression, would be unsuccessful. If every member of the household should invariably insist on his own rights, and the exact performance of every act of duty should be strictly enforced by the father, would such family be well governed? In family government, much must be left to the discretion of the parent. But how unfortunate have been those nations which have left everything to the kindness and paternal care of their rulers, and have not insisted on their own rights!

§ 5. But the principles of civil government have come to be better understood. The doctrine that one man has a divine right to rule a whole nation, or, that one is born to command, and all others are bound to obey, is believed only where the people are too ignorant to appreciate the blessings of freedom. As light and knowledge have advanced among the nations, the great truth has been gaining ground, that all men have a natural and equal right to a voice in the government; and that the *will of the people* is the true *foundation* of all just government, and the *good of the people* its true *object*.

§ 6. The fundamental principles of government are correctly stated in the Declaration of Independence. It is therein declared that "all men are created equal." The equality here meant is equality of political rights; all being entitled to an equal measure of political power, as well as to an equal share in the benefits of the government. Whence, then, does any man, or any number of men, get the right to rule over their fellow men? The same declaration gives the true answer: "All governments derive their just powers from the *consent of the governed*." All rightful authority to govern is in the people, and is either exercised directly by the people, or is delegated by them to others chosen for that purpose.

§ 7. Hence we conclude, that a democracy is the most natural form of government. All men's being created equal in respect to political rights, implies that they are *by nature* fitted for the exercise of political power, and, consequently, that a democratic form of government is best adapted to the nature of mankind, and is designed by the Creator for the regulation of civil society.

§ 8. The most natural and simple idea of a free government, is that of the people's meeting in their own persons for consulting, debating, and enacting laws for the regulation of their conduct, and the protection of their rights. But all the people cannot unite in making laws. Hence the necessity of government by representation. Also, the inhabitants of a town or small district are best acquainted with their own wants and interests, and can better judge of the qualifications of candidates for office residing in their immediate neighborhood, wherefore; a state is divided into districts of suitable size for the election of representatives.

§ 9. But in order to insure a faithful representation, the people must be independent of their representatives, and have the power to control them. Here, again, we see the necessity of a constitution. By their constitution, the people delegate to their representatives the necessary powers of government; and by the same instrument, they reserve to themselves the right to restrain their representatives and other officers as they may deem necessary.

§ 10. If it is the true object of government to promote the good of the whole and not of a few, then the government ought to be one in the formation of which all the people are consulted. But all will not agree in opinion and judgment; and the consent of all the citizens to any form of government might never be obtained. Hence the necessity of the rule which prevails in all popular governments and deliberative assemblies: *the will of the majority must govern.* Without such rule, no free government could be either established or sustained.

CHAPTER IX.

THE DIVISION AND DISTRIBUTION OF THE POWERS OF GOVERNMENT.

§ 1. Having explained the nature of a constitution, and shown how it is made and adopted, it will be next in order to show how the powers of government under a constitution are divided. The excellence of a form of government consists essentially in a proper separation and distribution of power.

§ 2. One of the chief excellencies of the American constitutions, is the separation of the political and civil powers. The words political and civil are generally used as having the same meaning. Thus, in speaking of the system of government and laws of a country, we use the general term, "political institutions," or "civil institutions;" either being deemed correct. But the words civil and political have also a particular signification. The same distinction is observed here as was made in a preceding chapter between the constitution, or political law, and the municipal or civil laws; the political power being that which is exercised by the people in their political capacity in adopting their constitution, and electing the officers of government; the civil power that which is exercised by the officers thus elected in administering the government.

§ 3. In an absolute government, no such distinction exists; all power being centered in the supreme ruler. There is no political law binding on him. The rules by which the powers of his government are exercised, consist of certain customs and usages for which his subjects have even a higher regard than for his own authority. Yet being himself subject to no positive laws or regulations that have been adopted by the people, or that may be altered by them, the people enjoy no political rights.

§ 4. In a mixed government, or limited monarchy, political power is exercised to some extent. Although there is, in most governments of this kind, no written constitution adopted by the people, as in a republic, the members of one branch of the law-making power are elected by the people;

and in such election they are said to exercise political power.

§ 5. The civil power in well constructed governments, is divided into three departments, the legislative, the executive, and the judicial. The *legislative department* is that by which the laws of the state are made. The legislature is composed of two bodies, the members of which are elected by the people. In limited monarchies, or mixed governments, only one branch of the legislature is elective; the other being an aristocratic body, composed of men of wealth and dignity, as the British house of lords.

§ 6. The *executive* department is that which is intrusted with the power of executing, or carrying into effect, the laws of the state. In each of the several states of this union, the executive department consists of a governor, assisted by a number of other officers, some of whom are elected by the people, and others are appointed in some manner prescribed by the constitution and laws. It is the duty of the governor to see that the laws are duly executed. He oversees the general business of the state, and recommends to the legislature such matters as he thinks ought to receive their attention.

§ 7. The *judicial* department is that by which justice between citizens is administered, and embraces the several courts of the state. All judges and justices of the peace are judicial officers. It is their business to judge of and apply the laws in cases brought before them for trial. There are several courts in a state; some of lower, others of a higher order. The manner in which these courts are constituted, is not precisely the same in all the states; but their general powers, and the manner of conducting trials, are the same.

§ 8. Experience has shown the propriety of the division of the civil power of a state into these three departments, and of keeping them separate and distinct, and of confining the officers of each to the powers and duties belonging to their respective departments. Those who make the laws ought not to exercise the power of executing or enforcing them; nor should they who either make or execute the laws, sit in judgment over those who are brought before them for justice. A government in which the different powers of making, executing, and applying the laws should be united in the same hands, whether consisting of one man or a single body of men, however numerous, would be little better than an absolute despotism. It was one of the main defects of some of the ancient republics, that the powers of government were not properly divided and balanced.

§ 9. Again, the law-making department of the civil power is divided into several branches. The plan of dividing the legislative power, which existed in some of the ancient republics and in Great Britain, and also in the American colonies while subject to that country, has been adopted and continued in the constitutions of all the states in this union, with some modifications in some of them.

§ 10. The best governments among the ancient republics, and those which existed longest, and were most firm and stable, were upon this plan. The law-making power was vested in a chief magistrate, lords, and a representative assembly. These several branches, holding a check upon each other, are more likely to enact good and wholesome laws, than if the whole power were in the hands of one man, or a single representative assembly. A government of this kind was constituted at Sparta by Lycurgus, which lasted above eight hundred years; whereas the government established by Solon at Athens, which was a simple democracy, was of short duration, about one hundred years. Not only was the government of the Spartans more durable, but the citizens were better governed.

§ 11. Under the Roman constitution was formed the noblest people and the most powerful nation that had ever existed. The supreme power was vested in two consuls, (chief magistrates,) a senate, and the people. But if all the powers of these several branches had been united in a single assembly, whether consisting of the whole body of freemen, or of their representatives, it is not probable that the people would have been long free, or the nation ever great. The distribution of power, however, was never accurately and judiciously made in that constitution. The executive was never sufficiently separated from the legislative; nor was the control which these powers were to have upon each other defined with sufficient accuracy.

§ 12. The framers of our American constitutions, who had before them the various systems of government, ancient and modern, and were well acquainted with their nature and operation, have happily preserved what was good in those systems, and avoided their defects. And in nothing is the superiority of our plan of government more manifest, than in the wise division and distribution of its powers.

§ 13. There is another division of power. A single set of officers in each of the several departments, legislative, executive, and judicial, residing at the seat of government, can not regulate all the minute affairs of every neighborhood throughout the state. Business in which the people of a small community alone are interested can be better done by some local authority. For this purpose, a state is divided into counties and towns, in each of which there are officers elected to exercise certain powers of government. (See Towns and Counties.)

§ 14. There is another reason for the division of a state into small territories. The people, in the exercise of their political power, must act *collectively*, which can be done only in small districts, as towns. In all elections for choosing state, county, and town officers, and for voting upon the question of adopting a constitution, the people act in town meetings.

CHAPTER X.

CAUSES OF THE REVOLUTION, AND OF THE ESTABLISHMENT OF OUR PRESENT FORM OF GOVERNMENT.

§ 1. The people of the United States, as is probably known by the youngest reader of this work, have not always lived under their present excellent form of government. For more than one hundred and fifty years after the first settlement of this country, they were subject to the government of Great Britain. In 1776, the American colonies, now states, separated themselves from the parent country, and claimed the right to establish a government for themselves.

§ 2. This country was first settled by the English, who

claimed it by right of discovery, they having discovered it in 1497, about five years after Columbus had discovered the West India islands. The first permanent settlement, however, was not made until the year 1607, when a colony of 105 persons settled at Jamestown, in Virginia. A few years afterward, (1620,) a colony was planted in Plymouth, in Massachusetts. After this the number of colonies rapidly increased to twelve, the last of which, Pennsylvania, was settled in 1681. About fifty years thereafter, (1732,) Georgia was settled; the last of the thirteen colonies which declared themselves free and independent states.

§ 3. The governments of the colonies, during their connection with Great Britain, were not such as the colonists chose for themselves, but such as the king was pleased to prescribe for them in their charters. The word *charter* is from the Latin *charta*, which means paper. The instruments of writing by which the king granted privileges to individuals or corporations, were written on paper or parchment, and called charters. The colonial charters granted to individuals and companies the right to trade and settle in this country, and prescribed the limits of the territory granted to each. And either the same or a separate charter contained rules for the government of the colony.

§ 4. The governments of the several colonies, though not alike in every particular, were on the same general plan. The powers of government were vested in a governor, a council, and an assembly of representatives chosen by the people. These three branches corresponded to the king, the nobles, and the commons in Great Britain. Power was therefore divided in those governments in nearly the same manner as it is in the states at present; there being in every state a governor, a senate, and a representative assembly.

§ 5. There is, however, an important difference between those governments and the present. The people of the colonies were not allowed to choose a constitution or form of government; nor had they the privilege of choosing the officers of the different departments of the government. The governors were appointed either by the king, or by such persons as had authority from the king to appoint them; and they were generally under the control of the king, by whom they might be kept in office or dismissed at pleasure.

§ 6. The council was composed of a small number of men, also appointed by the king, and subject to his pleasure. This body constituted one branch of the legislature. The judges and magistrates, and other officers, were appointed by the governors or by the king, or other persons who appointed the governors.

§ 7. Hence it appears that only one branch of the law-making power was chosen by the people, while the other two, the governor and council, were appointed by the king, or were subject to him. And as every measure proposed by the representatives required the concurrence of the governor and council, just and necessary laws were often denied the people. Besides, a measure thus concurred in, must be sent to England for the approval of the king before it could become a law.

§ 8. In a few of the colonies, however, the people enjoyed greater political privileges. In Massachusetts, Rhode Island and Connecticut, for many years before the revolution, they elected their governors and both houses of the legislature. Yet even in these colonies, no laws might be enacted that were contrary to the laws of England. And the privileges which the people enjoyed were granted by the king, and might be taken away from them at his pleasure.

§ 9. Not only were the colonists denied the benefits of liberal and just legislation at home; many of the laws enacted by parliament and approved by the king, were highly oppressive. These laws were designed to secure to Great Britain exclusively the benefit of the trade of the colonies. A law was enacted declaring that no goods should be imported into the colonies but in English vessels. If brought in other vessels, both the goods and the vessels were to be forfeited to the British government. Another law required such articles produced here as England wanted, to be transported to that country, and to other countries belonging to Great Britain. The colonists were permitted to ship to foreign markets such products only as English merchants did not want. They were prohibited from selling abroad any wool, yarn, or woolen manufactured goods. Another law declared that no iron wares of any kind should be manufactured in the plantations.

§ 10. Thus was it attempted to suppress manufactures in

the colonies. In short, it was the policy of the British government to compel the colonists to buy of England all the goods they wanted which they did not themselves produce, and to sell to England the surplus productions of the colonies. For this purpose, heavy duties were laid upon goods imported into the colonies from other countries than Great Britain and her possessions. These duties were taxes levied upon goods brought into the colonies from abroad, and were collected by officers here from persons importing the goods.

§ 11. The nature and effects of these duties will more plainly appear to the young reader from the following facts:—The colonists traded with the West India islands. Some of these islands belonged to France, some to Spain, others to Great Britain. Now to prevent the colonists from buying goods at the French and Spanish Islands, parliament enacted a law compelling them to pay high duties on the molasses, sugar, and other articles from these islands.

§ 12. Great Britain did not stop here. Not satisfied with these acts by which English traders had been enabled to enrich themselves, parliament claimed the right to tax the colonies "in all cases whatsoever;" and an act was passed accordingly, laying duties upon all tea, glass, paper, and painters' colors, imported into the colonies; and the money thus collected was put into the British treasury. The colonists remonstrated against these unjust laws. Petitions were sent to the king, and memorials to both houses of parliament, praying that these laws might be repealed, but in vain. At length, the colonists resolving no longer to submit to such laws, and the British government attempting to enforce them, a war between the two countries was the consequence.

§ 13. The war commenced in 1775. On the 4th of July, 1776, the congress declared the colonies to be free and independent states. Congress was a kind of legislative body, composed of a few delegates or representatives from each of the several colonies. A description of this congress will be given in another part of this work; also the declaration of independence, with the names of the men who signed it. After a severe struggle of about seven years, the war was ended, and Great Britain acknowledged the independence of the states. This change in our relations with that country, and the establishment of independent governments in the states, is called the *American Revolution.*

§ 14. Since the states declared themselves independent, one after another has changed its government, until all of the original thirteen have adopted new constitutions. During this period, eighteen new states have been admitted into the Union, making the present number thirty-one. Three others, Minnesota, Kansas, and Oregon, are now (1858) waiting for admission, and will soon be added to the number.

STATE GOVERNMENTS.

CHAPTER XI.

BY WHOM POLITICAL POWER IS EXERCISED IN THE STATES OF THIS UNION.

§ 1. The first act of political power is, as we have seen, the establishment of a constitution, or form of government. The next is the election of officers to administer the government. But prior to the exercise of this power, it must be determined to whom it shall be intrusted.

§ 2. In speaking of *the people* as acting politically, we do not mean all *persons;* but such only as are entitled by the constitution to vote at elections. It is the common opinion, that the duties which both nature and the custom of civilized countries have assigned to females, are such as to render it improper for them to take an active part in public affairs. Nor ought males to be permitted to do so, until they shall have had time to acquire the requisite knowledge and judgment to exercise power discreetly. And that they may act independently, they ought to have attained the age and condition of *freemen.* None, therefore, but free male citizens of the age of twenty-one years, are allowed to vote at elections.

§ 3. That a man may vote understandingly, he ought also to have resided long enough in the state to become acquainted with its government and laws, and with its citizens, from whom he is to select those for whom he is to vote. All our state constitutions require, as one of the qualifications of every elector, that he shall have resided in the state for a specified period of time; which period is not the same in all the states, varying in the different states from three months to two years. In most of the states, he must also have resided for some months in the county, and be a resident of the town in which he offers to vote.

§ 4. Under the early constitutions of the old states, the right of voting, otherwise called the *right of suffrage*, and *the elective franchise*, was restricted to those who owned property, or paid rent or taxes to a certain amount. In the election of the higher state officers, freeholders only were entitled to vote. A *freeholder* is an owner of real estate, that is, property in lands, which he may hold in his own right and transmit to his heirs. In the constitutions of the newer states, the possession of property has not been made a qualification of an elector; and in the amended constitutions of the old states this restriction upon the elective franchise has been removed, until it has nearly ceased to exist in the United States. The right of voting is now enjoyed by all independent white male citizens, with few exceptions, in almost every state of the Union.

§ 5. All *male citizens*, as the term is here used, does not mean every *man* twenty-one years of age. Foreigners, or *aliens*, are not in law called citizens, nor entitled to the political privileges enjoyed by persons born in this country. Their knowledge of our government is deemed to be too limited to qualify them immediately for the proper exercise of political power; nor is it presumed that they will feel a sufficient interest in our government until they shall have become permanently settled in this country. A way is provided by which, after a residence here for a term of years, they may be admitted to all the privileges of native citizens. Their becoming thus invested with the rights of natural born citizens, is called being *naturalized*. (See Naturalization.)

§ 6. Also persons convicted of certain infamous crimes are denied the privilege of voting thereafter at elections, unless they have been pardoned before the expiration of the term for which they were sentenced to be imprisoned, or unless the disqualification be removed in some other way prescribed by law. Paupers, idiots, and insane persons, are in some state constitutions expressly disqualified.

§ 7. It will be seen by reference to the several state constitutions, that "*white* male citizens" only are mentioned as entitled to the right of suffrage, in most of the states. In the New England states, except Connecticut, there is no exclusion of colored citizens from the right of voting. And in New York, male citizens of color owning a freehold estate of the value of $250, are qualified electors. The justice or propriety of excluding persons of color from a participation in the government, has always been questioned, and has been the subject of much discussion in the several state conventions by which the constitutions have been framed, as well as by the people at large. But hitherto, attempts to enfranchise colored citizens have generally proved unsuccessful.

CHAPTER XII

ELECTIONS.

§ 1. Elections are annually held in each state for electing officers to serve in the several administrations of state, counties, and towns. Town meetings for the election of town officers are usually held in or near the months of March and April. Most officers elected by the people, other than town officers, are chosen at the general state election, which, in most of the states, is held in the month of October or November.

§ 2. Elections are conducted by persons designated by law, or chosen by the electors of the towns for that purpose. It is their duty to see that order is preserved, and that the business at elections is properly done. They are usually called judges of elections, or inspectors of elections. Persons also, (usually two,) are appointed to serve as clerks Each clerk keeps a list of the names of the electors voting at the election, which is called a poll-list. *Poll* is a Saxon word, signifying *head,* and has come to mean person. Hence, so much "a head" means so much for every person. By a still further change, it is made to signify an election, because the persons there voting are numbered. Thus, "going to the polls" has obtained the same meaning as going to an election, or to the place of voting.

§ 3. When the hour appointed has arrived, and the officers of election are ready to receive votes, the polls are said to be open; and one of the officers makes it known by a proclamation, or public announcement. Each elector hands to one of the inspectors a ballot, which is a piece of paper, on which are written or printed the names of the persons he votes for, and the title of the office to which each is to be elected. *Ballot,* from the French, means a *little ball,* and is used in voting. Ballots are of different colors; those of one color signifying an affirmative vote; those of another color, a negative vote. Hence, the application of the word to the written or printed ticket now generally used in voting.

§ 4. If no objection is made to an elector's voting, and the inspectors are satisfied that he is a lawful voter, the ballot is put into the box; and the clerks enter his name on the poll-list. If the inspectors have reason to suspect that a person offering to vote is not a qualified elector, they may, before receiving his ballot, question him upon his oath in respect to his qualifications as to age, the term of his residence in the state and county, and his citizenship. Any bystander also may question his right to vote. This is called *challenging.* A person whose vote is thus challenged, is not allowed to vote until the challenge is withdrawn, or his qualifications are either proved by the statement of other persons, or sworn to by himself.

§ 5. In the New England States, a list is kept of all persons in each town who, upon examination, have been ascertained to be duly qualified voters; and those only whose names are thus registered are allowed to vote. Thus is avoided much of the confusion and delay often caused in other states, by the examination of voters at the time of voting; and much illegal voting is prevented. Voters in those states are also required to take what is called the "elector's oath," in which they promise to be true and faithful to the state and its government, and also to the constitution of the United States; and to give their votes as they shall judge will conduce to the best good of the same.

§ 6. After the polls have been closed, the box is opened, and the ballots are counted. If the number of ballots agrees with the number of names on the poll-lists, it is presumed no mistake has been made, either in voting or in keeping the lists. The number of votes for each candidate being ascertained, a statement is made of the names of all the persons voted for, and of the number of votes given for each, and signed by the officers of election. This statement, or a copy of it, is deposited with the town clerk, either to be kept on file or recorded. If the election is one for the choice of town officers, it is there determined who are elected, and their election is publicly declared.

§ 7. The election of county and state officers can not, of course, be determined by the canvassers in the towns. The statement of votes given for the several candidates in each town, is sent to the board of county canvassers, who determine and declare the election of officers chosen for the county. To determine the election of state officers, and such others as are elected for districts comprising more counties than one, a statement of the votes for the candidates for these officers is sent by the several boards of county canvassers to the state canvassers at the seat of government, who, from the returns from the several counties, determine and declare the election of these officers.

§ 8. In some of the states, voting at popular elections is done openly, or *viva voce.* Viva voce means, literally, living voice. In voting in this manner, the elector pronounces the name of the person for whom he votes.

§ 9. In most of the states, the election of officers is effected by a plurality of votes. An election by *plurality* is when the person elected has received a higher number of votes than any other, though such number should be less than a majority of all the votes given. If, for example, out of 1,000 votes divided among three candidates, one should receive 450, another 300, and the third the remaining 250 votes; the first, having received the highest number, though not a majority, would be elected. In the New England states, a *majority*, that is, more than half, of all the votes given, is necessary to an election Hence, the least number of votes out of 1000 by which a person can be chosen, is 501. There are some exceptions to the majority principle in these states ; certain officers being elected by plurality.

§ 10. Both these modes are liable to objection. Where a simple plurality effects a choice, 1,000 votes may be so divided upon three candidates, as to elect one of them by 334 votes ; or, of four candidates, one may be elected by 251 votes. Thus a person may be elected who is the first choice of but a small portion of the people of his district. Artful politicians, taking advantage of this mode of election, have sometimes secured the election of a favorite candidate by a small plurality of votes. An objection to the other mode is, that if no person receives a majority of all the votes, a new election must be held ; and sometimes several unsuccessful trials are made before a choice is effected ; thus subjecting the electors to much inconvenience, and leaving offices for the time vacant. Cases have occurred in which the people of a district have been for a long time without a representative in the state or national legislature.

CHAPTER XIII.

STATE LEGISLATURES ; HOW CONSTITUTED.

§ 1. The legislature of every state in the union, is composed of two houses, a senate and a house of representatives. The latter, or lower house, in the states of New York, Wisconsin, and California, is called the assembly ; in Maryland and Virginia, the house of delegates ; in North Carolina, the house of commons ; and in New Jersey, the general assembly. In most of the states, the two houses are called the general assembly.

§ 2. The senate, as well as the other house, is a representative body ; its members being elected by the people to represent them. Perhaps the reason why the lower house is usually designated "the house of representatives," is, that under the colonial governments, this was the only representative branch of the legislature ; our present senate being in the place of the old council, the members of which were appointed by the king. Or, as the members of the lower house are, in most of the states, chosen for shorter terms than senators, are more numerous, and consequently represent smaller districts, they may be considered as more fully and more immediately representing the people.

§ 3. Senators are chosen annually in the six New England states and in Georgia. In the other states they are elected for terms of two, three, or four years. In most of the states in which senators are elected for longer terms than one year, the senators are not all elected at the same time ; but are divided into classes ; those of one class going out of office one year, and another class another year ; so that only a part of the senators are elected every year, or every two, three, or four years.

§ 4. The senate is sometimes called, by way of distinction, the upper house ; being a more select body, composed of men generally chosen with reference to their superior ability, or to their greater experience in public affairs.

§ 5. Senators are differently apportioned in different states. In some states they are apportioned among the several counties, according to their population. In others they are elected by districts ; the state being divided into as many districts as there are senators, and a senator being chosen in each district, as at present in New York. In a few of the states, the senatorial districts being unequal in size and population, more senators are apportioned to some districts than to others.

§ 6. Representatives are, in most of the states, elected annually, and are apportioned among the several counties or districts, or (in the New England states) the towns, according to the number of inhabitants in each. In nearly one half of the states, (including most of the southern and western states,) representatives are elected, and sessions of the legislature held every second year. The rules of apportioning senators and representatives, are not the same in all the states. (See Synopsis of State Constitutions in the Appendix.)

§ 7. From the more rapid increase of population in some counties or districts than in others, their proportional representation becomes unequal. It is therefore provided by the constitution, that at the end of certain periods, the inhabitants of the state shall be numbered, and a new apportionment of senators and representatives made, according to such enumeration, so that each county and district may have its just proportion of senators and representatives. The periods of time between the enumerations are not the same in all the states, varying from four to ten years. An enumeration of the people is usually called *census*, which among the Romans, meant the valuation of a man's estate, and the registering of himself and his family.

§ 8. To be eligible to the office of senator or representative, the constitution requires that a person shall have resided in the state for a certain term of years. In most of the states senators, and in some of them representatives, must be of greater age than twenty-one years; and in some they are also required to be freeholders.

§ 9. If a senator dies, or resigns his office, before the term expires for which he has been elected, the vacancy is filled by the election of another person at the next election of senators, or in such other manner as the constitution may provide. But the person chosen to fill a vacancy, holds the office only for the remainder of the term of him in whose stead he was chosen.

CHAPTER XIV.

ORGANIZATION OF LEGISLATIVE BODIES; PRIVILEGES OF MEMBERS, &C.

§ 1. The legislature composed of the senate and house of representatives, meets as often as the constitution requires, to consider the condition of the state, and to enact such laws as may be necessary to promote the public welfare. Meetings of the legislature are held at a place permanently fixed by the constitution, or by act of the legislature; at which place the principal state officers keep their offices Hence it is called the seat of government, or more fre quently the *capital* of the state. The building erected for the accommodation of the legislature and other state officers, is called the *capitol.*

§ 2. The two houses having assembled, each in its own chamber, every representative and every new senator is required, before proceeding to business, to take the oath of office, in which he solemnly swears that he will support the constitution of the United States, and the constitution of his own state ; and that he will discharge the duties of his office according to the best of his ability. All persons elected to the more important and responsible public offices, are required to take such oath. An *oath* is a solemn declaration, in which the person appeals to God to bear witness to the truth of what he declares. Oaths are required because it is presumed that persons under the obligation of an oath, will be more likely to act conscientiously. Many, however, even under these solemn obligations, discharge their duties very unfaithfully. The faithful discharge of public duties is best secured by the election of good men.

§ 3. The constitution declares what number of members shall constitute a quorum. *Quorum* means such number of any body of men as have power to act. It seldoms happens that all the members of a numerous body can be present at the same time ; constitutions therefore declare what number of members of each house shall constitute a quorum to do business. In most of the states, a majority of all the members constitutes a quorum; in others, two-thirds. A smaller number than a quorum, however, have power to adjourn from time to time, and to compel the attendance of absent members.

§ 4. All legislative bodies have certain rules of order for doing business. The constitution allows each house to determine the rules of its own proceedings ; and for the information of the public, each house is required to keep a journal of its proceedings, and to publish the same, except such parts as ought to be kept secret. And that persons so desiring may witness its proceedings, the door of each house must be kept open, except when the public welfare requires secrecy.

§ 5. To prevent any hinderance to the public business, and to secure to the people the services of their representatives, most of the state constitutions provide, that members of the legislature shall not, except for certain crimes and misdemeanors, be arrested on civil process, or be in any manner subjected to prosecutions at law, either during the session of the legislature, or in going to or returning from the same. In some states, this privilege is enjoyed also for several days before going and after returning.

§ 6. Each house has power to expel any of its members, and punish its members and officers for disorderly behavior, by imprisonment. And each house may also punish other persons as well as its members, for contempt or insult offered to the house; for disorderly conduct tending to interrupt its proceedings; for publishing false and malicious reports of the proceedings, or of the conduct of the members; and for sundry other offenses.

§ 7. After the members have been sworn into office, they proceed to the appointment of officers of their respective houses. Each house elects one of its members as chairman, who is usually called *speaker*. The lieutenant-governor, in states where there is one, presides in the senate, and is called *president of the senate*. In the absence of a presiding officer, a temporary speaker or president is elected, who is called speaker or president *pro tempore;* commonly abbreviated, *pro tem.*, which is a Latin phrase, meaning *for the time.*

§ 8. It is the duty of the person presiding to keep order, and to see that the business of the house is conducted according to its rules. And when a vote is to be taken he puts the question, which is done by requesting all who are in favor of the proposed measure to say "aye," and those opposed to say "no;" and when a vote has been taken, he declares the question to be carried or lost, as the case may be. This part of a speaker's business is similar to that of the chairman of an ordinary public meeting.

§ 9. Each house also chooses a *clerk* to keep a record or journal of its proceedings; to take charge of papers, and to read such as are to be read to the house; and to do such other things as are required of him; a *sergeant-at-arms*, whose duty it is to arrest members or other persons guilty of disorderly conduct, to compel the attendance of absent members, and to do other business of a like nature; also one or more *door-keepers*. The officers mentioned in this section are not selected from the members of the house, but from the citizens at large.

CHAPTER XV.

MANNER OF ENACTING LAWS.

§ 1. When the two houses, having been duly organized, are ready for business, the governor sends to both houses a *message,* which is read to each house by its clerk. The governor exhibits in his message the condition of the affairs of the state, and recommends such measures as he judges necessary and expedient.

§ 2. Soon after the legislature has commenced its business, the committees of each house are appointed. A legislative committee generally consists of either three, five, or seven members, who consider and act upon matters intrusted or *committed* to them. The committees are usually appointed by the presiding officer of the house, and are numerous. Some or all of the following committees are appointed in the legislature of every state ; a committee on finance, or the funds and other money matters of the state ; a committee on agriculture ; a committee on manufactures ; also committees on the incorporation of cities and villages ; on banks and insurance companies ; on rail-roads ; on canals ; on education ; and on sundry other subjects.

§ 3. The object of appointing these committees is to expedite the business of the house. So great a number and variety of subjects are presented for the action of the legislature, that they could not all be disposed of during the session, if the whole house were occupied in the investigation of every subject. But as all the information necessary to enable the house to act understandingly, may as well be obtained by a committee composed of a few men as by the whole house, inquiries into many of these subjects may be going on at the same time.

§ 4. Applications for the establishment of banks are referred to the committee on banks, to inquire into their necessity ; subjects relating to schools, are referred to the committee on education ; those relating to rail-roads, to the committee on rail-roads, &c. Thus is every subject referred to its appropriate committee. If at any time a matter arises having no relation to those subjects upon which standing committees are appointed, it is usually referred to a *select* committee, appointed for the special purpose of considering such subject.

§ 5. The members of the several committees meet from time to time during hours when the house is not in session, to consider the matters referred to them. At the meetings of a committee, any person wishing to be heard in favor of or against a proposed measure, may appear before the committee for this purpose. Persons from all parts of the state are usually in attendance, during the sessions of the legislature, to urge or oppose the passage of laws in which they are interested.

§ 6. After due inquiry and consideration, committees make their reports to the house. A report of a committee contains a statement of the facts that have been ascertained, and of the reasons why the law prayed for ought or ought not to be passed. If a committee reports against a measure, the house generally dismisses the subject; if the committee reports in favor of a measure, it usually brings in a bill with the report. A *bill* is a draft or form of an intended law.

§ 7. Not all bills, however, which are brought before the house, are reported by committees. Any member of the house desiring the passage of a law, gives notice that he will, on some future day, ask leave of the house to introduce a bill for that purpose; and, at the time specified, if the house shall grant leave, he may introduce the bill. But at least one day's previous notice must be given of his intention to ask leave, before leave can be granted to introduce a bill.

§ 8. A bill must go through many stages and forms of deliberation before it can become a law; all of which it is not deemed important to detail in this place. These forms of deliberation and action are, with some unimportant exceptions, the same in all legislative bodies in the union. Before a bill is passed, it must be read three times; but it may not be read oftener than once on the same day without the consent of the whole house, in some states; in others, three-fourths or two thirds of the house. Nor can it be altered or amended before its second reading.

§ 9. After a bill has been read twice, it is referred to a

committee of the whole house, to be taken up for discussion and amendment. When a house resolves itself into a committee of the whole to consider a bill thus committed, the speaker appoints another member to the chair, and the speaker takes part in the debate, if he chooses, as an ordinary member. When either house is in committee of the whole, the person presiding is addressed as "chairman." When not in committee of the whole, the person temporarily occupying the chair, is addressed as "speaker," or "president," as the permanent presiding officer would be addressed, if he were himself in the chair.

§ 10. After a bill has been fully discussed and amended, it is proposed to be engrossed, and to be read on a future day the third time. To *engross* a bill is to copy it in a large, fair hand, after it has been amended in committee of the whole. On the proposition to engross a bill for the third reading, is the proper time for those opposed to the bill to take their stand against it. If the question on the engrossment and third reading of a bill is not carried, the bill is lost, unless revived by a vote of the house to reconsider. But if the question to read a third time is carried, the bill is accordingly read on a future day, and the question taken on its final passage. Further amendments are sometimes made to a bill on its third reading.

§ 11. When the final vote is to be taken, the speaker puts the question: "Shall the bill pass?" and requests those in favor of it to say "aye," and those opposed to say "no." If a majority of the members present vote in the affirmative, (the speaker also voting,) the bill is passed; if a majority vote in the negative, the bill is lost. Also if the ayes and noes are equal, it is lost, for lack of a majority in its favor. In a senate where a lieutenant governor presides, not being properly a member, he does not vote, except when the ayes and noes are equal: in which case there is is said to be a *tie*. He then determines the question by his vote, which is called the *casting vote*. In some states, on the passage of a bill, a bare majority of the members present voting in the affirmative is not sufficient to pass it, unless every member happens to be present. The constitution requires a majority of *all the members elected* to each house.

§ 12. When a bill has passed one house, it is sent to the

other to be considered and acted upon in the same manner; and if agreed to by that house also, without alteration, the bill is passed. If a bill is amended in the second house, it must be returned to the first, and the amendments agreed to, or the bill is lost. Some bills are sent several times from one house to the other with amendments, before they are agreed to by both houses.

§ 13. In a majority of the states, a bill, after it has passed both houses, is to be sent to the governor to be approved and signed by him, as in Great Britain bills passed by parliament, are sent to the king for his approval. In refusing to sign a bill, he is said to *negative* or *veto* the bill. (Chap. V. § 4.) No executive, however, in this country, has the power of an *absolute* negative upon acts of legislation, as in monarchies, where no laws can be enacted without the approval of the executive. Our constitutions provide for the enactment of laws, notwithstanding the veto of the governor; hence he has only a *qualified* negative.

§ 14. If a governor refuses to sign a bill, he must return it to the house in which it originated, stating his objections to it; and if it shall be again passed by both houses, it will be a law, without the governor's approval. But in such cases greater majorities are usually required to pass a law. In some states, a majority of two-thirds of the *members present* is required to pass a bill returned by the governor; in others a majority of *all the members elected* to each house. Or if the governor does not return a bill within a certain number of days, it becomes a law without his approval, or without being considered a second time.

§ 15. It may be asked, Why should bills be sent to the governor for his approval? For the same reason as that for which a bill passed by one house is sent to the other. Bills are sometimes passed hastily, and without due information. Legislatures are therefore divided into two branches; and a bill having passed one house is sent to the other, where any mistakes may be detected, and the bill either amended or rejected. But errors are sometimes committed by both houses. Therefore to guard still more effectually against the enactment of bad laws, it is provided that the governor also shall examine bills. But as it would be unsafe to invest any one man with an absolute negative upon all bills, the governor is required to return such as he does not approve, to be passed, if possible, in the manner prescribed by the constitution.

§ 16. To prevent sessions of the legislature from being protracted to an unnecessary length, a few state constitutions limit them to a certain number of days, or state the number of days for which the members shall receive pay. But the expediency of such a provision is doubted. Important measures are often hurried through without due consideration, or are arrested in their passage by an untimely adjournment.

§ 17. The compensation of members of the legislature is fixed by the constitution, in some states, in others by law, and paid out of the treasury of the state.

CHAPTER XVI.

EXECUTIVE DEPARTMENT.—GOVERNOR AND LIEUTENANT-GOVERNOR; SUBORDINATE STATE OFFICERS.

§ 1. The chief executive power of a state is, by the constitution, vested in a governor. He is assisted in the administration of the government by several subordinate executive officers. The governor is chosen at the general annual election; in South Carolina by the legislature. The terms of office are not the same in all the states. In the six New England states, the governor is chosen annually; in the other states for different terms of two, three, and four years.

§ 2. The qualifications of governors are also different in different states. To be eligible to the office of governor, a person must have been for a certain number of years a citizen (in some states a native born) of the United States; and for a term of years preceding his election a resident of the state. He must also be above a certain age, which, in a majority of the states, is at least thirty years; and in some of the states he must be a freeholder.

§ 3. The powers and duties of a governor are numerous. Some of those usually mentioned in a constitution are the following : He sends to the legislature at the beginning of every session, a message, containing a statement of the general affairs of the state, and recommending such measures as he shall judge to be expedient. It is his duty also to see that the laws are executed, and to transact all necessary business with the officers of government.

§ 4. A governor has power also to grant reprieves and pardons, except in cases of impeachment, and in some states, of treason also. To *reprieve* is to postpone or delay the execution of the sentence of death upon a criminal. A *pardon* annuls the sentence and exempts him from punishment. A governor may also *commute* a sentence ; which is to exchange a penalty or punishment for one of less severity.

§ 5. The governor has power also, in some states, with the consent of the senate, to appoint the higher militia officers, and certain civil officers in the executive and judicial departments. In a few of the states, there are executive councils, whose advice and consent are required in such cases. In making such appointments, the governor nominates, that is, he *names* to the senate, in writing, the persons to be appointed. If a majority of the senators present consent, the person so nominated is appointed. Many other powers and duties are by the constitution devolved upon the governor, as will be seen hereafter.

§ 6. The duties of a lieutenant-governor are not numerous. He is president of the senate, as has been stated, but has only a casting vote therein. The principal object in electing this officer seems to be, to provide a suitable person to fill the office of governor in case of vacancy. In nearly one half of the states, the office of lieutenant-governor does not exist.

§ 7. When the lieutenant-governor acts as governor, the senate chooses from its own number a president. And if the offices of both the governor and lieutenant-governor should become vacant, the president of the senate must act as governor. In states where there is no lieutenant-governor, the duties of the governor, in case of vacancy, devolve upon the speaker of the senate ; and if the office of the speaker of the senate also becomes vacant, then the speaker of the house of representatives acts as governor.

§ 8. Among the executive officers who assist in the administration of the government, there are in every state either some or all of the following : a secretary of state ; a controller, or auditor ; a treasurer ; an attorney-general ; and a surveyor-general. The mode of appointment and the terms of office, are prescribed by the constitution or by law. In some states, these officers are appointed by the governor and senate ; in others by the legislature ; and in others they are elected by the people. These officers keep their offices at the seat of government of the state.

§ 9. The *secretary of state* keeps a record of the official acts and proceedings of the legislature and of the executive departments, and has care of all the books, records, deeds of the state, and parchments, and of all the laws enacted by the legislature, and all other papers and documents required by law to be kept in his office.

§ 10. It is the duty of the secretary of state to see that the laws are published. He causes accurate copies to be made of all the laws passed by the legislature, and published in one or more papers, as directed by law. And after the close of each session of the legislature, he also causes the laws to be printed and bound together in a volume, and distributed. Copies of the laws thus bound, are deposited in the public offices of the state, for the use of the officers of the government ; and a copy is sent to each county and town clerk, to be kept in their offices for the use of the people who wish to examine the laws. Copies are also sent to certain officers of the government ; and one or more copies are exchanged with each of the states, for copies of their laws to be kept in the state library. Various other duties devolve upon the secretary of state.

§ 11. The *state auditor*, in some states called *controller*, manages the financial concerns of the state ; that is, the business relating to the money, debts, land, and other property of the state. He examines and adjusts all accounts and claims against the state, and superintends the collection of moneys due the state. When money is to be paid out of the treasury, he draws a warrant (a written order) on the treasurer for the money, and keeps a regular account with the treasurer of all moneys received into and paid out of the treasury. He reports annually to the legislature a statement of the funds of the state, and of its income, and its expenditures during the preceding year.

§ 12. The *treasurer* has charge of all the public moneys that are paid into the treasury, and pays out the same as directed by law. And he is required to keep an accurate account of such moneys, specifying the names of the persons from whom received, to whom paid, and for what purposes. He also exhibits annually to the legislature a statement of moneys received and paid out by him during the preceding year, and of the balance in the treasury.

§ 13. Auditors and treasurers, and other public officers intrusted with the care and management of money or other property, are generally required, before they enter on the duties of their offices, to give bonds, in sums of certain amount specified in the law, with sufficient sureties, for the faithful performance of their duties. The sureties are persons who become responsible to the state for all damages arising from neglect of duty on the part of the officers, not, however, exceeding the sum mentioned in the bond.

§ 14. The *attorney-general* is a person learned in the law, appointed to manage law-suits in which the state is interested. He prosecutes persons indebted to the state, and causes to be brought to trial persons charged with certain offenses. He also gives his opinion on questions of law submitted to him by the governor, the legislature, and the heads of the departments. In some states, there is no attorney-general; suits in which the state is concerned being conducted on the part of the state by the state's attorney for each county.

§ 15. The *surveyor-general* superintends the surveying and selling of lands belonging to the state. He keeps in his office maps of the state, describing the bounds of counties and towns; and when disputes arise respecting the boundaries, he causes surveys to be made, if necessary, to ascertain such bounds. These and other similar duties he is by law required to perform. In some states there is no surveyor-general, the duty of that office being devolved upon a county officer.

§ 16. There is also, in many states, a state *superintendent of common schools*, or as he is sometimes called, *superintendent of public instruction*, whose general duties are described in a subsequent chapter.

§ 17. There are in every state one or more persons employed to do the public printing. A printer chosen for this purpose, is called *state printer.* It is his business to print the journal, bills, reports, and other papers and documents of each house of the legislature, and all the laws passed at each session to be distributed by the secretary of state as the law requires. State printers are either chosen by the legislature, or employed by persons appointed for that purpose; or the printing is let to the person or persons offering to do it at the lowest prices. Printers are required to give bonds, with sureties, for the faithful performance of the work.

§ 18. There are sundry other officers in the service of the state, properly called executive officers, among whom are the following: persons having the care of the *public buildings* and other property of the state; a *state librarian,* who has charge of the state library, consisting of books containing matter of a public nature, such as the laws of the state, laws of the United States and of the several states, enacted from year to year; together with a large collection of miscellaneous works; superintendents of state prisons, lunatic asylums, and other state institutions; whose duties are indicated by their titles, and need no particular description.

CHAPTER XVII.

COUNTIES AND COUNTY OFFICERS; POWERS AND DUTIES OF COUNTY OFFICERS.

§ 1. The necessity of dividing a state into small districts of territory, has already been mentioned. (Chap. IX., § 13, 14.) The first division is into counties; these again are divided into towns. These territorial divisions are the same as in England, the country from which the colonies were chiefly settled.

§ 2. Counties in England were formerly districts governed by *counts* or earls; hence the name of *county.* A county was also called *shire;* and an officer was appointed by the count or earl to perform certain acts in the principal town in the county, which town was called *shire town,* and the officer *shire-reeve*, or *sheriff*, whose powers and duties were of a nature similar to those of the sheriff of a county in this country. The shire town is that in which the court-house and other county buildings are situated, and where the principal officers of the county administration transact their business. In some counties there are two such towns, which are called *half-shires*.

§ 3. Counties and towns are bodies corporate, or bodies politic. A *body politic*, or corporation, is a number of persons united and authorized by law to act under one name, and as a single person, in the transaction of business. Hence a community of people, united for the purpose of government, is a body politic. Persons associated for any purpose without being incorporated by law, are not called a corporation. The object of incorporating an association by law, is to give its members the power to make certain rules for their government, and to enforce those rules ; and the power to sue and the capacity to be sued, and to hold and sell property, as one person.

§ 4. Although the names of the officers of the county administration, and the distribution of power therein, are in some respects different in the different states, the powers and duties of these officers are nearly the same in all the states. County officers are generally elected by the people of the counties at the general election.

§ 5. As a county possesses various corporate powers, there must necessarily be among its officers some in whose name these powers are to be exercised, and all acts and proceedings by and against it are to be done. In some of the New England states, Ohio, and others, there is a board of *county commissioners*, (usually three,) who exercise corporate powers. In New York and Michigan, these powers are exercised by and in the name of the *board of supervisors*, which is composed of the supervisors of the several towns, there being one supervisor in each town. This board of officers has power also to examine and settle the accounts against the county, and to order money to be raised to defray its expenses ; to make orders or contracts in relation to the building or repairing of the court-house, jail, and other county buildings ; and to perform such other acts as the laws require.

§ 6. There is also a *treasurer* in each county, to receive

and pay out the money required to be collected and paid out in the county. There is also an *auditor* in some states, to examine and adjust the accounts and debts of the county, and to perform certain other duties. The duties of county auditors, in their several counties, are similar to the duties of a state auditor. In states in which there is no county auditor, his duties are in part performed by the county treasurer, or some other county officer or officers.

§ 7. There is also a *register* or *recorder*, who provides suitable books, and records in them all deeds, mortgages, and other instruments of writing required by law to be recorded. In New York, and perhaps in some other states, the business of a register or recorder is performed by the *county clerk*, who is also clerk of the several courts held in the county, and who serves in the capacity of clerk or secretary to certain boards of county officers. In some states, deeds, mortgages, &c., are recorded by the town clerks of the several towns.

§ 8. Another county officer is a *sheriff*, whose duty it is to attend the sittings of all courts held in the county; to execute all warrants, writs, and other processes directed to him by the proper authority; to apprehend persons charged with crime; and to take charge of the jail and the prisoners therein. It is his duty also to preserve the public peace; and he may cause all persons who break the public peace within his knowledge or view, to give bonds, with sureties, for keeping the peace, and for appearing at the next court to be held in the county, and commit them to jail if they refuse to give such bonds. In the performance of these and other duties, he is assisted by deputies. Sheriffs are generally elected by the people.

§ 9. There are elected in each county one or more *coroners*, to inquire into the cause of the death of persons who have died by violence, or suddenly, and by means unknown. Notice of such death is given to the coroner, who orders a jury to be summoned, and witnesses subpœnaed, and repairs to the place of such dead person to inquire into the cause and manner of the death. Such examination is called a *coroner's inquest*. The fees of sheriffs and coroners are fixed by law.

§ 10. In some states there is a *county surveyor*, whose duties within his county are similar in their nature to those of a state surveyor-general.

§ 11. An attorney, elected or appointed for the purpose, attends all courts in which persons are tried in the county courts for crimes, and conducts all prosecutions for crimes tried in such courts. In states where there is no attorney-general for the state, the prosecuting attorney for each county serves in this capacity, in trials in which the state is a party. As all breaches of the peace, and all crimes, are considered as committed against the state, and prosecuted in its name, this attorney is sometimes called *state's attorney*.

CHAPTER XVIII.

TOWNS AND TOWN OFFICERS; POWERS AND DUTIES OF TOWN OFFICERS.

§ 1. The territories into which a county is divided, are usually called *towns*. In some states they are called, and perhaps more properly, *townships;* and the name of *town* is given to an incorporated village, or a city. We shall, however, in this work, apply to these territorial divisions the name of *town*.

§ 2. The people of the several towns meet once a year for the election of town officers, and for the regulation of certain town affairs. The electors of a town have power, at their annual town meetings, to order money to be raised for the support of the poor, for the building and repairing of bridges, and for other town purposes; to make regulations concerning fences; to fix the compensation of town officers in certain cases; and to perform such other acts as come within the usual powers of towns.

§ 3. The principal officers generally elected in towns, are the following: one or more persons who have the general oversight and direction of town affairs, called by some name corresponding to the nature of their duties; a town clerk; one or more assessors; one or more overseers of highways; overseers of the poor; officers to manage school affairs ; constables ; collectors of taxes ; treasurer ; fence-viewers ; pound-keepers, &c. In some states, there are also sealers of weights and measures ; persons to measure and inspect wood, lumber, bark, and other commodities.

§ 4. The officers first mentioned in the preceding section, are, in the New England states, called *selectmen*, of whom there are at least three, and in no state more than nine, in each town. In Ohio, and perhaps a few other states, they are called *trustees of townships*, and are three in number. In New York and Michigan, there is in each town one such officer, called *supervisor*.

§ 5. The powers and duties of these officers are more numerous and extensive in some states than in others. They have power to lay out roads, and lay out and alter road districts ; and to do certain acts relating to roads, bridges, taxes, common schools, the support of the poor, &c., and to examine and settle all demands against the town. In some of the states, however, some of these duties are in whole or in part performed by other officers.

§ 6. The *town clerk* keeps the records, books, and papers of the town ; records in a book the proceedings of town meetings, and the names of the officers elected at these meetings, and such other papers as are required by law to be recorded. In some states, deeds and other conveyances are recorded by the clerks of towns.

§ 7. The duties of *assessors* and *collectors* relate to the assessment and collection of taxes, and are described in another chapter.

§ 8. The persons having the general care and superintendence of highways, have power to lay out roads, and to lay out and alter road districts ; to assess the labor to be performed in the several districts ; to pay out the money raised for repairing bridges, &c. In some states, these duties are devolved upon other officers.

§ 9. Each town is divided by the proper officers into as many road districts as may be judged convenient ; and a person residing in each such district is chosen, called *overseer* or *supervisor* or *surveyor of highways*, whose duty it is to see that the roads are repaired and kept in order in his district. In some states, a tax is laid and collected, sufficient to keep in repair the highways, each person assessed being allowed to perform labor or furnish materials to the amount of his tax. In other states, road taxes are assessed upon the citizens in days' labor, according to the value of their property; every man, however, being assessed at least one day for his head, which is called a *poll-tax*. Persons not wishing to labor, may pay an equivalent in money, which is called *commuting*.

§ 10. It is the duty of *overseers of the poor* to provide for the support of all poor and indigent persons belonging to the town, who need relief, and have no near relations who are able to support them.

§ 11. The principal duties of a *constable* are, to serve all processes issued by justices of the peace in suits at law for collecting debts, and for arresting persons charged with crimes. The business of a constable in executing the orders of a justice of the peace, is similar to that of a sheriff in relation to the county courts.

§ 12. The *town treasurer* receives all moneys belonging to the town, and pays out the same as they may be wanted for town purposes, and accounts yearly to the proper officers. This office does not exist in all the states.

§ 13. The duties of *fence-viewers* relate chiefly to the settling of disputes between the owners of adjoining lands concerning division fences; the examining or viewing of fences when damage has been done by trespassing animals; and the estimation of damages in such cases.

For a particular description of the duties of town officers, reference must be had to the statutes of the several states.

CHAPTER XIX.

INCORPORATION AND GOVERNMENT OF CITIES, VILLAGES, &C.

§ 1. Cities and villages have governments peculiar to themselves. It is evident that places containing a large population, need a different government from that of ordinary towns or townships. Many of the laws regulating the affairs of towns sparsely inhabited, are not adapted to a place where many thousand persons are compactly settled

Besides, the electors in such a place would be too numerous to meet in a single assembly for the election of officers, or for other public business.

§ 2. Whenever, therefore, the inhabitants of any place become so numerous as to require a city government, they apply to the legislature for an act incorporating them into a city. The act or law of incorporation is usually called a *charter*. The origin of this word has been given. (Chapter X. § 3.) The word charter, in this country, is now commonly used to designate an act of the legislature conferring powers and privileges upon cities, villages, and certain other corporations.

§ 3. The chief executive officer of a city is a *mayor*. A city is divided into wards of convenient size, in each of which are chosen one or more *aldermen*, (usually two,) and such other officers as are named in the charter. The mayor and aldermen constitute the *common council*, which is a kind of legislature, having the power to pass such laws, (commonly called *ordinances*,) and make such orders and regulations, as the government of the city requires. The mayor presides in meetings of the common council, and performs certain judicial, and numerous other duties. There are also elected in the several wards, assessors, constables, collectors, and other necessary officers, whose duties in their respective wards are similar to those of like named officers in country towns.

§ 4. The people in cities, however, are not wholly governed by laws made by the common council. Most of the laws enacted by the state legislature, are of general application, and have the same effect in cities as elsewhere. Thus the laws of the state require that taxes shall be assessed and levied upon the property of the citizens of the state to defray the public expenses ; and the inhabitants of the cities are required to contribute their just proportion of the same ; but the city authorities impose and collect additional taxes for city purposes.

§ 5. In cities there are also courts of justice other than those which are established by the constitution or general laws of the state. A court for the trial of persons guilty of disturbing the peace, and of such minor offenses generally as are punished by imprisonment in the county jail, exists in cities, and is called a *police court*. It is held by a *police jus-*

tice, who is either elected by the people or appointed in such manner as the law prescribes. In some of the larger cities, there are courts of *civil* as well as criminal jurisdiction, differing from those which are common to counties generally.

§ 6. The government of incorporated villages is not in all respects like that of cities. The chief executive officer of such villages is in some states called *president*. The village is not divided into wards ; the number of inhabitants being generally too small to render such divisions necessary. Instead of a board of aldermen, there is a *board of trustees*, or *directors*, who exercise similar powers. The president of a village is usually chosen by the trustees from their number. In Ohio, and some other states, incorporated villages are called *towns*, and their chief executive officer is called *mayor*.

§ 7. In some states, there is a general law under which the inhabitants of any village may form themselves into such corporation, with the necessary powers of government, without a special law of incorporation.

§ 8. Not only is every city, town, and county, a corporation, but the state itself, whose citizens are united for the purpose of government, is one great corporation. The latter, however, is not formed by an act of the legislature as other corporations are, but by the people themselves in establishing the constitution or political law of the state.

§ 9. Besides these *territorial corporations*, as counties, towns, cities, &c., for purposes of government, there are *incorporated companies* for carrying on business of various kinds, as turnpike and rail-road companies, and companies for purposes of manufacturing, banking, insurance, &c. These several kinds of business, to be carried on extensively and successfully, usually require a larger amount of money than a single individual possesses. A number of persons therefore unite their capital, and ask for an act of incorporation, granting them powers which they could not have in the capacity of an ordinary business partnership. A more particular description of some of these corporations will be given in another chapter.

§ 10. One of the characteristics of a corporation is, that it is perpetual. An ordinary business partnership must end on the death of any one or more of the partners. Not so with a corporation. When the persons who first composed the corporation are all dead, the corporation is still alive; for those who come after them have the same powers and privileges.

CHAPTER XX.

ASSESSMENT AND COLLECTION OF TAXES.

§ 1. As no government can be maintained without expense, and as every citizen is in some way benefited by the government, it is the duty of all who are able, to contribute to its support. Every government must therefore have the power to provide the means of defraying its expenses. This is done chiefly by taxation. Taxes are assessed and levied principally upon the property of the citizens.

§ 2. All lands, and all personal property, are subject to taxation, except public property; as the corporate property of the state, of counties, and towns, including the buildings in which the public business is done, the prisons, jails, asylums, &c., and the lands attached to them; also school-houses and meeting-houses with lands attached; burial-grounds; and the property of literary and charitable institutions; these several kinds of property being exempt from taxation. *Lands, real property,* and *real estate,* have the same meaning, and include land, with all buildings and other articles erected or growing thereon. *Personal estate,* or *personal property,* includes all household furniture, money, goods, chattels, and debts due from solvent debtors.

§ 3. As each citizen is to be assessed in proportion to the value of his property, it is necessary, first, to make a correct valuation of all the taxable property. For this purpose, the assessor or assessors pass through the town and make a list of the names of all the taxable inhabitants, and the estimated value of the property, real and personal, of each; and returns of the same are made to the proper county officers, who cause the tax list for each town to be made out, and order the taxes to be collected.

§ 4. In some states, every person liable to taxation is

himself required to furnish a list of all his taxable property; printed blank lists having been previously distributed among the taxable inhabitants for this purpose. To secure accuracy in the lists, the assessors (called also *listers*) may require persons to make oath that they have made a true statement of their property, real and personal, and of its estimated value. In states where the polls of the tax payers are assessed, these also are set down in the lists at such sums as the law directs to be affixed to each poll.

§ 5. Before a tax list can be made out, it must be known what amount is to be collected in each town. The amount is made up of three parts: first, the sum wanted to defray the expenses of the town; secondly, its share of the county expenses; and thirdly, its proportion of the expenses of the state government, or of what is to be raised for state purposes.

§ 6. The apportionment of the state and county expenses among the several towns, is made according to the amount of property in each as valued by the assessors. The state auditor or controller, having received from the several counties returns of the aggregate value of the property of each county, is enabled to apportion to each its quota of the amount to be raised for state purposes. To each county's share of the state expenses is added the sum to be raised for county purposes, and the amount is apportioned among the towns. Then adding to each town's share of the county and state expenses, the amount to be raised for town purposes, gives the amount to be collected in the town.

§ 7. Having thus ascertained the sum to be raised in each town, the officers whose duty it is, cause a tax list to be made out, containing the names of all taxable persons in the town, and the amount of each person's tax opposite his name. The tax list of each town, certified and signed by the proper persons, is put into the hands of the collector, with a warrant ordering the same to be collected.

§ 8. In some states, town, county, and state taxes are, or may be collected separately, and whenever they shall be ordered by the proper authorities. In other states, however, the whole amount to be raised for state, county, and town purposes, for the year, is made out in a single rate bill. The money collected for county and state purposes, is paid to the county treasurer, who pays to the state treasurer the amount of the state tax ; and the remainder is applied to the payment of the county expenses. And the amount collected for town purposes is paid to such persons in the town as are by law authorized to receive the same.

CHAPTER XXI

THE MILITIA.

§ 1. To defend a country against foreign enemies, and to put down insurrections and rebellion against the government by its own citizens, it is the practice of governments to keep their respective countries prepared for events of this kind. For this purpose, men are required to meet every year on certain days for instruction in the art of war.

§ 2. All white male citizens of the United States, between the ages of eighteen and forty-five years, are liable to do military duty in the states in which they reside, except such persons as are exempt by the laws of the state and of the United States. Persons exempt by the laws of the state, are usually the following : Ministers of the gospel ; commissioned officers of the militia having served a certain number of years ; members of uniformed companies having served for a specified term ; members of fire companies ; certain public officers while in office ; and in some states, teachers and students of colleges, academies and common schools ; and a few others. Persons exempted by the laws of the United States, are the vice-president and all executive and judicial officers of the government of the United States ; members of congress and its officers ; custom-house officers and their clerks ; post-officers and drivers of mail stages ; ferrymen employed at ferries on post-roads ; pilots and mariners.

§ 3. It will be seen that the president of the United States, and the governor of the state, are not mentioned among the persons who are free from military duty. By the constitution of the United States, the president is commander-in-chief of the army and navy of the United States; and of the militia of the several states also, when called out into actual service; and by the constitution of the state, the governor is the commander-in-chief of the militia of the state.

§ 4. Persons who, having been duly notified, refuse to appear at military parades, or, appearing, are not equipped as the law directs, are tried by a military court, called *court martial*, consisting usually of three military officers, or of such other persons as may be appointed according to the law of the state. If the persons tried do not show good cause for their delinquency, they are fined in such sum as the law prescribes. In certain cases, courts may consist of more than three members.

§ 5. The highest militia officer next in rank to the governor, is the *adjutant-general* of the state; who keeps a list of all the higher commissioned officers, containing the date of their commissions, their rank, the corps they belong to, the division, brigade and regiment, and the places of their residence. He distributes all orders from the commander-in-chief to the several divisions; attends public reviews where the commander-in-chief shall review the militia; and obeys all orders from him relative to carrying into execution the system of military discipline established by law.

§ 6. There is also, in some states, a *commissary-general*, who has the care of the arsenals and magazines, and the articles deposited in them. An *arsenal* is a building in which are kept cannon, muskets, powder, balls, and other warlike stores; all of which are to be kept in repair and ready for use. The commissary also furnishes the officers of the militia such articles as they are entitled to receive for the use of their companies.

§ 7. There are persons who, believing all wars to be wrong, can not conscientiously do military duty. As it is the object of our government to secure to every person the liberty of conscience as well as other rights, the constitutions of the states provide, that those who are averse to bearing arms, may be excused by paying annually a sum of money as an equivalent for the service required by law. But it may well be doubted whether compelling a man to pay such equivalent is not itself a violation of the rights of conscience. Persons conceiving it no less morally wrong to commute for the service than to perform it, have refused to do either, and have submitted to the forcible collection of the commutation money, and, in some instances, even to imprisonment. Hence, in some states, all persons belonging to the society of Friends, usually called Quakers, are exempt without the payment of an equivalent.

§ 8. By the laws of New York and Ohio, the rank and file of the militia in these states are not required to train in time of peace. Persons subject to do military duty, except those connected with the uniformed companies, are enrolled in the militia ; and instead of doing duty, they annually pay a small tax, which, in New York, is fifty cents, and in Ohio fifty cents, or a day's highway labor.

§ 9. Laws abolishing trainings and musters of the great body of the militia, are growing into favor, and for these, among other reasons : first, the militia system produces no material improvement in discipline ; secondly, the time spent in these useless exercises, and the money expended for arms and equipments, are burdensome to many citizens ; and thirdly, there is no probability of an occasion requiring a large portion of the militia to be called into immediate service. The volunteer companies and the standing army of the nation, are deemed sufficient for any supposable emergency.

§ 10. Happily, the practice of settling controversies between nations by war, is becoming less popular in civilized and Christian communities. War is a fearful evil, and ought to be discouraged, and, if possible, avoided. Were governments so disposed, they might in most cases settle their differences peaceably and honorably, as individuals do. If the love of military honor were less encouraged, and the principles of peace duly inculcated, the time would be hastened when "nations shall learn war no more."

CHAPTER XXII.

EDUCATION; SCHOOL FUNDS; SCHOOLS, &C.

§ 1. The object of a good government is to promote the happiness and welfare of its citizens. To protect them in the enjoyment of life and the fruits of their labor, is not its whole duty. It should go further, and make express provision for improving the condition of the people, especially the less favored portions of them.

§ 2. The prosperity and happiness of a people depend essentially upon their education. In many of the eastern countries, the people, for the want of intelligence, are degraded and miserable. They are governed by a despot, who rules over them with great rigor. Such is their ignorance, that they know not that there could be any improvement in their condition: consequently, they could not govern themselves as the people of this country do. It is only where the people are well educated, that a free government can be maintained. Therefore, if we would secure a continuance of the blessings of good government, the advantages of education must be enjoyed by the citizens generally; and it is the duty of the government to provide the means for promoting the general diffusion of useful knowledge. The states have accordingly instituted school systems for the instruction of children and youth of all classes.

§ 3. But the states do not all provide these means in the same manner, nor to the same extent. In most of them the schools are supported only in part, in a few of them wholly, at the public expense. In some states, a fund has been provided, the income of which is annually applied to this object. A *fund*, in general, is a sum of money used for carrying on business of any kind. The money, or capital stock, which a merchant employs in trade, is a fund. Also the moneys and other property of a state, which are set apart for paying the expenses of the government, or for the construction of canals, roads, and other public improvements, are called funds. The interest of these funds, and the income from other sources, are called the *revenue*.

§ 4 In some states, school funds are provided by appropriating the public lands, which are lands owned by the state as a corporate body; the proceeds of which, from sales or rents, constitute a part or the whole of the school fund, the interest of which is annually applied to the support of schools. If the income from the school fund is insufficient for this purpose, the deficiency may, as is done in some states, be supplied, in whole or in part, by taxation, or from the state treasury. In several of the states, the common schools are wholly supported at the public expense.

§ 5. Many of the new states have large school funds. At an early period, while most of the territory from which these states have been formed was yet the property of the United States, and uninhabited, congress passed an act, designating a particular section of land (number sixteen) in every township, for the support of schools therein. By this act, one-thirty-sixth part of the lands within each of these states, has been thus appropriated, besides smaller portions granted for the benefit of a university in each state. These lands are in the charge of the proper officers, who dispose of them, and apply the proceeds as the law directs.

§ 6. The school funds of many of the states have been largely increased by certain moneys received from the United States. In 1837, there had accumulated in the national treasury, about thirty millions of dollars over and above what was needed for the expenses of the government. By an act of congress, this surplus revenue was distributed among the states then existing, to be kept by them until called for by congress. Although congress reserved the right to recall the money, it was presumed that it would never be demanded. That it never will be, is now almost certain. Many of the states have appropriated large portions of their respective shares for educational purposes. From its having been said to be only *deposited* with the states, this fund is sometimes called the *United States deposit fund.*

§ 7. School moneys coming from the state treasury, or state fund, are usually apportioned among the several towns of the state; and each town's share of the same, together with what may be raised in the town by taxation, or derived from its school lands, is divided among the several districts according to the number of children between certain ages in each, or in such other manner as may be directed by law. If the moneys thus received are insufficient to pay the wages of teachers, the deficiency is collected from the persons whose children have been taught in the schools, by rate bill.

§ 8. The towns, or townships, are divided into districts of suitable size for schools, which are called *district schools.* They are also called *common schools,* from their being supported by a common fund, and designed for the common benefit; and perhaps also from the lower and more common branches only being taught in them. One or more *trustees* or *directors* are annually chosen to manage the affairs of the district; also a *district clerk,* to record the proceedings of all district meetings; and a *collector* to collect taxes assessed upon the inhabitants for building and repairing school-houses, and all rate bills for the payment of teachers.

§ 9. The highest common school officer is the *state superintendent of common schools.* The superintendent collects information relating to the schools; the number of children residing in each district, and the number taught; the amount paid for tuition; the number of school-houses, and the amount yearly expended in erecting school-houses; and other matters concerning the operations and effects of the common school system. If there is no other officer whose duty it is, the superintendent also apportions the money arising from the state funds among the several counties. He reports to the legislature at every session the information he has collected, and suggests such improvements in the school system as he thinks ought to be made.

§ 10. There is in each county an officer who receives from the state superintendent the money apportioned to his county, and apportions the same among the several towns of the county. He also reports to the state superintendent the number of children in the county; and performs such other duties as the law requires. In some states, there is no such officer; but the money is apportioned by the state superintendent among the towns; and the reports from the towns are made directly to the state superintendent.

§ 11. In the towns there are officers whose duties are, to examine teachers, visit schools, apportion the school moneys among the districts, and to collect the lists of the number of children in the several districts, with such other information as the law requires, and report the same to the county officer, or if there is none, to the state superintendent. In some states, there is in each county an officer, or a board of officers, for the examination of teachers, and for the performance of certain other duties relating to the schools of the county.

§ 12. Academies and colleges also receive aid from the state, to a limited extent. A distinct fund is created in some states for their benefit; in others, they are aided by special appropriations from the state treasury.

CHAPTER XXIII.

CANALS; RAIL-ROADS, &C.

§ 1. In further carrying out the purposes of government, provision ought to be made to secure to the citizens the means of obtaining a suitable reward for their industry. As all must contribute to the support of the government from the avails of their labor, the government ought, by all just and proper means, to render the labor of all, as nearly as may be, equally profitable.

§ 2. The people of a large state do not all possess equal advantages. Those who reside near navigable waters and good roads, are better rewarded for their labor than others who reside at a greater distance from them. A farm in the vicinity of a good market, may possess double the value of another of equal size and fertility, in a remote part of the state; because a large portion of the value of the products of the latter is expended in transporting them to market. And those who reside far in the country must also pay higher prices for the goods they purchase, to remunerate the merchants for the cost of transportation. Hence the necessity of good roads, canals, or other means of facilitating intercourse between distant parts of the state.

§ 3. Among the works of public utility, canals are perhaps the most useful, and are to be preferred wherever their construction is practicable. *Canals* are sometimes constructed by incorporated companies ; but generally these works, especially those of considerable magnitude, are constructed by the state, and are the property of the state. Although there are some states in which there are no canals of the latter description, it may be interesting to young persons to know how so important a state work is accomplished.

§ 4. To raise the money necessary to make a canal, the legislature might levy a general tax upon the property of the citizens ; but this would be inexpedient ; because, first, the payment of so large a sum within the time in which it would be desirable to complete the work, would be burdensome ; and secondly, the burden must fall alike upon the people of all parts of the state, whereas those residing most remotely from the line of the work, would derive from it no material advantage.

§ 5. When, therefore, a great work of this kind is undertaken by a state, the law authorizing the work usually provides a *fund*, the income of which is to be applied to this object. This fund consists of such lands, property, and moneys as the legislature may grant for this purpose. A fund was thus constituted in Ohio, at the commencement of the canal enterprise in that state ; to which fund congress subsequently made a grant of 840,000 acres of the public lands of the United States lying in that state. Similar grants of land in other western states, have, it is believed, been made for canals or other public improvements.

§ 6. These funds, however, furnish but a part, some of them only a small part, of the money necessary to complete the work : and all the states undertaking public improvements, may not have the lands or other property to constitute such a fund. The state, therefore, obtains the money, chiefly or wholly, by borrowing the same for a long term of years, relying on the income of the canal fund, and the proceeds of tolls collected on the canals when completed, to repay the cost of their construction. Should the income of the canals and canal fund prove insufficient, the deficiency may be supplied by taxation. The original cost of the Erie canal in the state of New York, completed in 1825, was reimbursed by the revenue arising from tolls and the canal fund, about ten years after its completion, without the necessity of taxation ; and its enlargement now in progress, (1858,) at a cost of nearly $25,000,000, will, it is presumed, be ultimately reimbursed in the same manner.

§ 7. The business of borrowing the money is done, on the part of the state, by persons duly authorized, who give for the money borrowed the bonds of the state, which are written promises to pay the money at the time specified, with interest at the rate agreed on ; the interest generally to be paid semi-annually. These bonds are usually given in sums of $1,000 each. The debts of a state thus contracted by issuing bonds, are called *state stocks*, as the capital or stock required to construct any state work, is obtained by the sale of these bonds. These bonds, like the certificates of stock in a rail-road or turnpike company, are transferable, and may be bought and sold as promissory notes, and constitute an important article of trade.

§ 8. These stocks are taken by men who have large sums of money to lend, and who consider the state a responsible debtor ; because, if it has no other means of paying its bonds, the legislature has power to raise the money by taxation. Most of the states have contracted debts in this manner for various purposes ; and many of them are largely indebted, not only to American capitalists, but to those of European countries, whence many millions have been sent to the United States to purchase state stocks.

§ 9. Officers are appointed according to law to manage the canal fund, and others to superintend the canals. There are also officers at suitable distances along the canals to collect the tolls, which are charges paid by the masters or owners of boats for the use of the canal.

§ 10. The states of New York, Pennsylvania, Ohio, and some other western states, have prosecuted the canal enterprise on a large scale. And although large debts have been incurred by the construction of these canals, the benefits derived from them more than compensate for the vast expense of their construction.

§ 11. *Rail-roads* are constructed by companies incorporated for that purpose. The necessity for an act of incorporation is readily seen. Rail-roads pass through the lands of private individuals ; and without the authority of law, the land of no person can be taken for such purpose ; nor can a law authorize it to be taken unless the work is one of public utility ; nor even in such case, unless compensation is made to the owner for his land ; for it is declared by the constitutions of the several states, that "private property shall not be taken for public use without just compensation."

§ 12. If, therefore, the legislature deem such road to be of public utility, they incorporate the company with the requisite powers to construct the road, on making compensation for the land, the value of which is to be estimated in such manner as the law prescribes. The law also prescribes the manner in which the general affairs of the road are to be conducted.

§ 13. The amount of capital to be employed by the company, is mentioned in the act, and is raised in this way : The amount of capital, or stock, is divided into shares of $50 or $100 each. Persons wishing to invest money in the road, subscribe the number of shares they will respectively take. When all the shares are thus sold, and the money is paid in, the company is ready to proceed to the construction of the road. The owners of these shares are called *stockholders*, who choose from among themselves such number of *directors* as the act of incorporation authorizes. The directors elect from their number a *president*.

§ 14. A person buying shares, receives a certificate signed by the proper officers, stating the number of shares he has purchased. The holder of these certificates, if he wishes to make some other use of the money he has invested in the business, may sell his stock to some other person, to whom he passes his certificate, which is evidence of the amount of stock so purchased. Thus these certificates are bought and sold as promissory notes.

§ 15. Stockholders depend, for the reimbursement of their capital, upon the money to be received for the transportation of passengers and freight. Such portion of the income of the road as remains after paying all expenses of running and repairs, is divided semi-annually among the stockholders. Hence the sums thus divided are called *dividends*. The returns from some roads are so large as to make the investment a profitable one ; so that the holder of shares is enabled to sell them at a profit. When shares in the stock of any institution are bought and sold at their nominal value, stocks are said to be at *par*. If above or below the nominal value, they are said to be above or below par. In large commercial cities, as New York, Boston and Philadelphia, the purchase and sale of stocks in rail-roads, banks, insurance companies, &c., is a regular and extensive business of capitalists.

CHAPTER XXIV.

BANKS AND INSURANCE COMPANIES.

§ 1. We are informed that the first institution of bank was in Italy, where certain Jews kept benches in the market places for the exchange of money and bills; and *banco* being the Italian name for bench, banks took their title from this word. The first banks are supposed to have been only places where money was laid up or deposited for safe keeping. But banks at the present day are not used for depositing alone.

§ 2. Banks in this country can be established only by authority of law. If the inhabitants of a place want a bank, they petition the legislature to incorporate a banking association. The act of incorporation prescribes the manner in which the company shall be formed, how its business shall be done, and the amount of capital or stock to be employed. The capital of a bank is raised by the sale of shares and issue of certificates, as in the case of railroads, (Chap. XXIII, §13, 14.)

§ 3. The stockholders elect of their number, usually thirteen directors, who choose one of themselves to be president. The president and directors choose a cashier and clerks.

§ 4. A part of the business of banks is still that for which they were originally established, namely, the receiving of money on *deposit*. Merchants and others in commercial places, deposit in a bank, for safe-keeping, the money they receive in the course of business, and then draw it out on their written orders as they have occasion to use it. An order of this kind is called *check*. Persons depositing money only occasionally, and intending to draw for the same at once, usually receive from the cashier a *certificate of deposit*, which states the name of the depositor, the sum deposited, and to whose order it is to be paid. For the use of money deposited for any considerable period, banks agree to pay interest, usually, however, less than the established or ordinary rate. Certificates of deposit may, by indorsement, be made transferable as other negotiable paper, and are often remitted to distant places, where, by presentation at a bank, they may, for a trifling compensation, be converted into money.

§ 5. Another kind of business done by banks is, to assist merchants and others in transmitting money to distant places. An operation of this kind is performed thus: A, in Boston, wishing to send $1,000 to B, in Philadelphia, puts the money into a bank in Boston, and takes for it an order, or draft, on a bank in Philadelphia, for that amount, to be paid to B. The draft is sent by mail to B, who calls at the bank and receives the money; and the bank charges the amount to the Boston bank.

§ 6. But how does the bank in Philadelphia get the money from the bank in Boston? There are in Philadelphia business men who have occasion to remit money to Boston, and who pay their money into the Philadelphia bank, and take drafts on the bank at Boston. The banks at both places are constantly receiving money and drawing upon each other. Thus the transmission of millions of dollars may be performed every year through the banks, without any expense except the small charge of the banks for transacting the business: and a vast amount of travel, and the risk of loss by accident or robbery, which attends the conveyance of money in person, are avoided.

§ 7. A material part of the business of banks is to lend money. A person wishing to borrow money at a bank, makes a note for the sum wanted, which is signed by himself, and indorsed by one or more others as sureties. For this note the cashier pays the money, usually in the bank's own bills, retaining the interest on the sum so lent, instead of waiting to receive it when the note becomes due. This is called *discounting* a note.

§ 8. Banks are allowed to issue their own bills as money. A bank bill or note contains a promise to pay the bearer a certain sum on demand, and is signed by the president and cashier. It passes as money, because the bank is bound to pay it in specie, if it is demanded. Paying notes thus is called redeeming them. When a bank is unable to redeem all the bills it has issued, it is said to fail, or to be broken. In such case, the bill-holders suffer loss, unless some security has been provided.

§ 9. For the security of bill-holders, the stockholders of banks are, in some states, made individually responsible for the redemption of their bills; that is, their individual property is liable to be taken for that purpose. In a few states, *safety funds* have been provided for redeeming the bills of broken banks. A yearly tax is levied upon the several banks of the state, until a sum has accumulated which is deemed sufficient to meet all supposable failures. When this fund has been exhausted, it is replenished by renewed taxation.

§ 10. But a system of banking, called *free banking*, has more recently been adopted in some states. This system is designed to provide more effectually for the security of bill-holders, and throws open the business of banking to all, by a *general law.* Any person, or any number of persons, may, by complying with the conditions of this general law, establish a bank without a special law for this purpose. Persons, before commencing business under this law, are required to put into the hands of the proper state officers, ample securities for the redemption of their bills; and they may not issue bills to a greater amount than the amount of their securities. These securities must consist of approved state stocks, or United States' stocks, or partly of public stocks and partly of real estate. When a bank fails, the lands and stocks held in pledge by the state are sold, and the avails applied to the redemption of bills. This system of banking seems to be growing into public favor.

§ 11. *Insurance companies* also are authorized by law. Their business is to insure persons against loss by fire. The corporators, on being paid a small sum, consisting of a certain per centage on the amount for which the property is insured, agree to pay such amount if the property shall be destroyed by fire. There are companies also for insuring ships and other vessels at sea; and *life insurance companies*, that agree to pay, in case of the death of the person insured, a certain sum for the benefit of his family, or of some other person or persons named in the policy.

§ 12. The profits to the stockholders of an insurance company, consist of the excess of premiums received over the amount paid out for losses. Thus, if a company has issued 2,000 policies, each covering property of an average amount of $1,000, the amount of risk is $2,000,000 ; and if the rate of insurance is one per cent., the amount received in premiums is $20,000. Hence, if none of the 2,000 buildings insured are burned within the year, this sum is gained. If ten of them should be burned, the gain would be $10,000 less. If twenty should be destroyed, there would be no gain, but an actual loss to the amount of the necessary expenses of the concern, to be paid out of the capital stock of the company.

§ 13. But from the average number of losses annually during a long course of years, companies are enabled so to fix the rates of insurance, as to secure to the stockholders a fair profit on their capital. The rates of insurance are not the same on all property ; a higher per centage being charged on that which is deemed hazardous ; that is, more exposed to fire, than is charged on that which is less exposed. The profits on the business of the company, are annually or semi-annually divided among the stockholders in proportion to the amount of their respective shares, and are called *dividends.*

§ 14. There is another kind of insurance companies, which differ materially from the *stock* companies described in the preceding sections. They are called *mutual insurance* companies. They are so called because the members unite in insuring each other. Every person having his property insured by such a company, is a member of it. He has his buildings and the property in them valued ; and he pays a certain rate per cent. on such valuation. A fund is thus raised, out of which any member suffering loss by fire is paid the value of the property lost. Whenever the fund is exhausted, it is again supplied by a tax assessed upon the members in proportion to the value of each one's property insured.

CHAPTER XXV.

JUDICIAL DEPARTMENT; JUSTICES' COURTS.

§ 1. In the preceding chapters it has been shown how the laws of the state are made, and how the government is administered; and also what are the powers and duties of officers in the legislative and executive departments of the government. There is another class of officers, whose powers and duties remain to be described, called *judicial officers.* Their business is to administer justice to the citizens; and when sitting for that purpose, they are called a *court.*

§ 2. It is the legislature of the state which determines what acts shall be deemed public offenses, and what shall be considered right and just between the citizens; but to judge of and interpret the laws, and decide whether they have been violated, and to determine the proper measure of justice, is, as has been observed, wisely committed to a separate and distinct department. (Chapter IX, § 8.)

§ 3. A government without some power to decide disputes, to award justice to the citizens, and to punish crime, according to the laws of the state, would be incomplete. It would be improper to allow every man who thinks himself injured to be judge in his own case, and to redress his own wrongs. Justice is best secured to the citizens by establishing courts for the redress of injuries, and for the punishment of crimes; and that no injustice may be done to any member of the community, constitutions require, that in all cases of crime, however openly committed, the offender shall have a fair and impartial trial.

§ 4. There are several courts in each state. Some are of a higher, others of a lower order: by which is meant, that some have greater jurisdiction than others. In speaking of the jurisdiction of a court, reference is had to its power to pronounce the law. The word *jurisdiction* is composed of two Latin words, *jus*, law, or *juris* of the law, and *dictio*, speaking; hence juris dictio, a speaking or pronouncing of the law. The jurisdiction of a court therefore means its power to determine questions in law.

§ 5. Some courts have power only to try civil causes; others have jurisdiction in causes both civil and criminal. Some have jurisdiction in cases arising in any part of the state; others only in cases arising within the county. As most suits at law are tried in justices' courts, and as cases may be carried up from them to the higher courts, we will begin with the lowest and proceed to the highest.

§ 6. *Justices' Courts.* Justices of the peace are in most of the states elected by the people in the towns; but their jurisdiction extends throughout the county. Justices of the peace usually have power only to try civil causes in which limited sums are claimed, and criminal causes in which the lowest offenses are charged. Causes are called *civil*, when money is claimed; *criminal* when persons are tried for crime. Causes, actions, and suits, are words generally used to signify the same thing, meaning prosecutions at law, or lawsuits. The party that sues is called *plaintiff*; the party sued is the *defendant*.

§ 7. Actions may be commenced by the parties going voluntarily before a justice; but this is seldom done. They are generally commenced by compulsory process. *Process* sometimes means the whole course of proceedings in a suit, from the beginning to the end. It also denotes a particular stage of the proceedings, as the *original* or *commencing process*; the *mesne* (pronounced *mean*) *process*, intervening between the beginning and the determination of a suit; and the *final process*, or process of execution. The word is applied to the written instruments issued by judicial officers to enforce proceedings at law. The process by which a suit is commenced, is a writ, or *summons*; and the action is considered commenced, when the summons is delivered to the constable.

§ 8. A summons issued by a justice of the peace, is addressed to a constable of the town, in some states to any constable of the county, commanding him to summon the defendant to appear before the justice on a day and at an hour specified, to answer the plaintiff in a suit, the nature of which is mentioned in the summons. If the defendant is found, the constable serves the summons by reading it; and if the defendant requests it, the constable must give him a copy of it. If he is not found, a copy must be left at his place of abode, with some one of the family of suitable age. The constable returns the summons to the justice, at or before the time named for trial, with an indorsement on the back of it, stating the time it was served, and also whether personally served, or served by copy.

§ 9. Either party may appear in person, or by attorney, a person appointed to answer and act for him. When parties have appeared and answered to their names, they make their pleadings ; that is, the plaintiff declares for what he brings his suit ; and the defendant declares the nature of what he has to *offset* against the plaintiff's demand, or pleads payment, or denies the demand altogether. These acts of the parties are called *joining issue.*

§ 10. The declaration of a party is not taken as evidence in his own favor in a court of justice : he can not establish a fact without *witnesses.* The justice, therefore, at the request of either party, issues a *subpena,* which is a writ commanding persons to appear and give evidence. Subpenas may be served by a constable or other person, who must pay, or tender to the witness, the legal fee for a day's attendance, or the witness is not obliged to attend.

§ 11. If a person duly subpenaed, whose testimony is material, does not appear, the justice may issue an attachment, commanding the constable to bring the witness before the court ; and the witness may be charged with the fees of the constable and justice, or fined in some other way, as the law provides, unless he shall show good cause for not attending. Also a witness who, without a reasonable excuse, does not appear, or appearing, refuses to testify, may be fined by the justice, and is liable to pay the damage sustained by the party in whose behalf he was subpenaed.

§ 12. At the time of trial, the justice proceeds to try the issue. The witnesses are sworn to testify truly to what they know ; and after hearing the testimony on both sides, the justice decides according to law and equity, as the right of the case may appear. If a defendant does not appear at the time of trial, the justice may hear the proofs and allegations of the plaintiff, and determine the case according to what shall be made to appear by that party alone. If anything is found to be due to either party, the justice enters judgment against the party indebted, for the amount due the other, with the costs of suit, which consist of the fees of the justice, constable and witnesses. If nothing is found to be due the plaintiff, judgment is entered against him for the costs.

§ 13. If at the time of joining issue, the parties, or either of them, for want of material witnesses, or for other sufficient reasons, can not safely proceed to trial, the justice may *adjourn* the trial to a future day.

§ 14. A plaintiff may discontinue or withdraw his action before judgment is rendered; in which case the justice enters judgment of *nonsuit*, which means a stoppage of the suit. A plaintiff is also nonsuited for not appearing when his name is called in court at the time appointed for trial, or for some other default. In all cases of nonsuit, and also when a trial is had and no cause of action is found, judgment is rendered against the plaintiff for costs.

§ 15. A debtor may avoid the expense of a lawsuit, by *confessing judgment*. The parties go before a justice, and the debtor acknowledges the claim of the creditor, and consents that the justice enter judgment accordingly. In some states, the confession and consent must be in writing, and signed by the debtor. The sum for which judgment may be confessed, is limited by law.

CHAPTER XXVI.

TRIAL BY JURIES; COLLECTION OF JUDGMENTS; APPEALS.

§ 1. One of the most valuable privileges enjoyed by the people of this country, is the right of trial by jury. A justice may be suspected of partiality or incompetency; or it may sometimes be deemed unsafe to submit a cause to the judgment of a single individual who enjoys in a high degree the public confidence. Our constitutions therefore guaranty to every citizen the privilege of having a jury to try a cause to which he is a party.

§ 2. A *jury* is a number of men who sit on a trial, and are sworn to try a matter of fact, and to declare the truth according to evidence. This declaring of the truth is called *verdict*, which means a true saying. A jury in a justice's court consists of six men, all of whom must agree in their verdict.

§ 3. The manner of selecting the jurors is prescribed by law, and is not the same in all the states. After issue is joined, and before testimony is heard, either party may demand of the justice that the cause be tried by a jury. Whereupon the justice issues a *venire*, which is a writ or precept commanding a constable to summon such number of duly qualified men as the law directs, to appear before the justice to make a jury to try the cause between the parties named in the venire. As is the practice in some states, a greater number than six is summoned, and from that number the six are drawn who are to constitute the jury. In some states, freeholders only are lawfully qualified to serve as jurors.

§ 4. After hearing the proofs and arguments on both sides, the jurors are put under the charge of a constable, who is sworn to keep them in some convenient place, without meat or drink, except such as the justice may order, till they agree on their verdict, or till discharged by the justice; and not to allow any person to speak to them during such time, nor speak to them himself, except by order of the justice, unless to ask them whether they have agreed on their verdict. When they have so agreed, they return, and deliver the verdict, in open court, to the justice, who enters judgment according to the finding of the jury. If the jurors do not all agree after having been out a reasonable time, they are discharged; and a new venire is issued, unless the parties consent that the justice render judgment on the evidence. Persons summoned as jurors may be fined for not appearing, or for refusing to serve.

§ 5. After a judgment has been rendered, the justice issues an *execution*, which is a writ commanding the constable to collect the amount of the judgment, and, if necessary, to take and sell the goods and chattels of the debtor, and make returns to the justice within the time required. If the money can not be collected, the execution is returned as not satisfied. A justice of the peace can not issue an execution against real estate. If a constable, through negligence, fails to collect a judgment as required by the execution, or if he neglects to return the execution to the justice within the time mentioned therein, the constable himself and his sureties become liable to pay the amount of the judgment.

§ 6. There are certain articles of personal property which are exempt from execution, and which poor men are allowed to retain for the use and comfort of themselves and their families; such as necessary household furniture, apparel, beds, and the tools or implements of trade. Besides reserving these articles of personal property, the law, in many states, exempts from execution a house and lot of limited value. The practice, once generally prevalent in this country, of imprisoning debtors who were unable to satisfy executions, has been abolished, except for fines and penalties.

§ 7. The foregoing description of the proceedings of a justice's court is that of a prosecution in ordinary cases. But there are other modes of prosecution in certain cases, one of which is by *attachment.* An attachment is a writ directing the property of a debtor to be taken, and kept till a trial can be had, and judgment obtained. This mode of proceeding is adopted when the plaintiff has reason to believe that a debtor conceals himself to avoid being prosecuted by summons, or is about to remove his property or himself from the county, or intends in some other way to defraud his creditors.

§ 8. In case of an absent or concealed debtor, the constable, as is the common practice, leaves a copy of the attachment, with an inventory of the property attached, at the defendant's last place of residence; or, if he had none in the county, the copy and inventory are to be left with the person in whose possession the property is found. If the defendant does not appear on the day of trial, the plaintiff may proceed to prove his demand, and take judgment. An execution is then issued against the property attached.

§ 9. *Appeals.* If either party is dissatisfied with a judgment rendered in a justice's court, he may have the cause removed to the county court. In some states, there are certain cases in which no appeal from a justice's court is allowed. When the removal is made by *appeal*, the whole cause is removed; the witnesses again give their testimony; and the facts are submitted for a rehearing. When a cause is removed by a *writ of error*, the witnesses are not required to attend the trial in a higher court. The substance of the testimony and proceedings before the justice is produced before the court, and upon this the judges give judgment, as the right of the case may appear. If they decide the judgment of the lower court to be correct, they are said to *affirm* such judgment; but if they find it wrong, they *reverse* it.

CHAPTER XXVII.

COURTS OTHER THAN JUSTICES' COURTS.

§ 1. There is in every county a court, called *county court*, or *court of common pleas*, consisting of one or more judges, elected by the people of the county, in most of the states, in others, appointed either by the legislature, or by the governor, with the advice and consent of the senate. In this court are tried civil causes in which are claimed sums of greater amount than a justice of the peace has jurisdiction of, and the lower crimes committed in the county. Also causes removed by appeal or otherwise from a justice's court, are tried in this court.

§ 2. There are other courts having different names and jurisdiction in different states; as *circuit court*, *superior court*, *supreme court*, and *court of appeals*. A circuit court seems to derive its name thus: A state is divided into judicial districts, and one of the judges of the supreme court or some other judge or judges, go from county to county, holding a court once a year, or oftener, in each of the counties composing a judicial district. A part of the business of this court is to try appeals from the county court, and such of the higher crimes as a county court has not the power to try. Courts in which crimes are tried, are sometimes called courts of *oyer and terminer*.

§ 3. Every county court, and every circuit court having similar jurisdiction, has a jury to try issues of fact, and a grand jury. An *issue of fact* is when the *fact* as to the indebtedness or the guilt of the party charged is to be determined from the testimony. It is so called to distinguish it from an *issue of law*, in which the *law* in the case is to be determined, which is done by the court instead of a jury. This jury is usually called a *petit jury*, as distinguished from a *grand jury*.

§ 4. It is one of the excellencies of our government, that the liberty and lives of the people, as well as their property, are protected by a constitutional provision, securing to every person the right to be tried by a jury of his equals. As liberty and life are more valuable than property, they ought to be most carefully guarded. Hence the constitution of the United States, and the constitutions of the several states, declare that no person shall be put upon trial for a capital or other infamous crime, without the previous judgment of a grand jury that he ought to be tried.

§ 5. The manner of selecting and drawing grand and petit jurors, is prescribed by law. A number of judicious men in each town are selected by some person or persons authorized by law to do so, whose names are written on separate pieces of paper, and put into a box in each town, and kept by the town clerk; or, as is the practice in some states, the names of the persons designated as jurors in the several towns, are sent to the county clerk and by him kept in a box. Previous to the sitting of each court, the requisite number is drawn out of the box, and the persons whose names are thus drawn, are summoned to attend as jurors.

§ 6. A jury to try a cause in these courts consists of twelve men; and all must agree in a verdict. The number of grand jurors is not the same in all the states; nor is it required that a grand jury shall always consist of a definite number of men; nor that their judgment shall be unanimous, in order to put a person upon trial.

§ 7. On the opening of the court, the jurors are sworn to make a true presentment of all things given them in charge. The judge then gives them a charge, and appoints one of their number as foreman; and the jurors retire to a private apartment to attend to their duties. They hear all complaints brought before them, against persons for crimes and breaches of the peace; and examine witnesses who appear to testify; and when it is requested, they have the assistance and advice of the state's attorney. If they think any person complained of ought to be tried, they draw up a writing, in which they charge him with the offense of which they think him guilty. This is called an *indictment*. It is signed by the foreman, endorsed, "a true bill," and carried by the jury into court.

§ 8. If the person has not before been arrested, he may

now be arrested, to be put upon trial. As all crimes are considered as committed against the peace and order of the community, the offender is complained of and tried in the name and in behalf of the people of the state, who are the prosecuting party. The prosecution is managed by the prosecuting attorney for the county, whose appointment and general duties have been mentioned. (Chapter XVII, § 11.)

§ 9. The *supreme court* is the next higher, and in most states, the highest state court. This court differs somewhat in the different states, both in its structure and its jurisdiction. It is believed, however, that, in most or all of the states, it has both original and appellate jurisdiction, civil and criminal. By *original* jurisdiction is meant, that a suit may *originate* or commence in this court, or that it has the power to try a suit in the first instance. By *appellate* jurisdiction is meant the right to adjudge cases brought before it by appeal from other courts. In the state of New York, there is a higher court, the highest in the state, which has appellate power only. Its business is to review cases from the supreme court.

§ 10. A *court of chancery* is in its nature different from all other courts. It is sometimes called a *court of equity*, being designed to enable persons to obtain what is right and equitable, when they can not obtain the same in ordinary *courts of law*. In ordinary courts, a man is not allowed to be a witness for himself; but in this, the parties may be put on oath. In other courts, a person can not be compelled to fulfill a contract; he can only be made to pay damage for default; but in a court of equity, a man may, in certain cases, be compelled to fulfill the contract itself.

§ 11. If a debtor has property held in trust for him by another; or has money, notes, or other obligations or debts owing to him; this court may compel him to discover and give up such property to satisfy an execution against him; and it may prevent his debtors from paying him such debts. It has power also to restrain banks and other corporations and individuals from doing fraudulent acts; to dissolve corporations; to stop proceedings at law in certain cases; and to do many other things of a like nature, by way of relief, when relief can not otherwise be had.

§ 12. Suits in equity are not commenced as suits *at law*

The plaintiff prepares a bill of complaint, called a *bill in chancery*, the facts in which are sworn to by the plaintiff. The bill, which contains a petition or prayer that the defendant, the party complained of, may be summoned to make answer on oath, is filed with the clerk of the court, who issues a subpena, commanding the defendant to appear before the court on a day named. A trial may be had on the complaint and answer alone; or witnesses may be introduced by the parties. The case is argued by counsel, and a *decree* is pronounced by the court, which the court has power to carry into effect.

§ 13. Courts of chancery, or courts of equity, separately organized as such, no longer exist in many of the states. The power to try suits in equity is exercised by the judges of the common law courts.

§ 14. *Court of Probate.* In each county there is a *judge of probate*, whose duties relate to the proving of wills, and the settling of the estates of persons deceased. A *will* is a writing in which a person gives directions for the disposal of his property after his death. The Latin word *probatus* means proof; hence the application of the word probate to the proving of a will. (See Wills and Testaments.) In the state of New York, this officer is called *surrogate.*

§ 15. *Court of Impeachment.* There is no law court by this title. The name is applied to the senate when sitting on a trial of impeachment. An *impeachment* is a charge against a public officer for corrupt conduct in office. For example, a member of the legislature who should, for money, or some other consideration offered as a bribe, vote for or against a proposed law; or any other officer who should act corruptly in his official capacity, would be liable to impeachment. The constitutions of the several states, and the constitution of the United States, give to the house of representatives the power *to impeach*, that is, to make the charge or accusation, and to the senate the power *to try* the impeachment. This practice has come from Great Britain, where the impeachment is made by the house of commons, and the house of lords is the high court of impeachment.

§ 16. The mode of commencing a trial of this kind, as prescribed by law, is as follows: The house of representatives makes the charge, and delivers it to the president of the senate, who causes the court to be summoned. The accused is then brought before the court to answer to the charge, and is entitled to counsel to assist him. When the issue is joined, the court appoints a time and place for trial. Before the trial commences, the clerk administers to the president of the senate, and the president to the other members, an oath truly to try and determine the charge according to evidence. The trial is conducted as trials are in courts of justice. If two-thirds of the members present concur in a conviction, the accused is convicted; if not, he is acquitted. If the person is convicted, the court may remove him from office, or disqualify him from holding any office thereafter, in the state, or both remove and disqualify him; but no other judgment can be pronounced by this court. But if the act committed by the offender is a crime, he may also be indicted, tried, and punished in a court of common law, as any other person.

CHAPTER XXVIII.

CRIMES AND MISDEMEANORS; PROSECUTION OF OFFENDERS.

§ 1. The statutes of each state define the crimes of which its laws take cognizance. The definitions given in this chapter, agree substantially, it is presumed, with those of similar crimes in every state in the union. The statutes also prescribe the penalties, which are not precisely the same in all the states. Nor is there in any state an equal measure of punishment inflicted in all cases for the same offense. The laws usually declare the longest and the shortest terms of imprisonment, and the highest and lowest fines, leaving the exact measure of punishment, except for crimes punishable by death, to the discretion of the judges, to be fixed according to the aggravation of the offense.

§ 2. The laws of the several states differ in respect to the number of crimes made punishable by death. In some states the penalty of death is annexed to the crime of murder only. Treason is punishable by death; but as this offense is defined and made punishable by the laws of the United States, not all the states take cognizance of it. If committed in such states, it is tried in the courts of the United States. In New York, murder, treason, and arson in the first degree, are punishable by death. Few states make more than these crimes thus punishable. In two or three states, the penalty of death has been abolished, and imprisonment for life substituted.

§ 3. Crimes punishable by death, are called *capital* crimes, and their punishment is called *capital* punishment. The word capital is from the Latin *caput*, which means head; and so has come to signify the highest or principal. Hence, probably, the application of the word capital to the principal crimes receiving the highest punishment, which was formerly practiced extensively in other countries by beheading or *decapitating* the criminals.

§ 4. *Treason* is defined by statute to be, levying war in any state against the people of the state; or a combination of two or more persons, attempting by force to usurp or overturn the government of the state; or in adhering to enemies of the state while separately engaged in war with a foreign enemy, and giving them aid and comfort.

§ 4. *Murder* is the killing of a person deliberately and maliciously, and with intent to effect death; or killing a person in committing some other crime, though not with a design to effect death; or in killing a person purposely and without previous deliberation. The less aggravated cases of murder, are in some states distinguished as murder in the second degree, and punished by imprisonment for a long term, or for life.

§ 6. *Manslaughter* is killing a person either upon a sudden quarrel, or unintentionally while committing some unlawful act. The statutes of New York define four different degrees of manslaughter.

§ 7. *Arson* is maliciously burning any dwelling-house, shop, barn, or any other building, the property of another. Arson in the first degree, which is burning an inhabited dwelling *in the night time*, is in some states punishable with death.

§ 8. *Homicide* signifies mankilling. It is of three kinds: felonious, justifiable, and excusable. When felonious, it is either murder or manslaughter. *Justifiable* homicide is that which is committed in the necessary defense of one's person, house, or goods, or of the person of another when in danger of injury; or that which is committed in lawfully attempting to take a person for felony committed, or to suppress a riot, or to keep the peace. *Excusable* homicide is the killing of a person by accident, or while lawfully employed, without any design to do wrong. In the two last cases there is no punishment.

§ 9. Intentionally *maiming* another by cutting out or disabling the tongue or any other member or limb; inveigling or *kidnapping; decoying* and taking away children; *exposing children* in the street to abandon them; committing or attempting an assault with *intent to kill*, or to commit any other felony, or in resisting the execution of a legal process; *administering poison* without producing death; *poisoning any well* or spring of water; are all felonies, and punishable as such.

§ 10. *Burglary* is maliciously and forcibly breaking into and entering in the night time, any dwelling house or other building, with intent to commit a crime. Breaking into and entering a house by day, is considered a minor degree of burglary.

§ 11. *Forgery* consists in falsely making, counterfeiting, or altering any instrument of writing, with intent to defraud. The word *counterfeiting* is generally applied to making false coin or bank notes, or in passing them; or in having in possession any engraved plate, or bills unsigned, which are intended to be used for these purposes.

§ 12. *Robbery* is the taking of personal property from another in his presence and against his will, by violence, or by putting him in fear of immediate injury to his person. Knowingly to send or deliver, or to make for the purpose of being sent, a letter or writing, threatening to accuse any one of crime, or to do him some injury, with intent to extort or gain from him any money or property, is considered an *attempt to rob*, for which the offender may be imprisoned.

§ 13. *Embezzlement* is fraudulently putting to one's own use what is entrusted to him by another. To buy or receive property knowing it to have been embezzled, is to be guilty of the same offense. Embezzling is usually punishable in the same manner as larceny of the same amount.

§ 14. *Larceny* is theft or stealing. The stealing of property above a certain amount in value, is called *grand larceny*, and is a state prison offense. If the value of the property stolen is of less amount, the offense is called *petit larceny*, and is punished by fine or imprisonment in jail, or both.

§ 15. *Perjury* is willfully swearing or affirming falsely to any material matter, upon an oath legally administered. *Subornation of perjury* is procuring another to swear falsely: punishable as perjury.

§ 16. *Bribery* is promising or giving a reward to a public officer, to influence his opinion, vote or judgment. A person *accepting* such bribe, is punishable in the same manner, and forfeits his office, and, in some states, may never hold another public trust. This offense is not in all the states punishable by imprisonment in the state prison.

§ 17. *Dueling* is a combat between two persons with deadly weapons. Killing another in a duel is murder, and punishable with death. If death does not ensue, imprisonment. Challenging, or accepting a challenge to fight, or to be present as a second, imprisonment. Dueling is not a punishable offense in every state.

§ 18. Aiding or attempting to aid a prisoner committed for felony, to *escape from confinement*, or forcibly rescuing a prisoner charged with crime, from the custody of a public officer, is a crime. If the offense for which the prisoner is committed is less than felony, the punishment is imprisonment in jail, or fine, or both.

§ 19. *Bigamy* is the crime of having two or more wives, and is also called *polygamy*. But bigamy literally signifies having *two* wives, and polygamy any number more than one. These words, in law, are applied also to women having two or more husbands. A person having a lawful husband or wife living, and marrying another person, is guilty of bigamy. An unmarried person, also, who shall marry the husband or wife of another, is punishable in like manner.

§ 20. *Incest* is the marrying or cohabiting together as husband and wife, of persons related to each other within certain degrees.

§ 21. *Opening a grave* and removing a dead body for any unlawful purpose, or purchasing such body knowing it to have been unlawfully disinterred, is a crime. This offense is in some states punishable by imprisonment in a county jail, or by fine, and not in a state prison.

§ 22. Persons sometimes advise or are knowing to the commission of felonies but are not actually engaged in committing them. Such are *accessories.* He who advises or commands another to commit a felony, is called an *accessory before the fact,* and is punished in the same manner as the principal. If he conceals the offender after the offense has been committed, or gives him any aid to prevent his being brought to punishment, he is an *accessory after the fact,* and may be imprisoned or fined.

§ 23. *Assault and Battery* is unlawfully to assault or threaten, or to strike or wound another. Besides being liable to fine and imprisonment, the offender is liable also to the party injured for damages.

§ 24. A *riot* is the assembling together of three or more persons, with intent forcibly to injure the person or property of another, or to break the peace; or agreeing with each other to do such unlawful act, and making any movement or preparation therefor, though lawfully assembled. When riotous persons are thus assembled, and are proceeding to commit offenses, any judge, justice, sheriff, or other ministerial officer, may in the name of the state, command them to disperse. If they refuse, the peace officers are required to call upon all persons near to aid in taking the rioters into custody. Persons refusing to assist may be fined.

§ 25. A sheriff or other officer voluntarily suffering a prisoner charged with or convicted of an offense, to *escape* from his custody, is guilty of a misdemeanor. To *rescue* a prisoner thus charged or convicted, is punishable in a similar manner. It is also a misdemeanor to assist a criminal, with a view to effect his escape, though he does not escape from jail.

§ 26. A person taking upon himself to act as a public officer, and taking or keeping a person in custody unlawfully or without authority, is *false imprisonment;* for which the offender may be fined or imprisoned.

§ 27. The offenses mentioned in the last four sections, being of a lower grade than those defined in the preceding sections, and not being punishable in a state prison, are usually called *misdemeanors,* and are punishable by fine or imprisonment in a county jail. There are numerous other misdemeanors and immoralities, as profane cursing and swearing, betting and gaming, horse racing, disturbing religious meetings, sabbath-breaking, trespasses and injury to property, and many disorderly practices, all of which are punishable in like manner.

§ 28. Any judge or justice of the peace has power to issue process for apprehending any person charged with an offense. When a complaint is made to a magistrate, he examines the complainant on oath, and any witnesses that are produced; and if it appears that an offense has been committed, he issues a warrant, commanding the officer to whom it is directed to bring the accused before the magistrate.

§ 29. The magistrate first examines the complainant and witnesses in support of the prosecution; and next the prisoner, who is not on oath, and then his witnesses. If an offense has been committed, and the evidence of the prisoner's guilt is such as, in the opinion of the magistrate, to justify his being held to trial, the magistrate binds, by recognizance, the prosecutor and all material witnesses, to appear and testify against the prisoner, at the next court at which the prisoner may be indicted and tried.

§ 30. In some states the magistrate himself has power to try persons thus charged with offenses of the lowest grade. In certain other states, it is left to the choice of the prisoner to be bound over for trial at the county court, or to be tried by the magistrate, and thus to have the matter at once disposed of.

§ 31. If either the offender does not choose to be tried by the justice, or the justice has not power to try him; and if the offense is one for which he may be let to bail, the magistrate may take bail for his appearance at the next court. But if no bail is offered, or if the offense is not bailable, the prisoner is committed to jail until the next session of the court having power to try him. But he must be indicted by a grand jury before he can be tried. The reason why offenders are sometimes arrested and examined before their case is brought before a grand jury, is to prevent their escaping before the next county court, as grand juries sit only during the terms of courts.

§ 32. The way in which bail is taken is this: the accused gives a bond in such sum as the justice or judge shall require, with one or more sureties, who are bound for the ap pearance of the accused at the next court, or in case he shall not appear, then to pay the sum mentioned in the bond. The word *bail* is from a French word meaning to deliver, or to release. Hence, the justice *bails*, lets free, or delivers to his sureties, the party arrested. Hence, also, the surety is said to bail a person when he procures his liberation. The bond or obligation of the surety, is in law called a *recognizance*, as is also the bond given by the prosecutor and witnesses for their appearance against the prisoner.

GOVERNMENT OF THE UNITED STATES.

CHAPTER XXIX.

NATURE OF THE UNION.

§ 1. It has been attempted, in the foregoing chapters, to illustrate the principles of civil institutions, and to show the application of these principles to the government of the states. If the reader has carefully studied these chapters, it is presumed he now understands how the powers of the government of a state are divided; by whom and in what manner these powers are exercised; and what are his political rights and duties as a citizen of the state in which he resides.

§ 2. It will be next in order to treat of the government of the United States. The youngest student in political science probably knows, that while he is a citizen of a state, and is subject to its government and laws, he is at the same time a citizen of the United States. And as he is subject also to the laws and government of the United States, it is necessary to understand his rights as a citizen under this government, and the relation which the state governments and the government of the United States bear to each other.

§ 3. The government of this country is complicated. Not only is there a complete government in each of the states of the union, but the people of the several states are united in *one general government,* whose powers control, in certain matters, the people and the governments of the states. This government is similar, in form, to the state governments, its powers being divided into legislative, executive and judicial; and its constitution is called the "Constitution of the United States." The people of the states being incorporated into one great nation under a general constitution, this government is sometimes called the *national government.* The several states being united in a *confederacy,* the government is also called the *federal government;* the word federal being derived from the Latin, *fœdus,* and signifying a league, or contract, or alliance.

§ 4. In order to a correct understanding of the nature of the general government, and of our relations to it as citizens of the United States, we must consider the condition of the American colonies while subject to Great Britain. The colonies had then no political connection with each other. They were as independent of each other as different nations. Therefore the people were not then citizens of the United States; they were only citizens of the respective colonies in which they resided.

§ 5. During the controversy with Great Britain, it became necessary for the colonies to agree upon some general measures of defense. For this purpose, the first great continental congress, composed of delegates from the several colonies, met at Philadelphia on the 4th of September, 1774. The next year, in May, another congress met to propose and to adopt such further measures as the state of the country might require; and the same congress, on the 4th of July, 1776, declared the colonies to be "free and independent states."

§ 6. This declaration was called "The unanimous Declaration of the United States of America;" but the states were united only in certain measures of safety. There was no government which exercised authority over the states. The people were subject to their respective state governments only. They were not yet incorporated into one nation for the purpose of government, as now, under a constitution. Hence, they were not yet properly citizens of the United States.

§ 7. To effect the future security as well as the immediate safety of the American people, congress deemed it necessary that there should be a union of the states under some general government; and in November, 1777, that body agreed upon a plan of union. The articles were called "Articles of Confederation and perpetual Union between the States;" and were to go into effect when adopted by the legislatures of all the states. Some of the states were slow to agree to the articles; the last state not assenting to the plan until March 1, 1781, when the articles were adopted.

§ 8. But the union formed under these articles of confederation, was not such a union as that which exists under the present constitution, as will appear by considering a few points of difference between them. In the first place they were different in *form*. The confederation was merely a *union of states*. It had not, as the national government now has, the three departments of power, legislative, executive and judicial. It had only a legislature, and that consisted of a single body, called congress; in which the several states were entitled to an equal representation; the number of delegates from each state to consist of not less than two nor more than seven.

§ 9. The nature of that union as a mere confederation of states, appears, further, from the manner in which questions were determined by congress. Votes were taken by states. If a majority of the delegates of any state voted in favor of a measure, that state was set down in the affirmative; but if a majority voted against the measure, the state was placed in the negative. Thus each state gave but one vote; and a question having in its favor a majority of the states, was declared to be carried. If an equal number of the delegates of a state voted for and against a proposition, such state was said to be *divided*, and had no vote. So also a state lost its vote, if there were not at least two of its delegates present and voting.

§ 10. That government differed from the present also in regard to its *powers*. The confederation was a very weak government. Its powers were vested in a congress. The congress was to manage the common affairs of the nation, and to enact such laws (if laws they might be called) as should be deemed necessary; but a main defect in the system was, that congress had no power to carry its requisitions into effect.

§ 11. For example, it belonged to congress to ascertain

the number of men and the sums of money to be raised to carry on the war, and to call on each state to raise its due share; but congress could not enforce the requisition. It had no power to lay and collect taxes; it was dependent upon the states for raising the money to defray the public expenses. It could, and did, to some extent, borrow money in its own name, on the credit of the Union; but it had not the means of repaying the money so borrowed. The power being reserved to the states to lay the taxes, it depended upon the good will of the legislatures of the thirteen independent states to carry any measure of defense into effect. Indeed, by none of the states had the requisitions of congress been fully complied with.

§ 12. It may be asked how a union of the states could exist under so weak a government. But for the peculiar condition of the country at that time, it is doubted whether there would have been a sufficient compliance with the ordinances of congress to bring the war to a successful issue, which could be done only by union. It was a sense of danger from abroad, rather than any power in the government, that kept the states united. The plan of government was devised in a time of war, and had respect to the operations of war, rather than to a state of peace: and after the return of peace the inefficiency of this government very soon appeared.

§ 13. The condition of the states may be compared to that of individuals who unite in averting a common danger, or in pursuing a common interest, but whose union and friendship last only until the desired object has been attained. The war being over, the states did not long continue in harmony. Laws were enacted in some states giving their own citizens undue advantages over the citizens of other states; and in a few years, the mutual jealousies and animosities caused by these and other acts of partial legislation, became such as threatened to break up the union.

§ 14. It was now evident, that, to preserve the union, a government possessing more extensive powers was necessary; a government that could, in all needful cases, control the action of the state governments. After several ineffectual attempts to remedy some of the existing evils, congress, having been thereto requested, called a convention to revise and amend the articles of confederation. All the states, except Rhode Island, chose delegates, who met at Philadelphia in May, 1787, and framed the present constitution, which differs from the confederation, both in its form, or nature, and in the extent of its powers.

§ 15. The change effected in the nature of the federal government by the constitution, appears not only from the dissimilarity of the two plans, but also from the different modes in which they were formed and adopted, or the different authorities by which these acts were done. The articles of confederation were framed by congress, and ratified by the state legislatures. Hence, the adoption of these articles was the act of the *legislatures* of the states, and not of the *people* of the states ; and the confederation was a *union of states,* rather than a *union of the people* of the states.

§ 16. The constitution, on the other hand, was framed by men appointed expressly for that purpose, and submitted for approval, not to the state legislatures, but to the people of the states, and adopted by state conventions whose members were chosen for that purpose by the *people* of the several states. Hence, the constitution is virtually the act of the people ; and the union is not a mere confederation of states, but, as the preamble declares, "a more perfect union," formed by "THE PEOPLE OF THE UNITED STATES."

CHAPTER XXX.

HISTORY OF THE CONSTITUTION.

§ 1. THE brief description, in the preceding chapter, of the character of the confederation, designed merely to show the necessity of a change in the federal government, and to convey a general idea of the nature of the union, is deemed insufficient to prepare the political student for the successful study of the constitution. Therefore, before we proceed to the examination of the several provisions of that instrument, a more detailed history will be given of the practical workings of the confederation, and of the various efforts to relieve the country which terminated in the adoption of the constitution.

§ 2. The absence of all power in congress to raise money for public purposes, as one of the principal defects of the old government, has been mentioned. Congress was unable to enforce the collection of a revenue, either by direct taxation, or by duties on imported goods. Resolutions had at different times been passed by congress, recommending to the states to invest congress with the power to levy duties upon foreign goods imported into any of the states; but neither this nor any other plan proposed by that body for raising funds to support the war or pay the public debt, received the concurrence of all the states.

§ 3. Another serious defect of the confederation was the want of power to regulate commerce. We have noticed the restrictions imposed by Great Britain upon the trade of the colonies prior to the revolution. (Chap. X. § 8–10.) The restrictive policy of that country was designed not only to secure a market for her manufactures and other productions, but also to increase her shipping. By her memorable navigation acts of 1651 and 1663, it was ordained, that "no commodity of the growth or manufacture of Europe, should be imported into any of the king's plantations in Asia, Africa, or America, but what had been shipped in England, Wales, or the town Berwick, and in English built shipping, whereof the master and three-fourths of the mariners were English, and carried directly thence to the plantations."

§ 4. After the return of peace and the consequent revival of trade between the two countries, the effects of the unequal footing upon which our commerce was placed, by the laws of Great Britain, soon reäppeared. Although the rigor of her ancient policy had been in some measure abated, both our goods and our vessels were subject to onerous duties in British ports, while congress had no power to meet the legislation of Great Britain with similar restrictions upon her commerce. The attention of congress having been called to this subject, a resolution was passed, (April 30, 1784,) requesting the states to invest congress, for fifteen years, with the power to prohibit the importation or exportation of goods in vessels belonging to, or navigated by, the subjects of any foreign power with whom the states had not formed treaties of commerce; and also to prohibit foreigners, unless authorized by treaty, from importing into the United States any goods except such as were the produce of the country of which they were citizens; all acts of congress passed in pursuance of these powers to take effect when approved by nine states.

§ 5. Considerable time necessarily elapsed before reports from the several states were received by congress. From the report of a committee of congress, (March 3, 1786,) it appears that acts complying either fully or partially with the recommendation of congress, had been received from ten states. But some of these acts were so dissimilar in some of their provisions, and others were so inconsistent with the recommendations of congress, that they were not deemed compliances. Congress therefore called again upon the three non-complying states to grant the powers desired, and requested those other states (six) whose acts were defective, to conform them to the recommendation. Acts were at length received from all the states; but some of them were still imperfect, and their amendment was again requested.

§ 6. While these efforts were in progress, and with a view to the same object, a proposition was made in congress to submit to the states an alteration of one of the articles of confederation, conferring upon congress the power "of regulating the trade of the states with foreign nations and with each other, and of levying such imposts and duties upon imports and exports as might be necessary for the purpose; the duties to be collected under the authority, and to accrue to the use of the states in which they were payable." But congress deeming it advisable that amendments of the confederation should originate with the state legislatures, the proposition was not submitted to the states for ratification.

§ 7. In the same year, (Nov. 1785,) a resolution was introduced into the house of delegates of Virginia, instructing its delegates in congress to propose a recommendation to the states to invest congress with the power to regulate trade. A resolution to this effect was favorably received, and once passed that house. It was afterward reconsidered for the purpose of amendment, but no vote upon its passage was again taken. Subsequently, however, (Jan. 1786,) the general assembly of that state adopted a resolution appointing commissioners to meet commissioners to be appointed by the other states, to take into consideration the situation and trade of the United States, and the necessity of a uniform system of commercial regulations; and to report to the several states such an act as, when ratified by them, would enable congress effectually to provide for this object.

§ 8. A meeting was accordingly held at Annapolis, in Maryland, September 11, 1786; but as only five states, New York, New Jersey, Pennsylvania, Delaware, and Virginia, were represented, the commissioners deemed it unadvisable to proceed to business relating to an object in which all the states were so deeply concerned; but they united in a report to the several states and to congress, recommending a general meeting of the states in a future convention to be held at Philadelphia on the second Monday of May next, and expressing the opinion that, as there were numerous acknowledged defects in the system of federal government, the powers of the deputies should be extended to other objects than those of commerce, with a view "to render the constitution of the federal government adequate to the exigencies of the union."

§ 9. In pursuance of this recommendation, the subject was taken up in congress; and on the 21st of February, 1787, a committee reported in favor of a convention. The report, after some amendment, was agreed to, as follows:

"Whereas there is provision in the Articles of Confederation and perpetual Union for making alterations therein, by the assent of the United States and of the legislatures of the several states; and whereas experience hath evinced that there are defects in the Confederation; as a mean to remedy which, several of the states, and particularly the state of New York, by express instructions to their delegates in congress, have suggested a convention for the purposes expressed in the following resolution; and such convention appearing to be the most probable mean of establishing in these states a firm national government:

"*Resolved*, That, in the opinion of Congress, it is expedient that, on the second Monday in May next, a convention of delegates who shall have been appointed by the several states, be held at Philadelphia, for the sole and exclusive purpose of revising the Articles of Confederation, and reporting to Congress and the several legislatures such alterations and provisions therein as shall, when agreed to in Congress, and confirmed by the states, render the Constitution adequate to the exigencies of government and the preservation of the Union."

§ 10. Several of the states, namely, Virginia, North Carolina, New Jersey, Pennsylvania, and New York, had already, in compliance with the recommendation from Annapolis, taken action upon the subject. The act of Virginia was passed November 24, 1786, and her deputies were appointed the 4th of December. New Jersey appointed a portion of her delegates as early as the 23d of November. The recommendation of congress was followed by acts of appointment in all the other states except Rhode Island; and the delegates met pursuant to appointment, on Monday the 14th of September, 1787. The convention, however, was not organized until the 25th, that being the first day upon which a representation of a majority of the states appeared.

§ 11. A few days only had elapsed, when a great difference of opinion was found to exist among the members. Two plans of government, embodying the leading features of the present constitution, were submitted, and a resolution offered, declaring "that a *national government* ought to be established, consisting of a supreme legislative, judiciary, and executive." This resolution was opposed by members, who not only objected to such a government, but denied the power of the convention to change the general plan of the existing government; the convention having been called, as expressed in the resolution of congress, "for the sole and express purpose of revising the articles of confederation;" and that the acts of the several state legislatures for the appointment of delegates were in conformity to that resolution.

§ 12. To these objections it was replied, that the powers of the convention were not thus restricted; that the convention was expressly authorized, by the resolution of congress referred to, to report such alterations, as should "render the federal constitution adequate to the exigencies of the government and the preservation of the Union;" and that this object could not be effected by the mere alteration of a few of the articles of confederation. The convention, it was further said, could *conclude nothing*, as no proposed alterations could have effect unless confirmed by the states; but it could *propose any thing* which the "exigencies of the

Union" were supposed to demand. After considerable debate, the resolution was adopted; and one of the plans previously presented for consideration of the convention, was taken as the basis of its action in the proposed new government.

§ 13. But, although the present government, with its three complete departments, legislative, executive, and judicial, controlling, in matters of general concern, the action of the state governments, and operating directly upon individual citizens, is properly called a national government; yet it is not wholly such, but partly national and partly federal. As in all pure confederacies, the states had an equal voice in the government. Some of the federal features of the confederation have been retained in the constitution, as will appear on a further examination of that instrument. Hence, the union is still called, with propriety, the *federal union*, and the government, the *federal government*.

CHAPTER XXXI.

LEGISLATIVE DEPARTMENT.—HOUSE OF REPRESENTATIVES.

§ 1. All the legislative powers granted in the constitution, are "*vested in a congress of the United States, consisting of a senate and house of representatives.*" (Art. 1, sec. 1.) We have elsewhere mentioned, as an object of dividing a legislature into two branches, to guard against the passage of ill-considered and unjust laws. (Chap. XV, § 15.) Whatever reasons there may be for dividing a state legislature into two distinct and independent branches, apply with equal force to the structure of the legislature of the union. The check given to each house upon the acts of the other is necessary, not only to guard against unintentional errors, but against the influence of private interest upon the conduct of representatives. The danger of unwise and corrupt legislation is greatly diminished by giving to the two branches a negative upon each other's proceedings.

§ 2. The *house of representatives* is composed of members *chosen every second year* by the people of the several states;

and the electors in each state have the qualifications requisite for electors of the most numerous branch of the state legislature. (Art. 1. sec. 2.) Under the confederation, delegates were appointed for one year, and were at any time subject to recall by the state legislature. Elections so frequent, especially elections by the people, would bring together a great number of men without the requisite experience in national business. Measures originated at one session would often be determined by new members unaided in their decisions by the light of previous investigation. Wise legislation is best secured by a term of office which will enable the same set of men to mature and finish the business they have begun. Hence two years was considered a proper term for a national representative.

§ 3. The convention readily acceded to the proposition to transfer the choice of representatives from the state legislatures to the people. It is proper that a representative should derive his power from those whose wants he is to make known, and whose rights he is to guard.

§ 4. In determining the qualifications of the electors of representatives, regard was had to the supposed preferences of the states. In some of them, property, or the payment of taxes, was made a qualification. In others, none but freeholders were voters. In others, the senate and governor were elected by freeholders, while in the election of the other house freemen generally were allowed to vote. In others, again, the right of suffrage was almost universal. It was presumed that no state would object to a rule which it had established, or might thereafter establish, for electing the popular branch of its own legislature.

§ 5. A representative, to be eligible, must have attained the age of twenty-five years, and been seven years a citizen of the United States ; and he must be, when elected, an inhabitant of the state in which he is chosen. (Art. 1, sec. 2.) Few men at an earlier age than twenty-five years, have that knowledge of public affairs, or that degree of caution and prudence, which is requisite in the exercise of so important a trust. Aliens can hardly be supposed to feel that attachment to our institutions, and that regard for the public interest, which are felt by our own citizens. A residence for a less period than seven years after they shall have become citizens, could hardly enable them to acquire sufficient knowledge of our government and of the various interests of the country, to fit them for the duties of legislators. For equally wise reasons is a representative required to be an inhabitant of the state he is chosen to represent. The business of a state is more safely intrusted to a representative whose residence in the state has made him more familiar with its interests, and who must himself be affected by the measures he may support.

§ 6. The next clause of the constitution prescribes the rule of apportionment. No part of the labors of the convention was more difficult than the settling of the principle of representation. It was proposed in the plan under consideration, that the vote of each state should be in proportion to its quota of contribution to the general revenue, or to the number of its free inhabitants, as the one or the other might seem best in different cases. To this the smaller states objected. One of the states, (Delaware,) had expressly instructed her delegates not to surrender the right of an equal vote in congress. A proportional representation, or unequal suffrage, it was said, would give the large states undue influence. A combination of three or four such states would enable them to enact whatever laws they pleased, however oppressive to the others. Not only so; they could even control the appointment of the president, the judges, and other officers of the government.

§ 7. It was urged, on the other hand, that there was no similarity of interests which would be likely to unite the larger states against the small ones; that there was quite as much danger of combinations of the smaller states, or of some of them with one or more of the larger states; and that the number of small states (small in population) would soon be increased by the admission of new states formed from the western territory. Union was indispensable to the welfare and safety of all. Especially did the small states need the protection of the federal government. But no other than a radical change, similar to the one proposed, could preserve the union; and it was evident that the convention would agree to no plan which should retain the right of the small states to an equal vote in the legislature.

§ 8. The difficulty of an arrangement was increased by the proposition to exclude slaves from the representative population. Although slavery existed in most of the northern as well as in the southern states, the number of slaves in the former was comparatively inconsiderable. These states, therefore, very naturally favored the proposed exclusion of slaves. The slaveholding states strenuously insisted on their being included in the basis of representation. The debate was warm and protracted. Indeed, so inflamed did the controversy become, and so unyielding were the parties, as to cause fears of a sudden dissolution of the convention.

§ 9. Against the computation of slaves in fixing the rule of apportionment, it was urged, that slaves, having neither personal liberty, nor property, nor being permitted to acquire property, but being themselves property, and, like other property, at the will of the master, they ought not to be counted. They were not represented in the states; why should they be represented in the general government? If they were men, let them be made citizens and voters. If they were property, why should the property of the free states be excluded? Besides, the admission of slaves into the representation would indirectly encourage the slave trade, which was a violation of the most sacred laws of humanity.

§ 10. There being no hope of settling this exciting question but by compromise, it was at length agreed that, in ascertaining the number of the representative population, three-fifths of the number of slaves should be added to the number of free persons; that is to say, every *five slaves* should be counted as *three free* persons. The advantage to the slaveholding states of this arrangement is clearly shown by the following example: Suppose a state to contain 600,000 free persons and 500,000 slaves. Adding three-fifths of the number of slaves (300,000) to the number of free persons, gives 900,000 as the number of the representative population: and the state would be entitled to *three* representatives for every *two* that a state would have which contained 600,000 free inhabitants and no slaves.

§ 11. In return for this advantage, the slaveholding states consented that, in the apportionment of direct taxes among the states, the same rule should be observed: so that a state gaining every third representative by the computation of its slaves, as in the case supposed, (§ 10,) would, in cases of direct taxation, contribute to the national treasury *three* dollars for every *two* which it would pay if its slaves were not counted. But this expected advantage has not been realized by the non-slaveholding states, as the treasury of the United States is supplied by the revenues derived from other sources, chiefly by duties on imports. Congress has found it necessary to exercise its power of direct taxation only two or three times since the adoption of the constitution.

§ 12. The constitution does not limit the house to any definite number of representatives; it only declares that the number shall not exceed one for every 30,000 inhabitants. It requires an enumeration of the inhabitants every ten years; and the next congress thereafter determines the ratio of representation and the number of representatives and apportions them among the states. But as a representative for every 30,000 inhabitants, after the population has become very numerous, would make the house too large to transact business with equal dispatch, the ratio of representation has been increased with the increase of population. After the census taken in 1790, the ratio was fixed at 33,000, which gave the house 106 members. After the census of 1800, the same ratio made the number of members 142. After 1810, the ratio was 35,000; the number of members, 182. After 1820, the ratio was 40,000; the number of members, 213. After 1830, the ratio was 47,700; the number of members, 240. After 1840, the ratio was 70,680; the number of members, 223. After 1850, the ratio was 93,000 and a fraction, making the number of members, 233; of which number California had one; but by special enactment an additional member was given to that state, making in all, 234. Minnesota has since been admitted as a state with two representatives, (1858,) and the admission of other new states will take place before the next apportionment.

§ 13. Representatives are chosen by districts. Each state is divided by the legislature into as many districts, called congressional districts, as there are representatives to be elected in the state; and one representative is chosen in each district. In most of the states, representatives are chosen at the general state election. In some of them, there are special elections for choosing representatives.

§ 14. The constitution secures to the smallest states a

representation in the house of representatives. It declares that each state shall have at least one representative. Without such a provision, and with a ratio large enough to keep the house within a proper size, the smallest states might be deprived of a representation in this branch. By an act of congress, every territory also, belonging to the United States, in which a government is established, is entitled to a delegate, who has the right of debating, but not of voting.

CHAPTER XXXII.

THE SENATE.

§ 1. THE *senate of the United States is composed of two senators from each state, chosen by the legislature for six years; and each senator has one vote.* (Art. 1, sec. 3.) The division of the legislature into two branches was decided at an early period of the session, and apparently without serious opposition: but as to the structure of the senate, there was a great diversity of opinion. For the election of senators, several modes were proposed. One proposition was, that the members of the second branch should be elected by those of the first, out of a proper number of persons nominated by the individual legislatures; another, that they should be chosen by the state legislatures; another, by the people of each state, in districts; another, by a body of electors chosen for that purpose by the people; and another still, that they should be appointed by the executive magistrate out of a proper number of persons nominated by the individual legislatures. The last two modes, however, seem to have found no favor beyond their respective movers.

§ 2. The election of senators by the state legislatures appears to have been agreed to without much difficulty. It was proposed by those who thought it expedient to assimilate our national legislature, as nearly as might be, to that of England, by placing the election of one branch one remove from the direct choice of the people. It was acceptable also to those who were desirous of preserving state distinction in the general government. In one branch the people would be represented *individually*, in the other *collectively*.

§ 3. We notice also the term of office of senators. As has been observed, one object of a second branch is to provide a check upon the popular or democratic branch; and with a view to the greater efficacy of this check, not only was the election of senators given to the state legislatures but the senate was made a more durable body than the other. In the principle of a permanent senate, the convention was nearly unanimous; but as to the precise duration of the term of service, there were many different opinions. Terms of four, five, six, seven, and nine years were proposed, and even a term during good behavior, which is virtually for life.

§ 4. One object of a permanent senate is independence. A representative who may be soon displaced by a new election, is more likely to be swayed in the discharge of his official duties, by a desire to secure a reëlection, than one who holds his office more securely. The longer the term, the more independent, it is presumed, will be his action. A durable senate also secures greater stability in the government. Frequent changes of legislatures are generally attended with corresponding changes in the laws. A fluctuating policy is an evil to be avoided. For instance, what man would hazard his capital in a business which might be suddenly prostrated by a change in legislation? Popular excitements are incident to democratic governments, and are often encouraged by demagogues in hope of political gain; and under these impulses the people may call for measures which afterward they would themselves be most ready to lament and condemn. As a safeguard against these excesses of democracy, a long term was adopted.

§ 5. On the other hand, a very long term, it was apprehended, might render that body too independent. Firmly seated in power, senators might become regardless of the wishes and interests of their constituents. Hence, the medium term of six years was supposed to be long enough to give due stability to the law-making power of the government, and yet short enough to insure a proper sense of responsibility on the part of the members of this body.

§ 6. We notice next the principle of representation in the senate. This was involved in the general question of the rule of apportionment which was the subject of the excited controversy mentioned in the preceding chapter. The advocates of the proposed national government contended for a proportional representation in both branches; the adherents to the confederation strenuously insisted on *equal* suffrage in both. As on the question of slave representation, so on this, a compromise was the only means of effecting an agreement; and the convention finally agreed to the proposition, that in the first branch there should be a proportional representation; and that in the second the states should be equally represented. Thus was effected what may be called the second great compromise of the constitution.

§ 7. It will be perceived, however, that, although the states are equally represented in the senate, the *vote* in this body is not taken in the same manner as it was under the confederation, namely, by states. The proposition, as at first offered, provided that each state should have one vote; but it was so modified that, instead of voting by states, the members should vote *per capita*, each senator having one vote.

§ 8. There is a manifest propriety in having the seats of one-third of the senators vacated every two years. The renewal of the entire body at once might be attended by too sudden a change of public measures; or it might place a salutary change of policy for too long a period beyond the power of the people. A wise and politic measure enacted near the close of the term of one senate, might be unexpectedly repealed or materially modified by their successors; or the operation of a bad law passed at the commencement of a senatorial term, might be prolonged for six years. The present arrangement enables the people to prepare for any anticipated changes in legislation, and leaves at all times in the senate a majority of experienced members, acquainted with the unfinished business of previous sessions, and with public affairs generally.

§ 9. That the interests of a state may suffer no injury from the want of a full representation in the senate of the United States, vacancies that happen during the recess of the state legislature, may be filled by the executive of such state, until the next meeting of the legislature. An appointment, however, may not be made before the vacancy actually happens. The term of James Lanman, a senator in congress from the state of Connecticut, expired with the session which closed on the 3d of March, 1825, at a time when the legislature of that state was not in session. As it was necessary for the senate to reässemble on the 4th of March, to act on the nominations of the newly elected president, and as the legislature had failed to appoint a successor to Mr. Lanman, the governor, in order to prevent a vacancy, reäppointed that senator a few days before the expiration of his term. It was decided by the senate, that, as no vacancy had happened when the appointment was made, Mr. Lanman was not entitled to a seat.

§ 10. A person to be eligible to the office of senator, must have attained to the age of thirty-five years, and been nine years a citizen of the United States; and he must be when elected, an inhabitant of the state for which he is chosen. (Art. 1, sec. 3.) The propriety of these qualifications of age and citizenship has been considered. (Chapter XXXI, § 5.) In fixing the qualifications of senators, it was deemed proper to require greater age and experience, and a longer term of citizenship, than in the case of representatives; and to increase the independence of this body, and perhaps also to infuse into it some degree of the aristocratic principle, by making it the representative of wealth, it was proposed to superadd the property qualification. A majority, however, appear to have been opposed to such restriction upon the eligibility of a candidate for any office in the general government.

§ 11. The remainder of this section, and most of the four succeeding sections, so nearly resemble those of a similar nature in state constitutions; and the propriety of the other portions of these sections is so readily perceived, that no particular notice of them is deemed necessary.

§ 12. The powers and the regulations of the two houses in relation to impeachments, the election of officers, the elections and qualifications of members, adjournments, rules of proceeding, punishment of members, &c., described in this first article of the constitution, are nearly the same as are provided by the constitutions of the several states for the government and practice of their respective legislatures.

§ 13. The 7th section of the 1st article of the constitu

tion provides for the passage of bills negatived by the president. Bills returned by him with his objections become laws when passed by majorities of two-thirds of both houses. They also become laws if not returned by him within ten days (Sundays excepted) after they have been presented to him, unless their return is prevented by the adjournment of congress.

CHAPTER XXXIII.

POWERS OF CONGRESS.—TAXATION, AND BORROWING MONEY.

§ 1. Having seen how the legislative department of the general government is constituted, we proceed to the consideration of its powers. Liberty can be secure only where the rights of the people and the powers of the government are clearly defined and well understood ; since, without this knowledge, the people are incapable of keeping the government within the limits of its constitutional powers.

§ 2. In respect to the origin and extent of the powers of the state governments and the general government, there is an important difference. The general government derives its powers from the states, or the *people of the states*, and can exercise such powers only as the people have *delegated* to it by the constitution ; whereas, the states, originally possessing entire sovereignty, may exercise all powers which they have not surrendered to the general government. That is to say, the national government is *limited* to the powers granted ; the power of the state governments is *unlimited*, except so far as they have parted with any of their original powers.

§ 3. Most of the important powers of the government of the United States are vested in congress, and are expressed in the 8th section of the 1st article of the constitution. Perhaps the want of none of these powers was so sensibly felt under the confederation, as the first three here mentioned : and it is probably for this reason that they were placed at the beginning of the list. The first of these is the power "*to lay and collect taxes, duties, imposts and excises;*" the objects of which power are declared to be, "*to pay the debts, and provide for the common defense and general welfare of the United States.*"

§ 4. Congress had been obliged to borrow large sums of money to defray the expenses of the war. Several millions were borrowed from France and Holland. But congress had no power, as has been observed, to raise money by taxation. The government could not pay its debts, nor support itself. But by the power here given, it may raise money to any amount necessary for the objects stated in the constitution, either by *direct taxation;* that is, by laying the tax directly on the property of the citizens; or by *indirect taxation*, which is by duties, imposts, and excises.

§ 5. *Duties* or *customs*, and *imposts*, have nearly the same meaning. The last, however, are properly taxes on goods *imported* only; the first apply to taxes on goods exported as well as on those imported. But as our government does not impose duties on exports, these three words practically signify the same thing. But *excise* has no reference at all to the exportation or importation of goods; it is a tax laid upon an article manufactured, sold or consumed, *within* the country. Such, for example, is the duty paid by keepers of taverns and groceries for the privilege of selling liquors.

§ 6. The power of taxation is qualified by the provision, that "all duties shall be uniform throughout the United States." This is necessary to prevent the giving of unjust preferences to any one or more states over others. Without this restriction upon the exercise of this power, a few states might, by a combination of their representatives in congress, secure to themselves undue advantages in certain branches of trade and business.

§ 7. Notwithstanding congress has power to raise money by taxation in several ways, it has seldom been found necessary to exercise it in any other way than by laying duties on foreign goods, and on the vessels in which they were imported. How effectual this mode of taxation has been will appear from the following facts: At the close of the revolutionary war, the national debt amounted to $42,000,000, on which congress could not so much as pay the interest. Two years after the constitution went into effect, the debt had risen to $75,000,000; in 1804, to $86,000,000. From that time it gradually diminished until the commencement of the late war, in 1812, when it was reduced to $45,000,000. By that war, the debt was again increased, being, in 1816, $127,000,000.

§ 8. The raising of so large a sum, by a direct tax, would have been very oppressive. Wherefore congress exercised its power of taxation almost exclusively in laying duties on imports; and from the revenue thus raised, not only have the yearly expenses of the government been defrayed, but this vast national debt has long since been paid, leaving in the treasury a large surplus of more than thirty millions of dollars, which, by an act of congress in 1836, was apportioned among the several states, to be kept and used by the states until called for by congress. Probably the return of the money will never be demanded.

§ 9. Equally necessary is the power next mentioned, "*to borrow money on the credit of the United States.*" Large sums of money are sometimes wanted to pay a debt before they can be raised from the revenues or regular income of the nation; and sometimes immediately, as in case of war. In such case, congress must either tax the people, or borrow the money. But who would lend the government, if it had not the means of paying? Hence we see the utility of both these powers. Capitalists now have confidence in the credit of the government; because, if other means of fulfilling its engagements are insufficient, it has power to raise the money by direct taxation.

CHAPTER XXXIV.

POWER OF CONGRESS, IN RELATION TO COMMERCE.

§ 1. THE power "*to regulate commerce with foreign nations,*" which is next in the list, seems to be in a measure connected with the first, "*to lay duties.*" It will be remembered that, before the war of the revolution, the colonies were dependent on Great Britain for manufactured goods. (See Chap.

X.) By that war, the direct trade with that country was interrupted. But when peace was restored, our markets were again open to British goods ; while upon American produce and American vessels entering British ports, heavy duties were levied. Thus was the trade of the two countries placed on an unequal footing. We wanted English goods, but England would not take the produce of our labor in exchange without subjecting it to heavy duties.

§ 2. Some explanation may be necessary to enable young persons to understand the objects and unequal operation of this measure of British policy. One object was to secure a market at home for the products of agricultural labor. To show how this is done by taxing foreign products, let us suppose the cost of raising a bushel of wheat in England to be one dollar, and the cost of producing it here and transporting it to that market to be the same. If now a duty of 40 cents a bushel is laid by Great Britain upon foreign wheat, the English consumer, instead of buying it with this duty added, will buy of the English producer. But the American farmer has wheat for which he must find a market abroad ; and in order to sell it in the English market, he must pay 40 cents on every bushel to the British government ; or, which is the same thing, he must sell it for so much less than its value to the British purchaser, who pays the duty to that government.

§ 3. The people of this country being nearly all employed at that time in agriculture, and consequently dependent upon foreign markets for the sale of the surplus products of their labor, they were compelled to submit to these duties. As the result of this system, the consumers in Great Britain obtained their supplies partly at home and partly from abroad ; and the British government thus accomplished the two-fold object of encouraging and rewarding agricultural labor at home, and of drawing a large revenue into its treasury by taxing the same kind of labor in this country.

§ 4. Not possessing the means at that time of manufacturing to any considerable extent, the country was flooded with goods from Great Britain, for which our citizens must either pay in money, or in produce heavily burdened with duties. Hence, some measures for regulating foreign trade became necessary. But congress had not the power to regulate commerce ; the power belonged to the states. The states, acting separately, could not effect the object desired; and they were unable to agree upon any general system of measures. A history of the attempts which were made to remedy the evils complained of, and which resulted in the formation of the constitution, in which the power to regulate commerce was inserted, has been given. (Chap. XXX.)

§ 5. It has just been remarked, that the two powers "to lay duties" and "to regulate commerce" seem to have a connection. Indeed, the former has been used to carry into effect the latter. One of the means by which it was intended to regulate our foreign trade, was the laying of duties upon foreign goods, with a view to check the excessive importation of them, and to encourage and aid our own citizens in supplying the deficiency by manufacturing for themselves.

§ 6. That the power to lay duties was intended to be used for this purpose, appears from its immediate exercise by congress. The first law, except one, passed under the present constitution, authorized "duties to be laid on goods, wares and merchandises imported," and for purposes, one of which was declared to be, "the encouragement and protection of domestic manufactures." It was by such regulations of her foreign trade that England had strengthened her manufacturing interests, and acquired such advantages over other nations; and it was intended, by the adoption of a similar policy, to render this country less dependent upon others.

§ 7. It may be proper, however, here to observe, that, for many years, congress did not find it necessary to exercise this power to a very great extent. Soon after the constitution went into effect, the principal nations of Europe became engaged in war, in which England also was involved. A large portion of the population of those countries having been withdrawn from agricultural pursuits to serve in the armies, a foreign demand was created for the productions of our soil; and our people were enabled to supply themselves at less disadvantage with manufactures from abroad.

§ 8. But after peace had been restored in Europe, and people had returned to their wonted employment, the principal foreign demand for our breadstuffs ceased; and the severe effects of large importations of goods began again to be experienced. Congress now deeming it necessary to exercise, to a greater extent, its power to regulate trade, by discouraging importations and encouraging domestic manufactures, commenced an effective system of protection, in the year 1816. Although duties were imposed upon many articles, the great interest encouraged by the act of that year, was the manufacture of cotton goods, especially those of the coarser kinds.

§ 9. Since that period, laws have from time to time been passed, extending the like favor to the manufacture of iron and iron wares, woolen, and a great variety of other goods. Manufacturing is now carried on very extensively in this country; our citizens being supplied in great part—with some articles almost exclusively—by our own manufacturers. A large portion of the people having thus been drawn into manufacturing and mechanical employments, and become consumers instead of producers of agricultural products, a market has been created at home demanding more of the grain, meat, and other products of agricultural labor, than is usually required to supply all foreign demand.

§ 10. Congress has power also *"to regulate commerce among the several states."* Without this power, each state might adopt regulations favorable to its own citizens, and injurious to those of other states. This was actually done under the confederation; and to restore and preserve harmony, and to secure equal justice to the citizens of all the states, which could be done only by one uniform system for the whole, this power was given to the general government.

§ 11. Under the power to regulate commerce, congress has also made *navigation laws*—laws relating to the shipping of the nation. The want of a power in congress to retaliate the navigation acts of Great Britain, has been mentioned. Since the adoption of the constitution, congress has at different times laid discriminating *tonnage* duties. An act of this kind was passed by the first congress, imposing a duty of fifty cents a ton upon foreign vessels, and upon American vessels six cents a ton. Laws have from time to time been passed, modifying these duties as circumstances and the regulations of other nations required, until they have become unnecessary.

§ 12. Laws, however, still exist, requiring vessels to be measured to ascertain their tonnage, and prescribing the manner in which they are enrolled or registered and licensed, and in which they are to enter and leave ports, the duties of masters of vessels, what papers they are to carry, &c. The laws also prescribe regulations for collecting the revenue arising from foreign commerce. There is in every port of entry a *collector of customs*, who superintends the collection of duties. When a vessel arrives, it is submitted, with the cargo, and all papers and invoices, to the inspection of the proper officers; and the goods subject to duty are weighed or measured, and the duties estimated according to law.

§ 13. On some articles a *specific* duty is charged, which is a duty of a certain amount on a pound, yard, or gallon; as, two cents on a pound of iron, or fifty cents on a yard of cloth. Others are charged with an *ad valorem* duty, which is a duty according to the value, being a certain percentage on the value of an article; as forty per cent. on what costs one dollar would be forty cents; or thirty per cent. on one hundred dollars would be thirty dollars.

§ 14. Our foreign commerce has become very extensive, and the revenue derived from it is large. The average value of the goods imported during the last ten years, ending June 30, 1857, is $225,000,000. The average amount of duties collected on the same, is about $50,000,000. The duties on imports, and the proceeds of the sales of public lands, which have averaged during the same time, $5,000,000 annually, constitute nearly the whole revenue, from which are paid the salaries of officers and other expenses of the general government.

CHAPTER XXXV.

POWERS OF CONGRESS IN RELATION TO NATURALIZATION, BANKRUPTCY, MONEY, COPY-RIGHTS AND PATENTS.

§ 1. Another power given to congress, is the power "*to establish a uniform rule of naturalization.*" It has already been stated, that foreigners, or aliens, are not entitled to the privileges of citizens till they become naturalized. Before the constitution was adopted, every state established its own rules for naturalizing foreigners. But as a person, on being made a citizen in any state, becomes a citizen of the United States, it is evident that there should be but one rule of naturalization.

§ 2. An alien must have lived in the United States five years before he can become a citizen. Two years before he is admitted as a citizen, he must declare, on oath, in writing, before a proper court, that he intends to become a citizen of the United States, and to renounce his allegiance to his former government; and he must declare, on oath, that he will support the constitution of the United States. Then, two years thereafter, the court, if satisfied as to his moral character and his attachment to the constitution, may admit him as a citizen.

§ 3. On his being naturalized, a man's minor children, if dwelling in the United States, also become citizens. If a man has lived at least three years in the United States before he becomes of age, he may, at the expiration of the five years' residence, be admitted by the court, without having previously made a declaration of his intention to become a citizen.

§ 4. In the same clause is given the power to establish "*uniform laws on the subject of bankruptcies throughout the United States.*" A *bankrupt* is an insolvent debtor, that is, a person unable to pay all his just debts. A *bankrupt law* is a law which, upon an insolvent's surrendering all his property to his creditors, discharges him from the payment of his debts. Such laws, by securing to honest and unfortunate debtors the enjoyment of their future earnings, encourage them to engage anew in their industrial pursuits. And as such laws, if judiciously framed, compel a full surrender of the debtor's property, they do not operate to the injury of his creditors. This humane provision of the constitution will be the more favorably regarded, when it is considered that debtors were formerly liable to an indefinite term of imprisonment for their debts. But however beneficent to the unfortunate poor, these laws have afforded to dishonest and fraudulent debtors the means of procuring a release from their obligations.

§ 5. The power to pass bankrupt laws was intended to remedy the inconvenience of the dissimilar and conflicting laws of the different states. And yet, important as this power was deemed, there is no existing law on the subject. Laws have at three different times been enacted, the last of them in 1841; but all were repealed soon after their enactment. That which had the longest existence was passed April 1800, and repealed December 1803.

§ 6. The absence of uniform and general bankrupt laws has brought into question the constitutionality of state insolvent laws. The constitution prohibits the states from passing laws impairing the obligation of contracts; and does not the discharge of a debtor weaken, or make entirely void, his obligation? Cases involving the constitutionality of state insolvent laws have come before the supreme court of the United States. It has been decided by this court, (1.) That, until congress shall establish a system of bankruptcy, a state may pass such insolvent laws as shall not impair the obligation of contracts. (2.) That a state has no authority to pass a law discharging a debtor from the obligation of a contract made before the law was passed. (3.) That a discharge is valid only between citizens of the state by which the law was passed, and that a debtor removing into another state, and there taking the benefit of an insolvent law, is not discharged from debts contracted before his removal.

§ 7. But the question arises, can there be a discharge from the payment of a debt, without impairing the obligation of a contract? It has been held that the obligation of a contract made *after* the law was passed, was not impaired in the meaning of the constitution, because the parties had reference to the laws existing when the contract was made. But it is questioned by some eminent jurists, whether the discharge of a debtor from even such a contract can be constitutionally authorized.

§ 8. The power *"to coin money and regulate the value thereof,"* is properly given to congress. Formerly the system of reckoning was by pounds, shillings, and pence; the value of which was different in different states. For instance, in the New England states, six shillings made a dollar, in New York eight, in Pennsylvania seven shillings and sixpence. This rendered dealing between the people of different states highly inconvenient. The present decimal mode of calculation, by dollars and cents, established by congress, together with the use of decimal coins, has removed the former inconvenience.

§ 9. Money is coined at the *mints*. The principal mint in the United States, and the first that was established in this country, is at Philadelphia. The business of coining is under the superintendence of a director. The principal persons employed under him are a treasurer, an assayer, a chief coiner, an engraver, and a melter and refiner. The gold and silver, before it is coined, is called *bullion*. Individuals, as well as the government, may get money coined at the mint. There are also branch mints in New Orleans, at Charlotte, in North Carolina, at Dahlonega in Georgia, in California, and in the city of New York. In the last named place, gold is assayed, but not coined.

§ 10. Congress has also the power *"to fix the standard of weights and measures."* The facility and convenience of commercial intercourse between the states requires that there should be a uniform standard of weights and measures. The object of this power, however, has never been carried into effect by congress. Each state fixes its own standard; but the standards of the different states, it is presumed, very nearly agree.

§ 11. The power next mentioned is *"to provide for the punishment of counterfeiting the securities and current coin of the United States."* By "securities" here are meant bonds and other written evidences of debt. It is manifestly proper that, as the general government has the power to borrow money and to coin money, it should also have power to provide for punishing those who forge its written obligations for the payment of the money borrowed, and who counterfeit its coin. Hence, these offenses are tried in courts of the United States.

§ 12. Congress has power *"to establish post-offices and post-roads."* The post-office department, from the facilities which it affords for the circulation of intelligence and the transaction of business, is an institution of incalculable value to the people of the union. It is impossible to conceive all the difficulties which would attend the exercise of this power by the different states. A uniform system of regulations is indispensable to the efficiency of this department, and could be secured only by placing the power in the hands of congress.

§ 13. Another power of congress is, "*to promote the progress of science and useful arts, by securing, for limited times, to authors and inventors, the exclusive right to their respective writings and discoveries.*" Useful arts and sciences are much aided by new inventions or discoveries, and by new books. But if every man had the privilege of printing and selling every book or writing, there would be little encouragement to men of ability to spend, as is often done, years of labor in preparing new works for the public. Nor would men of genius be likely to spend their time and money in inventing and constructing expensive machinery, if others had the same right as the inventors to make and sell the same. Congress has therefore enacted laws for the benefit of authors and inventors.

§ 14. The exclusive right of an author to the benefits of the printing and sale of his books or writings, is called *copy-right*, and is obtained thus: The author sends a printed copy of the title of his book to the clerk of the district court of the United States of the district in which the author resides. The clerk records the title in a book, for which he receives fifty cents, and gives the author, under the seal of the court, a copy of the record, for which also he receives fifty cents.

§ 15. The author must also, within three months after the publication of the work, deliver a copy of the same to the clerk of the district court. And he must cause to be printed on the title page or page immediately following, of every copy of the book, words showing that the law has been complied with. (See the 2d page of this book.) This secures to the author the sole right to print and sell his work for twenty-eight years; at the expiration of which time, he may have his right continued for fourteen years longer, by again complying with the requirements of the law as before, provided it be done within six months before the expiration of the first term, and a copy of the record published in a newspaper for the space of four weeks.

§ 16. If an author disposes of his interest in his work before a copy-right is secured, the person becoming the proprietor of the work procures the copy-right in his own name. A proprietor or owner of a copy-right may at any time sell and assign his right to another person; in which case the assignment is to be recorded in the office whence the copy-right was issued.

§ 17. *Patents* for new inventions are obtained at the patent office at the seat of government, which office is connected with the department of the interior. (See Chap. XLI, § 4.) The commissioner of patents superintends the granting of patents, under the direction of the secretary of the interior. To secure an exclusive right to an invention, the inventor must deliver to the commissioner of patents a written description of his invention, and specify the improvement which he claims as his own discovery ; and he must swear that he believes he is the true discoverer thereof.

§ 18. Before the petition of an inventor is considered, he must pay the sum of thirty dollars. If the commissioner, upon examination, does not find that the invention had been before discovered, he issues a patent therefor. Patents are granted for the term of fourteen years, and may be renewed for a further term of seven years, if the inventor has not been able to obtain a reasonable profit from his invention.

CHAPTER XXXVI.

POWERS OF CONGRESS, IN RELATION TO PIRACY AND OFFENSES AGAINST THE LAW OF NATIONS, WAR, MARQUE AND REPRISAL, ARMY AND NAVY, DISTRICT OF COLUMBIA ; IMPLIED POWERS.

§ 1. Congress has power "*to define and punish piracies and felonies committed on the high seas, and offenses against the law of nations.*" *Piracy* is commonly defined to be forcible robbery or depredation upon the high seas. But the term *felony* was not exactly defined by the laws of England ; and its meaning was various in the different states ; being sometimes applied to capital offenses only ; at others, to all crimes above misdemeanor. For the sake of uniformity, the power to define these offenses is given to congress : and as no state has jurisdiction beyond its own limits, it is proper that congress should have the power to punish, as well as define, crimes committed on the high seas.

§ 2. Nor are offenses against the law of nations more clearly defined : therefore the power to define these are with equal propriety given to congress. As our citizens are regarded by foreign nations as citizens of the United States, and not as citizens of the states ; and as the general government alone is responsible to foreign nations for injuries committed on the high seas by citizens of the United States, the power is granted to congress.

§ 3. The power "*to declare war*" is properly given to congress. It would be dangerous to allow a single state to make war ; and to depend on the state governments to provide the means of prosecuting a war, had already been found to be unsafe. And as the people of all the states become involved in the calamity and expense of a war, the power to declare war ought to belong to the representatives of the nation.

§ 4. Congress has also the power "*to issue letters of marque and reprisal.*" *Marque* means passing the frontier or limits of a country ; *reprisal*, taking in return. Letters of marque and reprisal give to persons injured by citizens of another nation, the liberty to seize the bodies or goods of any of the citizens of such nation, and detain them until satisfaction shall be made. It is not clear that such license ought ever to be given. Although it is designed to enable citizens of one country to obtain redress for injuries committed by those of another, without a resort to war, its tendency is to provoke rather than prevent war. Besides, it does not appear just to seize and detain the bodies or goods of unoffending persons. If the power to grant such license is ever to be exercised, it is properly vested in congress.

§ 5. If congress has the power to declare war, it follows that it should have command of the land and naval forces, and all other means of national defense ; for without this, the power to declare war would be nugatory. The command of the militia is necessary also to insure the execution of the laws and to suppress insurrections. It became necessary soon after the government was organized under the constitution, to call out a military force to quell an insurrection in the western part of Pennsylvania, which had risen to resist the execution of a law of congress imposing an excise duty on domestic distilled spirits. In pursuance of the power to provide for calling forth the militia for such purposes, congress has authorized the president to raise such force as he shall at any time deem necessary.

§ 6. Congress has power "*to exercise exclusive legislation over such district* (not exceeding ten miles square) *as may, by cession of particular states, become the seat of government.*" The "ten miles square," as appears from the language of the clause, was not yet in possession of the national government: but it was in contemplation, by the states of Maryland and Virgina, to cede it to the United States for the purpose mentioned. As it is the property of the nation, it is proper that it should be under the exclusive control of the general government. It is called the District of Columbia. That part of it which was ceded by Virginia, was in 1846 retroceded by congress to that state. Like authority is exercised by congress over all places acquired "*for the erection of forts, magazines, arsenals, dock-yards, and other needful buildings.*" The public safety evidently requires that these places should be subject to no other legislation than that of congress. p. 272.

§ 7. The power last mentioned in this section is the power "*to make all laws necessary and proper for carrying into execution the foregoing and all other powers vested*" *in the general government and its officers.* As it was impossible to enumerate every particular power which congress might find it necessary to exercise, certain powers were expressly granted; to which was added this general grant of power to pass laws for carrying those certain powers into effect.

§ 8. It is the opinion of some eminent statesmen, that the powers of congress are not enlarged by this clause; that the power therein granted is necessarily *implied* in, and incidental to, the powers expressly granted. For example: The power to construct break-waters and light-houses, and to remove obstructions from navigable rivers, is included in the power "to regulate commerce;" and congress might make such improvements without an express grant. So also the power "to establish post-offices," implies the power to punish the robbery of the mail. It is the doctrine of the most eminent expounders of the constitution, "that wherever the end is required, the means are authorized; wherever a general power to do a thing is given, every particular power for doing it is included."

§ 9. The express grant, however, of the power under consideration, was deemed useful in order to prevent any doubts which might be raised upon the subject. Time and experience have proved its utility. Many important measures have been enacted by congress, which, but for this clause, would have been defeated by doubts as to their constitutionality. Under the confederation, congress could exercise no powers but such as were "*expressly* delegated." This stringent provision was at times attended with great inconvenience, and prevented the adoption of effectual measures of relief; and the embarrassments to the action of congress which it had occasioned, had probably no small influence in procuring the insertion of this declaratory clause, to avoid the scruples of those who might deny to congress all powers not expressly granted. Several other important powers are in other parts of the constitution conferred upon congress, which will be hereafter considered.

CHAPTER XXXVII.

POWERS PROHIBITED TO CONGRESS.

§ 1. While the constitution grants to the general government all powers deemed necessary to be exercised for the general welfare, it imposes upon congress certain important restrictions, most of which are contained in the 9th section of the 1st article of the constitution. The prohibition first mentioned is in these words: "The *migration or importation of such persons as any of the states, now existing, shall think proper to admit, shall not be prohibited* by the congress prior to the year one thousand eight hundred and eight; but *a tax or duty may be imposed on such importation*, not exceeding ten dollars for each person."

§ 2. This provision, which was intended to reserve to the states, for the time specified, the right to import slaves, was the subject of much debate in the convention of framers; and has ever since been the fruitful occasion of popular discussion. It has ever been a cause of wonder and regret to many of the American people, that this inhuman traffic should have been permitted by the constitution, even for a limited period. Like certain other provisions, however, it is the result of concession and compromise, as will appear from the following sketch of the proceedings of the convention on the subject.

§ 3. A section had been reported, declaring that "no tax or duty should be laid by congress on articles exported from any state ; nor on the migration or importation of such persons as the several states should think proper to admit ; nor should such migration or importation be prohibited." As the southern states were the principal exporting states, it is evident that the whole section was intended as a concession to those states. The clause prohibiting the laying of duties on exports, was, after considerable discussion, adopted, 7 states voting in the affirmative, and 4 in the negative. The latter were New Hampshire, New Jersey, Pennsylvania, and Delaware.

§ 4. It was then proposed, though by a delegate from a southern state, (Luther Martin, of Maryland,) to vary the article so as to allow a prohibition or tax on the importation of slaves, for the reason, first, that as five slaves were to be counted as three freemen in the apportionment of representatives, the clause, as reported, would leave an encouragement of this traffic ; secondly, that slaves weakened one part of the union which the other parts were bound to protect ; and thirdly, that such a feature in the constitution was inconsistent with the principles of the revolution, and dishonorable to the American character.

§ 5. The opposition to this proposition was principally from the three extreme southern states, these being the only states which had not abolished the foreign slave trade : and one of these, (North Carolina,) had discouraged the trade by imposing duties on slaves imported. Their delegates insisted on the privilege of continuing the importation. They did not apprehend insurrections among their slaves, and would readily exempt the other states from the obligation to protect the southern states. Religion and humanity had nothing to do with this question. Interest was the governing principle with nations. The true question was, whether the southern states should or should not be parties to the union ; and the opinion was expressed, that they would not be, if the slave trade should be prohibited. It was urged, also, that the northern states would be benefited by the importation, as it would give additional employment to their shipping. It was further said, that, if left at liberty, these southern states might, by degrees, do of themselves what was wished, as Maryland and Virginia had already done.

§ 6. Certain northern delegates, particularly those from Connecticut, though disapproving the slave trade, urged that the matter should be left with the states; that there should be as few objections as possible to the proposed government; and that the abolition of slavery was going on, and would probably, by degrees, be completed by the good sense of the several states. Taxing the importation was objected to, as that implied that slaves were property.

§ 7. There being little hope of a speedy agreement, it was proposed by delegates from South Carolina to refer the subject to a committee, with a view to making slaves liable to an equal tax with other imports. The clause prohibiting the taxing of exports having been previously adopted, the two remaining clauses of the section, together with the section relating to navigation laws, were referred to a committee, in the hope, as was said, of "forming a bargain among the northern and southern states." The necessity of a power to regulate commerce by duties on foreign goods and shipping, in order to protect our own, has been mentioned. (Chap. XXXIV.) It was therefore to be expected that congress would exercise this power in passing navigation acts: but in compliance with the wishes of southern delegates, who apprehended that the taxing of foreign shipping would increase the cost of the transportation of their exports, a section had been inserted, prohibiting the passage of navigation acts, except by majorities of two-thirds of both houses.

§ 8. The committee to whom the subject had been referred, reported, as a substitute for the two clauses relating to the importation and taxation of slaves, a provision denying to congress the power to prohibit the importation of slaves prior to the year 1800, but allowing a tax or duty on the slaves imported, not exceeding the average of the duties laid on imports; and the section containing the restriction upon the passage of navigation laws was to be struck out. It was moved to insert 1808 in the place of 1800 To this it was objected, (by Mr. Madison,) that so long a term would produce all the mischief that could be apprehended from the liberty to import slaves, and would be more dishonorable to the American character than to say nothing about it in the constitution. In relation to taxes on slaves, he thought it wrong to admit in the constitution the idea that there could be property in men. Others, however, considered the tax as a discouragement to the importation. The year 1808 was finally fixed as the year when the restriction upon the power of congress to prohibit the slave trade was to cease.

§ 9. It now remained to dispose of the navigation clause. Southern delegates were still in favor of requiring a majority of two-thirds to pass navigation laws, alleging that the power of regulating commerce was a pure concession on the part of the southern states, and that they did not need the protection of the northern states. It was urged, on the other hand, that preferences to American ships would multiply them until they could carry the southern produce cheaper than it was now carried. A navy was essential to the security of the nation, particularly of the southern states, and could only be had by a navigation act encouraging American bottoms and seamen. Shipping was the worst and most precarious kind of property, and needed public patronage.

§ 10. Delegates from South Carolina at length proposed to yield this point. Although they regarded it as the true interest of the southern states to have no regulation of commerce, yet, considering the liberality of the eastern states, (in consenting to the importation of slaves,) and the interest which the southern states had in being united with the strong eastern states, they thought it proper that no fetters should be imposed on the power of making commercial regulations. At the worst, a navigation act could bear hard a little while only on the southern states. As they were laying the foundation for a great empire, they should look beyond the present moment. It was suggested also that a navigation act was necessary to secure the West India trade. The section containing the restriction on the power to pass navigation laws was accordingly struck out; and thus was effected the third great compromise of the constitution.

§ 11. Whether the interests or the honor of the nation

required this concession to the southern states, is a question upon which different opinions are entertained. It was desirable to secure the ratification of the constitution by all the states. To form a union of less than nine states, (Art. 7,) was thought inexpedient. If, as was feared, the three slave importing states, or but two of them, should reject the constitution without the prohibition mentioned, and but two or three other states, on account of objections to certain other parts of the plan, should fail to ratify, the great object of the convention would have been defeated. This consideration induced the northern states to consent to the compromise. It is, however, believed by many, that the southern states would eventually have acceded to the union, though the concession had not been made.

§ 12. The propriety of this concession depends materially upon the question, whether the power of congress, had it been left unrestricted, would have been earlier exercised for the abolition of the slave trade. This question it is, of course, impossible to determine. It is, however, a gratifying fact, that congress exercised its power for terminating this cruel and disgraceful traffic at the earliest possible period. A law was passed in 1807, to go into effect in 1808, making it unlawful, under severe penalties, to import slaves into the United States; and in 1820, the African slave trade was declared *piracy*, and made punishable by death.

CHAPTER XXXVIII.

POWERS PROHIBITED TO CONGRESS—CONTINUED.

§ 1. Among the restrictions on the powers of congress, is the prohibition to *suspend* "the privilege of the writ of *habeas corpus, unless when, in cases of rebellion or invasion, the public safety may require it.*" (Art. 1, sec. 9.) For the origin and meaning of this privilege, see Chapter XLV, § 9, 10.

§ 2. The next clause declares that "*no bill of attainder or ex post facto law shall be passed.*" A *bill of attainder* is an act of a legislature, inflicting the punishment of death upon a person pronounced guilty of some crime, without trial. If it inflicts a milder punishment, it is called a bill of pains and penalties.

§ 3. An *ex post facto law* is, literally, a law which has effect upon an act after it is done. It here means a law to punish, as a *crime*, an act that was lawful when it was done. Thus, if a law should be passed, by which a man should be made to suffer death for an act of justifiable homicide committed before the law was made, such would be an *ex post facto* law. A law is also an ex post facto law that inflicts a more severe penalty for an *unlawful* act than was imposed for such offense when committed. Thus, if a law were passed to-day, requiring that men awaiting trial for petit larceny heretofore committed, should, on conviction, suffer death, or imprisonment in state prison, such law would be an ex post facto law. Petit larceny not being thus punishable when the offense was committed, a more severe penalty could not be imposed after its commission.

§ 4. "*No attainder of treason shall work corruption of blood or forfeiture, except during the life of the person attainted.*" (Art. III, § 3, cl. 2.) To the young reader this sentence may need explanation. Literally, attainder means a taint, or staining, or corruption ; but it here signifies the same as judgment, or conviction. By the common law, the stain of treason was made to affect the *blood* of the traitor, so that he could not inherit property himself, nor could his heirs inherit from him ; but his whole estate was forfeited. The constitution properly abolishes a law by which the innocent were made to suffer for the crimes of others.

§ 5. Besides corruption of blood and forfeiture, the manner of inflicting the punishment was most disgraceful and inhuman. The offender was drawn to the gallows on a hurdle ; hanged by the neck, and cut down alive ; his entrails taken out and burned while he yet was alive ; his head cut off ; and his body quartered. Power being given to congress, in the clause above referred to, "*to declare the punishment of treason,*" congress has abolished this barbarous practice. Hanging, simply, is the punishment.

§ 6. "*Treason against the United States,*" as defined by the constitution, "*consists only in levying war against them, or in adhering to their enemies, giving them aid and comfort.*" A general proneness to construe crimes of a less aggravated char acter into acts of treason, rendered it proper that the constitution should define the crime. An assemblage of men for a treasonable purpose, such as war against the government, or a revolution of any of its territories, and in condition to make such war, constitutes a levying of war.

§ 7. War can be levied only by the employment of force; troops must be embodied; men must be openly raised; but there may be treason without arms, or the application of force to the object. To march in arms with a force marshaled and arrayed, committing acts of violence, in order to compel the resignation of a public officer, and thereby to render ineffective an act of congress, is high treason. When war is levied, all who perform a part, however remote from the scene of action, being leagued in the conspiracy, commit treason. But a mere conspiracy to levy war is not treason. A secret, unarmed meeting of conspirators, not in force, nor in warlike form, though met for a treasonable purpose, is not treason; but these offenses are high misdemeanors.

§ 8. "*No capitation or other direct tax shall be laid, unless in proportion to the census or enumeration herein before directed to be taken.*" (Art. I, § 9.) The word *capitation* is derived from the same Latin word as *capital*, which has been defined. (Chap. XXVIII, § 3.) It is a tax of a certain amount upon every head or poll, without respect to property; hence it is usually called a *poll-tax*. The above clause means, that if poll-taxes, which are a kind of direct taxes, should be laid in pursuance of the 3d clause, 2d section, and 1st article of the constitution, only three-fifths of the slaves are to be counted. Poll-taxes are not laid to any great extent, in any of the states.

§ 9. "*No tax or duty shall be laid on articles exported from any state.*" Probably no law could be devised which would operate equally upon the interests of the different states. Some states, for example, would be injuriously affected by a duty on cotton, rice, and tobacco; others by a duty on grain; and others by duties on manufactures, &c. But were it even possible to devise a plan which should be equal in its operation, it could hardly be expected to unite in its favor a majority of the representatives of the different and conflicting interests. As every necessary object of indirect taxation may be attained by duties on imports, exports are properly exempted. With a view to the same object, it is expressly provided, in the same clause, that "*no preference shall be given, by any regulation of commerce or revenue, to the ports of one state over those of another; nor shall vessels bound to or from one state be obliged to enter, clear, or pay duties in another.*"

§ 10. Of the two remaining clauses of this section, the one is designed to secure economy, regularity, and accountability in the expenditures of the public money; the other to secure respect for republican simplicity, and to guard against the corruption of the officers of the national government by foreign influence.

§ 11. Sundry salutary restrictions are also laid upon the states. "*No state shall enter into any treaty, alliance, or confederation.*" The articles of confederation contained the same prohibition. If every state were permitted to enter into engagements with one or more other states, or with foreign powers, the rights and interests of the other states might be seriously injured, and the entire policy of the national government counteracted. As the power to make treaties and alliances is vested in the general government, it is apparent that the same power in the state governments would endanger the very existence of the union. For a similar reason, the states may not "*issue letters of marque and reprisal.*" The power properly belongs to the general government, and can not therefore be safely intrusted to the state governments.

§ 12. The power to "*coin money*" was given to the general government, to secure a uniform currency. But this object could never be attained, if the power here prohibited were exercised by the states.

§ 13. A state may not "*emit bills of credit.*" These are defined to be promissory notes or bills issued by the authority of a state on the credit of the state, and designed to circulate as money. Both during and after the war of the revolution, a large amount of this paper money, almost worthless, was put into circulation by the continental congress, and by the states. Bank bills which circulate upon private credit, do not come under the prohibition. And it is the prevailing opinion that the prohibition does not apply to the notes of a *state* bank, drawn on the credit of a particular fund set apart for their payment. Some of the states had declared their irredeemable currency a legal tender. Hence the prohibition, in the same clause, "*to make any thing but gold and silver coin a tender in payment of debts;*" which means that no person shall be compelled to take in payment of a debt any thing *tendered* or offered but gold and silver coin.

§ 14. The states are forbidden also to pass any "*law impairing the obligation of contracts.*" Laws that would weaken the force of a contract, or release men from their obligations, would be contrary to the principles of justice, and give insecurity to the rights of property: they are therefore with great propriety prohibited.

§ 15. The power to pass "*bills of attainder*" and "*ex post facto laws,*" and the power to "*grant titles of nobility,*" are among the powers prohibited to the states in this clause. These acts are in the preceding section prohibited to congress; and being in their nature objectionable, they are with equal propriety prohibited to the states.

§ 16. The exercise, by the states, of the powers mentioned in the two remaining clauses of this section, is incompatible with the exercise of the same powers by congress; and they are therefore properly prohibited to the states.

CHAPTER XXXIX.

EXECUTIVE DEPARTMENT. PRESIDENT AND VICE-PRESIDENT; THEIR ELECTION, QUALIFICATIONS, &C.

§ 1. The executive power is vested in a president of the United States, who holds his office for the term of four years. A vice-president is chosen at the same time, and for the same term. (Art. 2, sec. 1.) The general duties of these officers are similar to those of the governor and lieutenant-governor of a state; and this department of the general government is constituted in a manner similar to that of a state government.

§ 2. The propriety of three separate and distinct departments of government, legislative, executive, and judicial, was so generally admitted, and the want of an executive power under the confederation was so sensibly felt, that every plan of government introduced into the convention provided for an executive department. In regard, however, to its organization and the extent of its powers, there was a great diversity of opinion.

§ 3. First, as to the number of persons of which it should be composed. An executive magistracy consisting of a number of persons, as some proposed, and divided in opinion as they would often be, could not act with the necessary vigor and promptitude. Measures involving the highest interests of the nation, and requiring speedy action, might be subjected to injurious delays, or be entirely defeated by divided councils. Unity in the executive, too, instead of tending to monarchy, as some apprehended, would rather be a safeguard against tyranny, by increasing the responsibility of the office ; for, where the whole responsibility of an act is thrown upon a single individual, it is impossible to shift any portion of deserved blame upon others.

§ 4. Secondly, as to the tenure of office. Specific terms of three, six, and seven years were proposed. It was also proposed to render the executive ineligible for a second term. A short term was considered necessary to insure responsibility ; and reëligibility would furnish a motive to good behavior. Against a short term it was urged, that it might induce an executive to shape his policy with a view to a reëlection rather than to the public good. A long term, it was argued, would secure greater firmness and independence in the discharge of his official duties, and enable him to mature and carry out his system of public policy. Eligibility for reëlection having been agreed on, the term of four years was adopted, as being most likely to secure, in an equal degree, the advantages of both a long and a short term.

§ 4. Thirdly, the mode of election. Several modes were proposed : (1.) Election by the national legislature. The main objection to this mode was, that it would render the executive too dependent upon the legislature. It would encourage bargain and intrigue. Votes would be given by members of the legislature, under promises or expectations of favors in return, either to themselves or their friends. (2.) Election by the people at large. Against this it was urged, that the people could not be sufficiently informed of the character of candidates ; that they would seldom or never give a majority of votes to any one man ; and that it would be attended with dangerous commotions. (3.) Election by electors chosen for that purpose. For the election of the electors, however, various modes were suggested ; namely, by the state executives ; by the state legislatures ; and by the people.

§ 6. The election of the president by electors was finally agreed to ; and each state was allowed to appoint its electors in such manner as the legislature should direct. (Art. 2, sec. 1.) In pursuance of the discretion here given, different modes were adopted in different states. In some the electors were appointed by the state legislatures ; in others they were elected by the people. Of the states which adopted the former mode, all but one have exchanged it for the latter. In all the states except South Carolina, presidential electors are now chosen by the people.

§ 7. These electors are, by the laws of the several states, to be chosen by general ticket. The names of two men, corresponding to the number of senators to which a state is entitled in congress, together with the names of as many others as there are representatives of the state in the lower house of congress, one to reside in each congressional district, are all placed upon the same ballot ; and every voter votes for the whole number of presidential electors to be chosen in the state. And by a law of congress, the electors are required to be chosen in all the states on the same day, which is the Tuesday next after the first Monday of November.

§ 8. The electors so chosen in each state meet in their respective states on the first Wednesday of December, and vote for president and vice-president ; and make and sign three certificates of all the votes given by them, and seal up the same. One of these certificates is to be sent by a person duly appointed by them, to the president of the senate at the seat of government, before the first of January next ensuing ; another is to be forwarded by mail, also directed to the president of the senate ; and the third is to be delivered to the United States judge of the district in which the electors are assembled.

§ 9. On the second Wednesday of February, the president of the senate, in the presence of all the senators and representatives, opens the certificates from all the states, and the votes are counted. The person having a majority of all the electoral votes for president is elected. If no person has a majority of the electoral votes, the house of representatives must choose the president from those candidates, not exceeding three, who had the highest numbers of the electoral votes. But in so doing, the members do not all vote together; but those of each state vote by themselves; and the candidate who receives the votes of a majority of the representatives of a state, has but one vote for each such majority; from which it appears that there are only as many presidential votes as there are states; and the person who receives the votes of a majority of the states, is elected.

§ 10. Of this mode of electing a president, the election of 1825 is a practical illustration. The votes of the electoral colleges had in December, 1824, been divided upon *four* candidates: Andrew Jackson having received 99 votes; John Quincy Adams, 84; William H. Crawford, 41; and Henry Clay, 37. Neither candidate having received a majority of all the electoral votes, the election of president devolved upon the house of representatives. Of the three candidates having received the highest numbers of electoral votes, Mr. Adams received the votes of thirteen states, Gen. Jackson, of seven states, and Mr. Crawford of four states. Mr. Adams having received the votes of a majority of all the states, he was elected.

§ 11. The present manner of electing a president and vice-president, which is prescribed by the 12th article of amendment, has been substituted for the original plan. (See Art. 2, sec. 1, cl. 3.) This alteration was probably induced by the difficulty of electing a president in 1801. Under the mode then existing, the electors did not designate the office to which either of the persons voted for was intended to be chosen. Of the electoral votes given in December, Thomas Jefferson and Aaron Burr had each 73 votes, the electors belonging to the same political party having unanimously voted for them both. The election must consequently be made by the house of representatives, where the balloting was continued many days, when, on the thirty-sixth ballot, Mr. Jefferson received the votes of a majority of the states. By the old mode, a tie must of necessity occur whenever the electors of the most numerous party vote unanimously for the candidates of such party. By requiring the persons voted for to be named for the offices for which they are respectively designed, the chances of an equal vote for two or more candidates for the same office are greatly diminished.

§ 12. To be eligible to the office of president or vice-president, a person must be a natural born citizen of the United States, thirty-five years of age, and must have been fourteen years a resident within the United States. (Art. 2, sec. 1, cl. 5. Amend. art. 12, cl. 3.) The reasons for requiring long terms of citizenship and residence, and mature age and experience, in the case of senators, apply with at least equal force in the office of president.

§ 13. The constitution properly provides for filling vacancies in the office of president, by devolving the powers and duties of the office upon the vice-president. The power of making further provision for supplying vacancies, is given to congress (Art. 2, sec. 1). In pursuance of the power here granted, it has been enacted, that in case of the removal, death, resignation, or inability, both of the president and vice-president, the president of the senate *pro-tempore* shall act as president · and if he, too, should die, resign, or become incompetent, the speaker of the house of representatives would assume the duties of the office. Since the adoption of the constitution, two vice-presidents have succeeded to the office of president : the first, in consequence of the death of President Harrison, in April, 1841 ; the second, in July, 1850, on occasion of the death of President Taylor.

§ 14. The increase and diminution of the salary of the president, as in the case of certain other officers, is properly prohibited. Without such prohibition, the compensation of a president might be reduced to a sum insufficient to meet his necessary expenditures, and afford a just remuneration for the services rendered. It would be impolitic to make the executive entirely dependent upon the legislature for his support. Control over his compensation would be little less than control over his will. On the other hand, if the emoluments of the office could be increased during his official term, he might be tempted to use undue influence to procure a needless augmentation of his salary.

§ 15. The president and vice-president go into office on the 4th day of March next after their election, and end their term on the 3d day of March, four years thereafter; the same days on which senators every six years, and representatives every two years, commence and end their regular terms of office.

CHAPTER XL.

POWERS AND DUTIES OF THE PRESIDENT; TREATIES; PUBLIC MINISTERS; APPOINTMENTS AND REMOVALS.

§ 1. The powers and duties of the president are enumerated in the 2d and 3d sections of the 2d article of the constitution. He is made the commander-in-chief of the army and navy of the United States, and of the militia of the several states when called into the actual service of the United States. It has been observed, that singleness of purpose, promptitude of action, and responsibility, are indispensable to a successful exercise of the powers and duties of an executive; and that these are supposed to be best secured by vesting the executive power in a single person (Chap. XXXIX. sec. 3.) To execute the laws, to suppress insurrections, and carry on war, are executive duties; and it is highly proper that the president should have the command of the public forces.

§ 2. The president has also the power to grant reprieves and pardons for offenses against the United States, except in cases of impeachment. The necessity of this power arises from the fallibility of courts of justice. Through partial or false testimony, errors in conducting trials, or the mistakes of judges and juries, a person may be unjustly convicted; or the offense may have been attended with palliating or mitigating circumstances. It is proper, therefore, that there should be lodged somewhere a power to mitigate the sentence, or postpone its execution, or to remit the punishment, as the case may seem to require; and in no other hands, it is presumed, would this power be more judiciously exercised than in those of the executive. Hence the same power is given to the governor of the states. (Chap. XVI, § 4).

§ 3. The next clause confers on the president the power by and with the advice and consent of the senate, to make treaties, to appoint embassadors, other public ministers and consuls, judges of the supreme court, and other officers. A *treaty* is an agreement between two nations. Treaties are made to restore or preserve peace, and sometimes to regulate trade, between nations. It is plain, therefore, that this power ought to be in the national government. In monarchical governments it resides in the king. To confide so important a trust to the president alone, would be imprudent. To associate the house of representatives with the president and senate, as in the enactment of laws, would render it impossible to act with the decision, secrecy, firmness and dispatch, which are sometimes necessary in negotiating treaties.

§ 4. The power of making treaties, being neither wholly executive, nor wholly legislative, but partaking of the nature of both, *a part* of the legislature—the body combining more of stability, energy, and experience, and, from its being less numerous, capable of acting more promptly, as well as being more easily convened, and at less expense—appears to be very properly associated with the executive in the exercise of this power. So the power "*to appoint embassadors, ministers,*" or other agents, by whom treaties are negotiated, seems to be with equal propriety placed in the same hands.

§ 5. In making a treaty, the terms are arranged and agreed upon by the agents of the governments; and the articles of agreement are sent to their respective governments to be ratified. Both governments must ratify, or the treaty fails. What is meant by the president and senate's making treaties, is their approving and sanctioning, or, as it is usually called, *ratifying* them. Treaties are sometimes negotiated by persons appointed by the two governments for that special purpose; at other times by the permanent representatives or ministers of the respective governments.

§ 6. Each of the principal civilized nations has some officer at home, who acts as agent in negotiating treaties and transacting other business with foreign governments; and has also a representative at the seat of each foreign government, to transact business for his nation, and to keep his government advised of what is done abroad. Hence, there are at the city of Washington, a minister from Great Britain, one from France, one from Russia, and one from each of the other principal governments of Europe and America. And our government has a minister residing at the seat of government of each of those countries. The officer of our government who corresponds with foreign ministers, and with our ministers abroad, is the secretary of state.

§ 7. Representatives at foreign courts are differently styled, embassadors, envoys, ministers, and charges des affaires, commonly written chargês d'affaires. An embassador who is intrusted with the ordinary business of a minister at a foreign court, is called an *embassador in ordinary*. An *embassador extraordinary* is a person sent on a particular occasion, who returns as soon as the business on which he was sent is done. He is sometimes called *envoy*; and when he has full power to act as he may deem expedient, he is called *envoy plenipotentiary*; the latter word signifying full power. An ordinary embassador resides abroad, and acts in obedience to instructions sent him from time to time.

§ 8. Agents sent by the United States to reside at foreign courts, are usually called *ministers*, especially those sent to the principal or more important countries. *Chargés d'affaires* are ministers of a lower grade, and are sent to inferior countries, or those with whom we have less important relations. The name is French, and is pronounced *shar-zha-daf-fair*, accented on the first and last syllables. It means a person having charge of the affairs of his nation.

§ 9. *Consuls* reside in foreign seaports. Their business is to aid their respective governments in their commercial transactions with such foreign countries, and to protect the rights, commerce, merchants, and seamen of their own nation. Hence much of their business is with masters of vessels, and with merchants. They also dispose of the personal estate left by the citizens of the United States, who die within their consulates, leaving no representative or partner in trade to take care of their effects.

§ 10. The president has power also, by and with the advice and consent of the senate, to *appoint judges of the su-*

preme court, the *head officers of the several executive departments*, and a great number and variety of other officers. The election of judges of the supreme court of the United States by the people, would be not only inconvenient but injudicious. And as a president is in a measure responsible for the acts of his subordinates in the several executive departments, and as without their coöperation and advice he could scarcely carry out his own measures ; the appointment is properly given to the executive ; and by being required to submit his choice to the body of senators, a sufficient safeguard is provided against the appointment of unworthy or incompetent men.

§ 11. The president has power to fill up all vacancies that may happen during the recess of the senate, by granting commissions which shall expire at the end of the next session. (Sec. 2, cl. 3.) Without such a power somewhere, the public interests would often suffer injury before the next regular session of the senate, or even before that body could be convened in extraordinary session. And as the president is responsible for the faithful performance of the duties of the subordinate executive officers, no danger was apprehended from his having the power alone to fill vacancies until the next session of the senate.

§ 12. In the exercise of powers claimed under the two preceding clauses, two important questions have arisen since the organization of the government. First : Is the consent of the senate required in the removal as well as in the appointment of an executive officer ? From the silence of the constitution on the subject of removal, it has been inferred by many of the ablest statesmen, including some who were most conspicuous among the framers of the constitution—that " the consent of the senate was as necessary to displace as to appoint :" otherwise the president might defeat the object of this provision, which was intended to guard against the abuse of the appointing power. He might, immediately after the close of each session of the senate, remove any officer at pleasure, and appoint some favorite who would hold until the expiration of the next session of the senate ; and if, to secure the consent of the senate, he should be compelled to nominate an acceptable person, he might, immediately after the adjournment of that body, remove the newly appointed incumbent, and reäppoint the obnoxious favorite. Or, if the senate should refuse to confirm an appointment made during the recess, he may, as some suppose, after the adjournment, reäppoint the same person or any other. Or he may thus reäppoint after the expiration of each session of the senate, even without having made any nomination during the session.

§ 13. This suggests the other question: Does the power to fill vacancies authorize such appointments? It has been alleged that, when an office expires, by its own limitation, with the session of the senate, a vacancy cannot be truly said to have *happened during the recess*, in the meaning of the constitution. The object of the framers doubtless was to prevent the continuance in office of any appointee, without the consent of the senate, after the close of the next session. In 1831, a vacancy was filled by the president, during the recess of the senate. At the ensuing session, the person appointed was three times nominated, and as often rejected—the last time on the last night of the session, and in the face of a previous declaration of the president, that he would nominate no other person. Immediately after the adjournment, the incumbent was reäppointed by the president. The constitutionality of the reäppointment was called in question, but was sustained by the opinion of the attorney-general. The mere opinion, however, of a single individual, holding his office at the will of the president, in the only case of the kind on record, is regarded by many as insufficient to settle this question.

§ 14. But the doctrine of the power of removal by the president alone, rests on a better foundation—the practice of the government. In organizing the auxiliary executive departments by the first congress, the question arose, whether the officers of these departments could be removed by the president, independently of the senate. It was argued, that, as the president and senate were associated in making appointments, the fair inference was, that they must agree in removals. This power in the hands of the president alone, it was further said, was dangerous to liberty, monarchical, and would convert executive officers into mere instruments of his will. In reply it was said, that the power of removal was completely executive. The president must see the laws faithfully executed; but this was impossible without the power of removing an officer whose coöperation was necessary to their execution. An immediate removal might become necessary ; and the public interest might suffer from the delay in convening the senate. After a full discussion of the question, it was decided in the affirmative. This construction is now settled in practice, although its correctness is not universally admitted.

§ 15. The powers and duties mentioned in the next section, are all properly devolved upon the president. (Art. 2, sec. 3.) Congress ought to have the benefit of the information in his possession of the state of the union ; and his recommendation of measures fixes upon him a responsibility for the policy of his administration, while it takes away from congress all ground of excuse for neglecting the consideration of necessary measures. The power to convene congress in sudden emergencies, and the power to adjourn congress in case of disagreement between the two houses, are necessary and convenient powers, and are with propriety given to the executive. The receiving of embassadors and other public ministers, is wisely made a duty. The refusal to receive a foreign minister is often regarded by his nation as highly disrespectful and offensive, and has a tendency to provoke war.

§ 16. By the next section, the president, vice-president, and all other civil officers of the United States, may be removed from office on impeachment for, and conviction of treason, bribery, or other high crimes and misdemeanors. A definition of impeachment, its objects, and a description of a trial of this kind, have been given. (Chap. XXVII.) The propriety of such a precautionary provision to secure a faithful discharge of public duties, can scarcely be doubted. Its efficacy, however, as a preventive of official delinquency, is far less, probably, than its authors supposed. The influence of party prejudice upon the minds of men, is such as would, in a majority of cases, protect a man against conviction for official misconduct by a court of impeachment, of whose members more than one-third were of the same political faith as the offender. So slight, indeed, is the probability of conviction, that impeachment for the most palpable political offenses is seldom attempted.

CHAPTER XLI.

AUXILIARY EXECUTIVE DEPARTMENTS.—DEPARTMENTS OF STATE, OF THE TREASURY, OF THE INTERIOR, OF WAR, OF THE NAVY, AND OF THE POST-OFFICE; ATTORNEY-GENERAL.

§ 1. THE general executive business of the nation, excepting what is done by the president in person, is performed in the several executive departments, of which the following are the head officers: the secretary of state, the secretary of the treasury, the secretary of the interior, the secretary of war, the secretary of the navy, the attorney-general, and postmaster-general. These officers are consulted by the president on important public matters; and hence they are called "the cabinet." They are appointed by the president and senate.

§ 2. The *secretary of state* performs many duties similar to those of a secretary of a state government. (Chap. XVI.) Besides these, he transacts much of the business with the governments of foreign countries. Instructions from the president to our public ministers abroad, are communicated by the secretary of state; and he also conducts the correspondence, and transacts the business to be done, with the ministers of foreign countries residing here. Hence he is sometimes called the *diplomatic* agent. *Diplomacy* signifies the forms of negotiation, or the customs and rules which govern the intercourse of nations through their respective ministers or agents. The secretary has a number of clerks.

§ 3. The *secretary of the treasury* conducts the financial affairs of the government. H's duties are nearly the same as those of the controller or auditor of a state. (Chap. XVI.) There are, in this department, two controllers and five auditors to examine and settle the public accounts, and collect the debts due the United States; a treasurer to keep and pay out the money; a register, who keeps accounts of the goods imported and exported, and of the shipping employed in our foreign trade; a solicitor; a recorder; and a large number of clerks.

§ 4. The *secretary of the interior* exercises all acts of supervision and appeal in regard to the office of the commissioner of patents, and the general land office; in relation to the acts of the commissioner of Indian affairs, the commissioner of pensions, and the commissioner of the public buildings: and he has supervision also over the lead and other mines of the United States; and he signs all requisitions for the payment of money out of the treasury on accounts relating to the several departments of his business.

§ 5. The department of the interior, called also the *home department*, was established in 1849. The business of this department was formerly transacted in the other departments. The patent office was connected with the department of state; the land office with the treasury department; and the business relating to our Indian affairs belonged to the department of war.

§ 6. On the war department formerly devolved also the business relating to military pensions. A *pension* is a yearly allowance to a person by the government for past services. In this country pensions are granted for services in war. Laws were early enacted by congress granting pensions to persons disabled in the war of the revolution so as to be unable to support themselves by manual labor. To the pension list were afterward added those who were disabled in the war of 1812. By later laws, the pension list has been extended to all who had served for six months at least in the army or navy during the war of the revolution, and to their widows during their lives. The usual allowance to pensioners is eight dollars a month. Those who were officers receive a greater compensation. Since the late war with Mexico, another class of pensioners has been added to the pension list. p. 273.

§ 7. The business of the *secretary of war* relates to the military affairs of the United States. The nation supports what is called a standing army, which consists, at present, of about 10,000 armed men, stationed in different parts of the United States, and ready for service when wanted. The secretary is assisted by a number of subordinate officers and clerks.

§ 8. The *secretary of the navy* superintends the business relating to the navy. A *navy* is the fleet, or ships of war, which a nation keeps to defend itself in time of war, and to protect the trade of its citizens on the high seas in time of peace. There are also employed in this department three *navy-commissioners*, and a number of clerks.

§ 9. The *attorney-general* prosecutes and conducts all suits in the supreme court in which the United States are concerned, and gives his advice upon questions of law, when requested by the president or heads of departments.

§ 10. The *postmaster-general* establishes post-offices, appoints postmasters, and provides for carrying the mails. The business of this department is very extensive. There is a postmaster in almost every town in the union; in some towns there are several; and the business of this vast number of officers, is under the general supervision of the department, and subject to its direction. p. 273.

§ 11. Every postmaster is required to keep an account of all the letters sent from and received at his office, and the name of the office to which each letter is sent, and of that from which it is received; also an account of all letters on which the postage is paid, and the amount paid on each, and of those which go free of postage. He is also required, at stated periods, to make out a list of all the letters remaining in his office, and to advertise the same. He sends quarterly to the general post-office an account of all letters sent and received, and of all moneys received for postage and paid out on the orders of the department. He sends also all letters which have been duly advertised and remain in the office, (called *dead* letters,) to the general post-office, where they are opened; and such of them as contain money or other valuable matter, are returned by mail to the writers of them. Letters also that have been *refused* at his office, are sent to the general post-office.

§ 12. Postmasters whose commission on postages has amounted to less than $200 during the preceding year, may receive and send, free of postage, letters on their own private business, and weighing not exceeding half an ounce; and members of congress, during their term of office, and until the first of December after its expiration, may send and receive letters and packages not exceeding two ounces, and all public documents, free. The person entitled to send matter free, must write on the outside his name and the title of his office. This is called *franking*. Civil officers at the seat of government also may frank matter relating to the business of their offices, by marking it outside, "official business." p. 274.

CHAPTER XLII.

JUDICIAL DEPARTMENT.

§ 1. The want of a national judiciary was a material defect of the confederation. Dependence upon the state courts for the means of enforcing the laws of the union, subjected the government to great inconvenience and embarrassment. A government that has a legislature and an executive, ought also to have a judiciary to judge of and interpret the laws. By the constitution, "*the judicial power of the United States is vested in one supreme court, and in such inferior courts as the congress may ordain and establish.*" (Art. 3, sec. 1.) And effect was given to this provision by the judiciary act of 1789, under which the several courts were organized.

§ 2. "*The judges of both the supreme and inferior courts hold their offices during good behavior.*" One of the best securities for a correct and impartial administration of justice, is the independence of the judges. To insure this independence, the tenure of the office was made permanent. Judges have now nothing to fear from a firm discharge of their duties. If they were liable to be displaced at short intervals, they would feel too much their dependence upon the appointing power. They are often called to judge of the validity or constitutionality of laws upon which the political parties of the country are divided; and it was deemed wise to take away from them every inducement to conform their decisions to the wishes of the appointing power, which generally represents the political opinions of the ruling party. The independence of the judges is further procured by the provision that their "*compensation shall not be diminished during their continuance in office.*"

§ 3. The first two clauses of the next section declare the jurisdiction of the judicial power. It is proper that all cases arising between citizens of the same state, as well as all crimes committed against its laws, should be tried in the courts of the state. But when cases arise under the laws of the United States, or between different states, or citizens of different states; or when crimes are committed on the ocean, or elsewhere beyond the jurisdiction of a state; it is evident that some other than a state court ought to try such cases. For example, if a person should violate the laws of congress made for the collection of duties on goods imported, he must be prosecuted in a court of the United States. So a murder committed at sea, beyond the limits of a state, is properly tried in a national court. Piracy, which is robbery on the high seas, is always tried in such court. And so the other cases mentioned.

§ 4. The next clause declares, that "*the trial of all crimes, except in cases of impeachment, shall be by jury.*" The importance of the right of trial by jury has been considered. (Chap. XXVI, § 1: XXVII, § 4.) It is required that "the trial be held in the state where the crimes shall have been committed." This is intended to secure the trial of the accused among his friends and acquaintances, and near the residence of his witnesses, whose attendance in a distant state could not be had without great inconvenience and expense, which might deprive him of the benefit of an important witness. It was proper to leave it to congress to direct where the trial should be in cases of crime committed beyond the limits of a state.

§ 5. The lowest national courts are the *district courts.* Every state constitutes at least one district; a few of the largest states, two each. In each district is a judge, called a *district judge*, who has power to hold a court. There are also in each district a *district attorney* to attend to suits on the part of the United States, and a *marshal,* whose duties in this court are similar to those of a sheriff in a state court. This court has four stated terms a year. It tries certain kinds of civil cases, and the lower crimes against the laws of the United States, committed on land and sea.

§ 6. The *circuits* embrace larger territories than the districts. There are nine circuits in the United States, each including several states. In each there is a *circuit judge,* who holds a court in his circuit twice a year. The judge of the district within which the court is held, sits with the circuit judge in holding a circuit court. Besides certain kinds of civil causes, this court tries the highest crimes against the laws of the United States; as murder within forts, arsenals, and other territory, the property of the United States, or on the high seas. It also tries some cases of appeal from district courts. In consequence of the late increase of the number of states and of population, an addition to the number of circuits has been proposed, and will probably soon be made.

§ 7. The *supreme court* consists of all the judges of the circuit courts, one of whom is the *chief justice* of the supreme court. There are but few causes which originate or commence in this court; its principal business is to rejudge cases that are brought up from the circuit courts. It holds one session annually, at the seat of government, commencing in January or February, and continuing about eight weeks.

§ 8. An important object of a supreme court of the United States, is to secure a correct and uniform interpretation to the constitution and laws of the United States. State laws, and decisions in state courts, are sometimes made which are supposed to be repugnant to the constitution and laws of the United States. And what may be pronounced constitutional by a court in one state, may be declared unconstitutional in another. Therefore, when any act or judgment in a case tried in the highest or last court in a state is deemed inconsistent with the constitution or laws of the United States, such case may be removed by writ of error to the supreme court of the United States, whose decision governs the judgment of all inferior courts throughout the union.

CHAPTER XLIII.

STATE RECORDS; PRIVILEGES OF CITIZENS; FUGITIVES, NEW STATES; POWER OVER TERRITORY; REPUBLICAN GOVERNMENT; AMENDMENTS; ASSUMPTION OF PUBLIC DEBTS; SUPREMACY OF THE CONSTITUTION; OATHS AND TESTS; RATIFICATION.

§ 1. THE constitution requires that "*full faith and credit shall be given in each state to the public acts, records and judicial proceedings of every other state;*" and gives to congress the power to prescribe the *manner of proving them,* and *their effect.* (Art. 4, sec. 1.) One object of this provision is to secure justice to judgment creditors in case of the removal of their debtors into other states. A person against whom a judgment has been obtained by due process of law, may remove with his property into another state, where, in consequence of the remoteness of his residence from that of the witnesses, or of the death or removal of material witnesses, he would be beyond the reach of justice by a new trial. Hence is seen the necessity of a provision requiring that the records of the court in which the judgment was had, shall be received in evidence, and have full credit, in every court within the United States.

§ 2. But there are numerous other cases which this provision is designed to meet; and in pursuance of the power here granted, congress has enacted, that a certificate under seal of the clerk of a court of record, may be transmitted to any state in the union; and wherever it shall be received, it shall be deemed evidence of the facts therein stated; provided, that the sealed certificate of the clerk to a judicial proceeding be accompanied by a certificate of the presiding judge or justice, that the attestation of the clerk is in due form. Acts of a state legislature must have the seal of the state affixed to them, in order to be entitled to credit in another state.

§ 3. "*The citizens of each state shall be entitled to all the immunities and privileges of citizens in the several states.*" (Art. 4, sec. 2.) This means that the citizens of any state going into other states, shall not, by the laws of those states, be deprived of any of the privileges of citizens; or that native born or naturalized citizens of any state removing into another, shall be entitled to the privileges which are enjoyed by persons of the same description in the state to which the removal is made. Without such a provision, any state might make laws, denying to citizens of other states coming into it, the right to buy and hold real estate, or to become voters, or to hold office, or to enjoy equal privileges in trade and business. But that provision does not prohibit a state from prescribing a certain term of residence therein as a qualification for voting at elections.

§ 4. The next clause of this section provides for apprehending "*a person charged with crime, who shall flee from justice, and be found in another state.*" The governor of the state from which such person has fled, sends a requisition to the governor of the state in which he is found, demanding his delivery to the proper officers, to be conveyed back for trial. Without such authority to apprehend criminals, the most atrocious crimes might be committed with impunity, as the perpetrators might easily escape justice, by taking shelter in an adjacent state.

§ 5. In the same section it is provided, that a "*person held to service or labor in one state,* (including slaves,) *escaping into another,*" shall not become free by any law of the state into which he flees, "*but shall be delivered up on claim of the party to whom such service or labor may be due.*" Before the constitution was adopted with this provision, a slave escaping into a non-slaveholding state became free, and could not be reclaimed. The owner of a runaway slave finding him in one of the free states, arrests him and brings him before a magistrate; and if he proves his title to the slave, to the satisfaction of the magistrate, the slave is delivered up to the owner or claimant.

§ 6. "*New states may be admitted by the congress into this union;* but no new state may be formed or erected within the jurisdiction of any other state; nor may a state be formed by the junction of two or more states, or parts of states, without the consent of the legislatures of the states concerned, as well as of the congress." (Art. 4, sec. 3.) This provision was rendered necessary by the large extent of vacant lands within the United States. The territory north-west of the Ohio river had been ceded to the general government by the states claiming the same; and a territorial government had already been established therein by the celebrated ordinance of 1787. There was also south of the Ohio river a vast tract, principally unsettled, within the chartered limits of Virginia, North Carolina, and Georgia, extending west to the Mississippi river; from which, it was presumed, new states would be formed. Justice, however, to these states, as well as to others, and in all future time, required the above general provision, that no state should be divided without the consent of its legislature and of congress.

§ 7. In pursuance of the power here given to congress, the following new states have been admitted: Vermont, in 1791. This state had formed a state constitution as early as 1777; but the territory being claimed by New York, congress refused to admit her into the confederation. In 1790, Vermont paid New York $30,000 to relinquish her claim, and was admitted the next year. Maine, a part of Massachusetts, was admitted in 1820. From the territory south of the Ohio, mentioned in the preceding section, the following: Kentucky was formed from Virginia by consent of her legislature given in 1789. The other southern states subsequently ceded to the general government their western lands, from which were formed Tennessee, Mississippi, and Alabama. From the north-western territory: Ohio, Indiana, Illinois, Michigan, Wisconsin. From the Louisiana territory purchased from France in 1803, Louisiana, Missouri, Arkansas, Iowa. From the Floridas, ceded by Spain to the United States, by treaty of 1819, the state of Florida. Texas, an independent republic, separated from Mexico, annexed to the union as a state, by resolution of congress. From territory acquired from Mexico, California—in all, eighteen states, admitted since the adoption of the constitution. This number of "new states" will, at no distant day, be largely increased from the vast extent of territory which still remains. Several of the organized territories have formed state constitutions, and are now (1858) ready for admission.

§ 8. The next clause authorizes congress "*to dispose of, and make all needful rules and regulations respecting the territory* and other property of the United States." But as titles to portions of the territory were disputed, a proviso was added, that nothing in the constitution should "prejudice any claim of the United States, or of any particular state." The right of the general government to exercise authority over its territorial possessions, is *implied* in the power to acquire them. This express grant establishes the right beyond doubt. In pursuance of the power here granted, congress has made "rules and regulations" for the government of the people of certain portions of the territory previously to their admission as states into the union.

§ 9. By the 4th section of the 4th article, the general government is bound to "*guaranty to every state in this union a republican form of government, and to protect each of them against invasion and domestic violence.*" The propriety of a power to prevent a state from changing its form of government is self-evident: and it is equally proper that a state, when invaded by a foreign enemy, or in case of an insurrection within its own borders, should have protection and aid from the general government; especially as the states have surrendered to it the right of keeping troops or ships of war in time of peace. (Art. 1. sec. 10.)

§ 10. The 5th article prescribes modes of *amending the constitution.* It will appear on examination of this article, that amendments can not be easily effected. The agreement of two-thirds of both houses of congress upon a proposition for an amendment, or the union of the legislatures of two-thirds of the states in requesting congress to call a convention for proposing amendments, will rarely occur. And when amendments are proposed, their ratification by the legislatures of three-fourths of the states, or by conventions in three-fourths of them, would be still more improbable. Had an easy mode of amending the constitution been provided, its strength might have been impaired, and its permanency endangered, by injudicious alterations. Although twelve articles, styled amendments, have been adopted, most of them are mere additions, and do not alter any of the provisions of the constitution.

§ 11. The 1st clause of the 6th article, is an acknowledgment of the obligation of the government to pay "*all debts contracted before the adoption of the constitution.*" As has been observed, congress had borrowed large sums of money, for the payment of which it had not the power to provide; and one object to be attained by a change of government, was to make provision for fulfilling the engagements of the nation. This clause, it is said, was also intended to allay the fears of public creditors, who apprehended that a change in the government would release the nation from its obligations.

§ 12. The next clause declares, that "*this constitution, and the laws made in pursuance thereof, and all treaties* made under the authority of the United States, *shall be the supreme law of the land*," and binding above all state authorities. If it were not so—if all state authorities were not bound by the constitution of the United States, nothing would have been gained by the union. If the laws made by congress were not to be the supreme law, why give congress the power to make them? Or if treaties could be nullified by any power in a state, why was power to make them given to the general government? Hence, the judges of every state are bound by the laws and treaties of the United States, whatever may be found in the laws or constitution of any state to the contrary.

§ 13. The remaining clause of the 4th article requires certain officers, both of the United States and of the several states, to "be bound by oath or affirmation to support this constitution; but *no religious test shall ever be required* as a qualification to any office or public trust under the United States." Binding the conscience of public officers by oath or solemn affirmation, has ever been considered necessary to secure a faithful performance of their duties. They are generally required to swear not only to support the constitution, but also to discharge the duties of their offices to the best of their ability. Religious tests are forbidden. *Test* here means an oath or a declaration in favor of or against certain religious opinions, as a qualification for office. In England, all officers, civil and military, were formerly obliged to make a declaration against transubstantiation, and assent to the doctrines and conform to rules of the established church. Desirous of securing to all the full enjoyment of religious liberty, the introduction of tests was properly prohibited.

§ 14. By the last article, the constitution, when *ratified by* "*the conventions of nine states*," was to be established between the states so ratifying it. The ratification of the constitution by all the states was doubtful; therefore entire unanimity was not required; and a union of less than nine states was deemed inexpedient. The framers closed their labors in September, 1787; and in July, 1788, New Hampshire, the ninth state, sent its ratification to congress. Congress appointed the first Wednesday of January, 1789, for choosing electors of president in the several states, and the first Wednesday of February for the electors to meet in their respective states to elect the president. Gen. Washington was unanimously chosen, and on the 30th of April was inaugurated president. Proceedings, however, commenced under the constitution on the 4th of March, preceding. The ratifications of North Carolina and Rhode Island were not received by congress until the following year. The ratification of the former was received in January, 1790; that of the latter in June of the same year.

CHAPTER XLIV.

AMENDMENTS TO THE CONSTITUTION.

§ 1. Much of the opposition to the constitution arose from the absence of express guaranties of certain rights. The ratifications of several of the state conventions were accompanied by the expression of a desire, that in order to prevent misconstruction or abuse of the powers of the constitution, some declaratory and restrictive clauses should be added. Accordingly, the first congress, at its first session, proposed twelve amendments, ten of which, being the first ten in the list of amendments, were ratified by the requisite number of states. Vermont having been admitted since the adoption of the constitution, the ratifications of eleven states were necessary. Virginia, the eleventh state, ratified the 15th of December, 1791. The amendments had been proposed at the session which commenced the 4th of March, 1789. Most of these articles of amendment are the same as are found in the "bills of rights" in the constitutions of the states.

§ 2. The 1st article of amendment guaranties *freedom in religion; freedom of speech and of the press;* and *the right of petition.* The first two of these rights are elsewhere considered. (Chap. XLV.) The other, which is "the right of the people peaceably to assemble, and to petition the government for a redress of grievances," is so essential to civil liberty, and so evidently just, that it can be hardly presumed that any interference with it would ever receive the sanction of law, had no declaration of the right been made.

§ 3. The 2d article declares "*the right of the people to bear arms.*" Without this right on the part of the people, ambitious men might, by the aid of the regular army, subvert public liberty, and usurp the powers of government.

§ 4. The 3d article declares that "*no soldier shall, in time of peace, be quartered in any house without the consent of the owner, nor in time of war, but in a manner to be prescribed by law.*" An important right of the common law is, that "a man's house is his own castle." Among the grievances enumerated in the Declaration of Independence against the king of Great Britain, was one "for quartering large bodies of armed troops" among the people of the colonies. To secure the people against intrusions of this kind, is the object of this prohibition.

§ 5. Article 4th guaranties "*the right of the people to be secure in their persons, houses, papers, and effects, against unreasonable searches and seizures.*" But such security there could not be, if persons could be arrested under a general authority given to an officer, or if warrants could be issued upon a bare application. Innocent men would often be subjected to much trouble and perplexity; and unjust suspicions would be thrown upon their characters. It is therefore properly provided, that "no warrants shall issue, but upon probable cause, supported by oath or affirmation, and particularly describing the place to be searched, and the persons or things to be seized."

§ 6. Article 5th declares that "*no person shall be held to answer for a capital or other infamous crime, unless on a presentment or indictment of a grand jury,*" except in certain extraordinary cases. Grand juries and their duties have been described. (Chap. XXVII.) The chief object of an indictment before trial is not to guard against the conviction of innocent persons, but to prevent their being subjected to the trouble of defending themselves in cases of prosecution originating in mere suspicion, or instigated by malice or revenge. "*Nor shall any person be subject, for the same offense, to be twice put in jeopardy of life or limb.*" But it is not considered a second trial, in the sense of the constitution, when the jury on the first prosecution has been discharged without giving a verdict, or when a new trial is granted in behalf of a person convicted, before the judgment of the former trial has been executed. The propriety of securing to the people, beyond doubt, the remaining rights mentioned in this article, and those stated in the next, is evident upon the slightest consideration.

§ 7. "*In suits at common law, where the value in controversy shall exceed twenty dollars, the right of trial by jury shall be preserved.*" (Amend. art. 7.) The right of trial by jury in civil cases had not been declared in the constitution; and to allay the fears caused by the want of an express guaranty of this right, this amendment was proposed. By "suits at common law" are meant those tried in the ordinary courts of law, as distinguished from those tried in courts of equity and courts of admiralty. It is further declared, that "*no fact tried by a jury shall be otherwise reëxamined in any court of the United States, than according to the rules of the common law.*" This means, that when a court of the United States exercises appellate jurisdiction, the fact, if tried by a jury in the lower court, must be reëxamined in the appellate court according to the rules of the common law; that is, by a new trial by jury.

§ 8. The 8th amendment declares that "*excessive bail shall not be required, nor excessive fines imposed, nor cruel and unusual punishments inflicted.*" Without the first of these restrictions, the sums in which persons charged with crime shall be required to give bail, might be fixed so high as to prevent their procuring the necessary sureties; thereby depriving them of the privilege of enjoying their liberty until the time of trial, and often subjecting innocent persons to a long imprisonment. It is therefore properly left to the court to determine the sum, which should correspond to the nature and aggravation of the offense. The same discretion is given to the courts as to the precise measure of punishment to be inflicted in each particular case of crime.

§ 9. The 9th article of amendment declares, that "*the enumeration, in the constitution, of certain rights, shall not be construed to deny or disparage others retained by the people.*" There were persons who feared that, because the constitution enumerated certain rights as belonging to the people, those not included in the enumeration were to be considered as having been surrendered to the general government. Although the nature of the constitution does not afford just ground for such an inference, the article was inserted to remove the scruples of those whose jealousy for the rights of the people had induced them to look upon the constitution with disfavor.

§ 10. The 10th amendment has nearly the same object as the preceding. "*The powers not delegated to the United States by the constitution, nor prohibited by it to the states, are reserved to the states respectively, or to the people.*" It has already been observed, that the constitution of the United States is an instrument of delegated, and consequently of limited powers; and that, as its powers are derived from the states, or from the people of the states, it necessarily follows, that all powers not delegated or conferred, are withheld, and belong to the states, or to the people. This article, therefore, is useful merely as declaring a rule of construction of the constitution, and as removing a material ground of opposition to it. But the granting of any power to congress does not forbid the exercise of a similar power by the states. The states retain such power, unless the constitution has in express terms given it exclusively to congress, or unless its exercise is prohibited to the states, or unless its exercise by the states is inconsistent with its exercise by congress.

§ 11. The 11th amendment was proposed at the first session of the third congress, March 5, 1794, and the announcement of its ratification by the constitutional number of states, was made by the president to congress in a message dated the 8th of January, 1798. This amendment declares that *suits in law or equity shall not be "commenced or prosecuted against one of the states by citizens of another state."* The 2d section of the 3d article of the constitution, extends the judicial power of the United States to controversies "between a state and citizens of another state and of foreign states." It became a question whether, under this provision, suits could be brought *against* a state, as well as *by* it. A majority of the supreme court so decided. As many suits were pending against several of the states; and as their liability to be frequently harassed by suits brought against them created great alarm, this amendment was proposed and ratified, by which the right of private persons to bring or *commence* a suit *against* a state is taken away.

§ 12. The 12th and last amendment effects a change in the mode of electing the president and vice-president of the United States, and has been considered. (Chap. XXXIX.) This amendment was proposed at the first session of the eighth congress, December 12, 1803, and was adopted by the requisite number of states in 1804, according to a public notice by the secretary of state, dated the 25th of September of the same year.

COMMON AND STATUTORY LAW.

CHAPTER XLV.

RIGHTS OF PERSONS; FREEDOM OF SPEECH AND THE PRESS; HABEAS CORPUS; LIBERTY OF CONSCIENCE.

§ 1. In the foregoing chapters, we have taken a general view of the government of a state, and of the government of the United States. We have seen how, in each of these governments, the several departments, legislative, executive, and judicial, are constituted, and what are the powers and duties of the officers in these departments; and how the general affairs of these governments are conducted. We now proceed to give an abstract of the laws which more particularly define the rights, and prescribe the duties, of citizens in the social and domestic relations.

§ 2. The laws by which the rights of citizens are secured, and their social intercourse is regulated, are, first, *statute laws*, the laws enacted by the legislature, and duly published; secondly, the *common law*, which is not a code of written laws enacted by a legislature, but which consists of rules that have become binding by long usage and general custom. The comnon law of this country is the same as that of England, having been introduced and established here while the people were subject to that country; and it is still considered the law in all cases in which it has not been altered or repealed by constitutional or legislative enactments.

§ 3. The rights of citizens are either rights of person or rights of property. By the *rights of person*, or *personal rights*, we mean the right to be free to think, speak, and act as we please, and the right to be secure from injury to our bodies or persons and our good names. The *right of property* is the right to acquire, hold, and enjoy property. All laws may therefore be considered as being intended to secure either the one or the other of these classes of rights.

§ 4. Among the most valuable rights of person, is the right of every citizen "freely to speak, write, and publish his sentiments" on all subjects; usually termed, "*the liberty of speech and of the press.*" The word *press* is here used in its more comprehensive sense, denoting the general business of printing and publishing: hence, the liberty of the press is the free right to publish books or papers without restraint, except such as may be necessary to prevent infringements of the natural rights of other men.

§ 5. It was formerly common among the monarchical governments of Europe, to prohibit persons from speaking against the sovereign or his government. Books and papers could not be published until they had been examined and approved. The persons authorized to examine the manuscripts, were called *censors*. With the progress of free principles, however, these restrictions upon the freedom of speech and of the press have been, in most of these countries, essentially relaxed or entirely removed.

§ 6. In the United States, no law can be passed which shall prevent the humblest citizen from censuring the conduct of the highest officer of the government. Men may not, however, speak or publish against others whatever they please. While the constitution guaranties freedom of speech and of the press, it makes men "responsible for the *abuse* of that right." Without some restraint, men might, by false reports or malicious publications, injure the good name, the peace, or the property of others. Nor may they, in all cases, even speak the truth of others to their injury.

§ 7. To defame another by a false or malicious statement or report, is either slander or libel. When the offense consists in words spoken, it is *slander;* when in words written or printed, it is called *libel.* As a slander in writing or in print is generally more widely circulated, and likely to do greater injury, it is considered the greater offense. Hence damages may sometimes be recovered for slanderous words printed, when for the same words merely spoken, a suit could not be maintained. In case of slander, a man is liable only for damages in a civil action; but for libel, a person is not only liable for private damages, but he may also be indicted and tried as for other public offenses.

§ 8. By the common law of England, the libel was considered as great when the statement was true as when false, because the injury might be as great; therefore, when prosecuted for libel, a man was not allowed to prove to the jury the truth of his statement. But it may sometimes be proper to speak an unfavorable truth of others. In most of the states, therefore, it is provided by law or by their constitutions, that "the truth *may* be given in evidence to the jury; and if the matter charged as libelous is true, and was published with good motives and for justifiable ends, the party shall be acquitted." In the state of Vermont, however, and perhaps a few other states, if the party prosecuted proves the truth of his statement in any case, he is acquitted.

§ 9. Another valuable personal right is the privilege of the "writ of *habeas corpus.*" This is a Latin phrase, and means, have the body. This privilege was long enjoyed by the people of Great Britain before the settlement of the colonies, and by the colonists, as British subjects, to the time of their independence. It was natural, therefore, that the latter, in establishing governments for themselves, should insert in their constitutions a provision guarantying so valuable a right.

§ 10. A person committed, confined, or restrained of his liberty, for a supposed criminal matter, or under any pretense whatsoever, may, before the final judgment of a court is pronounced against him, petition a competent court or judge, stating the cause of complaint. The judge then issues a writ against the party complained of, commanding him to bring before the court or judge, the body of the person confined; and if he shall refuse to do so, he may be imprisoned. If, upon examination, it appears that the complainant has been illegally confined, the judge may discharge him.

§ 11. *Liberty of conscience* is the liberty to discuss and maintain our religious opinions, and to worship God in such manner as we believe most acceptable to him. History informs us of countries in which the people have been prohibited the enjoyment of this most valuable of all human rights. Even in some called Christian, thousands have been put to death for the expression of their religious opinions. But the rights of conscience are now more extensively tolerated. In some countries, however, there is still an established religion; that is, some religious denomination receives the support of the government, as in Great Britain. This is called "a union of church and state." But in this country, the government does not interfere in religious matters, except to secure to every denomination, "without discrimination or preference, the free exercise and enjoyment of religious worship."

CHAPTER XLVI.

DOMESTIC RELATIONS.—MARRIAGE, AND THE RELATION OF HUSBAND AND WIFE; PARENT AND CHILD; GUARDIAN AND WARD; MINORS; MASTERS, APPRENTICES AND SERVANTS.

§ 1. To make a marriage contract binding, several things are necessary: Persons must have sufficient understanding to transact the common business of life; hence, lunatics and idiots cannot bind themselves in marriage. The parties must not be nearly related to each other. The laws of the states generally declare at what degrees of relationship persons are forbidden to marry. Persons must be of sufficient age. In states where the age of consent, (as it is called,) is not fixed by statute, the common law must govern, which allows males to contract marriage at the age of fourteen years, and females at the age of twelve. Persons must act freely. If the consent of either party has been obtained by force or by fraud, the marriage may be declared void. p. 275.

§ 2. No person can lawfully marry who has a wife or husband living. Such second marriage is, by the common law, null and void. In some of the states, perhaps most of them, it is declared *polygamy*, and a state prison offense, except in certain cases; as when the husband or wife of the party who remarries is long absent, and the party remarrying does not know the other to be living within the time; or when the former marriage has been lawfully annulled or dissolved; or if the former husband or wife of the party remarrying has been sentenced to imprisonment for life, and perhaps a few other cases, differing somewhat in different states. In case, however, a marriage has been annulled or dissolved for the cause of adultery, the criminal party is, in some states at least, not allowed to remarry. Where there is no state regulation, the common law governs, which is that nothing but death, or the decree of a competent court, can dissolve the marriage tie. p. 276.

§ 3. The manner in which marriages are to be solemnized, and by whom, and the manner in which marriage licenses are obtained, or notices of marriage published, (which are required in some states,) are prescribed by the laws of the states in which such regulations exist. Marriages may be solemnized by ministers of the gospel, judges, justices of the peace, and certain other officers. But a simple consent of the parties, declared before witnesses, renders a marriage lawful. p. 276.

§ 4. The husband and wife are in law regarded as one person. By the common law, the husband has a right to the property of the wife which she had before marriage. He has a right to the use and profits of her real estate, during his life, if he shall die before his wife; in which case she takes the estate again in her own right. If the wife dies first, and there are no children, her heirs immediately take the estate. If there are children living, the husband holds the estate for life; and on his death it goes to the wife or her heirs.

§ 5. A husband cannot sell the real property of his wife, unless she joins with him in the deed. But her chattels real, which are leases for years, and all her personal estate, including debts due her by bond, note, or otherwise, when collected by him, become his ; and he may dispose of them as he pleases ; and they may be sold on execution for his debts. If he makes no disposal of the chattels real in his life time, he can not devise them by will ; and the wife, after his death, takes them in her own right. If he shall survive his wife, he acquires an absolute right to them.

§ 6. This provision of the common law which gives to the husband the possession and disposal of the property of the wife, has been repealed by special enactments in most of the states. By these state laws, the real and personal property of the wife owned by her before marriage, or lawfully conveyed to her by any other person than her husband after marriage, together with the rents and profits of such property, is declared to be her own, and not liable for the debts of her husband ; except in a few cases specified in the laws of each state : and she may dispose of the same by will, or otherwise. p. 277.

§ 7. As the husband, where the common law prevails, acquires, by marriage, an interest in his wife's property, he is obliged to pay her debts contracted before marriage ; but if they are not recovered of him during coverture, he is discharged. *Coverture*, in law, is the state of a married woman, considered as under *cover*, or under the power of her husband. p. 277.

§ 8. It is the duty of the husband to maintain his wife ; and he is bound to pay debts which she may contract for necessaries, but for nothing more. And it seems to be the law, that even if he forbids all persons to trust her, she can bind him for necessaries, if they have become separate through fault on his part. If they part by consent, and he secures to her a separate maintenance, and pays it according to agreement, he is not answerable even for necessaries. p. 278.

§ 9. The husband and wife can not be witnesses for or against each other in a court of justice ; but any declarations which a wife makes when acting as the agent of her husband, may be taken as evidence against him.

§ 10. It is the natural and reasonable duty of parents to maintain and educate their children, until they become of suitable age to provide for themselves. The age at which the obligations of parents, as guardians of their children, end, is twenty-one years, which is called the age of *majority*, when persons are said to be *of age*. Hence, under twenty-one they are in law called *infants*, or minors, and are said to be in a state of *minority*. In Vermont and Ohio, females at the age of eighteen years are of age.

§ 11. As parents are bound to support their minor children, they have a right to their labor ; and they may recover the money for the wages of their children, from any person employing them without their parents' consent. A parent is not bound to pay even for necessaries sold to a child, unless a child had authority from the parent, or unless the parent neglected to provide for the child, or forced him from home by severe usage. When a child is obliged to support himself, he is entitled to his own earnings. A second husband is not bound to support the children of his wife by a former husband. If, however, he receives such children into his family, he is liable to support them as his own.

§ 12. In ordinary cases, a father's obligation to maintain his children ceases when they become of age, however wealthy he may be. If, however, he has a poor, blind, or decripit child who, though in his majority, is unable to maintain himself, he is bound, if able, to support such adult child, and not allow him to become a public charge.

§ 13. The father is the natural guardian of a child, and after his death, the mother. But a father may, by his deed, or last will, dispose of the custody and tuition of a minor child, while under twenty-one years, to another person, who then has the care and management of the minor's personal estate, and of the profits of his real estate, during the time for which the disposal was made. Such person is then *guardian*, and the child is called *ward*.

§ 14. If the father dies before the child is of age, and does not by will appoint a guardian, the mother becomes the guardian of the child, and in some cases of his property also, until he arrives at the age of fourteen years, when he may choose a guardian for himself. When an infant becomes possessed of an estate in lands, if there is no father, the mother has the guardianship of the estate ; and if there is neither father nor mother, then the nearest and eldest relative takes the guardianship of such estate.

§ 15. The statutes of the several states do not declare how far minors may bind themselves by contract or agreement. In such case, the common law must determine. In general, a minor is not bound by a bargain which he may make ; but if he agrees, after becoming of age, to fulfill a contract which he made while a minor, he must do so. And if he has no father or other guardian, he is bound to pay for articles actually necessary for him. But the person who trusts him must make inquiry ; and if the minor has been properly supplied by his friends, the person trusting him can not recover ; nor can he in any case recover more than the actual value of the goods sold to the minor.

§ 16. But minors are responsible for the payment of fines ; and they may be prosecuted and tried for acts of fraud and crime. It is not easy, however, to determine, from the practice of courts of law, in what particular cases a minor is or is not accountable for fraudulent acts. His age, and the circumstances in which he was placed, might be such as to free him from obligation ; but for an act of gross and palpable fraud, committed by an infant who has arrived at the age of discretion, he would be responsible.

§ 17. In general, male infants, and unmarried females under eighteen years, may, of their own free will, bind themselves, in writing, to serve as *apprentices* or servants, in any trade or employment ; males, until the age of twenty-one, and females, until the age of eighteen, or for a shorter time. A minor thus binding himself must have the consent of the father ; or if the father is dead, or disqualified by law, or neglects to provide for his family, then consent must be had of the mother ; or if the mother is dead or disqualified, then of the guardian.

§ 18. Children that have become chargeable to the town or county for their support, may be bound out by the proper officers having charge of the poor And the laws of the states generally require, that a person to whom a child is bound, shall agree to cause such child to be taught to read and write, and also to be instructed in the general rules of arithmetic. The laws of some states do not require instruction in arithmetic in the case of female apprentices.

§ 19. The laws also provide for compelling both parties to fulfill their obligations. Masters have a right to correct their apprentices with moderation for negligence or misbehavior ; and they may recover damage at law of their apprentices for wilful absence. On the other hand, a master may be prosecuted for ill usage to his apprentice, and for a breach of his covenant. A master is liable to pay for necessaries for his apprentice, and for medical attendance; but he is not so liable in the case of a hired servant.

§ 20. When an apprentice becomes immoral or disobedient, investigation may be had of the matter by the proper authorities, and if good cause exist, the indenture may be annulled, and the parties discharged from their obligations. Upon the death of a master, an apprenticeship is dissolved.

§ 21. There is, it is believed, no statute law in any state particularly defining the rights and obligations of *hired servants* and the persons employing them. Both are obliged to fulfill their agreement. If a hired servant leaves the service of his employer, without good cause, before he has worked out the time for which he was hired, he can not recover his wages. And for immoral conduct, wilful disobedience, or habitual neglect, he may be dismissed. On the other hand, ill usage, or any failure on the part of the employer to fulfill his engagement, releases the laborer from his service.

§ 22. How far a master is answerable for the acts of his hired servant, is not clear. As a general rule, however, the master is bound by contracts made, and liable for injuries done, by a servant actually engaged in the business of his master, whether the injury proceeds from negligence or from want of skill. But for an injury done by a wilful act of the servant, it is considered that the master is not liable. If the servant employs another to do his business, the master is liable for the injury done by the person so employed. But a servant is accountable to his master for a breach of trust, or for negligence in business, or for injuring another person in his master's business.

CHAPTER XLVII.

RIGHTS OF PROPERTY.—TITLE TO PROPERTY BY DESCENT, OR INHERITANCE; WILLS AND TESTAMENTS.

§ 1. Every citizen of the United States may hold lands, and take the same by descent, devise, or purchase. To take land by descent, is to obtain it by inheritance. When a person, dying, makes no previous disposal of his property, it falls, or *descends*, by right, to his children or other relatives: hence they are said to become heirs to the property by *descent*. But a person may direct his property to be given, after his death, to whomsoever he pleases. This is called *devising* property, or *bequeathing* it; and the person receiving the property is said to have acquired it by *devise*. A person paying for property an equivalent in money or some other property, obtains it by *purchase*.

§ 2. But though every *citizen* of the United States may hold real estate, and convey it to others, the like privilege is not enjoyed by all *aliens*. By the common law, aliens can not hold and convey real property. In many states, however, laws have been enacted removing this disability. On declaring their intention to become citizens, and complying with certain regulations prescribed by law, an alien acquires the right to take and hold real estate to himself and his heirs forever.

§ 3. The laws of each state prescribe the order in which the property of intestates descends to their heirs. A *testament*, or *will*, is a written instrument, in which a person declares his will concerning the disposal of his property after his death. The word testament is from the Latin *testis*, meaning witness: hence the application of the word to this instrument, which is the witness or proof of a person's will. The person making a will is called *testator*; a person dying without making a will or testament, is called an *intestate*.

§ 4. The order in which the real estate of an intestate descends, being to a great extent determined by the laws of the states, is not uniform in this country. In general, however, the property of an intestate descends, first, to his lineal descendants; that is, persons descending in a direct line, as from parents to children, and from children to grand-children. The lineal descendant most nearly related to the intestate, however distant the relation may be, takes the property.

§ 5. If any children of an intestate are dead, and any are living, the inheritance descends to the children living, and to the descendants of the children dead; so that each child living shall receive such share as he would receive if all were living, and the children of those who are dead, such share as the parents would receive if living. Thus, suppose an intestate to have had three sons, one of whom is dead, but has left children. In this case, each of the sons living would share one-third of the property, and the children of the other son would have the remaining third.

§ 6. But if the children are all dead, and there are grand-children living, the grand-children share equally in the inheritance, though not an equal number are children of each parent. If, for example, A dies intestate, leaving two sons, B and C, both of whom die, the one leaving three children, and the other two, the five share equally in the estate. If, however, B, having three children, were living, and C were dead, leaving two children; then one-half of the property would descend to B, the son, and the other half to the two grand-children, the children of C. p. 278.

§ 7. The order of descent is so various in the different states, especially in cases in which there are no lineal descendants of an intestate, that it can be ascertained only by reference to the laws of each state. As a general rule, however, the inheritance passes, (1.) to the lineal descendants of the intestate; (2.) to the father; (3.) to the mother; (4.) to the collateral relatives. But even to this general rule, there are exceptions in the laws of some states. p. 278

§ 8. All persons of full age and sound mind, except married women, may give and bequeath real and personal estate by a last *will* and *testament*. In many of the states, perhaps in most of them, personal estate may be willed by persons at an earlier age. In a few states, females at eighteen may make a will of real and personal estate. In Connecticut, married women may dispose of real and personal estate by will, as any other person; and infants of either sex may bequeath personal estate at seventeen. In Ohio and some other states, personal estate may be willed verbally, if the will is reduced to writing within ten days after speaking the testamentary words, and subscribed by two disinterested witnesses.

§ 9. In most of the states, laws have been recently enacted, by which married women are allowed to hold, in their own exclusive right, all the property, real and personal, which they possessed at the time of marriage, and which they may acquire after marriage. (See Chap. XLVI § 6.) With the right of possession is also given, in most of these states, the power of disposing of the property by will.

§ 10. A will devising real estate must be subscribed by at least two attending witnesses, in whose presence the testator must subscribe the will, or acknowledge that he subscribed it, and declare it to be his last will and testament. In the six New England states, and several others, three subscribing witnesses are necessary. If the testator is unable to sign his will, another person may write the testator's name by his direction ; but he should sign his own name as witness to the will. p. 282.

§ 11. A testator may revoke or alter his will, by a later will or writing, executed in the same manner. But the second will, to revoke the former, must contain words expressly revoking it, or direct a different disposal of the property. A will may also be revoked by a sale of the property. And any alteration of the estate or interest of the testator in lands devised, by the act of the testator, is held to be an implied revocation of the will. Lands purchased after a will has been made, are not conveyed by it.

§ 12. As a general rule, a will is also revoked by the subsequent marriage of the testator and birth of a child. These circumstances, not contemplated at the time of making his will, and imposing upon him new duties and obligations, are presumed to have altered the testator's mind. If, however, the wife and child have been otherwise provided for, marriage and a child will not revoke a will. The will of an unmarried woman is revoked by her marriage.

§ 13. By the statutes of some states, a child born after the death of the testator, or born in his lifetime and after the making of the will, inherits a share of the estate, as if the father had died intestate. In other states, the statute goes further, and gives the same relief to all the children who are not provided for by will, and who have not had their portion in their parent's lifetime.

§ 14. A *codicil* is an addition, or supplement to a will, and must be executed with the same solemnity. It is no revocation of a will, except in the precise degree in which it is inconsistent with it.

§ 15. After the death of a testator who has bequeathed any real or personal estate, any executor, or any person interested in the estate, may have the will brought before the court for probate, which means *proof*. (See Chap. XXVII, § 14.) The court causes the witnesses to the will, and such others as any person interested may desire, to come before the court to be examined. An *executor* is a person named in the will of a testator, or otherwise appointed, to carry the will into effect.

§ 16. When a will has been duly proved and allowed, the court issues letters testamentary to the executor. *Letters testamentary* give to an executor authority to carry a will into effect, and to settle the estate of the deceased. If the person named in the will refuses to act, or is not lawfully qualified, the court appoints a person, who, in that case, is called *administrator*; and the court issues *letters of administration* with the will annexed. It is the duty of an executor to follow the directions of a will, so far as it goes; and in the rest of his duties, he must be governed by the law concerning administrators.

§ 17. Letters of administration are also issued in case of a person dying intestate. They give to the persons appointed to settle the estate of the intestate, the requisite authority. They are issued, first, to the widow or next of kin, or both, as the court may think fit. If such person or persons are incompetent or unsuitable, or if they refuse to serve, the letters of administration are granted to such other person as the law designates. The law prescribes particularly the manner in which the property of deceased persons shall be disposed of, and their debts paid.

CHAPTER XLVIII.

DEEDS AND MORTGAGES, AND THE PROOF AND RECORDING OF THEM.

§ 1. EVERY person capable of holding real property, may also dispose of and convey his right to such property to another person. Hence, the writing by which this right is transferred, is called a *conveyance;* but more frequently the instrument by which a title to land is conveyed, is called *deed,* and is held by the purchaser as evidence of his title to the land. Without a deed, he could not hold the land against a subsequent purchaser having a deed.

§ 2. Whenever, therefore, any real estate is to pass from one to another, the seller gives the buyer a deed. The deed mentions the names of the parties, the consideration or price paid, or to be paid, the place where the land is situated, and its boundaries; and in express words grants and conveys all the interest of the seller or grantor to the purchaser, and to his heirs for ever: and the seller affixes his name and seal to the instrument, usually in the presence of one or more subscribing witnesses. p. 283.

§ 3. But after a deed has been thus executed, the title of the purchaser is not secure, until the deed is recorded in the office of the proper recording officer of the county in which the land lies; or in the office of the town clerk, in those states in which conveyances are required to be there recorded. If the land should be conveyed by the seller to a subsequent purchaser who should get his deed first on record, such purchaser would hold the land, unless, before purchasing, he had had notice of a sale and deed to a prior purchaser. p. 284.

§ 4. In some states, however, a reasonable time is allowed a purchaser to get his deed on record, before he loses his right of possession by the earlier recording of another's deed. In some others the time is fixed by law, and varies in the different states from fifteen days to two years. But a deed, though not recorded, is good against the seller or grantor; and the dispossessed purchaser has a lawful claim against him for the value of the land. p. 284.

§ 5. Before a conveyance is recorded, the person executing it must acknowledge, before a proper officer, that he executed the conveyance; and the officer must certify in writing on the back or margin of the instrument, that the person did so acknowledge. In every state, either some or all of the following officers may take acknowledgment: judges of courts and justices of the peace; commissioners of deeds, appointed for that purpose; notaries public; mayors of cities and aldermen. Every deed duly acknowledged and delivered to the proper recording officers to be recorded, is, with the acknowledgment, copied at length, word for word, in a book provided for that purpose.

§ 6. The deed usually given is a *warranty deed*, in which the grantor agrees that he is seized of the premises in *fee-simple*, (is the absolute owner,) and that he will *warrant* and *defend* the premises in the quiet and peaceable possession of the purchaser and his heirs, forever. A *quit-claim deed* merely conveys the interest or claim of the grantor, without any warranty of title against any other claimant.

§ 7. A *mortgage* is a writing which conveys to another person a right to property as security for the payment of a debt, and is to have no force or effect when the debt is paid. A mortgage conveys land in the same manner as a deed; but a condition is added, providing, that if the debt for which the land is pledged shall be paid by a certain day, the instrument shall no longer have effect.

§ 8. When land is sold, and any part of the purchase money is to be paid at a future day, the seller usually conveys the land by deed to the purchaser; and the purchaser executes a mortgage to the seller, pledging the land as security for the payment of the money remaining unpaid. A mortgage also contains a condition, that if the money shall not be paid according to the agreement, the mortgagee, or person holding the mortgage, may sell the land to raise the money due; but if he sells it for more than the amount, the overplus must be paid to the mortgager.

§ 9. To effect a full conveyance of real estate, a wife must join with her husband by signing the deed with him; otherwise, if he should die in her lifetime, she would have for life the use of one-third of such estate. This right of a widow is called the right of *dower*. It is common, therefore, for the wife also to sign the deed; and she must also acknowledge, before the officer taking the acknowledgment, and apart from her husband, that she signed the deed freely, and without compulsion of her husband. In some states, the acknowledgment of the wife out of the presence of her husband is not required. p. 284–286.

CHAPTER XLIX.

INCORPOREAL HEREDITAMENTS; RIGHT OF WAY; AQUATIC RIGHTS; PARTY WALLS; DIVISION FENCES, &C.

§ 1. The term, *incorporeal hereditaments,* may need explanation to some readers. A *hereditament* is a thing capable of being *inherited.* Land, and all things attached to it by the course of nature, or the hands of men; as trees, herbage, water, buildings, &c., which are comprehended in the term real estate, are *corporeal* hereditaments. *Incorporeal* hereditaments are inheritable rights which grow out of corporeal inheritances, or which consist in their use and enjoyment; as, the right of pasturing a common; a right of passage over the land of another; a right to the use of waters, sometimes called *aquatic rights,* &c.

§ 2. A *right of way,* is a right of private passage over another man's ground. This right is sometimes granted by the owner of the soil; and to make it a freehold right, it must be created by deed, though it be only an easement upon the land of another, and not an interest in the land itself. An *easement* is, in general, an accommodation. In law, it is any privilege or convenience which one has of another, by grant or otherwise, as a right of way, &c. By the grant of an easement, the grantee acquires no other right than what is necessary to the fair enjoyment of the privilege.

§ 3. If it is a mere personal right, it can not be assigned to any other person, nor transmitted by descent. It is so limited, that the owner of the right can not take another person in company with him; and when he dies, the right dies with him. But a right of way belonging to an estate, may be conveyed when the land is sold. Thus if a man own lot A and lot B, and he used a way from lot A, over lot B, to a mill, or to a river; and if he sells lot A, with all ways and easements, the grantee will have the same privilege of passing over lot B as the grantor had.

§ 4. A right of way may arise from necessity. If a man sells a part of his land, and there is no other way to the remaining part, he is entitled to a right of way to it over the land sold. And if a man sells land wholly surrounded by his own land, the purchaser is entitled to a right of way to it over the other's ground, even though no such right is reserved. The right of way passes to the purchaser, as necessarily incident to the grant, or included in it.

§ 5. If one man should give another license to conduct water in lead pipes through his land, the man having such license may enter on the land, and dig therein, to mend the pipes. So if a person has a shop on another's soil by permission, he has, of necessity, a right of passage to and from it between the highway and the shop. The general rule is, that when the use of a thing is granted, every thing is granted which is necessary to the enjoyment of its use.

§ 6. A person has a temporary right of way over land adjoining a public highway, if the highway is out of repair, or is obstructed by snow, a flood, or otherwise. But the right of going upon adjoining lands does not apply to private ways. A person having a right to a private way over another's land, has no right to go upon adjoining land, even though the private way is impassable. The reason given is, that the owner of the way may be bound to repair it, and its impassable state may be owing to his own neglect. But if public roads become obstructed, it is for the general good that the public should be entitled to pass in another direction.

§ 7. A right of way sometimes arises by *prescription*; which is the right or title to a thing derived from long use and enjoyment. A person who is in possession of an interest or privilege which he and those from whom he received it, have enjoyed, undisturbed, for a long course of years, may, by virtue of this long use, have acquired a valid title to it: hence, he is said to hold it by prescription. A right similar to this, is that which a man acquires to land which has been peaceably held by himself, or by himself and pre ceding owners, for twenty years. Although the first occupancy was obtained without grant, the long free use of the land is, in law, equivalent to a grant, and implies a valid title.

§ 8. Another kind of easement is the right of the public to the use of *navigable waters.* The title of owners of land bounded on a river, extends to the center of a stream ; but the public, where the river is navigable for boats and rafts, have a right of passage therein as a public highway. The proprietors of the adjoining banks may use the land and water, but not in a way inconsistent with the rights of the public. On the other hand, neither the state, nor any individual, has the right to divert the stream from its natural channel, and render it less useful to the owners of the soil.

§ 9. Islands in a river belong to the persons who own the land on that side of the river to which they are nearest. If, however, they are so situated as to cover the middle of the river, they belong to the owner on each side.

§ 10. Where lands are bounded by the sea, or by navigable rivers where the tide ebbs and flows, the right of the soil extends to high-water mark ; and the shore below common, but not extraordinary high-water mark, belongs to the public.

§ 11. The owners of land adjoining highways, have a right to the soil to the center of the road : the public have only a right of passage while the road is continued. The owners of the soil may maintain a suit against any person who encroaches upon the road, or digs up the soil, or cuts down trees growing on the side of the road. They may carry water in pipes under it, and have every use of it that does not interfere with the rights of the public.

§ 12. A *party-wall* belonging equally to the owners of two houses, may be pulled down by the party wishing to erect a new house and a new wall ; but he must pull down and rebuild the new wall in a reasonable time, and with the least inconvenience : and if it is clearly necessary that the old wall should be repaired, the other party is bound to contribute ratably to the expense of the new wall ; but not a higher one than the old, nor one with more costly materials. All extra expense must be borne by the party building the new wall.

§ 13. Where the wall of the house to be pulled down belongs exclusively to the owner of the house, and stands wholly on his lot, yet if the beams of the other house rest upon the wall pulled down, and have done so long enough to establish an easement by prescription, the owner of such other house is entitled to have his beams inserted for a resting place in the new wall.

§ 14. The owner of a house in a compact town, intending to pull it down, and to remove its foundations, is not liable for injury to the adjoining house, if he gives due notice of his intention to the owner of such adjoining house, and removes his own with reasonable care.

§ 15. The subject of *division fences* between the owners of adjoining lands might, from its nature, seem to require notice in this place; but the obligations of the occupants of adjoining lands in regard to partition-fences, are almost exclusively the subject of statute regulations.

§ 16. Every proprietor of lands adjoining a stream, has naturally an equal right to the use of the water that flows in the stream adjacent to his lands, "as it was wont to run." Each may use the water while it runs upon his own land; but he can not unreasonably detain it, or give it another direction; and he must return it to its ordinary channel when it leaves his estate. He can not, by dams or any obstruction, cause the water injuriously to overflow the grounds of the neighbor above him, nor so use or apply it as materially to injure his neighbor below him.

§ 17. But this right to the use of waters, as an easement to the land, may be acquired and lost, or abridged and enlarged, by prescription. A man may diminish the quantity of the water, or corrupt its quality by the exercise of certain trades; and by such use of the water for a sufficient length of time, he is in law *presumed* to have acquired it by grant; and this presumption is the foundation of his right by prescription. The time of such use and enjoyment of water necessary to establish such right, is twenty years, except in states in which a different period is fixed by statute.

§ 18. It is a general and established doctrine, that an exclusive and uninterrupted enjoyment of water, or of light, or of any other easement, in any particular way, for twenty years, or for any period less than twenty years, which in any particular state is the established period of limitation, is a sufficient enjoyment to raise a presumption of title, as against the right of any other person. The time of enjoyment necessary for the prescription, is deemed to be uninterrupted, whether it has been continued from ancestor to heir, and from seller to buyer ; or whether the use has been enjoyed during the entire period by one person.

§19. As a right may be acquired by use, so also it may be lost by disuse ; and as an enjoyment for twenty years is necessary to found a presumption of a grant, and establish a right ; an absolute discontinuance of the use for twenty years, (where a less period is not fixed by law,) will raise the presumption that the right has been released or extinguished. Thus a title to land may pass from its actual owner by non-occupancy for twenty years ; and a title to it may be acquired by an undisturbed occupant, who shall hold it in peaceable and uninterrupted possession for the same number of years. p. 286.

CHAPTER L.

LEASES ; ESTATES FOR LIFE ; ESTATES FOR YEARS ; ESTATES AT WILL ; AND ESTATES BY SUFFERANCE ; RENT, &C.

§ 1. Real estate, the title to which is conveyed by deed, as distinguished from other estates in land, is called an *estate of inheritance.* An estate of inheritance, that is, an estate in lands that may be transmitted by the owner to his heirs, is a *fee.* No estate is deemed a fee, unless it may continue forever. When it is a pure and absolute inheritance, clear of any qualification or condition, it is called a *fee-simple.*

§ 2. An interest in lands which is to continue for a limited period, is usually conveyed by an instrument of writing, called *lease.* *To lease* means to let ; but generally, to let real estate to another for rent or reward. The word *demise* is often used instead of lease. The landlord, or person letting the estate, is called *lessor ;* and the tenant, or person to whom the land is leased, is called *lessee.* Leases for a term longer than one year, are usually required to be sealed, and in some states proved and recorded also, as deeds and mortgages.

§ 3. These limited interests in land are divided into estates for life, estates for years, estates at will, and estates by sufferance. An *estate for life*, is an estate conveyed to a person for the term of his natural life. Life estates held by lease, however, are not common in this country. Another kind of life estate is that which is acquired, not by the acts of the parties, as by lease, but by the operation of law. Such is the right of a husband to the real estate of his wife, acquired by her before or after marriage. Such also is the right of dower. (See Chap. XLVIII, § 9.)

§ 4. An *estate for years*, is a right to the possession and profits of land for a determinate period, for compensation, called *rent;* and it is deemed an estate for years, though the number of years should exceed the ordinary limit of human life. An estate for life is said to be a higher and greater estate than a lease for years, though the lease were for a thousand years; and if a lease should be for a less time than a year, the lessee would be ranked among tenants for years. Letting land upon shares for a single crop, is not considered a lease; and possession remains in the owner.

§ 5. A lessee for years may assign over his whole interest to another, unless restrained by agreement not to assign without leave of the lessor. And he may underlet for any less number of years than he himself holds; but he is himself liable to the landlord.

§ 6. A tenant for years, whose lease expires after the land is sown or planted, and before harvest, is not entitled to the crop, if the lease is for a certain period; for, knowing that his lease would expire before harvest time, he might have avoided the loss of his labor. It is believed that, in a few of the states, the tenant is entitled to the crop from grain sown in the autumn before the expiration of the lease, and cut the next summer after its expiration. But if the lease for years depends upon an uncertain event, the occurring of which would terminate the lease before the expiration of the term, the tenant would be entitled to the crop, if there were time to reap what has been sown, in case he should live.

§ 7. Where there is an express agreement to pay rent, the tenant can not avoid payment if the premises are destroyed, or if he is in any other manner deprived of their enjoyment and use, even without any default on his part. Hence, if land should be leased, with a flock of sheep, the tenant having agreed to pay a certain rent, and the sheep should all die, the full rent must be paid. So if the land should be destroyed by a flood, or the tenant driven from it by public enemies, he would be bound to pay rent. But if the land should be recovered from the tenant by a person having a better title than that derived from his landlord, he is not liable for rent after his use of the land has ceased.

§ 8. A tenant can not make repairs at the expense of the landlord, or deduct the cost of them out of the rent, if there has been no special agreement for that purpose. But if the premises, from want of repair, have become unsafe or useless, the tenant from year to year may quit without notice; and he would not be liable for any rent after the use had ceased to be beneficial.

§ 9. When rent is due, a tender of payment is good if made upon the premises; and if no place of payment has been agreed on, a personal tender off the land is also good. As to the time of payment, where there is no special agreement to the contrary, rent is due yearly, half-yearly, or quarterly, according to the usage of the country. Where there is no particular usage, the rent is due at the end of the year.

§ 10. An *estate at will*, is where land is let to another, to hold at the will of the lessor. Tenancies at will, strictly such, are not common. Such estates, when no certain term is agreed on, are construed to be tenancies from year to year; and each party is bound to give reasonable notice of an intention to terminate the estate. If the tenant holds over after the expiration of a lease for years, either by express consent of the landlord, or under circumstances implying consent, it is held to be evidence of a new contract without any definite period, and is construed to be a tenancy from year to year; and in those states in which the old English rule prevails, six months' notice must be given to the tenant to quit.

§ 11. What turns leases for uncertain terms into leases from year to year, is the landlord's reserving annual rent. A tenant placed on land without any terms prescribed or rent reserved, is strictly a tenant at will; and it has been held, that such tenant is not entitled to notice to quit; but the general rule now seems to be, that even in such case, the six months' notice is necessary; or, as in some states, a reasonable notice.

§ 12. An *estate at sufferance* is that which is acquired by a tenant who has come into lawful possession of land, but who holds over by wrong after his interest has ceased. He is not entitled to notice to quit; and where there is no special statute, he is not liable for rent; and the landlord may enter, and remove the tenant and his goods with such gentle force as may be necessary. If undue force is used, the landlord would be liable to an action for forcible entry and detainer

---

CHAPTER LI.

CONTRACTS IN GENERAL; AND WHAT IS NECESSARY TO THEIR VALIDITY.

§ 1. A CONTRACT is an agreement between two or more persons, by which the parties agree to do, or not to do, a particular thing. Contracts are *executory*, when the stipulations remain to be executed, or when one party agrees to sell and deliver, at a future time, for a stipulated price, and the other agrees to accept and pay. Contracts are express or implied. They are *express*, when the parties contract in express words, or by writing; *implied*, when an act has been done which shows that the parties must have intended to contract; as, when a person employs another to do some service, it is presumed that the party employing intended to pay for the labor performed.

§ 2. Contracts are also distinguished as specialties and simple contracts. A *specialty* is a contract under seal; as a deed, or bond. This class of contracts, however, it is not intended particularly to consider in this place. We shall here treat chiefly of that common class of contracts called *simple contracts*, or *contracts by parol*. *Parol* signifies by word of mouth. Applied to contracts, however, it not only means verbal contracts, but includes written contracts not under seal. Both are simple contracts ; and the only distinction between them is in the mode of proof. The mutual understanding of the parties to a verbal contract, may be proved by parol evidence ; but as the real intention of parties is more likely to be expressed in a written contract, the rule of law is, that parol evidence may not be admitted to contradict or vary the terms of a written instrument.

§ 3. Cases, however, sometimes arise, in which all that the parties intend is not comprehended in the terms of a written agreement, or in which the language of the writing is ambiguous or obscure. In such cases, parol evidence is admissible, not to vary the terms of a written instrument, but to explain what is doubtful, or to supply some deficiency. To deny such evidence in cases of this kind, would endanger the rights and interests of one or the other of the parties.

§ 4. To make a valid contract, *the parties must be capable of contracting*. They must be of sound mind. Hence idiots and lunatics are generally incompetent to make contracts. An *idiot* is a person born destitute of common sense, usually called a natural fool. A *lunatic*, or insane person, is one who has possessed his reason, but has been suddenly deprived of it. It was formerly supposed that this disease was produced by the influence of the moon. Hence, it is called lunacy, from *luna*, the Latin word for moon.

§ 5. If the lunacy is permanent, the lunatic is wholly incapable of contracting. But if it is merely intermittent, or by turns, a contract made during a lucid interval will be valid. If a person is a monomaniac, that is, one who is insane upon any one subject or class of subjects, he may contract in relation to subjects upon which he is sane. In the case of idiots, the general rule is, that if there is such a want of intelligence as to render the party incapable of acting in the ordinary affairs of life, or in the particular contract, his idiocy will annul his contract. To invalidate the contract, it must appear that the party contracting did not at the time understand what he was about.

§ 6. Contracts by lunatics and idiots may be considered as not necessarily void, but only *voidable;* the validity or invalidity depending upon facts to be proved. The person seeking to avoid a contract on the ground of mental imbecility, must prove that the person contracting was at the time incompetent. But if a general derangement is once established or conceded, the person is presumed to be incompetent; and the party seeking to enforce the contract, must prove the other to have been sane.

§ 7. Drunkards, also, are incompetent to contract while in a state of intoxication, provided the drunkenness is so excessive and absolute as to deprive them of reason for a time, and create impotence of mind. But for absolute necessaries, if the drunkard consumes them during his drunkenness, or keeps them after becoming sober, he is liable. Intoxication only renders a contract voidable, not void, as the party intoxicated may adopt it upon recovering his understanding.

§ 8. Another requisition to a valid contract, is the *mutual assent of the parties.* A mere offer by one party not assented to or accepted by the other, constitutes no contract. Assent must also be given freely. A contract entered into under duress, or compulsion, is not binding; as where assent is extorted by threats of personal injury. Assent must also be given with a knowledge of facts. A contract made under an injurious mistake or ignorance of a material fact, may be avoided, even though the fact is not fraudulently concealed. But a mistake made through ignorance of the law, will not render a contract void.

§ 9. A *valuable consideration,* also, is necessary to a valid contract. A *consideration* is what is given or done, or to be given or done, as the cause or reason for which a person enters into an agreement. Thus, the money given or offered, for which a man agrees to perform certain acts or labor, is the consideration of the agreement. So the consideration of a promissory note is the property for which the note is given. A consideration may be something else than money; it is sufficient if it is any thing that is either a benefit to the party promising, or some trouble or injury to the party to whom the promise is made.

§ 10. Mutual promises, also, are sufficient considerations; but to be obligatory they must be made at the same time: and it is not sufficient if they are made on the same day, and at different times. But if mutual promises are made simultaneously, they support each other: the promise by one party constitutes a sufficient consideration for a promise by the other party. To this rule, however, there are exceptions ; one of which is, when a proposal is made by means of agents or letters, in case the parties are distant from each other. In such cases, if the proposition is made in writing, and sent by mail, and an answer of acceptance is written and put in the mail, the contract is complete, unless, before the mailing of the letter of acceptance, a second letter has been received, containing a retraction of the proposal.

§ 11. Promises which are wholly gratuitous, are void ; because, being neither a benefit to the promisor, nor an injury to the promisee, they are not regarded, in law, as a valuable consideration. Hence, subscriptions to public works, and charitable, literary, and religious institutions, if they are merely gratuitous, can not be collected, unless they have operated to induce others to advance money, make engagements, or do other acts to their own injury.

§ 12. As gratuitous promises are void for want of consideration, so merely gratuitous services afford no consideration upon which payment for their value can be lawfully claimed ; there being no promise of compensation. Thus, voluntarily assisting to save property from fire, paying the debts of another without request, or securing beasts found straying, gives no lawful claim for recompense. But if a person knowingly permits another to do certain work, as plowing his field, or hoeing his corn, although the work may have been commenced without his order or request, his consent will be regarded, in law, as an *implied promise* to pay for the value of the labor, unless the circumstances of the case are such as to forbid the presumption.

§ 13. A consideration must not only be valuable ; it must be *possible*, and in accordance with law, sound policy, and good morals. A contract founded upon an *impossible* consideration, is void. No man can be lawfully bound to do what is not in the power of man to do. But it is otherwise, if the thing to be done is only at the time impossible in fact, but not impossible in its nature. Hence, inability from sickness to fulfill an agreement, or the impossibility of procuring an article of a certain kind or quality which a person has agreed to deliver, would not exempt him from liability in damages for the nonperformance of his contract.

§ 14. A contract, the consideration to which is *illegal* or *immoral*, may be avoided by either party. A man can not be held to an agreement to do acts forbidden by the law of God, or by the laws of the state. But if an illegal contract has been executed; that is, if the wrong has been already done, the party in the wrong cannot renounce the contract; for the general rule is, that no man can take advantage of his own wrong; and the innocent party alone has the privilege of avoiding the contract. If both parties are guilty, neither can, in ordinary cases, obtain relief on a contract that has been executed.

§ 15. The rule that a consideration is necessary to the validity of a contract, applies to all contracts and engagements not under seal, except bills of exchange and negotiable notes after they have passed into the hands of an innocent indorsee. (See Promissory Notes.) In contracts under seal, a consideration is necessarily *implied* in the solemnity of the instrument.

§ 16. It is declared by the English statute of frauds, which prevails generally in the United States, that no agreement that is not to be performed within one year from the time of making it, shall be valid, unless such agreement, or some memorandum or note thereof, is in writing, and signed by the party to be charged. The statutes of some of the states have adopted this provision of the English statute, and require, further, that a special promise to answer for the debt, default, or miscarriage of another person, and an agreement or promise upon consideration of marriage, except mutual promises to marry, shall likewise be void without such writing, in which the consideration shall be expressed. p. 287.

CHAPTER LII.

CONTRACTS OF SALE.

§ 1. The same general principles of law which apply to contracts in general, are applicable to contracts of sale The competency of the parties contracting; the sufficiency of the consideration in regard to its value, its legality and morality; the assent of the parties; and the absence of fraud; which are requisite to the validity of the former, are necessary to that of the latter.

§ 2. A sale is a transfer of the absolute title of property for a certain price. Unless the absolute title is conveyed, the contract is merely a mortgage, or bailment, and not a sale. To make a sale valid, several things are necessary. The thing to be sold must have an *actual or a possible existence*, and be *capable of delivery*. Thus, if A sells a horse or certain goods to B; and if, at the time of the sale, the horse is dead, or the goods are destroyed; the sale is void. But if the goods are partially destroyed, the buyer may either take them at a proportionate reduction of the price, or abandon the contract.

§ 3. But, although the thing to be sold has no actual and present existence; yet if its future existence is possible, and if it is the product or increase of something to which the seller has a present right, it is a subject of sale. Thus, a man may sell the wool that shall grow on his sheep, the fruit that shall grow on his trees, or the future increase of his cattle. But he can not sell the products of the sheep or cattle which he may hereafter buy. A man may, however, agree to procure goods which he has not, and to furnish them at a future time for a certain price; and his contract will be good; though this is not strictly a sale, but only an agreement to sell.

§ 4. There can be no sale without a *price;* and the price must be fixed and definite, or susceptible of being ascertained by reference to some criterion prescribed in the contract, so as to render any further negotiation of the parties unnecessary. Thus, a man may agree to pay what shall be the market price at a particular time, or a price to be fixed by a third person. The price must also be payable in money or its negotiable representative, as notes or bills. One article given for another is merely a *barter*. The same principles of law, however, govern in both cases.

§ 5. There must be a *mutual consent of the parties;* and the contract is binding when a proposition made by one of the parties is accepted by the other. The negotiation of sale may be carried on by letter; and the sale becomes complete when the buyer puts into the mail his answer accepting the seller's proposition. But the buyer may retract his offer at any time previous to the mailing of the buyer's letter containing his assent. (See Chap. LI § 10.)

§ 6. In contracts of sale which are not perfected at once by payment and delivery, certain formalities are to be observed. These forms generally are prescribed by what is called the English statute of frauds, which requires, (1.) that the buyer shall accept and receive part of the goods sold; or (2.) give something in earnest to bind the bargain, or in part payment; or (3.) that some note or memorandum in writing of the bargain shall be made and signed by the party to be charged, or by his authorized agent. These provisions, however, apply only to cases in which the price of the goods is ten pounds sterling, or upward. The same rule prevails generally in this country, with slight variations: The price of the goods sold in cases to which the provisions of that statute apply, is fixed in each state by law. p. 287.

§ 7. To complete a contract of sale, and pass the title to the property to the buyer, there must be a *delivery of the goods sold.* When the goods are such as can not be manually or immediately delivered, or are not in the personal custody of the seller, the law does not require an actual delivery. But they must be placed in the power of the purchaser; or there must be such acts and declarations of the parties as imply a change of ownership. When the right of property has been transferred to the buyer, whether by an actual or only a constructive delivery, he immediately assumes the risk of the goods; so that if they shall be afterward injured or destroyed, he must bear the loss.

§ 8. When nothing is said at the sale as to the time of delivery, or the time of payment, the buyer is entitled to the goods on payment or tender of the price, and not otherwise; for, though he acquires the *right of property* by the contract of sale, he does not acquire the *right of possession*, until he pays or tenders the price. But if the seller delivers the goods absolutely, and without fraudulent contrivance on the part of the buyer, the buyer will hold possession of them.

§ 9. But when goods are sold upon credit, and nothing is said as to the time of delivery, the buyer is immediately entitled to the possession. If, however, it is ascertained, before the buyer obtains possession of the goods, that he is insolvent, or that he is so embarrassed as to disable him from meeting the demands of his creditors, the seller may stop the goods as a security for the price. But if they are stopped without good cause, or through misinformation, the buyer is entitled to the goods, and to damages which he may have sustained in consequence of their stoppage.

§ 10. In the sale of a chattel, if the seller has possession of the article, and sells it as his own, he is understood to *warrant the title.* A fair price implies a warranty of title; and the purchaser may have satisfaction from the seller, if he sells the goods as his own, and the title proves deficient. But if the possession is at the time in another, and there is no covenant or warranty of title, the party buys at his peril. It is thought, however, if the seller affirms that the property is his own, he warrants the title, though it is not in his possession.

§ 11. With regard to the *quality* of the thing, the seller is not bound to make good any deficiency, except under special circumstances, unless he expressly warranted the goods to be sound and good, or unless he made a fraudulent representation or concealment concerning them. The rule is, if there is no express warranty by the seller, nor fraud on his part, and if the article is equally open to the inspection of both parties, the buyer who examines the article for himself, must abide by all losses arising from latent defects equally unknown to both parties.

§ 12. But this rule does not reasonably apply to those cases in which the purchaser has ordered goods of a certain character, or in which goods of a certain described quality are offered for sale, and, when delivered, they do not answer the description. There being no opportunity of examining them, there is an implied warranty of the quality of the article. An intentional concealment or suppression of a material fact, when both parties have not equal access to means of information, is deemed unfair dealing, and renders the contract void. As a general rule, each party is bound to communicate to the other his knowledge of material facts, provided he knows the other to be ignorant of them, and they are not open and naked, or equally within the reach of his observation. The *moral law,* however, and fair dealing, require, in all cases, a full disclosure of all defects within the knowledge of the contracting parties.

CHAPTER LIII

FRAUDULENT SALES AND ASSIGNMENTS; GIFTS, &C.

§ 1. To protect the rights of the contracting parties alone, is not the only object of laws for the regulation of contracts. Contracts are often made which injuriously affect the rights of third persons, who are persons other than the contracting parties. Contracts by which third persons are most frequently injured, are those by which property is fraudulently conveyed by gift, sale, or assignment. A debtor, to place his property beyond the reach of his creditors, either transfers it to some other person by gift; or he sells or assigns it to another, under the false pretense of securing the payment of a debt; the property to remain with the assignor, with the secret understanding that the assignee is never to take it into his possession.

§ 2. Any agreement which operates as a fraud upon third persons, is void. It is a rule of common law, that all deeds of gift, and all transfers of goods and chattels made by any person to secure them for his future use, shall be void as against creditors; that is to say, such transfers shall not exempt the property from being taken to satisfy the demands of his creditors. And as a sale or an assignment is more likely to be fraudulent when the property remains with the seller or assignor, than when the assignee takes it into his own possession, it has long been a principle of law, that if property assigned or sold remains with the person assigning or selling it, the transaction is presumed to be fraudulent. But whether such conveyance of goods is only *prima facie* evidence of fraud, which the vendee or assignee may be permitted to rebut by proof, or whether the transaction is fraudulent in point of *law*, and void, is a question upon which the decisions of the courts in England as well as those in this country differ, and which, therefore, may be considered as not conclusively settled.

§ 3. Some have made a distinction between bills of sale and assignments that are absolute, and those that are conditional. The Supreme Court of the United States has affirmed the doctrine, that an absolute and unconditional bill of sale or conveyance, when the property is retained in possession, is of itself conclusive evidence of fraud ; in other words, it is presumed to be fraud in point of law, whatever it may be in fact. It has been held by the same court, that a conveyance with a condition that the property is to remain with the vendor until the condition shall be performed, or which is in the nature of a mortgage or security, expressing an agreement between the parties that the mortgager shall retain possession, is valid.

§ 4. In some states, the doctrine established by the courts is, that a continuance of possession is only *prima facie* evidence of fraud ; in which case, the mortgagee or assignee is allowed to show by proof, that the conveyance was made in good faith, and for a valuable consideration. In other states, the strict rule prevails, that, without a change of possession, the transaction is fraudulent *in law;* in which case the assignee, or person claiming the property under the assignment, is not permitted to show that, in point of *fact,* the transaction was *bona fide,* (made in good faith.)

§ 5. Although a rule that holds every conveyance to be fraudulent, unless followed by an immediate change of possession of the property conveyed, may be deemed necessary to prevent frauds upon third persons, it often operates to the injury or inconvenience of honest debtors. A debtor may be obliged to part with property, however convenient or needful its present use may be to him, in order to satisfy a debt ; when, but for this stringent rule of law, he might borrow the money to pay the debt, or procure a forbearance of it, by pledging property without losing the benefit of its use.

§ 6. Why this perplexing question has been left so long unsettled in the different states, it is not easy to perceive. In the state of New York, it has been set at rest by an express statute, declaring, that unless a sale or an assignment is accompanied by an immediate delivery, and followed by an actual and immediate change of possession, it shall be presumed to be fraudulent and void, as against creditors, and shall be conclusive evidence of fraud, unless the party claiming the property under the assignment, shall make it appear, that the same was made in good faith, and without any attempt to defraud. The essential provisions of this statute are believed to prevail at present in most of the states p. 287-289.

§ 7. In the sale of personal property, though there should be a judgment against the vendor, and the purchaser should have notice of it, that fact would not of itself render the sale fraudulent. But if the purchaser, knowing of the judgment, purchases with the view or purpose to defeat the creditor's execution, the transaction is fraudulent. The question of fraud depends upon the motive.

§ 8. Assignments are sometimes made by debtors for the benefit of their creditors. A person deeply indebted, or in embarrassed circumstances, assigns his property, in trust, to one or more persons, to be by them disposed of, and the avails to be applied to the payment of all his creditors, or of a part of them ; for the law which we have been considering, does not apply to assignments of this kind so as to forbid a debtor giving a preference to one or more creditors over others, provided the assignment is for a sufficient consideration. A debtor may directly assign or transfer all his property to a single creditor, and the assignment be valid : but if the value of the property is manifestly excessive, and disproportionate to the debt which it is intended to cover, the other creditors have a right to the surplus.

§ 9. When a debtor in embarrassed circumstances enters into an arrangement with all his creditors, to pay them a certain proportion of their claims, in consideration of a discharge of their demands, if he privately agrees to give a better or further security to one than to others, the contract is void ; because the condition upon which they agree to discharge the debtor is, that each creditor shall receive an equal benefit, and take a proportionate share.

§ 10. A gift or conveyance founded merely upon a consideration of affection, or blood or consanguinity, may be set aside by creditors, if the grantor was in embarrassed circumstances when he made it ; for a man is bound, both legally and morally, to pay his debts before giving away his property. But if he is indebted to only a small amount in proportion to his property, and wholly unembarrassed, the gift is not rendered voidable by his indebtedness, even though he should afterward become insolvent.

CHAPTER LIV.

PRINCIPAL AND AGENT, OR FACTOR; BROKER; LIEN, &C.

§ 1. A PRINCIPAL is one who employs another, as *agent*, to transact his business. A *factor* is an agent; but the word factor is generally understood to mean a *commercial* agent; that is, one who is employed by merchants residing in a distant place, to buy and sell, and transact business for them. Thus, country merchants send their wheat, flour, pork, and other country produce, to their agents in the cities, to be disposed of. The owners of the property are called *principals;* their agents are factors, or, as they are sometimes called, *commission merchants.* As receivers of property consigned to them, they are also called *consignees,* and the persons who consign or commit to them their property, are *consignors.*

§ 2. For the accommodation of the principal, the factor sometimes pays him a part of the value of the produce before it is sold. For the money thus advanced, the factor has a claim upon the property until the advance money shall be refunded, and all charges against the owner paid. And as a factor does not always know who is the actual owner, the person in whose name the goods are shipped, is to be deemed the owner.

§ 3. This claim which a factor has upon goods intrusted to him for sale, is called *lien;* and the factor may sell the goods, and retain out of the proceeds of the sale what is due him; and the remainder he must pay to the principal, or owner. But a person can not sell or pledge property committed to him for transportation or storage only; nor can a factor pledge goods intrusted to him for sale, as security for his own debts. A factor who disposes of any merchandise intrusted or consigned to him, and applies the avails to his own use, with intent to defraud the owner, may be punished by fine and imprisonment.

§ 4. How far, in ordinary business, a principal is bound by the acts of an agent, it is not easy to determine. As a general rule, however, a general agent, that is, one who either transacts all kinds of business for his employer, or does all acts connected with a particular business or transaction, or that relate to some particular department of business, so long as he keeps within the general scope of his authority, binds his principal or employer by all his acts, although in some special cases he has done an act which he was expressly instructed not to do.

§ 5. The justice of this rule is apparent. A large portion of the commercial business of every community, is transacted by agents; and if a principal who holds out to the public that his agent has general authority to act for him in a certain business, or a certain department of business, could quit himself from liability for acts of his agent whose authority he had limited by secret instructions, frauds would be frequent, dealings with agents would be unsafe, and the general business of the country would be greatly embarrassed.

§ 6. An agent is bound, in ordinary cases, to observe the instructions of his principal, even though an act in violation of such instructions should be intended for the benefit of the principal. The agent must bear, personally, all losses growing out of a noncompliance with his orders; and the profit accruing therefrom goes to the benefit of the principal. An agent, however, is excused from a strict compliance with his orders, if after receiving them, some sudden and unforeseen emergency has arisen, in consequence of which such compliance would operate as an injury to the principal, and frustrate his intention.

§ 7. When an agent receives no instructions, he must conform to the usage of trade, or to the custom applicable to the particular agency; and any deviation therefrom, unless it is justified by the necessity of the case, renders him solely liable for all the loss or injury resulting from it.

§ 8. An agent is bound to exercise ordinary diligence and reasonable skill; and he is responsible only for the want thereof. Ordinary diligence is that which persons of common prudence use in conducting their own affairs. Reasonable skill is the average skill possessed by persons of common capacity employed in the same business.

§ 9. If an agent exceeds the limits of his authority, he becomes personally responsible to the person with whom he deals, if the limitations of his authority are unknown to such person. So he is in like manner responsible, if he makes a contract in his own name; or if he does not disclose the name of the principal, so as to enable the party with whom he deals to have recourse to the principal, in case the agent had authority to bind him. And if the agent even buys in his own name, but for the benefit of his principal, and without disclosing his name, the principal also is bound, provided the goods come to his use. Also, if the principal is under age, or a lunatic, or otherwise incompetent to contract, the agent is liable.

§ 10. A *broker* is an agent who is employed to negotiate sales between parties for a compensation in the form of a commission, which is commonly called *brokerage*. His business consists in negotiating exchanges; or in buying and selling stocks, goods, ships, or cargoes; or in procuring insurances, and settling losses: and as he confines himself to one or the other of these branches, he is called an exchange broker, stock broker, insurance broker, &c. A broker differs from a factor. He has not the custody of the goods of his principal. He is merely empowered to effect the contract of sale; and when he has effected such sale, his agency ends. If a broker executes his duties in such a manner that no benefit results from them; or if he is guilty of gross misconduct in selling goods, he is not entitled to a commission or compensation.

§ 11. A *lien*, as has been stated, is the claim of a factor or agent upon property in his possession, as security for the payment of his charges. This right of lien extends to others than factors. It is intended also for the benefit of manufacturers and mechanics, and other persons carrying on business for the accommodation of the public. A merchant has a lien upon goods sold till the price is paid, if no credit has been stipulated for; and even when he agrees to give a credit, if the purchaser practices fraud in obtaining the goods, the seller may take them. These cases differ, however, from ordinary cases of lien, as the purchaser has not, in reality, acquired any lawful right to the property; and the merchant may dispose of the property as his own, which can not be done in other cases.

§ 12. A shoemaker receiving leather to manufacture into shoes, may retain the shoes until he is paid for the making; a tailor has a lien upon the garment made from another's cloth; a blacksmith upon the horse he shoes; an innkeeper upon the horse or goods of his guest ; and common carriers upon the goods they transport. But they can not hold the property for any other debt ; nor have they a right to sell it to satisfy their claim. Whenever a person allows property to go out of his possession, he loses his lien. p. 289.

CHAPTER LV.

PARTNERSHIP.

§ 1. A PARTNERSHIP is the association of two or more persons for the purpose of carrying on any business, agreeing to divide the profits and bear the loss, in certain proportions. Persons forming a partnership, unite their money or capital. Sometimes one furnishes money, and another performs the labor. Or, perhaps no money may be necessary, but each agrees to do his share of the labor.

§ 2. All the members of a partnership are bound by the act of any one of them, or by any contract which either of them may make. Although they agree to divide their gains and losses, either one of them is liable for all the debts of the partnership. If one of the concern buys property on his own account, for his individual use and benefit, he alone is liable ; but though he thus buys it, if it is afterward applied to the use of the partnership, all become liable.

§ 3. There are cases, however, when not all who share in the profits are responsible : as when a clerk or agent agrees to receive a part of the profits as a compensation for his service or labor ; or when one receives, as rent, a part of the profits of a tannery, tavern or farm. In these cases, although the parties share in the profits, there is no partnership ; and the persons who buy the stock and other materials, and hire the labor necessary to carry on their respective trades, are alone responsible.

§ 4. One partner can not bring a new partner into the firm, without the consent of all the others. If, therefore, a partner should desire to sell his interest to some other person who is to take his place in the partnership, he can not do so, unless all the partners consent to such sale.

§ 5. All the partners must unite in suing and being sued. Sometimes, however, there are secret or dormant partners, who conceal their names : these may not join in an action as plaintiffs, but they may be sued when discovered to be partners.

§ 6. As each partner is liable for all the debts of the concern, so each may, in the name of the firm, in ordinary cases, assign over the effects and credits to pay the debts of the firm.

§ 7. Any partner may withdraw when he pleases, and dissolve the partnership, if no definite period has been agreed on for the partnership to continue ; but if, by the terms of agreement, it is to continue for a definite period, it can not be dissolved before the expiration of the term, without the mutual consent of all the partners, except by the death or some other inability of one of them, or by a decree of the court of chancery.

§ 8. When a partnership is dissolved by the withdrawal of any of the partners, notice of dissolution ought to be duly published, or a firm may be bound by a contract made by one partner in the usual course of business, and in the name of the firm, with a person who contracted on the faith of the partnership, and who had no notice of the dissolution. The same notice is necessary to protect a retiring partner from continued responsibility. And even if due notice is given, yet, if he willingly suffers his name to continue in the firm, or in the title of the firm over the door of the shop or store, he may in certain cases be still liable.

§ 9. In some of the states, a partnership may be formed by a number of persons, some of whom are to be responsible only to a limited amount ; and their names are not to be used in the firm. But before a partnership of this kind can do business, a writing and certificate signed by the parties, stating the terms of partnership, and the amount for which the *special partners* (as they are called) are to be responsible, must be recorded. The terms of partnership must also be published in a newspaper.

§ 10. In partnerships thus formed, called *limited partnerships*, the special partners become liable only to the amount mentioned in the terms of partnership. The other partners, called *general partners*, whose names only are used, and who transact the business, are liable for all the debts contracted, as in ordinary partnerships. If such partnership is to be dissolved by act of the parties, before the time expires for which it was formed, notice of dissolution must be filed and recorded, and published in a newspaper.

CHAPTER LVI.

BAILMENT.

§ 1. Another class of rights and responsibilities are those which arise from delivering and receiving property in trust, to be kept or used, and redelivered, according to agreement. Such delivery and receiving includes giving and taking goods to be kept for and without reward, and in security for debt ; borrowing and lending ; letting for hire ; carrying, &c. These are comprehended in the word *bailment*, which is from *bail*, a French word, meaning to deliver.

§ 2. If a person takes goods to keep and return without reward, he must keep them with ordinary care, or, if they receive injury, he will be liable to the bailor for damage; in other words, a bailee without reward is responsible only for gross neglect. The person with whom goods are deposited, is also called in law, *depositary*. A depositary may not use the goods taken into his care.

§ 3. A *mandatary*, that is, a person who agrees to carry goods from place to place, or to do some other act or work upon or about them, without recompense, must use due diligence in performing the work ; he is responsible for gross neglect, if he undertakes and does the work amiss ; but it is thought that for agreeing to do, and not undertaking or doing at all he is not liable for damage. If he has been strongly persuaded to do the act, only a fair exertion of his ability is required.

§ 4. A borrower is liable for damage in case of slight neglect. If he applies the article borrowed to the use for which he borrows it, uses it carefully, does not allow another to use it, and returns it within the time for which it was borrowed, he is not liable.

§ 5. A person who receives goods in security for a debt or engagement, is liable for ordinary neglect. But if he bestows ordinary care upon the goods, and they should then be lost, he still has a claim upon the pawnor for the debt.

§ 6. When property is hired, that is, when something is to be paid for the use of an article, and it is injured by moderate usage, the owner bears the loss; but the hirer must not use it for any purpose but that for which it is hired, and he must return it promptly, or he is liable for damage.

§ 7. If an article is delivered upon which work is to be bestowed, the work must be properly done. A manufacturer who receives wool to make into cloth, or the tailor who takes cloth to make into a garment, must do the work well, or he is liable for damage. If the property should be lost or stolen, he is responsible for ordinary neglect.

§ 8. Innkeepers are, in general, responsible for all injuries to the goods and baggage of their guests, even for thefts. But for losses caused by unavoidable accident, or robbery, they are not liable.

§ 9. A common carrier, that is, one who carries goods for hire as a common employment, is responsible to the owner, even if robbed of the goods. But a person who occasionally carries goods for hire is not a common carrier, and is answerable only for ordinary neglect, unless he expressly takes the risk. A common carrier is one who holds himself out as ready to carry goods as a business, by land or by water, and is answerable for all losses, except in cases of public enemies, as in time of war, and in case of the act of God, as by lightning, storms, floods, &c.

§ 10. A common carrier is bound to receive from any person paying or tendering the freight charges, such goods as he is accustomed to carry, and as are offered for the place to which he carries. But he may refuse to receive them if he is full, or if they are dangerous to be carried, or for other good reasons. He may refuse to take them unless the charges are paid; but if he agrees to take payment at the end of the route, he may retain them there until the freight is paid. A carrier must deliver freight in a reasonable time; but he is not liable for loss by the freezing of a river or canal during his voyage, if he has used due diligence.

§ 11. Proprietors of a stage coach do not warrant the safety of passengers in the character of common carriers; and they are not responsible for mere accidents to the persons of the passengers, but only for want of due care. Slight fault, unskillfulness, or negligence, either as to the sufficiency of the carriage, or to the act of driving it, may render the owner responsible in damages for injury to passengers. But as public carriers, they are answerable for the loss of a box or parcel of goods, though ignorant of its contents; unless the owner fraudulently conceals the value or nature of the article, or deludes the carrier by treating it as of little or no value. Public carriers are responsible for the baggage of their passengers, though they advertise it as being at the risk of the owners.

CHAPTER LVII

PROMISSORY NOTES.

§ 1. A PROMISSORY *note* is a written promise to pay a specified sum, at a certain time, to a person named, or to his order, or to the bearer. A common form of a note is the following:

$100. ALBANY, June 9, 1858.

Three months after date, I promise to pay to James Smith, or bearer, one hundred dollars, value received.

JOHN BROWN.

§ 2. Notes thus written may be bought and sold as property in general, and perform, in many cases, the same office as money. But if in the above note the words "or bearer" were omitted, it would not possess the same qualities; or, as men say, it would not be *negotiable;* there being no promise to pay any other person than Smith. It might be sold; but the buyer, if obliged to sue, must sue in the name of Smith; in which case, Brown might offset any demands which he might have against Smith. The words *or bearer* should therefore be inserted, that any holder may collect it in his own name.

§ 3. Notes are also made negotiable by writing the words *or order* in the place of "or bearer;" but in this case, the person to whom a note is payable, who is called the payee, or promisee, must indorse it; which is done by writing his name on the back of it. Such indorsement is considered, in law, as his order to the maker or promiser to pay it to another person. Being thus indorsed, it is *negotiable;* that is, it becomes a subject of purchase and sale, and may pass from hand to hand by simple delivery, as if made payable to bearer, and may be sued in the name of any *bona fide* holder.

§ 4. It is usual to insert the words, "value received," as evidence that the note was given for a valuable consideration; for it will be recollected, that contracts are not valid without such consideration. But a note is good without these words. Whether they are inserted or not, the note is presumed to have been given for a valuable consideration; and the maker can not avoid his obligation to pay it, without making it appear that no value was received. In Connecticut, a note which is not negotiable in form, and not for value received, does not imply a consideration. Consequently, value must be proved by the holder. In Missouri, to make a note negotiable, it must contain the words, "for value received, negotiable, and without defalcation." (See § 12.)

§ 5. A note made by two or more persons may be joint, or joint or several. When it is written, "We promise to pay," it is only a joint note, and all must be sued together. If written, "We jointly and severally promise to pay," they may be sued either jointly or separately. Or if written, "I promise to pay," it is treated as a joint and several note. A note written, "We promise," and signed, A. B. principal, and C. D. security, is the joint note of both; and if written, "I promise," and signed in the same manner, it is the joint and several note of both.

§ 6. Any person having in possession a negotiable note, though a mere agent, is deemed the true owner, and may sue on it in his own name, without showing title. The *bona fide* holder can recover upon the paper, though it came to him from a person who had stolen or robbed it from the true owner; provided he took it innocently in the course of trade, for a valuable consideration, before it was due, and with due caution. If, however, suspicion is cast upon the title of the holder, by showing that the instrument has got into circulation by force or fraud, then the holder must show the consideration he gave for it.

§ 7. It has been observed, that a man can not convey to another a valid title to property which is not lawfully his own; and hence, that the purchaser of stolen goods must give them up to the lawful owner. The exception to this rule, in the case of promissory notes, seems, however, to be founded in reason and good policy. The use of negotiable paper in commercial transactions is of great public convenience: and it is proper that, for the sake of trade, protection should be given to the holder of such paper who receives it fairly in the way of business, though it has been paid, if he received it before it fell due.

§ 8. But it is equally material for the interests of trade, that the owner should have due protection. Hence, if a person takes a note from a stranger without inquiry how he came by it; or does not take it in the usual course of business, or for some responsibility incurred on the credit of the note, he takes it at his peril. But the owner, in order to place his right to relief beyond question, ought to use diligence in apprising the public of the loss of the note.

§ 9. The indorsement of a note, in the view of the law, amounts to a contract, on the part of the indorser, with the indorsee and every subsequent holder; (1.) That the note and the antecedent signatures are genuine; (2.) That he, the indorser, has a good title to the note; (3.) That he is competent to bind himself as indorser; (4.) That the maker is competent to bind himself for the payment, and will pay it when due; (5.) That if not so paid by the maker, he, the indorser, will, upon due notice given him that the note is dishonored, pay the same to the indorsee, or other holder.

§ 10. An indorsement made by writing the name only on the back of a note, is called a blank indorsement. A full indorsement is one which also points out the person to whom the note is to be paid. But a blank indorsement may be filled up at any time by the holder. For example: A note is payable to "John Jay, or order," or to "the order of John Jay," who indorses it in blank, which makes it payable to any other holder. But if the indorsee, the person to whom it is indorsed, wishes it paid to any particular person, he may fill up the blank by writing a request to that effect above the name of the indorser, thus: "Pay to George Bruce," or "Pay to George Bruce or order;" who, again, may by indorsement order it paid to some particular person. Or, by indorsing it in blank, or ordering it paid *to the bearer*, it would again pass, as at first, by mere delivery.

§ 11. In ordinary business transactions in the country, notes intended to be negotiable, are usually made payable to bearer, as in the form given, (§ 1.) And the young reader, inexperienced in business, may not know why they are not always so written. One advantage of making a note payable to order, is the protection which it affords to the holder or owner, in case the note should be lost or stolen. Take, for example, the note indorsed in blank in the case supposed in the last section. The owner, we will suppose, resides in Buffalo, and the maker in Detroit. The owner fills the blank over the name of John Jay with a request to "pay to George Bruce," also residing in Detroit, to whom it is sent by mail, to be by him presented to the maker for payment. And should the note by accident or fraud fall into the hands of another, it being payable to Bruce only, or to his order, the parties are protected from loss.

§ 12. A person buying a note after it has become due, takes it at his peril. Although the holder may sue it in his own name, the maker may offset any demands which he had against the promisee before it was transferred. But when notes in which no day of payment is expressed come under the operation of this rule, is a question to be determined by circumstances. In the states of New Jersey, Pennsylvania, Missouri, and perhaps others, the words "without defalcation or discount," or words to that effect, must be inserted in notes, or they may be met by offsets as notes that are bought after due. Also notes payable in some commodity are subject to the same rule.

§ 13. Notes payable *on demand*, are due immediately; and payment need not be demanded before the holder can sue. Also, if no time of payment is mentioned in a note, it is due when given, and no demand of payment is necessary. But a note payable *at sight*, or at a specified time after sight, must be presented for payment before it can be sued. If the words "with interest" are omitted, a note will not draw interest before the time at which it is due. If it is payable on demand, it will draw interest from the time payment is demanded.

§ 14. After the day on which a note is made payable, the maker is allowed three days for payment, which are called *days of grace.* The day on which the note becomes payable, is not to be counted one of the three days. Thus, a note dated the first day of January, having three months to run, is payable on the first day of April, which day is included in the three months, so that the last day of grace is the fourth day of the month. By general usage, a note does not become due on the day mentioned on its face, but on the last day of grace.

§ 15. We have seen the object of indorsements, and their binding effect upon the indorsers. Certain acts are necessary to fix responsibility upon an indorser of a note payable to order. The omission, or imperfect performance of these acts, has often operated to discharge indorsers from liability. In order to hold an indorser responsible, the holder must make a prompt demand of payment of the maker, and give reasonable notice of his default to the indorser. The object of such demand and notice is to afford the indorser opportunity to obtain security from those for whom he has become liable.

§ 16. Demand of payment must be made of the maker of a note on the last day of grace ; or, if such day falls on Sunday, or the fourth day of July, or any other day recognized by law as a holyday, or day of public rest, then the demand must be made on the second day of grace. If the third day of grace should fall on Sunday, and any holyday as Christmas, or fourth of July, should happen on Saturday, the demand must be made on Friday. As the holder may be required to prove that payment has been demanded, it must be done in presence of one or more witnesses. As to the time of day when the demand should be made, it is considered that the maker is entitled to the latest convenient time within the customary business hours of the place where the note is presented.

§ 17. If, in consequence of the removal of the maker before the note becomes due, or from any other cause, his residence is unknown, the holder must make endeavors to find it, and make the demand there ; though, if he has removed out of the state, it is sufficient to present the note at his former place of residence. If the maker has absconded, that will, as a general rule, excuse the demand.

§ 18. If payment has been demanded and refused, notice thereof must be given to the indorser; and one entire day is allowed the holder to give such notice. If the demand is made on Saturday, it is sufficient to give notice on Monday. If the indorser resides in the same town, he may be notified personally by the holder, or by a special messenger sent to his dwelling-house, where notice may be given personally, or left in a way likely to bring it to his knowledge. If the parties reside in different towns, notice may be sent by mail; in which case the notice must be put into the post-office, or mailed, as early as the next day after the third day of grace, so as to be forwarded as soon as possible thereafter. Or, notice may be sent by a private conveyance, or special messenger.

§ 19. Notes, on being transferred, are sometimes guarantied by indorsement. If a person simply write his name on the back, he is liable as an *indorser* only. If he guaranties the "payment" of the note, he is generally considered liable as an original *promisor*. If he guaranties the note "good" or "collectable," legal proceedings must be had against the maker, and indorsers also, if there be any, before the guarantor is liable. Strict notice to a guarantor is not required, as in the case of an indorser; but to hold him liable, it must be shown that he has not been prejudiced by the want of notice, or that the note was not collectable of the maker or indorsers when due. But the kind of liability incurred, whether that of indorser, original promisor, or surety, by indorsing a note or guarantying payment, is not the same in all the states. There are sundry other points in the law relating to promissory notes on which the statutes and judicial decisions are not uniform in all the different states.

CHAPTER LVIII.

BILLS OF EXCHANGE; INTEREST; USURY.

§ 1. A BILL *of exchange* is a written order or request to a person in a distant place to pay a third person a certain sum of money. The following is a common form:

$1,000. NEW YORK, April 10, 1858.

Twenty days after date, pay to the order of John Stiles, one thousand dollars, value received, and charge the same to account of

To GEORGE SCOTT, THOMAS JONES.
New Orleans, La.

§ 2. It will be seen that this is, in effect, the same as an order used in common business. But when drawn by merchants in commercial cities on persons in distant places, orders of this kind are called bills of exchange. They are often very convenient to persons in mercantile business. Bills drawn on persons in foreign countries, are called *foreign bills of exchange;* and those which are drawn on persons in distant places in our own country, are by way of distinction, called *inland bills of exchange.*

§ 3. The nature and operation of a bill of exchange are thus illustrated: A, in New York, has $1,000 due him from B, in New Orleans. A draws an order on B for that sum, and C, who is going to New Orleans, pays A the money, takes the order, and receives his money again of B. Thus A is accommodated by receiving his debt against B, and C has avoided the risk in carrying the money from place to place. A, who draws the bill, is called the *drawer.* B, to whom it is addressed, is called the *drawee.* C, to whom it is made payable, is the *payee.* As the bill is payable to C, or *his order*, he may, by indorsement, direct the bill to be paid to D; in which case C becomes the *indorser*, and D, to whom the bill is indorsed, is called the *indorsee*, or *holder.*

§ 4. If, when the bill is presented to the drawee, he agrees to pay it, he is said to *accept* the bill; and as evidence of the fact, writes his acceptance upon it. An acceptance may, however, be by parol. The acceptor of a bill is the principal debtor, and the drawer the surety. The acceptor is bound, though he accepted without consideration, and for the sole accommodation of the drawer. But payment must be demanded on the last day of grace; and, if refused, notice of nonpayment must be given to the drawer, as in the case of an indorsed note.

§ 5. No precise time is fixed by law at which bills payable at sight, or a certain number of days after sight, must be presented to the drawee for acceptance; though an unreasonable delay might discharge the drawer. A bill payable on a certain day after date, need not be presented for acceptance before the day of payment; but if presented before it becomes due, and acceptance is refused, it is dishonored; and notice must be given immediately to the drawer. If a bill has been accepted, demand of payment must be made upon the acceptor when the bill falls due; and it must be made at the place appointed for payment; and if no place is appointed, then at his house or residence, or upon him personally.

§ 6. A check upon a bank, (See Chap. XXIV, § 4,) is another kind of negotiable paper. It partakes more of the nature of a bill of exchange, than a promissory note. It is not a direct promise to pay; but it is an undertaking, by the drawer, that the drawee shall accept and pay; and the drawer is answerable only in case the drawee fails to pay. A check payable to bearer passes by delivery; and the bearer may sue on it as on an inland bill of exchange.

§ 7. When a foreign bill of exchange is to be presented for acceptance or payment, demand is usually made by a *notary public;* and in case of refusal, his certificate of the presentment of the bill, and of the refusal, is legal proof of the fact in any court. This certificate is called a *protest,* which means, *for proof.* A protest may be noted on the day of the demand; though it may be drawn up in form at a future period. Notaries are appointed in all commercial places of considerable business.

§ 8. A protest of an inland bill of exchange is not generally deemed necessary in this country; though it is the practice to have bills, drawn in one state on persons in another, protested by a notary. No protest is legal evidence in court, except in the case of a foreign bill. Yet it is expedient, in many cases of inland bills, to employ notaries when evidence is to be preserved, because they are easily found when wanted as witnesses. In some states, bills drawn in one state and payable in another, are deemed foreign bills ; and their protest as such is required. Notes payable at banks are also protested for nonpayment.

§ 9. *Interest* is an allowance for the use of money, or for the forbearance of a debt. Thus a person lends to another $100 for one year, and receives for the use of it $6, which is called the interest. Promissory notes are usually made payable with interest. The rate of interest is fixed by a law of the state, but is not the same in all the states.

§ 10. A higher rate of interest than that fixed by law, is called *usury*. Not only can no more be collected on any contract or obligation than the lawful rate, but in most of the states there is some forfeiture for taking usurious interest. In some states, the whole debt is forfeited ; in others, twice or thrice the excess above the lawful interest ; and in some, only the excess taken can be recovered. In the state of New York, no part of a usurious debt can be collected : but if it has been paid, only the excess above the lawful interest can be recovered. p. 290.

LAW OF NATIONS.

CHAPTER LIX.

ORIGIN AND PROGRESS OF THE LAW OF NATIONS ; THE NATURAL, CUSTOMARY, AND CONVENTIONAL LAWS OF NATIONS, DEFINED.

§ 1. In the course of this work, we have considered the necessity and nature of government and laws, and the different forms of government under which the people of different communities are associated, especially that which has been adopted by the people of this country ; and we have given an abstract of the principal laws by which their rights are defined, and their duties and mutual obligations, as individual citizens of the state and of the nation, are enjoined. As the people of the United States, in their national capacity, occupy an important position in the great community of nations, the author deems it proper to subjoin a compend of the rules by which intercourse between nations is regulated.

§ 2. The law of nations, in its present improved state, has not long existed. Ancient nations were little governed by the principles of natural justice. Little respect was paid by one nation to the rights of the persons and property of the citizens of another. Robbery on land and sea was not only tolerated, but esteemed honorable; and prisoners of war were either put to death, or reduced to slavery. By this rule of national law, commerce was destroyed, and perpetual enmity kept up between nations.

§ 3. No essential, permanent improvement in the law of nations seems to have been made until within the last three or four centuries. By the light of science and Christianity, the rights and obligations of nations have come to be better understood, and more generally regarded. Commerce also has done much to improve the law, by showing that the true interests of a nation are promoted by peace and friendly intercourse.

§ 4. Hence we find the nations of Europe and America recognizing the same rules of international law. And as the light of Christianity shall become more widely diffused, and its principles more generally practiced, the law of nations will undergo still further improvements. And may we not hope, that, as one of these improvements, the practice of settling national disputes by war will be abolished, and one more rational and humane be adopted, that of referring all difficulties which the parties are incapable of adjusting, to some disinterested power for adjudication?

§ 5. There is, in every nation or state, some acknowledged authority to make laws to protect the rights of the citizens, and courts of justice to try and punish offenders. But there is no tribunal before which one nation can be brought to answer for the violation of the rights of another. Every nation, however small and weak, is independent of every other. Hence, when injuries are committed by one upon another, the offended party, unless it chooses quietly to endure the wrong, must obtain redress, either by appealing to the sense of justice of the party offending, or by a resort to force.

§ 6. The equality and independence of nations, without respect to their relative strength or extent of territory, is a settled principle of national law. Each has a right to establish such government and tolerate such religion as it thinks proper, and no other nation has a right to interfere with its internal policy. To this general rule, however, writers make an exception. The natural right of every state to provide for its own safety, gives it the right to interfere where its security is seriously endangered by the internal transactions of another state. But it is admitted, that such cases are so very rare, that it would be dangerous to reduce them to a rule. The right of forcible interference is only to be inferred from the circumstances of the special case.

§ 7. So also cases seldom arise, when one nation has a right to assist the subjects of another in overturning or changing their government. It is generally agreed, that such assistance may be afforded consistently with the law of nations, in extreme cases ; as when the tyranny of a government becomes so oppressive as to compel the people to rise in their defense, and call for assistance. It is held that rulers may, by an unwarrantable exercise of power, violate the principles of the social compact, and give their subjects just cause to consider themselves discharged from their allegiance.

§ 8. When the subjects of any government have carried their revolt so far as to have established a new state, and to give reasonable evidence of their ability to maintain a government, the right of assistance is unquestionable. But it is not clear, that, prior to this state of progress in a revolution, the right to interpose would be justifiable. The assistance given by France to this country, during the war of our revolution, was not a violation of the law of nations. The states having thrown off their allegiance to Great Britain, and established a government of their own, any foreign nation had a right to assist the states in securing their independence.

§ 9. There is a sense, however, in which nations are not

wholly independent. The happiness of mankind, as has been observed, depends upon association. (Chap. I, § 5, 6.) Without the assistance which men in the social state derive from each other, they could scarcely support their own being. Similar to this is the mutual dependence of nations. Although the people of every nation have within themselves the means of maintaining their individual and national existence, their prosperity and happiness are greatly promoted by commerce with other nations. And as laws are necessary to govern the conduct of the individual citizens of a state, so certain rules are necessary to regulate the intercourse of nations.

§ 10. It has been observed, also, that the law of nature, which is in accordance with the will of the Creator as expressed in his revealed law, is a perfect rule for all moral and social beings, and ought to be universally obeyed; and that its observance conduces to their highest happiness. Equally binding is this law upon nations: nor is the general good of mankind less promoted by its application to the affairs of nations than by its application to the affairs of individual persons. It requires each nation to respect the rights of all others, and to do for them what their necessities demand, and what each is capable of doing, consistently with the duties it owes to itself.

§ 11. The law of nature applied to nations or states as moral persons, is called the *natural law of nations.* It is also called the *necessary law of nations*, because nations are morally bound to observe it; and sometimes the *internal law of nations*, from its being binding on the conscience.

§ 12. Although, as has been elsewhere remarked, (Chap. II, § 9,) the law of nature, as expressed in the law of revelation, is a correct rule of human conduct; yet, as much of this law consists of general principles from which particular duties can not always be deduced, positive human enactments are necessary to define the law of nature and revelation. So also an important part of the law of nations necessarily consists of positive institutions. Hence, some writers have divided international law under these two principal heads: the *natural law of nations*, and the *positive.*

§ 13. The *positive law of nations* is founded on usage or custom and agreement; and may be considered as properly divided into the *customary* law of nations, and the *conven-*

tional. The *customary law of nations* consists of certain maxims, or is founded on customs and usages which have long been observed and tacitly consented to by nations, and which thereby become binding upon all who have adopted them, so far as their observance does not require the violation of the law of nature.

§ 14. A *conventional law of nations* is one that has been established by a treaty or league. A *convention* is an assembly of persons who meet for civil or political purposes. But an agreement or contract between nations, though made without a formal meeting, is deemed conventional. The manner in which treaties are made, has been described. (Chap. XL, § 5.)

§ 15. Thus the rights and interests of nations do not depend for their security entirely upon the law of nature, which is liable to misconstruction. Nor, so far as they are dependent upon positive institutions, do they rest wholly upon the vague and uncertain law of usage or custom. *Conventional* law, because more definite, has been found to afford far greater security to the rights of commerce. Hence the practice, now common among nations, of regulating their intercourse by negotiation. Treaties of commerce have been formed between most of the principal commercial states in the world. Their utility in regulating trade between states, is no less than that of written agreements between individuals, by which the rights of the contracting parties are placed beyond dispute.

§ 16. One advantage of treaties of commerce is, that a nation may, if its interest demand, enter into treaties granting special privileges to one or more nations, without giving just cause of offense to others. Such special favors, however, should not be granted without good reasons. It is the duty of every nation to respect the rights of all others, and to cultivate that mutual good will which is the result of liberal, just, and impartial dealing.

§ 17. It may be said, that, if each nation is independent of every other, and if there is no constituted authority to enforce the fulfillment of treaty stipulations, the rights guarantied by treaties are still insecure. Few governments, however, are so devoid of a sense of honor, as, by a palpable violation of their treaty obligations, to incur the odium and condemnation of all mankind. Self-respect, and the fear of provoking a war, have generally proved sufficient incentives to the observance of treaties.

§ 18. The obligations of nations are sometimes called *imperfect*. A *perfect obligation* is one that can be enforced—one that exists where there is a right to compel the party on whom the obligation rests to fulfill it. An *imperfect obligation* gives only the right to demand the fulfillment, leaving the party pledged to judge what his duty requires, and to do as he chooses, without being constrained by another to do otherwise.

CHAPTER LX.

THE JURISDICTION OF NATIONS; THEIR MUTUAL RIGHTS AND OBLIGATIONS; THE RIGHTS OF EMBASSADORS, MINISTERS, &C.

§ 1. The seas are regarded as the common highway of nations. The main ocean, for navigation and fishing, is open to all mankind; and no nation can appropriate it to its own exclusive use. Every state, however, has jurisdiction at sea over its own subjects, in its own public and private vessels. The persons on board such vessels are protected and governed by the laws of the country to which they belong; and they may be punished by these laws for offenses committed on board of its public vessels in foreign ports.

§ 2. The question how far a nation has jurisdiction over the seas adjoining its lands, is not clearly settled. It appears to be generally conceded, that a nation has the right of exclusive dominion over navigable rivers flowing through its territory; the harbors, bays, gulfs, and arms of the sea; and such extent of sea adjoining its territories as is necessary to the safety of the nation, which is considered by some to be as far as a cannon shot will reach, or about a marine league. Different nations have at times claimed much wider jurisdiction into the sea; but such claim rests upon doubtful authority.

§ 3. It is the duty of a nation, in time of peace, to allow the people of other states a passage over its lands and waters, so far as it can be permitted without inconvenience, and with safety to its own citizens. Of this the nation is to be its own judge. The right of passage is therefore only an *imperfect right*, so called, because the obligation to grant the right is an *imperfect obligation*. (See Chap. LIX, § 18.) Whenever, therefore, the interests and safety of a nation require it, foreigners may be prohibited from coming within its territory.

§ 4. The right of a state to keep foreigners out of its territory, is incident to, or results from the right of domain. *Domain*, in a general sense, signifies possession, or estate, and is perhaps more frequently applied to lands. Applied to a state, it means its whole territory, with every thing included in it. And with respect to other states, the property of the individuals in the aggregate is to be considered as the property of the nation. The right of domain is unlimited; that is, the state has the sole and exclusive right to the dominion and control of the territory and other property within the state.

§ 5. In general, it is the duty of a nation to allow foreigners to enter and settle in the country. On being admitted into a state, the state becomes pledged for their protection, and they become subject to its laws while they reside in it; and in consideration of the protection they receive, they are obliged to aid in defending it, and in supporting its government, even before they are admitted to all the rights of citizens.

§ 6. But when persons who have committed crimes in one state, flee into another for shelter, the state into which they flee is not bound to rescue them from justice. A person charged with crime, can be tried only in the state whose laws he has violated. It is therefore the duty of the government to surrender the fugitive, on demand being made by the proper authorities of the state from which the person has fled, and after due examination by a civil magistrate, if it shall appear to the magistrate that there are sufficient grounds for the charge. The surrender of criminals is often provided for in treaties.

§ 7. That rule of the law of nations, which makes foreigners amenable to the laws of the state into which they remove, does not apply to embassadors. They are wholly exempt from all responsibility to the laws of the country to which they are sent, even when guilty of crime. All that can be done is, when their conduct is dangerous to the government and its citizens, either to deprive them of liberty by confinement, or to send them home, and demand their punishment.

§ 8. As the interests of nations are promoted by intercourse, it is necessary that there should be some means of treating with each other, with the view of maintaining friendly relations. This can be done in no other way so well as through the medium of persons representing their respective governments. Each nation having a right to treat and communicate with every other, it ought not to be deprived of the services of its representative. Hence, by the general consent of nations, the persons and property of embassadors and other public ministers, are held sacred and inviolable.

§ 9. Embassadors are, by the law of nations, entitled to the same protection in the countries through which they pass, in going to, and returning from, the government to which they are sent. And to insure them a safe passage, it has been the practice with some governments to grant passports, to be shown in case they were required. A *passport* is a written license from the authority of a state, granting permission or safe conduct for one to pass through its territory. Passports, though named in our law, are not known in practice, being deemed unnecessary.

§ 10. An embassador is entitled to protection, by the law of nations, on his entering the territory of the nation to which he is sent, and making himself known ; though he is not insured the enjoyment of all his rights until he is formally received by the sovereign, and has presented his credentials ; which are letters of attorney from his own sovereign, giving him his authority. In this country, ministers from abroad are received by the president.

§ 11. If a minister at a foreign court treats the sovereign with disrespect, the fact is sometimes communicated to the government that sent him, with a request for his recall. Or, if the offense is a more serious one, the offended sovereign refuses intercourse with him while his master's answer is awaited. Or, if the case is an aggravated one, he expels him from the country. Every government has a right to judge for itself whether the language or conduct of a foreign minister is offensive.

§ 12. Ministers at foreign governments, in their negotiations or business correspondence with those governments, sometimes consider themselves ill-treated, and their own nation dishonored, and take their leave and return home; or the minister informs his sovereign, who either recalls him, or takes such other measure as he shall think the honor and interest of his nation demand.

§ 13. The peculiar condition of a country, the nature of the business upon which an embassador is sent, or the personal character of the embassador, may be such as to justify a government in refusing to receive such embassador. But in order to preserve the amicable relations of the two countries, satisfactory explanations ought to be made, or good reasons offered for the refusal.

§ 14. Ministers have not power to bind their sovereigns to any treaty or agreement. An ordinary credential, or letter of attorney, does not authorize a minister to bind his sovereign conclusively. He could not do so without a special power, containing express authority so to bind his principal. Few governments would act so imprudently. Their ministers act under secret instructions, which they are not bound to disclose. Even the treaties signed by plenipotentiaries, (a word signifying *full power*,) are, according to present usage, of no force, until ratified by their sovereigns.

§ 15. We have used the words embassador and minister without distinction. The different titles applied to representatives at foreign courts, do not indicate any material difference between them as to their powers and privileges, but the different degrees of dignity and respectability which custom has attached to them. They are differently classed by different writers. Perhaps the following is correct: (1.) Embassadors. (2.) Envoys and ministers plenipotentiary. (3.) Ministers resident. (4.) Chargés d'affairs. The United States are represented abroad by ministers and chargés d'affairs. (See Chap. XL, § 6, 7.)

§ 16. Consuls are not entitled to the privileges enjoyed by ministers; but are subject to the laws of the country in which they reside. The principal duties of consuls have been described. The office of consul has been found to be one of great utility; hence, every trading nation has a consul in every considerable commercial port in the world. Their duties and privileges are generally limited and defined in treaties of commerce, or by the laws of the country which they represent. As in the case of ministers, consuls carry a certificate of their appointment, and must be acknowledged as consuls by the government within whose sovereignty they reside, before they can perform any duties pertaining to their office.

CHAPTER LXI.

OFFENSIVE AND DEFENSIVE WAR; JUST CAUSES AND OBJECTS OF WAR; REPRISALS; ALLIANCES IN WAR.

§ 1. Considering the immense cost of a war; the vast sacrifice of human life, and the misery and sorrow consequent thereon; and its demoralizing effects upon a people; men have formed the conclusion, that all wars are inconsistent with the principles of Christianity, and therefore wrong. But it is not our purpose to discuss the question of the lawfulness of war. The general opinion prevalent among Christian nations will be assumed; namely, that self-preservation, or the right of self-defense, is a part of the law of our nature; and that it is the duty of civil society to protect the lives and property of its members; and further, that such protection is an essential consideration on which they enter into the social compact.

§ 2. Wars are offensive and defensive. The use of force to obtain justice for injuries done, is *offensive war*. The making use of force against any power that attacks a nation or its privileges, is *defensive war*. A war may be defensive in its principles, though offensive in its operation. Thus, one nation is preparing to invade another; but before the threatened invasion takes place, the latter attacks the former as the best mode of repelling the invasion. In this case, the party making the attack would be acting on the *defensive*. (See § 13.) The contending parties are called *belligerents.* The word *belligerent* is from the Latin *bellum*, war, and *gero*, to wage, or carry on. Nations that take no part in the contest, are called *neutrals.*

§ 3. War ought never to be undertaken without the most cogent reasons. In the first place, there must be a *right* to make war, and *just grounds* for making it. Nations have no right to employ force any further than is necessary for their own defense, and for the maintenance of their rights. Secondly, it should be made from *proper motives;* the good of the state, and the safety and common advantage of the citizens. Hence, there may be just cause for war, when it would be inexpedient or imprudent to involve the nation in such calamity.

§ 4. The numerous objects of a lawful war may be reduced to these three : (1.) To recover what belongs to us, or to obtain satisfaction for injuries. (2.) To provide for our future safety by punishing the offender. (3.) To defend or protect ourselves from injury by repelling unjust attacks. The first and second are objects of an *offensive* war ; the third is that of a *defensive* war.

§ 5. Injury to an individual citizen of a state, by the subjects of another state, is deemed a just cause of war, if the persons offending, or the government of the state to which they belong, do not make reparation for the injury ; for every nation is responsible for the good behavior of its subjects. But, although this would, according to the law of nations, afford justifiable cause of war, neither the honor nor the true interests of a nation, require, that war should always be made for so slight a cause.

§ 6. The honor and dignity of a nation would, in some cases, be best maintained by its making indemnity to its injured citizens, if satisfaction is refused, and suffer the wrong to pass unredressed. An individual who, though under the sanction of law, should avenge every slight act of violence committed upon his person, by inflicting personal chastisement upon the offender, would forfeit the public esteem. Nor, as we suppose, is it necessary for a nation, in order to retain the respect of civilized nations, to seek redress for every trifling injury, by a resort to war. A just sense of duty would suggest forbearance, at least until remonstrance against the repetition of injuries should be found unavailing.

§ 7. A government that unnecessarily involves a whole nation in war, assumes a fearful responsibility. Generally, the injury sought to be redressed should be serious, and satisfaction be demanded and refused, before recourse is had to arms. And where there is a question of right between the parties, the government making war ought to have no reasonable doubt of the justice of its claim. And even when no such doubt exists, it would be the duty of such government to prevent a war, if possible, by proposals of compromise. And it is believed that, in no case ought war to be made until attempts have been made to effect an adjustment of difficulties by compromise, or by offers to submit them for arbitration.

§ 8. These sentiments, it is admitted, do not accord with the general practice of nations ; probably they will not receive the assent of every reader. But it is believed, that those who are well instructed in the precepts of revealed religion, and draw their ideas of moral obligation from that system of morality, will find in these sentiments nothing to condemn. In this enlightened, Christain age, almost all national controversies might be honorably settled without bloodshed, even when, according to the law of nations, just cause of war exists, if the party aggrieved should faithfully endeavor, by all proper means, to effect a peaceable adjustment.

§ 9. One of the means by which satisfaction is sought without making war, is that of *reprisals*. (See Chapter XXXVI, § 4.) If a nation has taken what belongs to another, or refuses to pay a debt, or to make satisfaction for an injury, the offended nation seizes something belonging to the former or to her citizens, and retains it, or applies it to her own advantage, till she obtains satisfaction : and when there shall be no longer any hope of satisfaction, the effects thus seized are confiscated, and the reprisals are complete. *To confiscate* is to adjudge property to be forfeited, and to appropriate it to the use and benefit of the state. But as the loss in this case would fall upon unoffending citizens, it is the duty of their government to grant them indemnity.

§ 10. But to justify reprisals by the law of nations, the grounds upon which they are authorized must be just and well ascertained. If the right of the party demanding satisfaction is doubtful, he must first demand an equitable examination of his claim, and next be able to show that justice has been refused, before he can justly take the matter into his own hands. He has no right to disturb the peace and safety of nations on a doubtful pretension. But if the other party refuses to have the matter brought to the proof, or to accede to any proposition for terminating the dispute in a peaceable manner, reprisals become lawful.

§ 11. By treaties of alliance, nations sometimes agree to assist each other in case of war with a third power. It is a question not clearly settled, whether the government that is to afford the aid, is bound to do so when it deems the war to be unjust. The reasonable conclusion seems to be, that, in cases simply doubtful, the justice of the war is to be presumed; and the government pledging its aid is bound to fulfill its engagement. The contrary doctrine would furnish a nation with too ready a pretext for violating its pledge. In cases only of the clearest injustice on the part of its ally, can a nation rightfully avoid a positive engagement to afford assistance.

§ 12. When, however, the object of the war is hopeless, or when the state under such engagement would, by furnishing the assistance, endanger its own safety, it is not bound to render the aid. But the danger must not be slight, remote, or uncertain. None but extreme cases would afford sufficient cause for withholding the promised assistance.

§ 13. When the alliance is defensive, the treaty binds each party to assist the other only when engaged in a defensive war, and unjustly attacked. By the conventional law of nations, the government that first declares, or actually begins the war, is considered as making *offensive* war; and though it should not be the first actually to apply force, yet if it first renders the application of force necessary, it is the aggressor; and the other party, though first to apply force, is engaged in a *defensive* war. (See § 2.)

CHAPTER LXII.

DECLARATION OF WAR; ITS EFFECT UPON THE PERSON AND PROPERTY OF THE ENEMY'S SUBJECTS; STRATAGEMS IN WAR.

§ 1. When a nation has resolved on making war, it is usual to announce the fact by a public declaration. In monarchical governments, the power to declare war, which of course includes the right of determining the question whether it shall be made, is vested in the king. In our own country, this power is, by the constitution, given to the representatives of the people, for reasons elsewhere stated. (Chap. XXXVI, § 3.)

§ 2. It was the custom of the Romans, first to send a herald to demand satisfaction of the offending nation; and if, within a certain period, (thirty-three days,) a satisfactory answer was not returned, and war was resolved on, the herald was sent back as far as the frontier, where he declared it. It was considered due to the people of the offending nation, that their chief, knowing the consequences of refusing satisfaction, might be induced to do justice, and to preserve the lives and peace of his subjects. War, without such demand and notice, was regarded as unlawful.

§ 3. Although the practice of all these formalities was not observed by nations in later times, it was usual to make a simple declaration, and communicate it to the enemy. But according to modern practice, war may lawfully exist without a formal declaration to the enemy. Any manifesto or paper from an official source, duly recognized by the government, announcing that the country is in a state of war, is considered sufficient. The act of recalling a minister has alone been regarded as a hostile act, and followed by war, without any other declaration. Such cases, however, have not been frequent. Under ordinary circumstances, the recall of a minister is not an offensive act.

§ 4. In the war between the United States and Great Britain, declared in 1812, the declaration was not communicated to the British government; but the war was actually commenced on our part immediately after the act of congress containing the declaration was passed. The purposes of a declaration are answered when due notice of a state of war is given by the government to its own citizens and those of neutral nations, that they may govern themselves accordingly; and the passage of the act of congress was deemed a formal official notice to all the world.

§ 5. The government of a state acts for and in behalf of all its citizens; and its acts are binding upon all. Hence, when a war is declared, it is not merely a war between the two governments; all the subjects of the government declaring it, become enemies to all the subjects of that against which it is declared.

§ 6. The severity of the rules of ancient warfare has been greatly mitigated. On the breaking out of a war in any state, the persons of the enemy found within the state, and their property, became immediately liable to be captured. And it is still held to be the right of a state to confiscate the property of such, and to detain the persons themselves as prisoners of war. Only *movable* property is thus liable to confiscation. Houses and lands continue to be the enemy's property; the income thereof only being subject to confiscation.

§ 7. Vattel, however, and some others, maintain, that neither the subjects of an enemy who are in a country when war is declared, nor their effects, can be rightfully detained. Permitting them to enter the state, and to continue therein, is a tacit promise of protection and security of return. They are therefore allowed a reasonable time to retire with their effects. Although this mild construction of the law is supported by high authority and extensive practice, and is consistent, it would seem, with reason and common justice; the question has been settled in this country in favor of the more rigid rule.

§ 8. By decisions of our national courts, war gives the sovereign power of the nation full right to take the persons and confiscate the property of the enemy wherever they may be found. But while these decisions claimed for congress the *right* of confiscation, the confiscation could not be made without a special law of congress authorizing it. So that, without any statute applying directly to the subject, the property would continue under the protection of the law, and might be claimed by the foreign owner at the restoration of peace.

§ 9. But whatever may be the true construction of the national law on this subject, the government of every nation may grant such privileges as it thinks proper, to the subjects of an enemy. Few civilized nations, at the present day, would, it is believed, deny such persons a reasonable time to retire with their property. It is probably owing, in a great measure, to the conflicting opinions of the writers on public law, that the privilege spoken of is now so generally secured by treaty.

§ 10. When war is declared, all intercourse between the two countries at once ceases. All trade between the citizens, directly or indirectly, is strictly forbidden ; and all contracts with the enemy, made during the war, are void.

§ 11. Although a state of war makes all the subjects of one nation enemies of all those of the other, all are not allowed, at pleasure, to fall upon the enemy. They can not lawfully engage in offensive hostilities without permission of their government. If they have no written commission as evidence of such permission, and if they should be taken by the enemy, they would not be entitled to the usual mild treatment which other prisoners of war receive, but might be treated without mercy as lawless robbers and banditti.

§ 12. The object of a just war is to obtain justice by force when it can not otherwise be had. When, therefore, a nation has declared war, it has a right to use all necessary means, and no other, for attaining that end. A just war gives us the right to take the life of the enemy ; but there are limits to this right. If an enemy submits, and lays down his arms, we can not justly take his life.

§ 13. Although all the subjects of a government are to be considered enemies, justice and humanity forbid that women, children, feeble old men and sick persons, who make no resistance, should be maltreated. Prisoners of war are not to be treated with cruelty. They may be confined, and even fettered, if there is reason to apprehend that they will rise against their captors, or make their escape.

§ 14. Prisoners of war are detained to prevent their returning to join the enemy, or to obtain from their government a just satisfaction as the price of their liberty. Prisoners may be kept till the end of the war. Then, or at any time during the war, the government may exchange them for its own soldiers, taken prisoner by the enemy ; or a ransom may be required for their release. It is the duty of the government to procure, at its own expense, the release of its citizens.

§ 15. Ravaging a country, burning private dwellings, or otherwise wantonly destroying property, is not justifiable, except in cases of absolute necessity. But all fortresses, ramparts, and the like, being appropriated to the purposes of war, may be destroyed.

§ 16. How far it is right to practice stratagems and deceit to obtain advantage of an enemy, we will not undertake to decide. To some extent they are justified by the law of nations ; but in general they are dishonorable and wrong.

§ 17. Spies are sometimes sent among the enemy, to discover the state of his affairs, to pry into his designs, and carry back information. This is a dishonorable office ; and spies, if detected, are condemned to death.

§ 18. The rights of a nation in war at sea are essentially different from those in war upon land. The object of a maritime war is to destroy the commerce and navigation of the enemy, with a view of weakening his naval power. To this end, the capture or destruction of private property is necessary, and is justified by the law of nations. Hence, for purposes of attack as well as defense, every nation of considerable power or commercial importance keeps a *navy*, consisting of a number of war vessels, which are kept ready for service.

§ 19. Besides these national ships of war, there are armed vessels owned by private citizens, which are called *privateers*. Their owners receive from the government a commission to go on the seas, and to capture any vessel of the enemy, whether it is owned by the government or by private citizens, or whether it is armed or not. And to encourage privateering, the government allows the owner and crew to keep the property captured as their own.

§ 20. This right being liable to great abuse, the owners are required to give security, that the cruise shall be conducted according to instructions and the usages of war ; and that the rights of neutral nations shall not be violated ;

and that they will bring in the property captured for adjudication. When a prize is brought into a port, the captors make a writing, called *libel*, stating the facts of the capture, and praying that the property may be condemned ; and this paper is filed in the proper court.

§ 21. If it shall be made to appear that the property was taken from the enemy, the court condemns the property as *prize*, which is then sold, and the proceeds are distributed among the captors. All prizes, whether taken by a public or private armed vessel, primarily belong to the sovereign ; and no person has any interest in it except what he receives from the state : and due proof must in all cases be made before the proper court, that the seizure was lawfully made. In this country, prizes are proved and condemned in a district court, which, when sitting for this purpose, is called a prize court.

CHAPTER LXIII.

RIGHTS AND DUTIES OF NEUTRAL NATIONS ; CONTRABAND GOODS ; BLOCKADE ; RIGHT OF SEARCH ; SAFE-CONDUCTS AND PASSPORTS ; TRUCES ; TREATIES OF PEACE, &c.

§ 1. A NEUTRAL nation is bound to observe a strict impartiality toward the parties at war. If she should aid one party to the injury of the other, she would be liable to be herself treated as an enemy. A loan of money to one of the belligerent parties, or supplying him with other means of carrying on a war, if done with the view of aiding such party in the war, would be a violation of neutrality. But an engagement made in time of peace to furnish a nation a certain number of ships, or troops, or other articles of war, may afterward, in time of war, be fulfilled.

§ 2. A nation is not bound, on the occurrence of a war, to change its customary trade, and to cease supplying a belligerent with any articles of trade which such belligerent was wont to receive from her, although the goods may afford him the means of carrying on the war. This rule applies also to the loaning of money. If a nation has been accustomed to lend money to another for the sake of interest, and the latter should become engaged in a war with a third power, the neutral nation would not break her neutrality if she should continue so to lend her money. The wrong in any case lies in the *intention* of aiding one to the detriment of the other.

§ 3. Vattel, however, in laying down this rule, supposes the case of a belligerent going himself to a neutral country to make his purchases. But in the case of a neutral nation *carrying goods* to the enemy of another, he does not appear to allow the same liberty. A nation in a just war, has a right to deprive her enemy of the means of resisting or injuring her, and therefore may lawfully intercept every thing of a warlike nature which a neutral is carrying to such enemy.

§ 4. A neutral nation's being permitted to continue her commerce with belligerent nations, and at the same time to furnish them with the means of war, renders it difficult sometimes to determine how far freedom of trade is consistent with the laws of war. In determining this question, it is necessary to distinguish correctly between goods that do not subserve the purposes of war, and those that do ; for nations should enjoy full liberty to trade in the former. To attempt to stop this trade would be a violation of the rights of neutral nations.

§ 5. Articles which are particularly useful in war, are those which a neutral is not allowed to carry to an enemy. The goods thus prohibited are called *contraband goods*. What these are, it is impossible to say with precision, as some articles may in certain cases be lawfully carried, which would be justly prohibited under other circumstances. Among the articles usually contraband, are arms, ammunition, materials for ship-building, naval stores, horses, and sometimes even provisions.

§ 6. Contraband goods, when ascertained to be such, are confiscated to the captors as lawful prize. Formerly the vessel also was liable to be condemned and confiscated ; but the modern practice, it is said, exempts the ship, unless it belongs to the owner of the contraband articles, or the carrying of them is connected with aggravating circumstances.

§ 7. One of the rights of a belligerent nation, and one which a neutral is bound to regard, is the right of blockade. *Blockade* is a blocking up. A war blockade is the stationing of ships of war at the entrance of an enemy's ports, to prevent all vessels from coming out or going in. The object of a blockade is to hinder supplies of arms, ammunition, and provisions from entering, with a view to compel a surrender by hunger and want, without an attack. A neutral vessel attempting to enter or depart, becomes liable to be seized and condemned. Towns and fortresses also may be shut up by posting troops at the avenues.

§ 8. A simple decree or order declaring a certain coast or country in a state of blockade, does not constitute a lawful blockade. A force must be stationed there, competent to maintain the blockade, and to make it dangerous to enter. And it is necessary, also, that the neutral should have due notice of the blockade in order to subject his property to condemnation and forfeiture. According to modern usage, if a place is blockaded by sea only, commerce with it by a neutral may be carried on by inland communication. Also, a neutral vessel, loaded before the blockade was established, has a right to leave the port with her cargo.

§ 9. To prevent the conveyance of contraband goods, the law of nations gives a belligerent nation the *right of search*; that is, the right, in time of war, to search neutral vessels, to ascertain their character, and what articles are on board. A neutral vessel refusing to be searched by a lawful cruiser, would thereby render herself liable to condemnation as a prize. Private merchant vessels only are subject to search; the right does not extend to public ships of war.

§ 10. To prove the neutral character of a vessel, she must be furnished with the necessary documents. The papers required are, sea-letters or passports, describing the name, property, and burden of the ship; the name and residence of the commander; and certificates containing the particulars of the cargo, and place whence the ship sailed, signed by the officers of the port. In a time of universal peace, the register of the vessel has been deemed sufficient.

§ 11. The property of an enemy found on board of a neutral vessel, may be seized, if the vessel is beyond the limits of the jurisdiction of the nation to which she belongs; but the vessel is not confiscated; and the master is moreover entitled to freight for the carriage of the goods. The *property of neutrals* found in an *enemy's vessels,* is to be restored to the owners.

§ 12. A neutral is forbidden, by the law and practice of nations, to permit a belligerent to arm and equip vessels of war within her ports. And our own government has, in conformity with the law of nations, declared it to be a misdemeanor for any of our citizens to fit out any vessel within the United States, or to accept or exercise a commission, or to enlist, or hire another to enlist, to go beyond the limits of the United States, to assist any people in war against another with whom we are at peace.

§ 13. It has been observed, that, in time of peace, the people of one nation are entitled to an innocent passage over the lands and waters of another. (Chap. LX, § 3.) It is held that this right extends to troops of war. But he who desires to march his troops through a neutral country must apply to the government of the neutral nation for permission; for it rests with the sovereign authority to judge whether the passage would be innocent. Such passage can scarcely be made without damage.

§ 14. If a passage is granted to the troops of one belligerent, the other has no just ground of complaint against the neutral state. But if a neutral nation grants or refuses a passage to one of the parties at war, she ought also to grant or refuse it to the other, unless she was previously bound to the former by treaty; in which case a passage can be justly claimed under the provisions of the treaty.

§ 15. It is sometimes agreed to suspend hostilities for a time. If the agreement is only for a short period, for the purpose of burying the dead after battle, or for a parley between the hostile generals, or if it regards only some particular place, it is called a cessation or *suspension of arms.* If for a considerable time, and especially if general, it is called a *truce.* By a partial truce, hostilities are suspended in certain places, as between a town and the general besieging it; and generals have power to make such truces. By a general truce, hostilities are to cease generally, and in all places, and are made by the governments or sovereigns. Such truces afford opportunities for nations to settle their disputes by negotiation.

§ 16. A truce binds the contracting parties from the time

it is made ; but individuals of the nation are not responsible for its violation before they have had due notice of it. And for all prizes taken after the time of its commencement, the government is bound to make restitution. During the cessation of hostilities, each party may, within his own territories, continue his preparations for war, without being chargeable with a breach of good faith.

§ 17. *Safe conducts* and *passports* are written licenses insuring safety to persons in passing and repassing, or insuring a safe passage of property. The right to grant safe conducts rests in the supreme authority of a state ; but the right is either expressly delegated to subordinate officers, or they derive it from the nature of their trust. If a person suffers damage by a violation of his passport, he is entitled to indemnity from him who promised security.

§ 18. War is generally terminated, and peace secured, by treaties, called *treaties of peace.* The manner of making treaties has been described. (Chap. XL, § 5.) A treaty of peace puts an end to the war, and leaves the contracting parties no right to take up arms again for the same cause. Hence, the parties agree to preserve "perpetual peace," which, however, relates only to the war which the treaty terminates ; but does not bind either party never to make war on the other for any cause that may thereafter arise.

§ 19. The contracting parties to a treaty of peace are bound by it from the time of its conclusion, which is the day on which it is signed ; but, as in the case of a truce, persons are not held responsible for any hostile acts committed before the treaty was known ; and their government is bound to order and to enforce the restitution of property captured subsequently to the conclusion of the treaty.

§ 20. War is sometimes terminated by *mediation.* A friend to both parties, desirous of stopping the destruction of human life, kindly endeavors to reconcile the parties. The friendly sovereign who thus interposes, is called *mediator.* Many desolating wars might have been early arrested in this way, had there always been among friendly powers generally a disposition to reconcile contending nations.

PARLIAMENTARY RULES

CHAPTER LXIV.

NECESSITY OF RULES OF PROCEEDING IN DELIBERATIVE BODIES; ORGANIZATION OF AN ASSEMBLY; DUTIES OF ITS OFFICERS; RIGHTS AND DUTIES OF MEMBERS.

§ 1. It must be apparent, upon the slightest consideration, that no deliberative assembly, consisting of any considerable number of persons, can transact business with facility or dispatch, without some established rules of proceeding. Their deliberations would almost unavoidably be protracted by needless debate; action upon any subject would be liable to interruption; and perhaps the assembly, incapable of preserving order, would break up in confusion.

§ 2. Hence, it has become the universal practice of political conventions and other assemblages for deliberative purposes, to observe some rules for conducting their deliberations. These rules are in all bodies nearly the same; so far, at least as the character of different meetings will admit; and, like many other institutions in this country, have come to us from England. From their having been originally adopted and practiced by the British parliament, they are called *parliamentary rules*; and the same term is still used, whether applied to the rules of legislative bodies, or to those of meetings for other purposes.

§ 3. These rules have been adopted by all legislative assemblies in this country, with such alterations and additions only as have been found necessary to adapt them to the peculiar circumstances of each assembly. And so far as they admit of general application, they regulate the proceedings of all public meetings. As every citizen has occasion to participate in public business, and as a large portion of the citizens are at times called upon to preside at meetings of some kind, a compendium of the principal rules of parliamentary practice, will, it is believed, add essential value to this "Manual," and will not be deemed incompatible with its design.

§ 4. Before an assembly proceeds to business, it must be duly organized; that is, it must be put into a suitable form for the transaction of business. It is done thus: One of the members of the meeting requests the others to come to order. The members having become seated, he requests them to nominate (name) some person to act as chairman. This being done, he declares that such person has been nominated, and puts the question, that the person named be requested to take the chair.

§ 5. It is not unusual for the person himself who calls the meeting to order, both to nominate a candidate for the chair, and to put the question to vote. Should the question be decided in the negative, (which, however, is seldom the case,) another person is nominated and the question is taken, until a choice is made. The person chosen to serve as chairman takes the chair, and proceeds to complete the organization of the meeting, by the election of a clerk, or secretary, in the same manner, and such other officers as the assembly shall think proper to appoint.

§ 6. When large conventions are assembled, and the importance of the business to be transacted seems to require a more deliberate choice of officers, the person calling the convention to order sometimes announces, that the organization is intended to be temporary, and preparatory to a permanent organization. And after such temporary organization, a committee is appointed to make a selection of persons as permanent officers of the meeting; who are generally a president, one or more vice-presidents, and one or more secretaries.

§ 7. The business of a vice-president is to take the chair in the absence of the president from the meeting, or when he leaves the chair to take part in the proceedings as an ordinary member. When, as is often the case at large conventions, a number of supernumerary vice-presidents and secretaries are chosen, it is done chiefly to give consequence and dignity to the meeting.

§ 8. In deliberative bodies composed of delegates chosen in the several towns, counties, or districts, to represent the people of these localities, it is necessary to ascertain before proceeding to business, who have been chosen as members, that those only who are authorized may take part in the proceedings, and that a list of the members may be made for the use of the meeting and its officers. A proper time for this investigation, is before the permanent organization, if the meeting was not permanently organized in the first instance.

§ 9. Sometimes also before, or immediately after, the permanent organization, besides the committee appointed to select permanent officers, committees are also appointed to arrange and report the order of business, and to fix the times for reassembling after adjournment; to prepare resolutions, and perhaps an address, to be presented to the meeting for consideration; and for such other purposes as may be deemed necessary. These committees are thus early appointed, that there may be no unnecessary delay in proceeding to business when the convention shall have become permanently organized. Legislative bodies have standing rules for the order of business, which are adopted by each successive legislature, and seldom with any essential alteration.

§ 10. Legislative assemblies can not do business without the presence of a quorum. The number of members constituting a quorum, is fixed by the constitution or by law. As ordinary public meetings are not to consist of any definite number of persons, it can not be known what number of members constitute a quorum. Hence, the business of such meetings is generally commenced, and from time to time resumed, after waiting a reasonable time for the attendance of members, without reference to any particular number.

§ 11. The principal duties of a presiding officer, are the following: To open each sitting by taking the chair, and calling the members to order; to announce to the assembly the business in order; to receive all communications, messages, motions, and propositions, and put to vote all questions which are to be decided by the assembly, and declare the result; to enforce the rules of order, and the observance of decorum among the members. The presiding officer may read sitting, but should rise to state a motion, or put a question. In many, especially small bodies, the formality of rising is more frequently dispensed with.

§ 12. It is the duty of a clerk or secretary, to take notes

of all the acts and proceedings of the meeting; to read all papers that may be ordered to be read; to call the roll of the assembly, and record the votes when necessary; to notify committees of their appointment and of the business referred to them; and to take charge of all papers and documents belonging to the assembly.

§ 13. It is the duty of every member to treat all other members with respect and decorum. In general, whispering or speaking to each other; standing up to the interruption of others; walking across the room, and especially passing between the presiding officer and a member speaking; to enter the room, or to remove from place to place, with hats on; are all violations of the rules of decorum. But to disturb each other by hissing, intentional coughing, spitting, or otherwise, is an aggravated breach of decorum, of which no member having a proper respect for himself or the assembly, will be guilty.

§ 14. It is the right of any member, and the special duty of the presiding officer, to call the attention of the assembly to any instance of disorderly conduct. A member charged with an offense against the assembly has a right to vindicate himself from the charge, and having been heard, he is to withdraw, unless, on his offering to withdraw, the assembly allows him to remain.

§ 15. No member, when his private interests, or his conduct as a member, are involved in a question under debate, ought to be present after having been heard in exculpation; but if he should remain, he should not be allowed to vote; or, if he should vote, his vote ought to be disallowed. The laws of decency, the honor of the assembly, and the rule that no man is to be judge in his own case, alike forbid the allowance of such vote.

CHAPTER LXV.

GENERAL ORDER OR ARRANGEMENT OF BUSINESS—INTRODUCTION OF BUSINESS, BY MOTION, PETITION, &c.

§ 1. When there has been no previous arrangement of the business of an assembly, the order in which the several matters are to be taken up, is left to the discretion of the presiding officer, unless the assembly, on a question, shall decide to take up a particular subject. In legislative bodies, there is a settled order of business; and the utility of such an order is found also in other meetings, which are to last a considerable time, and which have before them numerous subjects to be acted upon.

§ 2. Such an arrangement of business is desirable, both for the government of the presiding officer, and for restraining individual members from calling up favorite measures out of their just turn. Although, in the absence of a settled order, the consent of the assembly might be required in order to give precedence to any such favorite measure, an established order is useful in directing the discretion of the assembly, when it is moved to take up a particular matter to the injury of others which have a prior right to be attended to in the general order of business.

§ 3. It may be observed, in relation to a settled order of business, that the question of its necessity, and, if necessary, whether it shall be established according to some general rule, or by special orders relating to each particular subject, is to be determined by the nature and number of the matters before the meeting.

§ 4. When a meeting has been duly organized, and is open for business, any member may offer any proposition or communication which he may choose to make, consistently with the rules of the assembly. In order to do this, he must first "obtain the floor," as it is called. This is done by rising in his place, and addressing the presiding officer by his title; as, "Mr. President," or "Mr. Chairman," as the case may require. The presiding officer, hearing himself addressed, answers the call, by speaking the name of the member, that the assembly may take notice who it is that speaks. In legislative and other bodies representing large territories, such member is announced as "the gentleman from ——," naming the town or district which he represents.

§ 5. If two or more rise to speak nearly together, the presiding officer determines who was first up, and announces him; whereupon he proceeds, unless he voluntarily sits down and gives way to the other. If the decision of the president is not satisfactory, any member may call it in question, and have the sense of the assembly taken thereon; the question being first taken upon the name of the person announced by the president.

§ 6. A member introducing a proposition of his own, whether by resolution or otherwise, puts it into the proper form, and moves that it be adopted by the assembly. A proposition thus moved, is called a *motion;* and it is so called until it has been stated by the chair, and offered to the assembly for its adoption or rejection, when it is denominated a *question;* and when it is adopted, it becomes the *resolution*, *order*, or *vote* of the assembly.

§ 7. Motions are usually submitted in writing; and the president may refuse to receive any motion that is not in writing. Motions, however, which admit of being easily and correctly recorded by the secretary are often received, though not in writing. Or the chairman himself may, if he pleases, reduce a motion to writing before it is submitted.

§ 8. It should here be observed that principal motions only come under this rule. *Occasional* or *incidental* motions, and motions *subsidiary* to, or aiding a principal motion, are not offered in writing. Of these kinds of motions, are motions to adjourn, to postpone, to lie on the table, to take the previous question, to commit a subject; that is, to refer it to a committee. But a motion to amend, when additional words are to be inserted, must, if required, be in writing. These motions will be more particularly considered hereafter. (Chap. LXVIII.)

§ 9. A motion, to be entitled to the notice of the presiding officer, must have the approval of at least one member besides the person making it; which approval is expressed by his rising and saying that he *seconds* the motion. It is generally deemed inexpedient to take up time in considering a question which none but the mover regards with favor.

§ 10. When a motion has been seconded, it is stated by the president to the meeting. It then becomes a question for the decision of the meeting; and it is then, and not before, in order for any member to speak to it, or to make any other motion for the disposal of it.

§ 11. Communications, as memorials, petitions, remonstrances, from persons not members, are presented by members, as no person but a member has a right to speak to the assembly. A member presenting a petition, should be able to state the substance of it, and also prepared to say, if questioned, that it is written in proper and respectful language.

§ 12. According to the regular form, on presenting or offering a petition, a motion to receive it must be made and seconded, and a question put, whether it shall be received. In practice, however, the formality of a vote is generally dispensed with; and if no objection to its being received is made, the president takes it for granted that there is none. The petition is then brought up to the table, read by the clerk, and disposed of by the assembly. In legislative bodies, the mass of petitions are not even read on their reception, but are referred to the committees on the subjects to which the petitions relate. Other communications than petitions from persons not members, take a similar course.

CHAPTER LXVI.

MOTIONS—FOR THE PREVIOUS QUESTION; FOR POSTPONEMENT; TO LIE ON THE TABLE; TO COMMIT.

§ 1. When a question before an assembly is deemed useless or inexpedient, or is thought to have been sufficiently discussed, any member may stop the debate by moving the *previous question;* which is, *Shall the main question be now put?* If the question is decided in the affirmative, the main question is to be put immediately, without any further debate

§ 2. But the effect of a decision in the negative, is not everywhere the same. In some legislative bodies, the decision that the main question shall *not* be now put, is regarded as a determination that it shall not be put at any time during the present sitting; leaving the debate to continue through the same, unless the question shall be sooner disposed of. In the house of representatives, a negative vote on the previous question, has the contrary effect; that of *stopping* the debate for the day.

§ 3. To understand how it has come, that a negative decision should operate to *suppress* debate on a main question, when it is the object of an affirmative vote to effect a similar result, it is necessary to refer to the original use of the previous question. It is said to have been introduced in England, in 1604. It was then, Shall the main question *be put?* and a determination in the negative suppressed the main question for the whole session; for, if it could not be put at all, there was no use in continuing the discussion.

§ 4. But the previous question was afterward altered to its present form: Shall the main question be *now* put? and a decision in the negative, namely, that it shall not be now put, is to decide that it shall not be put that day. Hence, as the main question can not be put that day, or at the present sitting, the debate must be suspended during the same time.

§ 5. In the assembly of New York, and perhaps in some other legislative bodies, if the previous question is negatived; that is, if the main question can not be now put, the main question remains under debate. If the previous question is ordered, and if there are any pending amendments which have been adopted in committee of the whole, and not acted on in the house, the question is taken upon such amendments in their order, and without further debate or amendment, before the main question is put. In other bodies, all pending amendments are cut off and lost by taking the main question.

§ 6. In England, the object of the mover of the previous question, is to obtain a *negative* decision; because, although the effect would be, strictly, and according to its original intention, to suppress the main question for the day, it has, by parliamentary usage, come to be a disposal of the main question altogether, *without a vote* upon it; whereas, in this country, the object of the mover of the previous question, is to get a vote in the *affirmative*, with the view, *not* of suppressing the main question entirely, but of suppressing debate, either altogether, as in some assemblies, or, as in others, for the present time only. The effect of an affirmative decision is the same in both countries, namely, the putting of the main question immediately.

§ 7. When it is desired to suppress a main question for the whole session without having it come to a vote, the preferable course is, to move that the question be *postponed indefinitely;* which is a postponement without fixing a day for resuming the consideration of the question. This quashes the proposition for that session.

§ 8. When a question is before an assembly, which is deemed proper to be acted upon, but on which members are not prepared to act, either from want of information, or because something more pressing claims present attention, a motion is made to *postpone* the subject to some future day within the session ; or, if it is not thought proper to fix upon a day certain, the proper motion is, that the matter *lie on the table.* It may then be called up at any time when it is convenient to consider it. Such motion is sometimes intended to make a final disposal of a subject ; as such will be the effect, if it should not afterward be called up.

§ 9. If a proposition is so imperfect in its form as to need more amendment than can be conveniently made by the assembly, a motion is made to *commit* it ; that is, to refer it to a committee for amendment ; which committee may be the standing committee having similar subjects in charge, or a select committee appointed for this special purpose.

§ 10. But if the proposition is well digested, and seems to need but few and simple amendments, and especially if these are of leading consequence, the assembly itself proceeds to consider and amend the proposition. The modes of amendment are so various, and the different motions to amend so numerous, as to require a separate chapter for their consideration.

CHAPTER LXVII.

AMENDMENTS; DIVISION OF A QUESTION, AND ITS MODIFICATION; DIFFERENT MOTIONS TO AMEND; FILLING BLANKS; ORDER OF PROCEEDING IN CONSIDERING AND AMENDING PAPERS.

§ 1. When a proposition or a question contains more parts than one, it may, by consent of the assembly, be divided into two or more questions. So also, if there are several names in a proposition, they may be divided, and put one by one.

§ 2. The mover of a proposition is sometimes allowed to *modify* it, after it has been stated as a question by the presiding officer. And sometimes, after an amendment has been moved and seconded, the mover of the original proposition consents to the amendment, and it is accordingly made. But if objected to, such modification and amendment can only be made by permission of the assembly, by a motion and vote. Nor may the mover of a proposition, after it has been stated as a question, withdraw it, without similar leave.

§ 3. One way of amending a proposition, is by *striking out* certain words, or a paragraph. Before a question is put on a proposed amendment by striking out, those desiring to retain the paragraph, should amend it, if it needs amendment, before the vote on striking out is taken; as it can not be restored, if struck out, nor amended, if retained.

§ 4. When it is proposed to amend by *inserting* or *adding* a paragraph, or a part of one, its friends should make it as acceptable as they can, by amendments, before the question is put for inserting; as it can not be amended by inserting the same words afterward. If, however, the same words are connected with others, so as to make a different proposition, a motion to insert the same words is in order.

§ 5. When it is moved to amend by striking out or inserting certain words, or a paragraph, the manner of stating the question is, first, to read the whole passage to be amended as it stands; then the words proposed to be struck out or inserted; and lastly the passage as it will be when amended.

§ 6. Another form of amending a proposition is, to *strike out* certain words *and insert* others in their place. The manner of stating a question of this kind, is, first, to read the passage as it stands at present; then the words to be struck out; next those to be inserted; and lastly, the passage as it will stand if amended. If desired, the question may then be divided by a vote of the assembly: if divided, the question is first taken on striking out; and, if carried, it is next put on inserting the words proposed. If that question is lost, it may be moved to insert others.

§ 7. If a motion to amend by striking out and inserting, is put, undivided, and decided in the negative, the same motion can not be made again; but it may be moved to strike out the same words, and insert others of a tenor different from those first proposed. If this motion is negatived, it may be moved to strike out the same words, and insert nothing. Motions may, in various other ways, be made to amend by striking out or inserting words formerly proposed to be struck out or inserted, or a part of them; provided they are so connected with others not before proposed, as to make a different proposition.

§ 8. If a motion to strike out and insert is decided in the affirmative, it can not be moved, either to insert the words struck out, or a part of them, or to strike out those inserted, or a part of them; but the words struck out, or a part of them, may be inserted with others; and the words inserted, or a part of them, may be struck out with others.

§ 9. A proposed amendment may itself be amended; but a motion to amend an amendment to an amendment of a main question, is not admitted. Such an accumulation, or piling of questions, would embarrass the action of an assembly. The same result must be sought by deciding against the amendment of the amendment in the form proposed, and then moving it again as it is wished to be amended. In this form it becomes only an amendment of an amendment. A person desiring to amend an amendment should give notice, that, if rejected in its present form, he will move it again in the form in which he wishes it adopted; in which case, those who prefer the latter may join in rejecting the former.

§ 10. Propositions are sometimes introduced with blanks, purposely left by the mover, to be filled with times and numbers by the assembly. The matter to be inserted, however, is not properly considered as an amendment to a question, but rather as an original motion, to be decided before the principal question. Motions may be made to fill blanks, and the question put on each before another is made. But the usual and better mode is, to have several propositions first made, and then take the question on them in regular order.

§ 11. In filling blanks, it is not the rule in all assemblies, as some suppose, that the largest sum or number, and longest time, are always to be first put to the question ; although such is probably the general rule. A better rule is said to be this : In all cases of time or number, if the *larger* comprehends the *lesser*, we must begin with the greatest, and go down until an affirmative vote is obtained. But if the lesser includes the greater, the question must be first put on the least, and go up until a vote is reached.

§ 12. But it is not, in all cases, easy to determine, whether the larger includes the lesser, or the lesser the greater ; as will appear from the fact, that Mr. Jefferson, in his Manual, mentions, among others, as belonging to the former class, the question, to what day a postponement shall be ; and to the latter, the question, on what day the session shall be closed by adjournment. Another author assigns to the former class, the amount of a fine ; and to the latter, the amount of a tax. In these and other cases mentioned, the distinction might not, at first thought, appear to every presiding officer.

§ 13. Therefore, in explanation of this rule, it is said, that the object is, not to begin at that extreme number or time, which, and more, being within every man's wish, none can vote against it ; and yet, if it should be carried in the affirmative, every question for more would be precluded ; but at that extreme which will unite few, and then to advance or recede, until a number or time is reached that will unite a majority.

§ 14. To illustrate : Take the question of postponement, (§ 12,) and suppose three days named to fill a blank, the first, tenth, and twentieth of any month. Here the greater includes the lesser ; because, if the time of postponement extends to the furthest day named, it of course extends to or beyond the earliest ; or, the earliest or a later day is within every man's wish. But if the above named days were proposed as days on which to adjourn, the lesser would include the greater ; for, if the assembly adjourns on the first day of the month, it will of course be adjourned on the twentieth : and as all wish for the adjournment as early as the twentieth, or earlier, the beginning should be at the other extreme. But the difficulty of applying this rule in many cases, is perhaps a reason why it is the general rule to take the question first on the largest number and longest time.

§ 15. The natural order in considering and amending any paper containing several distinct propositions, is to begin at the beginning, and proceed through it by paragraphs ; and it is not in order to go back and amend any former part. This, however, is sometimes allowed, especially in small bodies, where a strict adherence to the rule is less necessary.

§ 16. To the above rule there is an exception. In the case of a resolution, or series of resolutions, or other paper, having a preamble or title, the preamble or title is postponed until the other parts are gone through with. Also the title of a bill in a legislative body is so postponed. The reason is, that such alterations may be made in the body of the bill, as shall require an alteration of the title.

§ 17. In considering a paper consisting of several paragraphs, as a bill, resolutions, draft of an address, &c., the whole paper is to be read, first by the clerk, and then by the presiding officer, by paragraphs, pausing at the end of each, and putting questions for amending, if amendments are proposed ; and when the whole paper has been gone through with, the question is taken on agreeing to or adopting the whole paper, as amended, or unamended.

§ 18. In considering a paper which has been referred to a committee, and reported back to the assembly, the amendments only are read, in course, by the clerk. The presiding officer then reads the first, and puts it to the question, and so on, until all are adopted or rejected, before any other amendment is admitted, except an amendment to an amendment. When the amendments reported by the committe have been disposed of, the presiding officer pauses for amendments to be proposed to the body of the paper. So also he pauses for this purpose if the paper was reported without amendments, putting no questions but on amendments proposed. Having gone through the whole, he puts the question on agreeing to or adopting the paper, as the resolution or order of the assembly.

CHAPTER LXVIII.

ORDER OR PRIORITY OF QUESTIONS; PRIVILEGED QUESTIONS; SUBSIDIARY AND INCIDENTAL PRIVILEGED QUESTIONS.

§ 1. It is a general rule, that the question first moved and seconded, shall be first put. But this rule gives way to what are called *privileged questions;* and these privileged questions again have priority among themselves.

§ 2. A motion to adjourn takes place of all others. But this motion can not be received after another question is put, and the assembly is engaged in voting. Nor, after a motion to adjourn is negatived, can the motion be renewed, until some other proceeding has taken place.

§ 3. Orders of the day take the place of all other questions, except for adjournment, and the incidental question, the question of privilege. (§ 15.) Orders of the day are subjects which have, by an order of the assembly, been assigned for a particular day. Hence, when the day fixed for the consideration of these subjects arrives, they are privileged questions for that day. But a motion for the orders of the day, to give it precedence, must be for the orders generally, if there is more than one, and not for any particular one; and, if carried, they must be read and gone through with, in the order in which they stand, unless some particular subject is taken up out of its regular order, by a special vote.

§ 4. Another class of privileged questions, are those which

are secondary to the principal question ; and as they are used to assist in disposing of a principal question or motion, they are sometimes called *subsidiary questions.* Subsidiary motions, are motions for the previous question, to lay on the table, to postpone, either indefinitely or to a day certain, to commit, and to amend.

§ 5. The nature and use of these motions, and their operations as applied to a main question, have been explained. We will here speak briefly of their different degrees, the privileges which they have among themselves, and of their effect upon each other.

§ 6. It is a general rule, that subsidiary or secondary questions can not be used to dispose of or to suppress one another ; the common principle, "first moved, first put," applies to them. If, for example, a motion has been made to postpone, commit, or amend a main question, it can not be moved to suppress that motion by the previous question. Or, if there is a motion for the previous question, or for the commitment or amendment of a main question, it can not be moved to postpone the motion for the previous question, or for the commitment or amendment of the main question.

§ 7. There are several reasons for this rule. It would be a piling of questions on one another, which, to avoid embarrassment, is not allowed. Besides, it is useless, as the same result may be had more simply, by voting against the motion itself, which is sought to be disposed of by another secondary motion.

§ 8. To this rule, however, there are exceptions. A motion *to amend* may be applied to a motion to postpone, to commit, or to amend, a principal motion. The reason why the secondary motion to amend has a privilege which is not given to other secondary and privileged motions, is its useful character. It is not used to dispose of or suppress, but to carry out and improve the motion to which it is applied. But it can not be applied to motions for the previous question, and to lie on the table, for the reason that these motions, being already as simple as they can be, do not admit of any change or amendment. There are a few other exceptions. (§ 14, 15.)

§ 9. A motion to lie on the table takes precedence of and supersedes the other subsidiary motions ; namely, for the previous question, to postpone, to commit, and to amend; and if carried, removes the principal motion, and all the other subsidiary and incidental motions connected with it, from before the assembly, until it is again taken up.

§ 10. The previous question is of the same degree with all other subsidiary questions, except that of lying on the table, and, consequently, if first moved, can not be superseded by a motion to postpone, commit, or amend; and if moved first and put, the others can not be made at all; for, if the previous question is decided in the affirmative, the main question must be immediately put; and it would not be in order to postpone, commit, or amend; if negatived, that is, if the main question is not to be now put, it is taken out of the possession of the assembly for the day; so that there is nothing to postpone, commit, or amend; (except in assemblies, where the negativing of the previous questions has a different effect.)

§ 11. The motion to postpone is of the same degree as the motions for the previous question, to commit, and to amend; and, if first made, can not be superseded by them. A motion to postpone indefinitely may be amended so as to make it to a day certain; and a motion to postpone to a certain day, may be amended so as to make the postponement indefinite, or to a different day certain.

§ 12. A decision to postpone a proposition, leaves no ground for any other subsidiary motion; but if it is decided not to postpone, a motion for the previous question, or to commit, or to amend may be applied.

§ 13. A motion to amend stands in the same degree with the previous question, and indefinite postponement; but it gives way to a motion to postpone to a day certain, and without a violation of the rule before mentioned, (§ 9,) that these subsidiary motions may not suppress one another. The reason is, that the postponement to a day certain is not a suppression of a question, but leaves it before the assembly, to be resumed at the time to which it is adjourned.

§ 14. A motion to amend gives way also to a motion to commit; for the reason that the latter, instead of suppressing, aids and facilities the former.

§ 15. There is another class of privileged questions, which, arising out of other questions, are called *incidental questions*, and must be put before the questions out of which they arise. They are questions of order, questions of privilege, questions incident to the reading of papers, questions for the suspension of a rule, on the withdrawal of a motion, and amendment of amendments. The two last have been considered. (Chap. LXVII, § 2.)

§ 16. It is the duty of a presiding officer to enforce the rules and orders of the assembly; and it is the right of every member taking notice of the breach of a rule, to insist upon its enforcement. If a question arises as to the fact of there being a violation of a rule, it is called a *question of order;* and the subject out of which it arises, must give way until the incidental question of order is disposed of.

§ 17. A question of order is first decided by the chairman, without debate or delay. If the decision is not satisfactory, any member may *appeal* from that decision, and have the question decided by the assembly. The question is then stated by the chairman: Shall the decision of the chair stand as the decision of the assembly? It is then debated and decided as other questions; and the chairman himself may take a part in the debate, at least so far as to state the reasons for his decision.

§ 18. A *question of privilege* is one that concerns the rights and privileges of an assembly and of its individual members; as when a quarrel arises between two members; or when some other disturbance takes place to interrupt the business of the assembly. When a question of privilege arises, it supersedes, for the time, all others, except questions of adjournment, and must be first disposed of.

§ 19. When papers are laid before an assembly, every member has a right to have them once read. When the reading is called for, the presiding officer directs it to be done by the clerk. If the reading is objected to, it must be put to the question. But a member has not the right to read, or to have read; any paper or document, having no relation to a question under consideration, without the consent of the house. This would consume too much time.

§ 20. Formerly, it was the practice in legislative bodies, on referring papers to committees, to have them first read; but of late, any part of a paper is seldom read, except the title, unless the reading is insisted on by a member. If a question arises on its reading, this question has the privilege of being first decided.

§ 21. If action upon a subject can not be had, by reason of some special rule prohibiting it, a motion may be made to dispense with, or *suspend the rule*, in order to permit the action desired: and the motion to suspend must be first decided. The rules of legislative bodies usually require the consent of a greater number than a bare majority for the suspension of a rule. Where no rule exists, it is presumed general consent is necessary.

CHAPTER LXIX.

COMMITTEES—THEIR APPOINTMENT AND REPORT; COMMITTEE OF THE WHOLE.

§ 1. The nature and general duties of committees in all deliberative assemblies are similar to those of legislative committees, which have been briefly described. (Chap. XV.) The number of members constituting the several standing committees of legislative bodies generally, is permanently fixed, either by usage, or by an express rule. The number of a select committee is determined at the time of its appointment. Such is usually the case in ordinary assemblies, in the appointment of all committees.

§ 2. In fixing upon the number of a committee, different numbers are sometimes proposed by different members, which are separately put to the question, beginning with the highest. Sometimes the person moving the appointment of a committee, includes the number in his motion; and a different number may be moved as an amendment of the motion.

§ 3. The mode of selecting the members, is either by appointment by the presiding officer, by ballot, or by nomination and vote of the meeting. In legislative assemblies, and others sitting for a considerable time, it is usually provided by a standing rule, that, unless specially ordered otherwise, all committees shall be named by the chair.

§ 4. In appointing a committee to which a subject is to be referred, the committee ought to be so constituted that a majority of its members shall be favorable to the proposed measure; the mover and seconder being usually of course appointed. The object of referring or committing a bill or other paper, is to make it acceptable to the assembly; but a committee opposed to it would totally destroy it. And when a member who is against a measure, hears himself named as one of the committee, he ought to ask to be excused. Persons, however, who take exceptions to some particulars in the bill, or other paper, may, and perhaps ought, to constitute at least a part of the committee.

§ 5. The members of a committee have the right to appoint their chairman; but as a matter of courtesy, the person first named on a committee is usually permitted to act as chairman, who presides over it, and reports its proceedings to the assembly.

§ 6. The order in which committees are to consider and amend papers referred to them, is substantially the same as that practiced by the assembly. (Chap. LXVII.) It is, however, less strictly observed; nor, indeed, does the same strictness in committee seem to be necessary.

§ 7. When a paper is referred to a committee, they may not erase, interline, or disfigure it; but they must, in a separate paper, set down the amendments they have agreed to report, stating the words to be inserted or omitted, and where, by reference to the paragraph, line, and word. Or, if the amendments are numerous, they may be reported in the form of a new draft.

§ 8. When a committee have agreed on a report, it is moved by some member, and voted, that the chairman, or some other member, make their report to the assembly.

§ 9. In making a report, the chairman of the committee, standing in his place, informs the house, that the committee to whom was referred such a bill, or subject, have according to order, had the same under consideration, and have directed him to report the same without amendment, or with sundry amendments, (as the case may be,) which he is ready to do when it shall please the house to receive it; and he or any other member may then move that the report be now received.

§ 10. If, however, no objection is made, the report is received without the formality of a motion and vote. So also the reading of a report by the chairman, and again by the clerk, as required by the rule, is usually dispensed with, until it is taken up for consideration. The printing of reports in legislative bodies, generally renders the reading unnecessary.

§ 11. When the report of a committee is received, the committee is dissolved, and can act no more without a new power. But it may be revived, and the same matter recommitted to them ; which, however, is not done, except in important cases, and for special reasons. If a report is not received, the committee is not discharged, but may be ordered to sit again. The first part of this section applies only to committees in ordinary public meetings, and to legislative *select* committees. Standing committees in a legislature continue during the session, and are not subject to be dissolved and revived.

§ 12. The report of a committee, when taken up for consideration, may be amended, and otherwise acted on, as other propositions. And when it is to be disposed of by a final vote, the question is stated to be on its adoption ; and, if adopted, the whole report becomes the statement, resolution, or act of the assembly. It is the practice, at least to some extent, in ordinary public meetings and conventions, on receiving a committee's report, and before it is taken up for consideration, to take the question on its acceptance, as a formal discharge of the committee.

§ 13. All legislative bodies sometimes act as a *committee of the whole ;* and while sitting as such they are not called by their usual name, as the senate, or the house, but are addressed or spoken of as *the committee.* And the presiding officer is not called speaker or president, but chairman. (Chapter XV, § 9.) Ordinary meetings or conventions do not at any time assume the name of committee of the whole ; nor do they, in form, resolve themselves into such committee ; yet, in many of their proceedings, they are allowed the same freedom as is usually enjoyed by a legislative committee of the whole.

§ 14. The form of going from the house into committee of the whole, is for the presiding officer, on motion made and seconded, to put the question, that the house, or the senate, do now resolve itself into a committee of the whole, to take under consideration such a matter, naming it. If the question is determined in the affirmative, he leaves the chair, naming some member to act as chairman, and takes a seat elsewhere ; and the person appointed chairman, takes his seat at the clerk's table. In some legislative bodies, he takes the chair of the presiding officer.

§ 15. Matters of great concern are usually referred to a committee of the whole house. In committee of the whole, the executive message is discussed, and the several subjects embraced in it are arranged and prepared to be referred to the appropriate standing committees, and to select committees, if any need to be appointed. Important bills reported to the house, are also referred to such committee to be considered and amended before they are finally disposed of by the house. One object of instituting a committee of the whole, is to afford greater freedom of discussion. The sense of the whole can be better taken in committee, where every one speaks as often as he pleases, provided he can obtain the floor.

§ 16. A committee of the whole can not adjourn as others may ; therefore, if their business is unfinished at a sitting, some member moves that the committee rise, report progress, and ask leave to sit again. If the motion prevails, the chairman rises, and the presiding officer resumes the chair ; and the chairman of the committee then informs him, that the committee of the whole have, according to order, had under their consideration such a matter, and have made some progress therein ; but not having time to go through with the same, have directed their chairman to ask leave to sit again. Whereupon the question is put on their having leave, and sometimes also on the time when the house will again resolve itself into a committee.

§ 17. No previous question can be put in a committee of the whole ; if, therefore, it is desired to stop or prevent debate, a motion may be made that the committee rise.

§ 18. If a committee of the whole have gone through with the matter referred to them, a member moves that the committee rise, and that the chairman report their proceedings to the house ; which being resolved, the chairman rises, the presiding officer resumes the chair, the chairman informs him that the committee have gone through with the business referred to them, and state what has been done by the committee. The question is then taken on agreeing to the report of the committee, unless postponed or laid on the table by a vote of the house.

CHAPTER LXX.

ORDER IN DEBATE.

§ 1. When the presiding officer is in the chair, every member is to be seated. The person occupying the chair, may not speak on the question in debate; but he may speak to matters of order, and be first heard; and he may, by leave of the assembly, state matters of fact for their information. He may also address the assembly when his decision on a question of order is appealed from. And when he rises to speak, any member standing ought to sit down; but a presiding officer may not interrupt a member who has the floor.

§ 2. When a person means to speak, he must stand in his place, and address the chairman. The manner of obtaining the floor, has been described. (Chap. LXV, § 4, 5.) A person speaking, should not mention a member present by his name, but describe him as him who last spoke, or on the other side of the question, or in some other way; or, as is common in legislative bodies, to designate another, as the gentleman from ——, naming the town, county, or district which he represents.

§ 3. If a member, before he has concluded his speech, gives up the floor for any purpose, he loses his right to it, even though it is yielded on condition that he shall have it again, or though it was given up to another only for an explanation. As a matter of favor, however, the person yielding the floor, is usually permitted to resume it.

§ 4. A person is not to use indecent language against the proceedings, or reflect upon any prior act or determination of the assembly, unless he means to conclude with a motion to rescind such determination. But reflections upon a proposition while under consideration, though it has even been reported by a committee, are no reflections on the assembly.

§ 5. No member may digress from his subject, and fall upon another member, and speak reviling or unmanly words of or to him. He may reprobate the nature or consequences of a measure in strong terms; but to arraign the motives of those who propose or advocate it, is a personality, and against order.

§ 6. A person speaking must confine himself to the question, and not speak impertinently, or beside the subject. So closely is this rule to be observed, that if at any time a secondary or an incidental question arises, as on an amendment, or a postponement, the person speaking must confine his remarks to the particular question then before the assembly, and not speak to the main question.

§ 7. When a member speaks irrelevantly, or beside the question, he may be interrupted by the chairman, or called to order by a member; and the question may be made, whether he shall be allowed to proceed in the manner in which he was speaking when interrupted. If no question is made, or if one is made and decided in the negative, he is still to be allowed to proceed in order; that is, keeping to the particular subject before the assembly.

§ 8. No member may, without the general consent of the assembly, speak more than once to the same question, until all who desire to speak have spoken. He may then speak a second time by leave of the assembly. This is the general rule, and is to be observed where no special rule provides otherwise. But those who have spoken on the main question, may speak again on secondary or incidental questions arising in the course of debate. And if a subject upon which a member has spoken is referred to a committee, he may speak again on the question presented by the report of the committee. In meetings other than legislative assemblies, greater freedom is allowed.

§ 9. A member may also be permitted to speak a second time to clear a matter of fact; or merely to explain himself in some material part of his speech, or to the orders of the assembly; keeping himself to that matter only. But he can not interrupt another who is speaking, in order to make the explanation.

§ 10. No member is to disturb another in his speech, by hissing, coughing, speaking, or whispering; nor by passing between the member speaking and the chair, or by walking across the room; nor by any other disorderly behavior. But if a member finds that the assembly are not inclined to hear him, and that by conversation or any other noise they endeavor to drown his voice, it is the most prudent way to submit to the pleasure of the house, and to sit down; for it seldom happens, that members are guilty of this piece of ill manners without some reason; or that they are so inattentive to one who says anything worth their hearing.

§ 11. If repeated calls do not produce order, the chairman may call by his name any member obstinately persisting in irregularity; whereupon the assembly may require him to withdraw. He is then to be heard in exculpation, and to withdraw. Then the chairman states the offense committed, and the assembly considers the kind and degree of punishment to be inflicted.

§ 12. If a member uses disorderly, offensive, or insulting words, he is interrupted by another member or by several members rising and calling him to order. The member complaining of the words and desiring them to be taken down by the clerk, must repeat them; and the chairman may then direct the clerk to take them down in his minutes. But if he thinks them not disorderly, he delays the direction. If the call becomes pretty general, he orders the clerk to take them down as stated by the objecting member. They are then part of his minutes, and, when read to the offending member, he may deny that they were his words, and the assembly must then decide by a question whether they were his words or not: and the words, as written down, may be amended so as to conform to what the assembly thinks them to be.

§ 13. Then the member may either justify the words, or explain the sense in which he used them, or apologize. If the assembly is satisfied, no farther proceeding is necessary But if two members still insist on taking the sense of the assembly, the member must withdraw before that question is stated, and then the sense of the assembly is to be taken If the offending member is allowed to conclude his speech, and any other member speaks, or other business intervenes, after offensive words are spoken, they can not be taken notice of for censure. This is for the common security of all, and to prevent mistakes, which are likely to happen, if words are not taken down immediately.

CHAPTER LXXI.

TAKING THE QUESTION; MANNER OF VOTING; RECONSIDERATION.

§ 1. When the debate upon a question is ended, and the final vote is to be taken, the presiding officer states the question, and puts it, always first in the affirmative, in words differing slightly in form in different bodies; but substantially as follows; *Gentlemen, all of you who are in favor of*—repeating, as nearly as may be, the words of the question—*say aye;* and after the answer of ayes, *All those who are opposed, say no.*

§ 2. The presiding officer then, judging by the sound which voice is the greater, declares to the assembly that *the ayes have it,* or the *noes have it,* as the case may be; or, as in some assemblies, *it is carried,* or, *it is lost.* If he is doubtful as to the majority, he may put the question a second time before declaring the result. If he is still unable to decide, or, having decided, if any member is not satisfied with the decision, the presiding officer directs the assembly to divide, that the members on each side may be counted.

§ 3. In some places, the members vote by holding up their right hands. Such is said to be still the practice in legislative bodies in the New England states.

§ 4. The most convenient mode of dividing a house, is to direct the members to rise, first those in the affirmative, and then those in the negative, and be counted. Every member present when the question is stated, is, according to the general rule, required to vote; and, on the other hand, none can vote who was not then in the room.

§ 5. Another form of taking the question, is by taking the *yeas* and *nays.* This mode is practiced in legislative bodies in this country. The form of stating a question to be thus taken, is, *All who are in favor of,* &c., *will, when their names are called, answer in the affirmative;* and, *All those who are opposed, will, when their names are called, answer in the negative.* The roll is then called in alphabetical order, by the clerk, who notes the answer of each member, yes or no. The yeas and nays are then counted, and the result is declared.

§ 6. Except on the final passage of a bill, questions generally are not taken in this manner, unless called for by members, who, for certain reasons, desire to have the yeas and nays entered on the journal. The constitution of the state declares what number of members shall request the yeas and nays, in order to require them to be taken. The constitutions of some states, require the yeas and nays on the final passage of all bills and resolutions.

§ 7. According to the strict rule of parliament, a question once put and decided, can not be brought up again at the same session, but must stand as the judgment of the house. This rule prevails in this country also, but with a modification which has often been found useful in relieving an assembly from great inconvenience and difficulty otherwise unavoidable.

§ 8. When a question has been decided in the affirmative or negative, it is in order to move that the vote be *reconsidered.* If such motion prevails, the matter is restored to the state in which it stood before the vote reconsidered was taken. In many legislative bodies, there is a special rule, providing that a motion to reconsider may be made only on the same or the next day, and by a member who voted with the majority. But this rule, like other special rules, is binding only where it has been expressly adopted.

SUPPLEMENTARY NOTES.

*** The following Notes are supplementary to the Chapters and Sections of the same numbers in the body of the work.

CHAPTER XXVI.

§ 6. Persons only who are householders are entitled to the benefits of the homestead exemption. The laws of different states, though not uniform in every particular, generally secure to the head of a family, and after his decease, to his wife and children, a lot of land and buildings thereon, not exceeding a certain amount in value, to be occupied as a residence or homestead. The following named states have enacted laws of this kind, exempting from execution such property to the amount of the sums annexed to the names of the states respectively :

Maine, $500 ; New Hampshire, $500 ; Vermont, $500 ; Massachusetts, $800 ; New York, $1,000 ; New Jersey, $500 ; South Carolina, $500 ; Florida, a farm of 40 acres, of which ten are cultivated ; land and improvements not to exceed in value $200 ; Alabama, homestead with 40 acres of land, not exceeding in value $500 ; Mississippi, 160 acres and buildings, not in any city, town, or village ; or, in a city, town, or village, land worth $1500 exclusive of buildings and improvements ; Texas, 200 acres not in a town or city, or any town or city lots to the value of $2,000 ; Arkansas, 160 acres, or one town or city lot ; Tennessee, homestead, $500 ; Ohio, $500 ; Michigan, 40 acres, not within a town-plat, city, or village, or a lot in a town, city, or village, $1,500 ; Indiana, real or personal property, or both, $300 ; Illinois, lot and buildings, $1,000 ; Iowa, farm of 40 acres, the buildings not to be in a city, town, or village ; or one-fourth of an acre in a town, city, or village ; Wisconsin, same as Iowa ; Minnesota, $1,000 ; California, $5,000.

In Georgia, it was enacted, that, on contracts made after May, 1, 1842, 20 acres, and for each child under fifteen years, five acres additional, were exempted ; provided no part of it was the site of a city, town, village, mill or factory ; the 20 acres to include the dwelling-house and improvements of the original tract ; the value of the house and improvements not to exceed in value $200—the same being extended to cities, towns, and villages. By a later act, 50 acres were exempted on contracts made after January 1, 1844 ; the land being liable, however, for the purchase money, which is probably the case in all the states.

CHAPTER XXXVI.

§ 6. The necessity of giving to congress complete and exclusive power at the seat of government, is shown by a certain occurrence near the close of the revolutionary war, which probably suggested the incorporation of this provision in the constitution. At the time alluded to, the old congress, then sitting at Philadelphia, was surrounded and insulted by a small body of mutineers of the continental army. The executive authority of Pennsylvania, (then vested in a council of thirteen members,) wanting the requisite energy and courage, failed to afford protection ; and congress removed to Princeton, in the state of New Jersey. After having remained there for some time undisturbed, they adjourned, for the sake of greater convenience, to Annapolis, in Maryland. It is hence evident, that the members of the general government ought not to be dependent upon a state for protection in the discharge of their duties.

The establishment of a permanent seat of government, after the treaty of peace with Great Britain, received the early attention of congress. In October, 1783, it was resolved, that buildings for the use of congress should be erected on the banks of the Delaware. A few days later it was resolved, that buildings for a similar purpose should be erected on the Potomac, with the view of reconciling the conflicting wishes of the northern and southern states, by establishing two seats of government. In December, 1784, it was further resolved, that a district should be purchased on the banks of the Delaware for a federal town ; and that contracts should be made for erecting a house for the use of congress and the executive officers, and suitable buildings for the residence of the president and the secretaries of the several departments. But the appropriation of the necessary funds for these purposes, requiring the assent of nine states, was prevented by the southern interest. In 1790, a compromise was made, by which the friends of Philadelphia, in consideration of having the seat of government at that city during ten years, the time estimated to be necessary to erect the public buildings, agreed that the seat of government should be permanently fixed on the Potomac.

CHAPTER XLI.

§ 6. By more recent acts of congress, the bounty of the government has been largely extended. In 1850, a "military bounty land bill" was passed, granting lands to the surviving soldiers, and to the widows or minor children of deceased soldiers, who served in the war of 1812, or in any of the Indian wars since 1790, and to the commissioned officers who served in the late war with Mexico, as follows: To those who engaged for twelve months, or during the war, and actually served nine months, 160 acres; to those who engaged for six months and served four months, 80 acres; and to those who served one month, 40 acres. Those honorably discharged in consequence of disability in the service before the expiration of their period of service, were to receive the same as if they had served out their terms. In 1852, the benefits of the act of 1850 were extended to state troops whose service had been paid for by the United States subsequent to the 18th of June, 1812; and by the act of 1855, persons having served in the navy were included; moreover, all who had served for any period, in the militia or the navy, were to be allowed 160 acres; and those who had received, under former acts, a less quantity, were to receive in addition enough to make, in the whole, 160 acres. Wagon-masters and teamsters employed by competent authority, were entitled to the same compensation.

§ 10. Postmasters whose commissions amount to $1,000 or more a year, are appointed by the president, by consent of the senate. The number of post-offices in the United States and territories, is about 30,000. From the report of the postmaster-general in 1857, it appears that the aggregate length of mail routes was 242,600 miles ; that the mails were transported 74,906,067 miles, at a cost of $6,622,046. The gross revenue from all sources, including receipts from letter carriers and foreign postages, together with $700,000 paid by the government for the transportation and delivery of matter franked by public officers, $8,053,951. The compensation to postmasters, $2,285,609 ; transportation, including foreign mails, $7,239,333 ; together with other expenses, make the total expenditures, $11,508,058.

§ 12. The transportation of the matter franked by the officers of the government, is paid for out of the public treasury, and the amount is included in the receipts of the post-office department.

The present rates of inland postage are, on every letter or package, not exceeding half an ounce in weight, sent not more than 3,000 miles, *three cents ;* over 3,000 miles, *ten cents.* Each additional half ounce, or fraction of half an ounce, is charged with an additional single postage. No letters sent unless the postage is prepaid. Drop letters, one cent each. On newspapers, periodicals, unsealed circulars, or other article of printed matter, sent to any part of the United States, weighing not over three ounces, *one cent ;* and one cent for each additional ounce.

Newspapers and periodicals, weighing not more than one ounce and a half, and not sent out of the state where published, are charged *half a cent.*

Small newspapers published monthly or oftener, and pamphlets containing not more than sixteen octavo pages, sent in single packages, to one address, and prepaid by postage stamps, when weighing at least eight ounces, *four cents*, and for each additional ounce, half a cent.

Books, bound or unbound, weighing not over four pounds, any distance not over 3,000 miles, prepaid, *one cent* for each ounce ; over 3,000, *two cents* an ounce. If not paid in advance, fifty per cent. additional is charged.

Weekly newspapers only, sent to subscribers within the county, *free.*

Newspapers and periodicals sent from the office of publication to actual subscribers, and paid quarterly in advance, are charged *one-half* the above rates. Quarterly payments in advance may be made either at the mailing office or at the office of delivery.

Transient matter, if not prepaid at the mailing office, is charged double the above rates.

Small newspapers, &c., when sent in packages of less than eight ounces, are rated singly.

All printed matter in covers or wrappers, must be open at the ends or sides, so that its character may be determined without opening the same.

Publishers of newspapers and periodicals may send to each other one copy of their respective publications, free of postage. Postmasters are not entitled to receive newspapers free of postage under their franking privilege.

The commissions of postmasters on the moneys received for postage, are as follows: On the first $100, sixty per cent.; on the next $300, fifty per cent.; on the next $2000, forty per cent.; on all over $2,400, fifteen per cent. On newspaper postages, fifty per cent. on all sums, large or small. On every free letter delivered by the postmaster, (except his own,) one cent. Stamped letters are considered as paid in cash. But no postmaster is entitled to retain more than $500 per quarter; and the surplus over $2,000 a year received in commissions by any postmaster, after deducting the expenses of the office, is to be paid to the postmaster-general. Also all that is received over $2,000 for boxes and pigeon holes, and for the delivery of letters in the city, or for keeping a branch post-office, is paid to the postmaster-general; so that no postmaster may receive for his services more than $4,000 a year.

CHAPTER XLVI

§ 1. In Ohio, Indiana, and Michigan, the age of consent has been raised to eighteen years in males, and fourteen in females; in Illinois to seventeen and fourteen; in Wisconsin to eighteen and fifteen. All the states do not specify the degree of relationship at which marriages are forbidden; and those that do, are not uniform. Some states have forbidden marriages which come within what are called the Levitical degrees; but these degrees have received different interpretations. In England particularly, the prohibition to marry within the Levitical degrees is said to rest on the ecclesiastical or canon law. These degrees, as interpreted by this law, not only forbid all marriages between relations in the ascending and descending lines, but between those in the collateral line to more distant degrees than is done in most of our states. The relation of uncle and niece, and of aunt and nephew, come within this rule.

Nor does the common and canon law make any distinction between connections by consanguinity and connections by affinity ; that is, relations by blood and relations by marriage. This would hold it as unlawful for a man to marry a deceased wife's sister as his own sister, or to marry a deceased brother's wife. It is contended, however, by many, that the Levitical law does not include such cases ; by others, that it is not binding as a municipal regulation. By the statutes of New York, only marriages between relations in the ascending and descending lines, and between brothers and sisters of the half as well as whole blood, are declared to be incestuous and void. In Ohio, marriages between persons nearer of kin than first cousins are unlawful.

§ 2. In Massachusetts, seven years of willful absence of either party exempts the other from liability to the penalty of the law for a second marriage. If one party has been absent a year or more, and is believed to be dead, the other does not incur the penalty by a second marriage. In Ohio, in case of three years' willful and continual absence of one of the parties, the penalty would not attach to a second marriage of the other. In New York, five years' absence of one party not known by the other to be living during that time, or being sentenced to imprisonment for life, would excuse from the penalty. But such second marriages, though excusable, would not be lawful. The first marriage contract would still be binding.

§ 3. To prevent the evils of clandestine and other improper marriages, the laws of Maine, New Hampshire, and Connecticut, require the publication of bans before marriage ; which is a notice of a marriage contract proclaimed in a church or other public place ; the object of which is, that any person may object, if he knows any good reason why the marriage should not take place. In Ohio, either such notice must be published on two successive days of public worship, or license must be obtained from the clerk of the county court, who must previously ascertain whether there is any legal impediment to the marriage. In Virginia, Indiana, and Wisconsin, a similar license is required. Like regulations exist in several other states; and in case of non-compliance with them, marriages have, in some states, been adjudged to be void. In Massachusetts it is only necessary to have a notice of the intended marriage registered by the clerk of the town.

§ 6. In the following named states, the property, real and personal, of a wife owned by her before marriage, and lawfully conveyed to her by any other person than her husband after marriage, is declared to be her own, and not liable for the debts of her husband: Maine, New Hampshire, Massachusetts, Rhode Island, Connecticut, New York, Pennsylvania, Maryland, Virginia, North Carolina, Florida, Alabama, Mississippi, Louisiana, Texas, Arkansas, Tennessee, Kentucky, Ohio, Michigan, Indiana, Iowa, and California. In Connecticut, the husband is entitled to the rents and profits of the wife's *personal* estate acquired by bequest or inheritance, but they are not liable for his debts. In Alabama, although the wife's property is not liable for the husband's debts, he has the control of it, as trustee of the wife, and is not liable to account to her for the proceeds. Also in California and Iowa, the control and management, and the rents and profits, remain with the husband. In several of the above named states, the husband must join with the wife in conveying real estate. In Florida and California, the wife's property must be inventoried and recorded. In Missouri, the property is not liable for debts of the husband contracted *before* marriage, or before the wife became possessed of the property. In Minnesota, the property of the wife acquired before marriage, is not liable during marriage for the husband's debts. In the states of Vermont, New Jersey, Delaware, South Carolina, Georgia, and Illinois, laws similar to the above have not, unless very recently, been passed.

§ 7. Some of those states which have abolished the common law right of the husband to the property of the wife acquired before marriage, have also abolished the common law obligation of the husband to pay the debts of the wife contracted before marriage. The wife's property alone is liable for such debts. The states in which such laws have been enacted, are, Massachusetts, Florida, Louisiana, Kentucky, California, and perhaps some others. In Indiana, the wife's property is first liable.

§ 8. In Pennsylvania and Alabama, the wife and husband become jointly liable for necessaries for the use and support of the family. In the former state, execution issues first against the property of the husband, and if none is found, then against the property of the wife. In Kentucky the wife is liable for debts by her and her husband jointly created in writing, for necessaries furnished any member of the family.

CHAPTER XLVII.

§ 6. The laws of Rhode Island, New Jersey, North Carolina, South Carolina, Tennessee, Louisiana, and Alabama, are exceptions to the rule which gives equal shares to descendants if they are all of equal degree of consanguinity to the ancestor. In these states, though the children of the intestate are all dead, the grandchildren do not take equal shares ; but those of each stock, or family, take the portion which their parent would have taken, if living.

§ 7. The real estate of intestates dying *without lawful descendants*, descends in the different states, according to the following rules :

In Maine, to the father ; but if the estate came to the intestate on the part of the mother, then to her and her kindred ; otherwise the mother shares equally with the brothers and sisters. If there is no widow, father, or brother or sister, the mother takes the whole. In New Hampshire the law is nearly the same as in Maine.

In Vermont the estate goes to the father ; but as the dower of the widow in this estate, if there are no children, is increased to one-half of the estate, the father takes but the other half. [It will be remembered, that a widow is, at common law, endowed of one-third part of all the real estate of her husband, of which she can not be deprived, even by his last will and testament. Hence, in speaking of the descent of an estate, only *two-thirds* are meant, except when a different portion is expressly mentioned.] In this state the mother takes equally with the brothers of the intestate. If there is no widow, father, or brothers and sisters, the mother has the whole estate.

In Massachusetts, the father, if there is one, always takes the estate; if none, it goes to the brothers and sisters, the mother sharing as one of them. If there is no brother or sister living, the estate goes to the mother in exclusion of the issue of deceased brothers or sisters.

In Rhode Island, the same as in Maine, when the estate came by the mother; otherwise to the father, if there is one; if not, to the brothers and sisters of the intestate; if none, nor father, then to the mother.

In Connecticut, the estate goes to the brothers and sisters of the whole blood; but if none, to the father and mother equally; or if but one of the parents is living, then the whole to that parent. Parents are preferred to half blood brothers and sisters. If the estate came by gift, devise, or descent, it passes to the kindred of the blood of the ancestor from whom it came.

In New York, to the father; but if the estate came by the mother, and there are brothers and sisters or their descendants, she takes an estate for life only; and if there are no brothers or sisters, or their issue, nor a father, the mother takes the inheritance in fee. [For definition of *fee*, see Chapter L, § 1.]

In New Jersey, brothers and sisters take in preference to parents; but if there are no brothers and sisters nor their issue, the father takes the estate in fee-simple; and if no father, the mother takes the estate for life; and after her death, it goes to the brothers and sisters of the half blood. If it came by devise, descent, or gift, it passes in all cases to the kindred of the blood of the ancestor from whom it came.

In Pennsylvania, the father and mother take jointly for life, and for the life of the survivor, if there is a brother or sister, or their issue of the whole blood; if none, the estate descends in fee to the father and mother, or to the survivor, if both are not living.

In Delaware, brothers and sisters take before parents; but in default of brothers and sisters, the estate goes to the next of kindred of the intestate who are in equal degree, meaning, probably, the parents, if living.

In Maryland, the father inherits; if there is no father, the brothers and sisters of the blood of the father and their descendants take the estate ; but if none, then the grandfather and his descendants ; and if that line fails, the estate goes in like manner to the mother and her descendants and maternal ancestors. If the estate came by descent from the mother, it goes to the mother or her kindred.

In Virginia, the father succeeds ; if no father, the mother shares equally with the brothers and sisters and their descendants. If the estate came to the intestate by his mother, it goes to the mother, or her kindred.

In North Carolina, to the brothers and sisters ; if none, the parents, or the survivor of them, take for life. If the estate came by gift, devise, or descent, it always goes to the kindred of the blood of the ancestor from whom it came.

In South Carolina, if there is no widow, the father, or if dead, the mother takes the estate with the brothers and sisters in equal shares.

In Georgia, the widow takes the whole estate ; if no widow, the father takes the whole ; if no father, the mother takes equally with the brothers and sisters.

In Alabama, the brothers and sisters ; if there are none, the father ; and if none, the mother takes the estate.

In Mississippi, the brothers and sisters are preferred to the parents ; but if there are no brothers and sisters or their issue, the father, or if none, the mother, takes the estate in fee.

In Louisiana, one-half goes equally to the father and mother, and the other half to the brothers and sisters or their issue. If only one parent survives, that parent takes only one-fourth ; if neither, the brothers and sisters take the whole.

In Kentucky, the father takes the estate ; if no father, the mother shares equally with the brothers and sisters and their descendants. If the estate came by the mother, it goes to her or her kindred.

In Tennessee, the whole goes to the brothers and sisters ; if none, to the father in fee, if living ; and if not, then to the mother for life, and then to the heirs on the part of the father ; but if there are none, then to the heirs on the part of the mother. If the estate was not acquired by the intestate, and there are no brothers and sisters, it goes in fee to the parent from whom it was derived. If the land was acquired by descent from the father, and there is no brother or sister, it goes to the uncles and aunts on the father's side.

In Ohio, the estate passes to the brothers and sisters of the whole blood and their representatives ; and if there are none of the whole blood, to those of the half-blood ; if none, then to the father ; if he is dead, to the mother. If the estate was not acquired by the intestate, it goes to the brothers and sisters of the blood of the ancestor from whom it came, whether of the whole or half blood ; but if there are none, and if it came by gift from an ancestor who is living, it goes back to him ; but if he is dead, it passes to his children if he has any ; if not, then to his brothers and sisters or their representatives ; but if such ancestor has none, then to the brothers and sisters of the intestate of the half blood and their representatives, though not of the blood of the ancestor. If all these fail, then to the next of kin to the intestate of the blood of the ancestor.

In Indiana, the father, or if dead, the mother, takes half of the estate, and the other half goes to the brothers and sisters of the intestate ; if no parents, the whole to the brothers and sisters ; but if none of these are living, the father, or if dead, the mother takes the whole. If there are brothers and sisters and no father, the estate is divided among the mother and brothers and sisters, the mother taking two shares.

In Illinois, half of the estate goes to the widow, and the residue, or if there is no widow, the whole, goes in equal parts to the parents, brothers and sisters, and their descendants ; and if only one of the parents is living, that parent takes, as survivor, a double portion. If there is neither widow, nor parents, nor brothers or sisters, or their descendants, it goes to the next of kin of the intestate.

In Missouri, the parents take equally with the brothers and sisters of the intestate.

In New Hampshire, Vermont, and North Carolina, uncles and aunts take equally with nephews and nieces, as being equal of kin. But as the statutes of the other states which have been mentioned in the foregoing notes to this chapter, place the brothers and sisters and *their descendants, or children* before any distinct branch of the grandparents' stock, it is presumed that in all these states nephews and nieces take in exclusion of uncles and aunts.

In Wisconsin, the estate goes to the widow during her natural life, and then to the father ; or, if there is no widow, the estate goes to the father. If there is no widow nor father, the brothers and sisters take the estate, the mother, if any, taking an equal share with them. If there is neither widow, nor father nor brothers or sisters, the mother takes the estate, to the exclusion, if any, of deceased brothers and sisters' children. In default of widow, father, mother, brothers and sisters, the estate descends to his next of kin in equal degree. If there is a widow and no kindred, the widow takes the estate.

In Iowa, one-half of the estate, (including the dower of the widow,) goes to the father of the intestate, and the other half to the widow ; and if there is no widow, the whole goes to the father. If there is neither father nor widow, the estate goes to his kindred, in the same manner as if he had died in possession of the estate. If there are no heirs in the male line, nor widow, the whole goes to the mother and her kindred. If there are no father nor mother nor their kindred, and there is a widow, the estate goes to the widow ; and if there is no widow, then to her heirs, if she has any ; if none, the property escheats to the state.

A more full description of the order of descent can not well be here given. A few of the new states are not includ ed in the list enumerated ; and it is not improbable that some changes have recently been made in the law of descent in some of those which have been mentioned. The manner of descent of personal estate differs in many, if not most of the states, from that of real estate ; and for information on the subject, reference must be had to the statutes of the states. In relation to the participation of widows in the personal property of their deceased husbands in some of the states, something may be found in the notes to Chapter XLVIII, § 9, relating to *dower.*

§ 8, 10. Wills must be subscribed either by the testator, or by some other person in his presence, and by his express direction. Three witnesses to a will are required in the six New England states, and in Maryland, South Carolina, Georgia, Florida, and Mississippi. In Mississippi, a will wholly written by the testator, and signed by him, need not be attested by any witness. In Missouri, wills must be recorded within thirty days after probate. In Louisiana, the regulations concerning the making of wills are materially different from those of the other states.

Nuncupative wills are such as are made by the verbal declaration of the testator, and depend merely on oral testimony for proof, though afterward reduced to writing. The object of authorizing wills of this kind is to enable persons to direct the disposal of property in their last illness under circumstances which do not admit of a compliance with the usual forms. They are generally restricted in the amount of property which may be bequeathed. Wills of this kind may be made in the following states; Alabama, for $500 ; Iowa, for $300 ; Wisconsin ; Minnesota ; Ohio. In the last mentioned state, personal estate only may be bequeathed verbally ; and the testamentary words must be reduced to writing within ten days. Two or more witnesses to nuncupative wills are necessary.

In Texas, a parent can not deprive his descendants by will of more than one-fourth of his or her property.

CHAPTER XLVIII.

§ 2. In Connecticut and Kentucky, the seal of the grantor is not required; nor in Alabama, if the maker acknowledges the execution before an officer. In nearly all the southern and western states, and in New Jersey and Pennsylvania, a scroll, or circle of ink, made with a pen at the end of a name, may be used as a substitute for a seal.

In most of the states deeds are to be subscribed by two or more witnesses. In Maine, Texas, Indiana, and Iowa, one is sufficient. As all conveyances of real estate must be acknowledged by the grantor, or proved, such acknowledgment would seem to be sufficient proof of their execution; and the principal object of witnesses may be presumed to be to prove the execution of a deed *in lieu* of an acknowledgment; or, if an acknowledgment is taken, to prove to the officer taking it, in case the grantor is not personally known to him, that the person offering to make the acknowledgment, is the person who executed the conveyance. Hence, in New York, Maryland, and Alabama, no witness is necessary in case a deed is duly acknowledged. In New York its execution may be proved by one witness; and in New York, New Jersey, Pennsylvania, Alabama,

Mississippi, Texas, Indiana, Minnesota, California, and perhaps a few other states, it is expressly provided, that a conveyance shall be either acknowledged by the party executing it, *or proved* by witnesses to have been executed in their presence; implying that the acknowledgment may be dispensed with.

§ 3. In Vermont, Rhode Island, Connecticut, and perhaps one or two other states, deeds are recorded in the office of the town clerk; in all the other states, in the office of a county register or recorder.

§ 4. In the following named states, specified periods of time are allowed for having deeds recorded, unless changes in some of them have been recently made: North Carolina, two years; Delaware, Tennessee, Georgia, and Indiana, one year; Virginia and Kentucky, eight months; Pennsylvania, Maryland, South Carolina, Alabama, Illinois, and Ohio, six months; Indiana, ninety days; Mississippi, three months. In Ohio, no time is fixed for mortgages. In states in which no time is prescribed, the deed must be recorded in a reasonable time. There are perhaps a few other states than those above mentioned, in which a certain time is allowed for recording.

§ 9. To entitle a wife to dower, the husband must have had a seizin of the land in *severalty* at some time during marriage; that is, he must have had possession alone, and not *jointly* with another person, which is called, in law, *joint seizin*. And the dower attaches whether it is a seizin *in fact*, that is, having actual or corporal possession, or whether it is a seizin *in law*, as where the law gives a title or ownership to a purchaser or an heir, but he has not yet entered on the lands. Also if a person seized in fee makes a lease for life, that is, for the life of the lessee, the wife of the lessor is dowable of the land, and defeats the lease by a paramount title. If, however, the lease was made before marriage, she is excluded from dower, unless the life estate terminated during coverture, because, prior to the death of the lessee, the husband was not seized of *the immediate* freehold. Nor does dower attach to lands mortgaged back to the grantor, or to a third person, to secure the payment of purchase money. In this case she is entitled to dower only in the surplus proceeds after satisfying the mortgage. Dower attaches to all real hereditaments, which include not only lands and tenements, but the rents and profits thereof.

At common law, which prevails in most of the states, the widow is endowed during her life, of a third of all the real estate of which her husband was seized *at any time during marriage*, and of which she had not been barred. But in the states of Vermont, Connecticut, Tennessee, North Carolina, and Georgia, the title to dower has been restricted to lands of which the husband was seized *at the time of his death;* consequently, a husband alone can convey the entire premises. In Georgia, however, lands having come to the husband by his intermarriage with his wife, are excepted ; and her dower in them can not be conveyed but by her own act. In Maine, New Hampshire, and Massachusetts, wild lands not connected with a cultivated farm are not subject to dower.

In Virginia, in addition to dower, the widow is entitled absolutely to one-third of the personal estate after payment of debts and charges, and for life to an estate in slaves. This additional right is modified and increased in case there are no children by the marriage. In Florida, besides dower, the widow, if there is no child or only one child, takes one-half of the personal estate absolutely ; if more than one child, one-third absolutely, excepting slaves, in which she takes a life estate.

In Arkansas, dower extends to personal estate also ; and if there are no lineal descendants, the widow takes one-half of both real and personal estate.

In Illinois, if there are no children and their descendants, the widow has one-half of the real estate, and the whole of the personal estate.

In Alabama, if there are no lineal descendants, the widow is endowed of one-half of the lands if the estate is solvent ; if insolvent, of one-third. If there are lineal descendants, then one-third, whether the estate is insolvent or not.

In Tennessee, if there are no heirs-at-law to inherit real estate, and there is a widow, she takes the estate in fee, subject to her husband's debts.

In Missouri, dower applies also to leasehold estate for the term of twenty years or more. Besides dower, the widow is entitled absolutely to implements of industry, household goods, kitchen furniture, and to other personal property to the value of $200 ; also, to a child's share of the personal estate absolutely; or, at her option, to one-third of the slaves for life, and one-third of the other personal property absolutely, subject to her husband's debts. If there are no descendants, she takes absolutely all the real and personal estate which came to the husband by the wife remaining undisposed of, and one-half of the real and personal estate belonging to the husband at the time of his death, subject to his debts. If the husband leaves descendants, but not by his last marriage, his widow may, in lieu of dower, take the real and personal property in his possession which came to him in her right by means of the marriage, subject to his debts.

In Louisiana, special provision is made for the widow or minor children of a deceased person left in necessitous circumstances. If they do no possess in their own right property to the amount of $1,000, they may demand from the succession of their deceased father or husband a sum sufficient to make up that amount; the use of which the widow has during her widowhood; and the money is then to go to the descendants of the deceased.

In Maine, New Hampshire, Vermont, Massachusetts, Connecticut, Wisconsin, and perhaps Florida and Louisiana, a private acknowledgment of the wife that she signed the deed freely, is not required.

CHAPTER XLIX.

§ 7, 18, 19. The periods fixed by the statutes of the states respectively in which a title to land may be acquired by uninterrupted possession, are as follows:—Twenty-one years in Pennsylvania and Ohio; twenty years in Maine, New Hampshire, Massachusetts, New York, New Jersey, Delaware, Indiana, Illinois, Iowa, Wisconsin, Minnesota; fifteen years in Connecticut, Virginia, Kentucky; ten years in South Carolina, Mississippi; seven years in North Carolina, Georgia, Florida; five years in California; ten years in Louisiana, when the possessor has been in good faith, and held by a just title, and thirty years without any title on the part of the possessor, whether in good faith or not In those states in which there is no express provision on the subject, it is presumed the common law term prevails, which is twenty years.

CHAPTER LI.

§ 16. The statutes of nearly all the states expressly provide, that, in the following cases, every agreement shall be void, unless the same, or some note or memorandum thereof, shall be in writing, and signed by the party to be charged therewith, or by his authorized agent: (1.) The special promise of an executor or administrator to answer damages out of his own estate; (2.) A special promise to answer for the debt, default, or misdoing of another person; (3.) Any agreement or promise upon consideration of marriage; (4.) Any contract for the sale of lands, or any interest in lands; (5.) Any agreement that is not to be performed within one year from the time of making it. Although the statutes of a few of the states omit, in their enumeration, one or more of the above cases, it is presumed that there is practically almost an entire uniformity in all the states.

In New York, Wisconsin, Minnesota, and California, the law requires that the written note or memorandum shall express the consideration of the agreement.

Also in these states, together with Michigan and Alabama, in the cases of agreements made in consideration of marriage, mutual promises to marry are excepted.

CHAPTER LII.

§ 6. The provisions of the English statute apply, in Maine, New Jersey, Arkansas, Iowa, and Missouri, to cases in which the price of the goods sold is $30 or more; in New Hampshire, $33.33; in Connecticut and Pennsylvania, $35; in Vermont, $40; in Massachusetts, New York, Michigan, Indiana, and Minnesota, $50; in Georgia, £10 sterling; in Alabama and California, $200; in Florida, sums of any amount. Not all the states have legislated on the subject; in such the English statute is presumed to govern.

CHAPTER LIII.

§ 6. These conditional sales or assignments of personal property, are commonly called *chattel mortgages*; and to render them valid against other persons than the parties thereto, when the mortgaged property remains in possession of the mortgager or assignor, they must be recorded or filed, in the following states, in the town or county in which the mortgager resides, or where the property is at the time of executing the mortgage.

In Maine, Massachusetts, Rhode Island, and New Hampshire, they are recorded by the town clerk ; and in New Hampshire, the parties must swear that the mortgage was made to secure the payment of an honest debt ; and the affidavit also is to be recorded.

In Connecticut, mechanical implements or machinery in a factory, or furniture in a dwelling, or hay in a building, mortgaged with the realty on which they are situate, and are particularly described in the mortgage, are held by the mortgager as effectually as if they were a part of the real estate, though he retains possession.

In New York, the mortgage is filed in the town clerk's office ; if in a shire town, then in the county clerk's office. Chattel mortgages hold for a year only, unless renewed within thirty days before the year expires.

In Maryland, acknowledged before a justice, and sworn to by the mortgager to be *bona fide*, and recorded within twenty days in the county records.

In North Carolina and South Carolina, recorded in the county records, and in North Carolina, also proved.

In Georgia, proved by the affidavit of the subscribing witness, and recorded by the clerk of the county court within three months.

In Florida, acknowledged and recorded by the proper county officer.

In Alabama and Mississippi, recorded in the county where the grantor resides, and the property is ; in Mississippi, within three months.

In Texas, the mortgage must be proved by two or more witnesses, or acknowledged, and recorded, as deeds of real estate, in the county in which the mortgager lives.

In Tennessee, proved and recorded, as mortgages on land.

In Kentucky, acknowledged and recorded as deeds.

In Ohio, to be deposited immediately with the county recorder, if in a shire town ; if not, then with the clerk of the township in which the mortgager resides. Such record is valid for a year only.

In Michigan, filed with the town clerk, and holds for one year only, unless, within thirty days before the expiration of the year, affidavit is made of the mortgagee's interest in the mortgaged property.

In Indiana, proved or acknowledged, and recorded in the county recorder's office within ten days.

In Illinois, acknowledged and recorded in the office of the county recorder. The mortgage must expressly provide for the possession of the property to remain with the mortgager. It is valid for two years.

In Missouri and Iowa, the mortgage must be acknowledged and recorded as deeds of land; in Iowa, within ten days.

In Wisconsin, a copy must be filed in the office of the town clerk where the mortgager resides, or, if he does not reside in the state, in the town where the property is at the time of executing the mortgage.

In Minnesota, a copy is filed in the office of the county register of deeds; or, if the mortgager is a non-resident of the territory, in the office of the register of the county in which the property is at the time of executing the mortgage.

In California, no mortgage of personal property is valid against other persons than the parties thereto, unless the mortgagee takes the property into his possession.

In those states in which there is no special law on the subject, the question of the validity of a chattel mortgage against third persons, when the property remains with the mortgager, is attended with uncertainty, depending upon the conflicting decisions of the courts.

CHAPTER LIV.

§ 11. Special laws have been passed in nearly all the states for the security of persons performing labor in the construction or repair of buildings, machinery, vessels, &c., and for furnishing materials for the same. They are called *mechanics' lien laws.* They give to contractors and master-builders a lien upon the structures, and upon the lots attached to them, until their claims shall be satisfied. The laws of the different states differ much in their details

The several periods for which these liens continue, vary from thirty days to several years, at the expiration of which period they cease, unless proceedings are commenced for enforcing them; which is done by attaching the property, or by bringing a suit, or by applying to the proper courts for authority to sell the property, as the one or the other mode of proceeding is prescribed by the law of the state. In most of the states, a lien of this kind does not hold unless the contract is in writing; in many of them they must also be recorded; and in a few, the filing of them is sufficient. In some states, sub-contractors and journeymen obtain the benefit of this law, by notifying the owner of the premises of their claims against their employers; in which case the owner may pay the journeymen, and retain the same on settlement with the contractor. Or a sub-contractor or a journeyman may, in some states, create a lien upon the premises, by giving written notice to the proprietor of his intention to furnish materials or perform labor on the building. Liens upon ships or other vessels are usually to be enforced within a few days after the liens shall have accrued.

CHAPTER LVIII.

§ 10. In Maine and Vermont, the legal rate of interest is *six* per cent. If more is agreed to be taken, only legal interest can be recovered. Usurious interest paid may be recovered back.

In New Hampshire and Massachusetts, the rate is *six* per cent. The party taking more forfeits three times the amount unlawfully taken.

In Rhode Island, the rate is *six* per cent. On a usurious contract, the principal and lawful interest can be recovered.

In Connecticut, *six* per cent. On a usurious contract, only the principal can be recovered. Persons taking usury, forfeit the whole of the interest, one-half to the prosecutor, the other half to the state treasury.

In New York, *seven* per cent. Contracts whereby a higher rate is reserved, are void. If, however, the principal and interest have been paid, only the excess car be afterwards recovered. Corporations can not set up the defense of usury in this state.

In New Jersey, *six* per cent. Usurious contracts are void. Persons taking more than the legal rate, forfeit the whole value of the subject matter of the contract, one-half to the state, and one-half to the prosecutor. In Hudson and Essex counties and the city of Paterson, the legal rate is *seven* per cent., if one or both of the parties reside therein.

In Pennsylvania, *six* per cent. Usurious interest can not be recovered; and if paid, may be recovered back.

In Delaware, *six* per cent. For taking more, the whole debt is liable to forfeiture, one-half to the state, and one-half to the prosecutor.

In Maryland, *six* per cent. If more is taken, only the excess over the legal rate can be recovered.

In Virginia, *six* per cent. Contracts for a greater rate are void; and a penalty is incurred of double the amount of the debt, one-half to the informer.

In North Carolina, *six* per cent. Contracts reserving a higher rate are void; and the party exacting it is liable to a forfeiture of twice the amount of the debt, one-half to the state, and one-half to the prosecutor.

In South Carolina and Georgia, *seven* per cent. If more is reserved, the entire interest is forfeited.

In Florida, *six* per cent., but may be *eight* by agreement. Usury is punishable by indictment and loss of the whole interest.

In Alabama, *eight* per cent. In usurious contracts, the principal only can be recovered.

In Mississippi, *six* per cent.; for the *bona fide* use of money, *eight* per cent. Any rate not exceeding *ten* per cent. may be taken by agreement in writing. Only simple interest can be recovered when a higher rate is reserved than is allowed by law.

In Louisiana, the legal rate is *five* per cent.; but may be *eight* by agreement. Bank interest is *six* per cent. For usury, the entire interest is forfeited.

In Texas, the legal rate is *eight* per cent.; but as high as *twelve* may be taken by agreement. If more is reserved than the law allows, no interest can be recovered.

In Arkansas, *six* per cent.; but any rate not exceeding *ten* per cent. may be contracted for. Usurious contracts are void.

In Tennessee, *six* per cent. For exacting more, a person may be fined not less than the amount unlawfully taken.

In Kentucky, *six* per cent. The usurious excess is void.

In Ohio, *six* per cent.; but any rate not exceeding *ten* per cent. may be taken on written agreement. If more is reserved, the excess is void.

In Michigan, *seven* per cent. Any rate not higher than *ten* per cent. may be agreed upon for a loan of money. Excess beyond these rates is void.

In Indiana, *six* per cent. A higher rate can not be recovered; and if paid, may be recovered back.

In Illinois, *six* per cent.; for money loaned, it may be *ten* per cent. Only the legal rates are collectable.

In Missouri, *six* per cent.; *ten* may be agreed upon. A person taking usury, forfeits ten per cent., to be paid for the benefit of the common school fund.

In Iowa, *six* per cent.; by agreement may be *ten*. Illegal interest paid, may be recovered.

In Wisconsin, *seven* per cent.; may be *twelve* by written agreement. A person paying more than legal rates, may recover treble the amount paid.

In Minnesota, *seven* per cent. Any rate may be taken by agreement.

In California, *ten* per cent. Parties may contract for any rate on money due, or to become due, cn any contract.

SYNOPSIS OF THE STATE CONSTITUTIONS.

MAINE

The District of Maine, formerly belonging to the state of Massachusetts, adopted in Convention, October 29, 1819, a constitution, preparatory to admission into the Union as a state, and was admitted as such, March 15, 1820. The constitution has received few alterations, among the more important of which are a change in the term of judicial officers from the term during good behavior, to the term of seven years, and a change of election of representatives in the legislature by a majority of votes, to election by plurality, or by the highest number of votes.

Electors. Every male citizen of the United States, of the age of twenty-one years, and upwards, excepting paupers, persons under guardianship, and Indians not taxed, having had an established residence in the state three months next preceding the election, is an elector for governor, senators, and representatives. Persons in the military, naval, or marine service of the United States, and students in seminaries, do not acquire a legal residence in any town. Electors, except in cases of crime, are privileged from arrest on the days of election, during attendance at, going to, and returning therefrom ; and are exempt from military duty on such days, except in time of war or public danger.

Legislature. The house of representatives consists of one hundred and fifty-one members, apportioned among the several counties according to population. Each town having 1,500 inhabitants, may elect one representative ; a town having 3,750 inhabitants elects two representatives ; a town having 6,750, elects three ; a town having 10,500, elects four ; a town having 15,000, elects five ; a town having 20,250, elects six ; a town having 26,250, elects seven. If the number of 1,500 shall at any time be too large or too small to apportion all the representatives to any county, it is to be so increased or diminished as to give the number of representatives according to the above rule. A representative must be twenty-one years of age, and must have been five years a citizen of the United States, one year a resident of the state, and three months next preceding his election a resident of the town or district which he represents.

The senate is to consist of not less than twenty, nor more than thirty-one members, elected in districts. They are elected by a majority of votes. If such election, in any district is not made by the electors, the senators elected, and the members of the house, elect, by joint ballot, from the two persons having received the highest numbers of votes. Senators must be twenty five years of age, and in other respects must have the same qualifications as representatives.

The annual meeting of the legislature is on the first Wednesday of January. Bills vetoed by the governor must be passed by two-thirds majorities to become laws.

Executive. The governor is elected annually. A majority of all the votes given is required. If no person is thus elected, the house of representatives, from the persons voted for, (not exceeding four,) having the highest numbers of votes, elects two, of whom the senate elects a governor. The governor must be thirty years of age, a native citizen, a resident of the state five years. There is a council, consisting of seven persons, to advise the governor in the executive part of the government. The counselors are chosen annually, on the first Wednesday of January, by joint ballot of the senators and representatives. The governor, with the advice and consent of the council, appoints judicial officers, coroners, and notaries public; also all other officers whose appointment is not by the constitution or by law otherwise provided for. There is no lieutenant-governor in this state.

A secretary of state, a treasurer, and an attorney-general, are chosen annually by joint ballot of both houses of the legislature; the treasurer not to be eligible more than five years successively.

Judiciary. The judicial power of the state is vested in a supreme judicial court, and such other courts as the legislature shall establish. Judges of the judicial court are appointed for seven years; judges and registers of probate are elected by the people of their respective counties for four years.

Education. The legislature is enjoined to require the several towns to make suitable provision for the support of schools in them. It is also the duty of the legislature to encourage and endow academies, colleges and seminaries of learning.

Miscellaneous Provisions. All civil officers may be *removed*, by impeachment, for misdemeanor in office ; and every person holding office may be removed by the governor and council, on address of both branches of the legislature. The credit of the state may not be loaned in any case. Nor may the legislature create any debts or liabilities, which shall, in the aggregate, exceed $300,000, except to suppress insurrection, to repel invasion, or for purposes of war.

Amendments to the constitution must be proposed by the legislature, two-thirds of both houses concurring, and ratified by electors at their next annual meeting. The votes of a majority of the electors voting on the question, is necessary to a ratification.

NEW HAMPSHIRE.

This state adopted a constitution in 1784. Its present constitution was adopted in 1792.

Electors. All male citizens, twenty-one years of age, except paupers, and persons excused from paying taxes at their own request, are voters.

Legislature. The two houses , together, are styled, the *general court.* The senate consists of twelve members, elected annually, in single districts. A senator must own a freehold estate of the value of £200 ; be thirty years of age ; have been an inhabitant of the state seven years immediately preceding his election ; and be an inhabitant of the district for which he is chosen. Representatives are chosen annually in towns ; each town having 150 ratable male polls twenty-one years of age being entitled to one representative, and an additional representative for every

300 additional ratable male polls. A representative must have resided in the state two years; must have an estate within his district of £100 value, one-half of it freehold. Senators and representatives must be of the Protestant religion.* A majority of each house constitutes a quorum.

The legislature may pass bills against the veto of the governor, by majorities of two-thirds. Bills also become laws if not returned by the governor within five days, unless the legislature, by their adjournment, prevent their return.

Executive. The governor is elected annually by a majority of votes. If no person receives a majority, the two houses, by joint ballot, elect one of the two persons having the highest numbers of votes. A governor must have been an inhabitant of the state seven years; must be thirty years of age; own an estate of £500, one half of it freehold; and be of the Protestant religion.* No lieutenant-governor. A council of five members, one in each district, is annually elected, by a majority of votes. If in any district no person has a majority, the senate and house elect one of the two having the highest numbers of votes. Counselors have the same qualifications as senators. The power of pardon, and the power of appointment, are exercised by the governor and council.

A secretary of state, a treasurer, and a commissary-general, are appointed by joint ballot of the senators and representatives.

Judiciary. All judical officers are appointed by the governor and council; justices of the peace for five years, the judges of the higher courts to hold during good behavior. Judges of courts and of probate become disqualified at the age of seventy years.

The attorney-general, solicitors, sheriffs, coroners, registers of probate, and naval and the higher militia officers, are appointed by the governor and council.

County treasurers and registers of deeds, are elected by the people of the several counties.

Education. It is made the duty of legislators and magistrates, to cherish the interests of literature and the sciences, and all seminaries and public schools; to encourage the promotion of agriculture, arts, trade, commerce, and manufactures; countenance and inculcate the principles of human-

* Property qualification for the legislature and governor, has been abolished.

ity and general benevolence, industry, honesty, sobriety, and all social and generous sentiments among the people.

Amendments. The sense of the people as to the necessity of a revision of the constitution is taken every seven years at an election; and if, by a majority of the votes, a revision is deemed necessary, the general court is to call a convention for that purpose; and any alterations proposed by the convention must be approved by two-thirds of the qualified voters who shall vote on the question of their adoption.

VERMONT.

THIS state was admitted into the Union in 1791, with a constitution formed in 1777; the present one was adopted in 1793, and has been several times amended.

Electors. Every citizen of the United States who has resided in the state one whole year before the election, and is of a quiet and peaceable behavior, is entitled to all the privileges of a freeman, by taking an oath, that, in giving his vote or suffrage, he will do it in such a manner as he believes will most conduce to the best good of the state.

Legislature. The senate consists of thirty members, elected annually. Each county is entitled to at least one senator, the remainder to be apportioned among the several counties according to their population, as ascertained by the last United States census, or by a state census taken for the purpose of such apportionment; regard being had in the apportionment to the counties having the greatest fractions, and giving to each county at least one senator. Senators must be thirty years of age, and freemen of the county in which they are elected. Representatives are elected in the several towns, each town being entitled to one representative; who must have resided two years in the state, the last of which in the town for which he is elected. A majority of either branch constitutes a *quorum;* for raising a state tax, two-thirds of the members elected must be present.

Bills negatived by the governor, become laws when repassed by majorities of both houses. Bills not returned within five days, become laws.

Executive The governor is elected annually; also a lieutenant-governor. If no person has a majority of votes, the election is made by joint ballot of the senate and house, from the three candidates (if there be so many) having the highest numbers of votes. The powers and duties of the governor are nearly the same as those of executives generally. He must have resided in the state four years. There is a lieutenant-governor in this state, qualified as the governor.

A secretary of state is chosen by the senate and house in joint assembly. A treasurer is elected at the same time, and in the same manner, as the governor and lieutenant-governor.

Judiciary. The judicial power of the state is vested in judges of the supreme court, and of the county courts, who are annually chosen by the senate and house; and in justices of the peace, who are elected by the freemen of their respective towns. Towns having less than 1,000 inhabitants, may elect any number of justices not exceeding *five*; towns having more than 1,000 and less than 2,000, may elect *seven*; towns having between 2,000 and 3,000, may elect *ten*; towns having between 3,000 and 5,000, may elect *twelve*; and towns having 5,000 or more, may elect *fifteen* justices.

Judges of probate are elected by the freemen of their respective districts. Assistant judges of the county court, sheriffs, and high bailiffs, and state's attorneys, are elected by the freemen of their respective counties.

Amendments. There is chosen, every seven years, by the people, a council of censors, thirteen in number, who examine into the different departments of the government, and who have power to call a convention to amend the constitution.

Miscellaneous Provisions. The constitution declares, that a competent number of schools ought to be maintained in each town, and one or more grammar schools supported in each county. No person not already a freeman of the state, may exercise the privilege of a freeman, unless he is a natural born citizen of one of the United States, or until he shall have been naturalized agreeably to the acts of congress.

MASSACHUSETTS.

THE constitution of this state was formed in 1780. It has been several times amended.

Electors. Every male citizen twenty-one years of age, (excepting paupers and persons under guardianship) having resided a year in the state, and six months in the town or district in which he claims a right to vote, and having paid a tax within two years, or is legally exempt from taxation, is entitled to the right of suffrage.

Legislature. The senate and house of representatives are, together, styled, the *general court.* The senate consists of forty members, chosen in districts. The number assigned to each district is to be in proportion to its population. Senators must have resided in the state five years, and must be, when elected, inhabitants of the districts for which they are chosen. Representatives are apportioned among the towns and cities. Every town or city containing 1,200 inhabitants is entitled to one representative, and for every 2,400 inhabitants above that number, to an additional representative. A town containing less than 1,200 inhabitants, may elect a representative as many times within ten years as the number 160 is contained in the number of its inhabitants. Such town may also elect a representative for the year in which the valuation of estates shall be settled. Whenever the population of the state shall exceed 770,000, the number of inhabitants entitling a town to one representative, and the number entitling it to each additional representative, are to be increased one-tenth ; and for every additional increase of 70,000 inhabitants, the same addition of one-tenth is to be made to the above numbers. Representatives must have resided a year in the towns they represent.

The general election is held annually on the 2d Monday in November. Sessions of the general court commence on the 1st Wednesday of January. Bills negatived by the governor become laws if passed by two-thirds majorities ; also if not returned by him within five days, unless the legislature by adjournment prevent their return.

Executive. The governor is chosen annually. He must

have been an inhabitant of the state seven years; and declare himself to be of the Christian religion. In case of no election by a majority of votes, the house elects two out of the four having received the highest numbers of votes, if so many have been voted for; if not, then out of the number voted for: and of the two so elected, the senate elects a governor. A lieutenant-governor is elected in the same manner as the governor. In exercising the pardoning power and the power of appointment, and in directing the affairs of the state generally, the governor acts in conjunction with an advisory council of nine members, elected annually by the senate and house in joint assembly. Counselors must have been inhabitants of the state five years.

The secretary, treasurer, receiver-general, commissary-general, notaries public, and naval officers, are chosen annually by the senators and representatives.

Judiciary. All judicial officers are nominated and appointed by the governor, with the consent of the council. The justices of the higher courts hold their offices during good behavior; justices of the peace for the term of seven years. The former may be removed by the governor and council on address of both houses of the legislature.

The attorney-general, the solicitor-general, sheriffs, coroners, and registers of probate, are appointed in the same manner as justices.

Education. The constitution makes it the duty of the legislature and magistrates to cherish the interests of literature and the sciences, and all seminaries of them; especially the university at Cambridge, public schools, and grammar schools in the towns.

Amendments are proposed in the general court by a majority of the senators and two-thirds of the representatives present and voting; and if agreed to by like majorities of the next general court, they are submitted to the qualified voters of the state for ratification.

RHODE ISLAND.

A CHARTER was granted in 1663, by Charles II, to the Rhode Island and Providence Plantations. The company to whom the grant was made, comprised a governor, a deputy-governor, and a council. To these were subsequently added a house of representatives, chosen by the people in towns, and a judiciary department, the judges of which were chosen annually by the people. This charter, thus modified, continued the basis of government until the year 1842, when the present constitution was adopted.

Electors. Every male (naturalized) citizen of the United States, twenty-one years of age, who has resided in the state one year, and in the town or city in which he offers to vote, six months; who owns real estate worth $134 over and above all incumbrances, or which rents for $7 a year over and above any rent reserved or the interest of any incumbrances thereon; also every male *native* citizen, who has resided two years in the state, and six months in the town or city where he offers his vote, whose name has been registered in the town or city clerk's office at least seven days, and who has within the year, and at least seven days before the election, paid a tax or taxes either assessed upon his estate, or paid by him voluntarily, to the amount of $1; or who, being so registered, has done military duty within the year; is a legal voter.

Legislature. The two houses together are called the *general assembly.* The sessions are held annually. The house of representatives may not exceed seventy-two members. They are apportioned among the towns according to population, allowing one representative for a fraction exceeding half the ratio; but each town or city is entitled to at least one member; and no town is to have more than one-sixth of the number to which the house is limited. The senate consists of the lieutenant-governor and one senator from each town or city in the state. The governor, and, in his absence, the lieutenant-governor, presides in the senate and in grand committee; but may vote only in case of equal division. Bills are not presented to the governor for revision in this state.

Executive. The governor and lieutenant-governor are elected annually. If no candidate receives a majority of votes, the two houses in joint assembly, (called the grand committee,) elect one of the two having received the highest numbers of votes.

A secretary of state, an attorney-general, and a general treasurer, are elected annually in the same manner as the governor; and their names, and the names of the persons voted for as governor and lieutenant-governor, are all placed upon one ticket.

Judiciary. A supreme court and such inferior courts as the general assembly shall establish. Judges of the supreme court are elected by the two houses in grand committee. Each judge holds his office until his place shall be declared vacant by a resolution of the general assembly.

Education. It is made the duty of the legislature to promote public schools, and to secure to the people the advantages of education. And the present fund, and all moneys and donations for the support of public schools, must be infallibly applied to such use.

Amendments to the constitution must be agreed to by two successive legislatures, (a majority of all the members elected to each house voting in their favor,) and must be approved by three-fifths of the electors of the state voting thereon.

CONNECTICUT.

The colony of Connecticut, comprising the territory of the present state, was formed by the union of several colonies under a charter granted by Charles II, in 1662. This charter was confirmed by England in 1688, and was continued as the basis of government until 1818, when the present constitution was adopted. This constitution was amended in 185–.

Legislature. The two houses, together, are styled, the *general assembly.* Representatives are apportioned among the towns according to population. Any elector is eligible to either house. Senators, not less than eighteen, nor more than twenty-four, are chosen in districts, the number of which is not to be less than eight, nor more than twenty-four; the districts to be alterable after each census of the United States. Election of senators is by plurality. A majority of each house is a quorum. Bills returned by the governor become laws when again passed by a majority of each house. Bills become laws also if not returned by the governor within three days after having been presented to him, unless the legislature, by adjournment, prevent their return.

Executive. A governor and a lieutenant-governor are elected annually. Any qualified elector, thirty years of age, is eligible. A majority of votes is necessary to elect the governor. In case of a failure to elect, the general assembly choose a governor from one of the two having the highest numbers of votes.

A treasurer, a secretary, and a controller of public accounts, are elected in the same manner as the governor and lieutenant-governor.

A sheriff is elected in each county for three years, and is removable by the general assembly.

Judiciary. A supreme court of errors, a superior court, and such inferior courts as the general assembly shall establish. The judges are appointed by the general assembly. Judges of the supreme court and of the superior court, hold their offices for the term of eight years; may be removed by the governor on the address of two-thirds of each house. Judges of probate are chosen annually by the electors in the several probate districts. Justices of the peace are elected in the several towns.

Electors. Every white male citizen twenty-one years of age, who has resided a year in the state, and six months in the town in which he offers himself to be admitted to the privileges of an elector, and who sustains a good moral character, shall, on his taking the oath prescribed by law, be an elector. He must also be able to read any section of the constitution of the state and of the constitution of the United States.

Amendments of the constitution are proposed by a majority of the house of representatives, approved by two-thirds of both houses of the next general assembly, and a majority of the electors at an election.

Education. The school fund is to remain a perpetual fund, the interest of which is to be inviolably appropriated to the support of the public or common schools throughout the state.

NEW YORK.

THE first constitution of this state was formed in 1777; the second in 1821, (adopted in 1822). The present constitution was formed and adopted in 1846.

Electors. Every white male citizen twenty-one years of age, who has been an inhabitant of the state a year, and for four months a resident of the county, may vote in the election district in which he resides; but he must have resided for thirty days in the district for which the officer is to be chosen for whom he offers to vote. Naturalized persons must have been admitted as citizens at least ten days before voting. Colored men must have resided in the state three years, and must own a freehold estate of the value of $250 over and above incumbrances, and have paid a tax thereon.

Legislature. A senate and an assembly. The senate consists of thirty-two members elected for two years, one in each senate district. The assembly consists of one hundred and twenty-eight members, apportioned among the several counties according to population. Counties entitled to more than one member are divided into as many districts as there are members; and a member is elected in each district.

The final passage of bills requires a majority of all the members elected to each house. Bills negatived by the governor are to be returned within ten days, and become laws by being again passed, by majorities of two-thirds of both branches. The compensation of members is $3 a day, and 20 cents a mile for traveling to and from the place of meeting; but they can receive pay for only one hundred days at a single session. A census is taken, and a new apportionment made every ten years.

Executive. The governor is elected for two years; must be a citizen of the United States, thirty years of age, and have resided in the state five years next preceding his election. A lieutenant-governor, qualified in the same manner, is elected at the same time.

A secretary of state, a controller, a treasurer, an attorney-general, and a state engineer and surveyor, are chosen for two years. Also three canal commissioners and three inspectors of state prisons, for three years, one of each to be elected every year.

Judiciary. A court of appeals, a supreme court, county courts, and courts held by justices of the peace. The state is divided into eight judicial districts, in each of which four justices of the supreme court are elected, for eight years, two of them every two years. The court of appeals is composed of eight judges, of whom four are elected by the electors of the state for eight years, one every two years, and the other four are selected from the class of justices of the supreme court having the shortest time to serve; that is, whose term of service is most nearly expired. The business of the court of appeals is to review cases brought from the supreme court. One or more of the justices of the supreme court hold special terms and circuit courts in the several counties; and one of them presides in the courts of oyer and terminer in each county. General terms of the supreme court are held in the several districts, by three or more of the justices.

A county court is held by a county judge elected for four years.

In holding criminal courts, two justices are associated with the county judge. These justices are elected by the electors of the county, and are selected from acting justices of the peace. The county judge is also surrogate, (called in other states judge of probate.) In counties having a population exceeding 40,000, a separate officer may be chosen as surrogate. County judges and surrogates hold their offices four years. Justices of the peace are elected in the several towns, and hold for the same term.

A clerk of the court of appeals, who is ex-officio clerk of the supreme court, is elected for three years. County clerks are clerks of the supreme court in their respective counties.

Judges of the court of appeals and justices of the supreme court may be removed by the legislature. County judges may be removed by the senate on recommendation of the governor.

There are, in cities, certain judicial officers and courts, distinct from those above mentioned.

Sheriffs, clerks of counties, coroners, and district-attorneys, are elected for three years, in the several counties. Sheriffs are ineligible for the next three years.

Education. The capital of the common school fund, (now more than $2,000,000,) the capital of the literature fund, and the capital of the United States deposit fund, are to be preserved inviolate. The revenue of the common school fund, and a large portion of the revenue of the United States deposit fund, are annually applied to the support of common schools ; the revenue of the literature fund to the support of academies.

Amendments to the constitution must receive the sanction of two successive legislatures, majorities of all the members elected to each house concurring, and be ratified by a majority of the votes of the electors voting thereon at an election. Every twentieth year, and at such other times as the legislature shall provide, the question of calling a convention to revise the constitution, shall be submitted to the electors of the state.

Miscellaneous Provisions. The legislature may not sell or lease the canals of the state, nor sell the salt springs. The credit of the state shall not be loaned for the benefit of any individual, association or corporation. Debts may be contracted to meet casual deficits or failures in revenue, or for other expenses not provided for ; but the aggregate of such indebtedness shall not any time exceed $1,000,000. Additional debt may be contracted to repel invasion, suppress insurrection, or to defend the state in war. Except the debts above specified, no state debt may be hereafter contracted, unless authorized by law for some single work or object, distinctly specified ; and the law must provide for the payment of the debt within eighteen years ; and, before it can take effect, must be submitted to and sanctioned by the people at an election.

Corporations must be formed under general laws, but may not be created by special act, except for municipal purposes, and in cases where, in the judgment of the legislature, the objects of the corporation can not be attained under general laws. The stockholders in any bank or other moneyed corporation, are individually responsible to the amount of their respective shares therein, for all its debts and liabilities contracted after the first of January, 1850. Bill-holders have preference in payment over other creditors of an insolvent bank.

NEW JERSEY.

New Jersey, as a colony, adopted a constitution in 1776, under which the state was governed until the present constitution, framed in 1844, was adopted.

Electors. All white male citizens, who have resided in the state a year, and in the county in which they claim the right to vote, five months, are qualified voters; except paupers, idiots, insane persons, or persons convicted of certain crimes.

Legislature. A senate and general assembly. The senate consists of one senator from each county, elected for three years. One-third of the senators are elected every year. A senator must be thirty years of age, and have been a citizen and an inhabitant of the state four years, and of the county one year, before his election. Members of the general assembly are apportioned among the counties according to the population. A new apportionment is made every ten years, after the taking of the United States census. The number of members may not exceed sixty. A member must have been a citizen and resident of the state two years, and of the county one year. A majority is a quorum.

The final passage of bills requires a majority of all the members elected to each house. The same majorities may pass bills disapproved by the governor. Bills become laws if not returned by the governor within five days, unless their return is prevented by the adjournment of the legislature. Legislature meets on the 2d Tuesday of January. Members of the legislature receive $3 a day for forty days, and $1,50 a day thereafter; and $1 for every twenty miles travel to and from the place of meeting.

Executive. The governor is elected for three years; and is ineligible for the next three years. He must be thirty years of age; must have been for twenty years a citizen of the

United States, and a resident of the state seven years next before his election. There is no lieutenant-governor. The pardoning power is exercised by the governor, in conjunction with the chancellor and the judges of the court of errors and appeals.

The state treasurer, and the keeper and inspectors of the state prison, are appointed annually by the senate and general assembly in joint meeting. The secretary of state, attorney-general, and prosecutors of the pleas, are appointed by the governor and senate, for five years.

Judiciary. A court of errors and appeals ; a court of chancery ; a prerogative court ; a supreme court ; circuit courts ; and such inferior courts as now exist, and as may hereafter be established by law. The court of errors and appeals consists of the chancellor, the justice of the supreme court, and six judges or a majority of them. The court of chancery consists of the chancellor ; who is also the ordinary, or surrogate-general, and judge of the prerogative court, to which appeals are made from the orphans' court.

The supreme court consists of a chief justice and four associate justices, which number of associate justices may be increased or diminished, but may not be less than two.

The circuit courts are held in every county, by one or more justices of the supreme court, or a judge appointed for that purpose, and have, within the county, common law jurisdiction concurrent with the supreme court, except in criminal cases ; and final judgments in circuit courts may be brought, by writ of error, into the supreme court, or directly into the court of errors and appeals. The justices of the supreme court and the chancellor hold their offices seven years ; the judges of the court of errors and appeals, six years ; and all are appointed by the governor and senate. The inferior court of common pleas shall have not more than five judges, one to be appointed every year, by the senate and general assembly.

Justices of the peace, from two to five, are elected in each township, and in each city ward, for five years. A township or ward containing 2,000 inhabitants, or less, may have two justices ; between 2,000 and 4,000, four justices ; over 4,000, five justices. Any township not voting in wards, and containing more than 7,000 inhabitants, may have an additional justice for each additional 3,000 inhabitants over 4,000.

Sheriffs and coroners are elected annually in their respective counties, and may be reëlected until they have served three years; after which they are ineligible for three years.

Education. The income of the fund for the support of free schools, except so much as shall be applied to an increase of the capital, is to be annually appropriated to the support of public schools, for the equal benefit of all the people of the state.

Amendments to the constitution must be agreed to by two successive legislatures, by majorities of all the members elected to each house, and be ratified by the electors at an election held for that purpose. The amendments, (if more than one,) must be voted on separately. Amendments may not be submitted to the people by the legislature oftener than once in five years.

PENNSYLVANIA.

A CONSTITUTION was adopted in 1776; another in 1790; and the present one in 1838.

Legislature. The senate and house of representatives are, together, called the *general assembly.* The representatives are chosen annually, and are apportioned every seven years among the counties according to the number of taxable inhabitants; the number to be fixed by the legislature, and not to be less than sixty, nor more than one hundred. A representative must be twenty-one years of age, have been, when elected, three years a citizen and inhabitant of the state, and the last year an inhabitant of the district he is to represent. Senators are chosen for three years, (one-third of them every year,) in districts, not more than two in any district, unless the taxable inhabitants in any city or county are such as to entitle it to elect more; but no city or county may elect more than four. The number of senators may not be less than one-fourth, nor greater than one-third of the number of representatives. A senator must be twenty-five years of age, and must have been a citizen and an inhabitant of the state four years, the last year of which an inhabitant of the district for which he is chosen.

Bills vetoed by the governor become laws if subsequently passed by majorities of two-thirds. Also bills not returned by him within ten days become laws without his approval, unless their return is prevented by adjournment.

Executive. The governor is elected for three years, and may not hold the office longer than six years in any term of nine years. He must be thirty years of age, and have been a citizen and an inhabitant of the state seven years. No lieutenant-governor.

A secretary of the commonwealth is appointed by the governor during pleasure. A treasurer is elected annually by the two houses in joint assembly.

Electors. Every white freeman, twenty-one years of age, having resided in the state one year, and in the election district where he offers to vote, ten days, next before the election, and within two years has paid a state or county tax assessed at least ten days before the election, is an elector. A qualified elector who shall remove from the state and return, becomes a voter by six months' residence in the state, and by the ten days' residence in the district, and the payment of taxes. White freemen between the ages of twenty-one and twenty-two years, are not required to have paid taxes. Electors, except in cases of crime, are privileged from arrest during their attendance on elections, and in going to and returning from them.

Judiciary. The judicial power of the commonwealth is vested in a supreme court, the judges of which are appointed for fifteen years; courts of oyer and terminer and general jail delivery in the several counties, of which the judges of the supreme court and court of common pleas are justices by virtue of their offices; a court of common pleas in each judicial district, no district to include more than five counties, the presiding judge of which holds his office for ten years, the associate judges for five years; a court of quarter sessions and an orphans' court for each county, held by judges of the common pleas; a register's court for each county, composed of the register of wills and judges of the common pleas; and courts held in the several townships, wards, and boroughs, by justices of the peace or aldermen elected by the voters therein, for five years. Judges of the supreme court are elected by the people of the state at large; others are chosen in the districts or counties over which they preside.

Prothonotaries of the supreme court are appointed by the court for three years. Prothonotaries and clerks of the several other courts, recorders of deeds, and registers of wills, are elected in their respective counties and districts, for three years.

Sheriffs and coroners are elected in their respective counties for three years. Sheriffs may not be twice chosen in any term of six years.

Not more than two justices of the peace or aldermen may be elected in any township, ward, or borough, without the consent of a majority of the electors therein.

Education. The legislature is required to provide for the establishment of schools throughout the state, in such manner that the poor may be taught gratis; and the arts and sciences are to be promoted in one or more seminaries of learning.

Amendments are proposed by a majority of all the members elected to each branch of the legislature, and agreed to in like manner by the next legislature, and ratified by a majority of the electors who shall vote thereon. If there are more amendments than one, they must be voted on separately; and no amendments may be submitted to the electors oftener than once in five years.

DELAWARE.

The first constitution of this state was adopted in 1776; the present, in 1831. It has received several amendments.

Legislature. A senate and house of representatives, called the *general assembly*. Representatives are chosen in counties for two years. They must be twenty-four years of age; must have been citizens and inhabitants of the state three years next preceding the first meeting of the legislature after their election, and of the county, one year Senators are elected in the several counties for four years: the number not to be greater than one-half, nor less than one-third of the number of representatives. A senator must be twenty-seven years of age, possess a freehold estate in the county of two hundred acres of land, or an estate in real and personal property, or in either, worth £1,000 at least; and have been a citizen and an inhabitant of the state three years, and the last year of the county for which he is chosen.

Bills are not submitted to the governor in this state, but are laws when passed by both houses. The legislature meets biennially on the 1st Tuesday in January.

Executive. The governor is elected for four years, and is not eligible a second time. He must be thirty years of age, and have been a citizen and an inhabitant of the United States twelve years, and the last six years of that term an inhabitant of the state. No lieutenant-governor.

A secretary of state is appointed by the governor during his continuance in office. A state treasurer is appointed biennially by the house of representatives, with the concurrence of the senate. [By this mode of election, the two houses do not meet in joint convention, as in certain other states; but they act separately, as in passing laws; a majority of each house being necessary to an appointment.]

Judiciary. The following courts are held by five judges, of whom one is chancellor of the state, and holds the court of chancery, and is president of the orphan's court. Of the other four, one is chief-justice of the state; the other three are associate justices, one of them to reside in each county.

The superior court consists of the chief-justice, and two associate judges; but no associate judge may sit in the county in which he resides. The court of general sessions of the peace and jail delivery is composed of the same judges, and in the same manner, as the superior court. The court of oyer and terminer consists of all the judges except the chancellor, and exercises the jurisdiction vested in the courts of oyer and terminer and general jail delivery. The court of errors and appeals issues writs of error to the superior court, receives appeals from the court of chancery, and determines finally all matters in error in the judgments and proceedings of the superior court. The court of errors and appeals upon a writ of error to the superior court, consists of the chancellor and two of the other judges. In other cases it is differently constituted. The orphans' court in each county is held by the chancellor and the associate judge residing in each county. The register's court in each county is held by the registers of the several counties. Judges of the above courts are appointed by the governor, and hold during good behavior. They may be removed by the governor on the address of two-thirds of all the members of each branch of the general assembly.

In pursuance of the power vested in the legislature to establish inferior courts, a court of common pleas is established in each county.

A competent number of justices of the peace in each county are appointed by the governor for seven years, and are removable by him on address of the legislature.

The sheriff and coroner of each county are chosen by the citizens thereof, for two years; but the sheriff may not be chosen twice in any term of four years. The legislature may vest the appointment of sheriffs and coroners in the governor; but no person may be appointed sheriff twice in any term of six years. The attorney-general, registers, and prothonotaries are appointed for five years, and are removable by the governor on address of the legislature.

Electors. Free white male citizens twenty-two years of age, having resided in the state one year, and the last month thereof in the county where they offer to vote, and having within two years paid a county tax assessed at least six months before the election. All white male citizens twenty-one years of age and under twenty-two, having so resided, may vote without payment of any tax. Electors are privileged from arrest during attendance on elections, and in going to and returning from them, except in cases of crime.

Amendments to the constitution are proposed by two-thirds of each house of the legislature, with the approbation of the governor, and ratified by three-fourths of each branch at the first session held after the next election of representatives. A convention to amend may be called by the legislature, in pursuance of the sense of the people expressed at a previous election.

MARYLAND.

A CONSTITUTION was adopted in 1776, which continued until 1851, when the present one was adopted.

Electors. Every white male citizen twenty-one years of age, having resided one year in the state, and six months in the county in which he offers to vote, may vote in the ward or election district in which he resides.

Executive. The governor is elected for four years. He must be thirty years of age; have been five years a citizen of the United States, and five years a resident of the state, and for three years a resident of the district from which he is elected. In case of vacancy, the general assembly elects some resident of the same district to be governor for the residue of the term. If the vacancy happens during the recess of the legislature, the president of the senate serves until the next session. There is no lieutenant-governor.

A secretary of state is appointed by the governor and senate, during the official term of the governor. A controller of the treasury is chosen by the electors of the state, for two years; and a treasurer and a state librarian are appointed by the legislature on joint ballot at each session.

Legislature. A senate and a house of delegates, styled, the *general assembly.* Senators, one from each county and the city of Baltimore, are elected for four years, one-half every two years. A senator must be twenty-five years of age, and a citizen, and must have resided three years in the state when elected, and a year in the county or city which he is to represent. Delegates are eligible at the age of twenty-one years; other qualifications the same as those of senators. They are elected for two years, and are apportioned among the counties according to population; the city of Baltimore to have four more delegates than the most populous county, and no county to have less than two delegates; the whole number not to be more than eighty, nor less than sixty-five.

The legislature meets on the first Wednesday of January, and is required to close its regular sessions on the 10th day of March next ensuing, unless both houses agree to adjourn at an earlier day. Bills must pass each house by a majority of all the members elected ; and when so passed and sealed with the great seal, the governor is required to sign them in the presence of the presiding officers and chief clerks of both houses.

Judiciary. The court of appeals consists of four judges, of whom one is elected in each of the judicial districts into which the state is divided. One is designated by the governor and senate as chief-justice. They must be thirty years of age, and have been citizens of the state five years. They hold their offices for ten years, and become ineligible at the age of seventy years. This court has appellate jurisdiction only. There are eight judicial circuits, in each of which, except the fifth, is elected a judge, called circuit judge, for the term of ten years. The judge of each circuit holds circuit courts in the several counties within his circuit. A circuit judge must have resided five years in the state, and two in his judicial circuit. The judges of this court have chancery powers.

There are in the city of Baltimore, a court of common pleas, and a superior court, each of which consists of one judge elected for ten years ; also a criminal court, held by a judge elected by the electors. And there are, in the city of Baltimore, and in each county, an orphans' court, consisting of three judges elected by the people for four years, and a register of wills, chosen for six years. Judges of the higher courts are removable by the governor on address by the legislature.

Justices of the peace and constables, the number to be fixed by the legislature, are elected for two years in each ward of the city of Baltimore, and in each election district in the several counties.

A sheriff is elected in each county and the city of Baltimore. The person having the highest number of votes is commissioned by the governor ; if two have an equal number, the governor may choose either of them. If a vacancy happens in the office, the governor commissions the person having had the next highest or equal number of votes Sheriffs are ineligible for the next two years.

A state's attorney is elected for four years in each county and the city of Baltimore.

Amendments. The constitution can be amended only by a convention, called by the legislature in pursuance of a vote of the people to be taken after each United States census.

Miscellaneous Provisions. Corporations may be formed only under general laws, except for municipal purposes, and in cases where the object of the corporation can not be attained without a special act. Lotteries are to cease after 1859. Duelists are disqualified for office. Members of the legislature are paid four dollars a day, and mileage ; the presiding officers of each house an additional dollar each. Ministers of the gospel may not be elected to the legislature. The contracting of state debts exceeding $100,000 at any time is prohibited ; and no debts may hereafter be contracted, unless provision is made for collecting taxes to pay them within fifteen years. The abolition of slavery is forbidden. Stockholders of banks are hereafter to be made individually liable to the amount of their respective shares.

VIRGINIA.

A CONSTITUTION was adopted in 1776 ; another in 1830 ; the present in 1851.

Electors. Every white male citizen, twenty-one years of age, who has been a resident of the state two years, and of the county, city, or town where he offers to vote, one year, is a qualified elector. In all elections votes are to be given openly, or *viva voce.* Dumb persons only may vote by ballot.

Legislature. The two branches are called *general assembly* The house of delegates consists of one hundred and fifty-two members, elected biennially in the several counties and election districts, each district comprising one or more counties ; but the districts are of unequal population, and not the same number of delegates is apportioned to each district. The senate consists of fifty members elected for four years, one-half to be elected every two years. The state is divided into fifty districts, in each of which one senator is chosen. Apportionments of members of both houses are to be made every ten years. Delegates are eligible at the age of twenty-one years; senators at the age of twenty-five.

Legislature meets once in two years. No session may continue longer than ninety days, without the concurrence of three-fifths of all the members elected to each house, in which case the session may be extended for a further period, not exceeding thirty days. Bills, to become laws, do not require the governor's approval.

Executive. The governor is elected for four years, and is ineligible for the next term. He must be thirty years of age, a native citizen of the United States, and have been a citizen of Virginia five years next preceding his election. A lieutenant-governor, who presides in the senate, but has no vote.

A secretary of the commonwealth, a treasurer and an auditor of public accounts, are elected for two years by the joint vote of the two houses. An attorney-general is elected by the voters of the state, for four years, at every election for governor.

Judiciary. A supreme court of appeals, district courts, and circuit courts. The state is divided into twenty-one judicial circuits, ten districts, and five sections. A judge for each circuit is elected for eight years, who holds circuit courts in the several counties composing his district. A judge of one circuit may be authorized to hold courts in another circuit. A district court is held by the judges constituting the section and the judge of the supreme court of appeals for the section to which the district belongs. The supreme court of appeals consists of a judge elected in and for each of the five sections, for twelve years. Judges may be removed by the general assembly. A county court is held monthly in each county, by not less than three nor more than five justices, except when the law shall require a greater number. Each county is divided into districts, in each of which four justices of the peace are elected for four years. The justices so elected choose one of their own body as presiding justice of the county court.

There are elected in each county, a clerk of the county court and a surveyor, for six years; an attorney for four years; a sheriff for two years; and constables and overseers of the poor as may be prescribed by law.

Amendments. The constitution contains no specific provision for its amendment. The last two constitutions have been framed by conventions authorized by acts of the legislature, and were ratified by the electors of the state.

Miscellaneous Provisions. Slaves hereafter emancipated forfeit their freedom by remaining in the state a year, and are reduced to slavery. The power of slave owners to emancipate may be restricted. The general assembly has no power to emancipate slaves. All property other than slaves must be taxed in proportion to its value. In assessing taxes, slaves over twelve years are to be valued at $300 each. A capitation or poll tax, equal to the tax assessed on land of the value of $200, is to be levied on every white male of the age of twenty-one years ; one-half to be applied to the purposes of education in primary and free schools. No debts may be contracted by the state on a credit of more than thirty-four years. Lotteries hereafter are prohibited.

The faith of the state shall not be pledged for the debts of any company or corporation. Loans may not be contracted, nor certificates of debt or bonds of the state issued, for a longer period than thirty-four years.

NORTH CAROLINA.

This state adopted a constitution in 1776, which was amended by a convention in 1835.

Legislature. A senate and a house of commons, denominated the *general assembly.* The senate consists of fifty members, chosen biennially, by districts, one in each district. The districts are laid off in proportion to the average amount of public taxes paid by the citizens during the five years preceding. Senators must have resided within their respective districts a year, and have possessed during that time, and continue to possess, within their districts, not less than 300 acres of land. The house of commons is composed of one hundred and twenty members, chosen biennially, and apportioned among the counties according to population, three-fifths of the slaves being added to the number of free persons. They must have resided a year in the counties they represent, and have possessed for six months, and continue to possess, within the same, not less than 120 acres of land.

The legislature meets biennially on the 3d Monday in November. Bills passed by both houses are laws without being presented to the governor.

Executive. A governor is elected every two years, and is eligible only four years in any term of six years. He must be thirty years of age; must have been a resident of the state five years; and must have in the state a freehold of the value of £1,000. No lieutenant-governor.

There is a council of state consisting of seven persons, to advise the governor in the execution of his office; a secretary of state; and a treasurer; all of whom are chosen by joint vote of the two houses, at each session, for two years. An attorney-general is chosen in the same manner for four years, unless for certain reasons the term shall be altered.

Judiciary. The judicial power is vested in judges of the supreme court, judges of the superior courts, judges of admiralty, and justices of the peace. The judges are appointed by the general assembly, by joint ballot, and hold their offices during good behavior. Justices of the peace, within their respective counties, are recommended to the governor by the representatives in general assembly, and are commissioned by the governor, and hold during good behavior.

Electors. White freemen of the age of twenty-one years, having been inhabitants of the state one year, and paid public taxes, are electors. Voters for senators are required also to own a freehold of fifty acres of land.

Amendments. A convention for making amendments may be called by the general assembly, two-thirds of all the members of each house concurring. Propositions for amendments may be made by three-fifths of the whole number of members of each house; and they become amendments when agreed to by a majority of two-thirds of the whole representation in each house of the next general assembly, and ratified by the qualified voters of the state.

Other Provisions. The legislature is required to establish schools, with such salaries to the masters, paid by the public, "as may enable them to instruct at low prices;" and all useful learning shall be duly encouraged and promoted in one or more universities. Atheists, infidels, or persons denying the divine authority of the Old or New Testament, or holding religious principles incompatible with the freedom or safety of the state, are ineligible to civil office. Clergymen, or preachers of the gospel, are ineligible as members of the legislature or of the council of state. All free males between twenty-one and forty-five years of age, and all slaves between twelve and fifty years, are subject to capitation or poll tax, which must be equal upon all individuals thus taxable.

SOUTH CAROLINA.

THE first constitution of this state was formed in 1775; the present one in 1790. The only essential amendments which it has received, were made in 1808.

Legislature. A *general assembly,* consisting of a senate and a house of representatives. The house is composed of one hundred and twenty-four members, elected for two years in districts, and apportioned according to the number of white inhabitants and the amount of taxes paid therein; one representative being allowed for every sixty-second part of the number of white inhabitants of the state, and one for every sixty-second part of the whole taxes raised by the legislature; and there must be at least one representative to every district. A representative must be a free white man twenty-one years of age; must have been a resident citizen of the state three years; and, if a resident of the election district, must have a freehold of 500 acres of land and ten negroes, or a real estate of the value of £150 sterling, clear of debt; if a non-resident, a clear freehold of £500 sterling. The senate is composed of forty-five members, elected by districts; each district, except one, being represented by one senator. Senators are chosen for four years, one-half of them every two years. A senator must be thirty years of age, and have been a citizen and resident of the state five years. If he is a resident in the district, he must have a clear freehold of £300 sterling; if a non-resident, a freehold in the district of £1,000

The legislature meets annually on the 4th Monday in November. Bills become laws when passed by both houses, signed by their presiding officers, and sealed with the great seal of the state.

Executive. The governor and lieutenant-governor are chosen by the legislature, for two years. To be eligible to either office, a person must be thirty years of age; must have been a resident citizen of the state ten years; and must have a settled freehold within the state of the value of £1,500 sterling, clear of debt. A governor is ineligible for the next four years after the expiration of his term.

Commissioners of the treasury, the secretary of state, and the surveyor-general, are elected by joint ballot of both houses, for the term of four years, and are ineligible for the next four years.

Judiciary. The judicial power is vested in such superior and inferior courts of law and equity as the legislature may establish. The judges are appointed by the legislature during good behavior.

Electors. Every free white male citizen, twenty-one years of age, is a voter, if he has resided in the state two years and owns a freehold of 50 acres of land, or a town lot, which he has owned six months; or, not having such freehold or town lot, has resided six months in the election district, and paid a tax the preceding year of three shillings sterling.

Amendments to the constitution may be made by a convention called by two-thirds of both branches of the whole representation. Alterations may also be made by like majorities of two successive legislatures.

Other Provisions. Religious freedom is established. Ministers of the gospel are ineligible to the office of governor, lieutenant-governor, or to the legislature.

GEORGIA.

A CONSTITUTION of this state was formed in 1777; a second in 1785; the present one was formed in 1798, and amended in 1839 and 1844.

Legislature. A senate and a house of representatives, styled, the *general assembly*. The members of both houses are elected biennially. The representatives are apportioned among the counties according to the population, including three-fifths of the slaves. Qualifications: age, twenty-one years; citizenship, seven years; inhabitant of the state three years, and of the county, one year. Senators are elected in districts, and must be twenty-five years of age; have been citizens nine years; inhabitants of the state three years, and of the district one year.

Legislature meets biennially, the 1st Monday in November. Bills rejected by the governor, if again passed by two-thirds of both houses, become laws. Also bills not returned within five days, become laws, unless their return is prevented by adjournment.

Executive. The governor is elected for two years. He must be thirty years of age; have been a citizen of the United States twelve years, and of the state six years. No lieutenant-governor.

A secretary of state, a treasurer, and a surveyor-general, are elected for two years.

Judiciary. A supreme court for the correction of errors, to consist of three judges chosen by the legislature for six years, one every two years; a superior court, whose judges are elected in their several circuits for four years; inferior courts, one in each county, consisting of five judges, elected by the people; and justices of the peace elected for four years. The clerks of the superior and inferior courts are elected by the people in their respective districts and counties.

Sheriffs are elected for two years, but may not be twice elected within any period of four years.

Electors are required to be white male citizens and inhabitants of the state, twenty-one years of age; to have resided in the county six months; and to have paid all the taxes required of them, and which they have had opportunity of paying, for the year preceding the election.

Amendments may be made by two successive legislatures, two-thirds of both houses concurring.

Miscellaneous Provisions. The legislature is required to aid in establishing seminaries for the promotion of the arts and sciences, and to provide for the improvement and security of the funds and endowments of such institutions. No laws shall be passed for the emancipation of slaves without the consent of their owners, nor for preventing immigrants from bringing their slaves with them from other states.

KENTUCKY.

This state was admitted into the union in 1792. Its first constitution, however, was adopted in 1790; another, in 1799; and the present in 1850.

Legislature. A house of representatives and a senate, styled, the *general assembly*. The house consists of one hundred representatives elected for two years, and apportioned among the counties according to the number of qualified voters. A representative must be twenty-four years of age, a citizen of the United States, and have resided in the state two years, and one year in the county for which he is chosen. When a city or town has a sufficient number of qualified voters, it may elect one or more representatives. The senate consists of thirty-eight members, one to be elected in each district, for four years, one-half every two years. Their qualifications are, age thirty years, residence in the state six years, and in the district one year.

Sessions of the legislature are held biennially, on the 1st Monday in November. Bills vetoed by the governor, if passed again by a majority of all the members elected to each house, become laws. Also if not returned by him within ten days, unless the return is prevented by adjournment; in which case they become laws, unless sent back within three days after the commencement of the next session.

Executive. The governor is elected for four years, and is ineligible for the next four years. Qualifications: age, thirty-five years, citizenship; and residence in the state six years. A lieutenant-governor, qualified and elected as the governor.

A treasurer, for two years, and an auditor of public accounts, a register of the land-office, and an attorney-general, for four years, are elected by the electors of the state.

Judiciary. A supreme court, styled court of appeals, circuit courts, county courts, courts held by justices of the peace, and such other courts inferior to the supreme court, as the legislature may establish. The court of appeals consists of four judges, one to be elected in each district for eight years, in such rotation that one may be elected every two years. If the number shall be changed, the principle of electing one judge every two years is to be preserved. A clerk of this court is chosen for eight years by the electors of the state. A circuit court is established in each county, to be held by a district judge, the state being divided into twelve judicial districts, and a judge elected in each, for six years. The number of districts may be increased, but may not exceed sixteen, until the population shall exceed 1,500,-000. Qualifications the same as those of the judges of appeals. In each county is a county court, composed of a presiding judge and two associate judges, elected for four years. They must have resided in the county one year.

For the election of justices of the peace, each county is divided into districts of convenient size, in each of which two justices are elected for four years, and a constable for two years; all having jurisdiction throughout the county. There are also elected, a state's attorney for each judicial district, a circuit court clerk for each county, and a county court clerk, an attorney, a surveyor, a coroner, and a jailer, for each county, for the same term as that of the presiding judge of the county court; and a sheriff for two years, who shall be reëligible for a second term; but shall not be reëligible, nor act as deputy, for the succeeding term.

Electors. Every free white male citizen, twenty-one years of age, who has resided in the state two years, and in the county, town, or city, in which he offers to vote, one year, and in the precinct in which he offers to vote, sixty days, may vote in such precinct, and not elsewhere.

Amendments by conventions only are provided for. But no conventions may be called by the legislature, until a majority of all the voters of the state shall have voted at two successive elections in favor of calling a convention.

Miscellaneous Provisions. The legislature may not pass laws for emancipating slaves without the consent of their owners, or without compensation; nor for preventing immigrants from bringing their slaves with them into the state; but may prevent slaves from being brought into the state as merchandise: and laws *shall* be passed permitting owners to emancipate their slaves, saving the rights of creditors, and preventing the emancipated slaves from remaining in the state, and also prohibiting free negroes from immigrating into the state. Clergymen, or teachers of any religious persuasion, are not eligible to the general assembly. The capital of the common school fund, consisting of nearly a million and a half dollars, is inviolably pledged to the support of a system of common schools. A superintendent of public instruction is elected for four years, at the time of electing the governor.

TENNESSEE.

This state was admitted into the union with its first constitution in 1796. The present one was formed in 1835.

Legislature. A general assembly, consisting of a senate and a house of representatives. Representatives are apportioned among the several counties or districts according to the number of qualified voters in each, and are not to exceed seventy-five, until the population of the state shall be 1,500,000, and may never exceed ninety-nine. They are eligible at the age of twenty-one, and must have been citizens of the state three years, and residents of the counties they represent, one year. Senators are apportioned as representatives; the number not to exceed one-third of the number of representatives. They are elected for two years, and are eligible at the age of thirty years; otherwise qualified as representatives.

General assembly meets biennially on the first Monday in October. Bills passed by the legislature are not presented to the governor for approval. Two-thirds of each house constitute a quorum.

Executive. The governor is elected every two years, at the time of the election of the members of the legislature. He may not hold the office more than six years in any term of eight years; must be thirty years of age, a citizen of the United States; and have been a citizen of the state seven years.

A secretary of state is elected by joint vote of the general assembly, for the term of four years; and a treasurer or treasurers, for two years.

Electors. Every free white man of the age of twenty-one years, a citizen of the United States, and a citizen of the county six months; also male persons of color, twenty-one years of age, who are competent witnesses in a court of justice against a white man.

Judiciary. A supreme court, and such inferior courts as the legislature may establish, and courts held by justices of the peace. The supreme court consists of three judges, one in each of the grand divisions of the state, and has appellate jurisdiction only, except in certain cases. Its judges are elected for twelve years, and are eligible at thirty-five. Judges of inferior courts are elected for eight years, and are eligible at thirty. For the election of justices of the peace, each county is divided into districts of convenient size, in each of which are elected two justices and one constable. A district containing a county town may elect three justices and two constables. Their jurisdiction extends throughout the county.

Attorneys for the state are elected by joint vote of both houses of the general assembly, for six years.

There are elected in each county by the electors, one sheriff, for two years, who is eligible six years in any term of eight years; one trustee for two years; and one register for four years. And the justices of the peace in each county elect one coroner and one ranger, for two years.

Education. The common school fund, and all lands and other property now and hereafter appropriated for the use of common schools, are to remain a *perpetual fund* for this purpose, the principal of which may never be diminished; and the interest is to go to the support of common schools, for the equal benefit of all the people of the state. And if hereafter there shall be any division of the public lands of the United States, or of the money arising from the sales thereof, the share coming to this state is to be devoted to the purposes of education and internal improvement.

Amendments to the constitution are proposed by a majority of all the members elected to each of the two houses, and must be approved by two-thirds of all the members elected to each house of the next legislature, and ratified by a majority cf the votes of all the voters for representatives.

Miscellaneous Provisions. A state census is to be taken every ten years. The legislature is required to pass laws exempting from military duty persons belonging to any religious sect known to be opposed to bearing arms. Ministers of the gospel are ineligible to a seat in the legislature. Atheists and persons denying a state of future rewards and punishments, may not hold civil offices. Dueling, and being in any way concerned in a duel, or in challenging to fight a duel, is a punishable offense, and disqualifies the offender for any office of honor or profit in the state.

OHIO.

THE first constitution of this state was adopted in 1802, preparatory to her admission into the union. The present constitution was adopted in 1851.

Legislature. General assembly, a senate and house of representatives. Senators and representatives are elected biennially in their respective counties or districts. They must have resided in the same one year. The ratio of representation in the house is ascertained by dividing the whole population of the state by the number one hundred; the quotient being the ratio for the next ten years. Every county having a population equal to one-half of the ratio is entitled to one representative; every county containing the ratio and three-fourths over, two representatives; counties containing three or more times the ratio, are not allowed a representative on any fraction. But a fraction not less than one-fifth of the ratio, is allowed a representative a proportional part of the ten years for which the apportionment is made. The ratio for a senator is ascertained by dividing the whole population by the number thirty-five. The same rule applies to the representation of fractions in senatorial districts as is applied to fractional representation in representative districts.

The legislature meets biennially on the 1st Monday of

January. Bills passed by both houses are laws without being submitted to the governor.

Executive. The executive department consists of a governor, a lieutenant-governor, a secretary of state, an auditor, a treasurer, and an attorney-general; all of whom are elected for two years, except the auditor, for four years. The supreme executive power is vested in the governor.

Judiciary. A supreme court, district courts, courts of common pleas, courts of probate, justices of the peace, and such other courts inferior to the supreme court in one or more counties, as the general assembly may establish. The supreme court consists of five judges chosen by the electors of the state at large. It holds at least one term in each year at the seat of government, and such other terms there or elsewhere as may be prescribed by law. The judges are elected for five years, one every year. The number may be increased or diminished by the legislature. The district courts are composed of one of the judges of the supreme court, and the judges of the court of common pleas of the respective districts; and are held in each county therein, at least once in each year; or, if deemed inexpedient to hold such court annually in each county, the legislature may provide that three annual sessions, in not less than three places, may be held in each district.

The state is divided into nine common pleas districts; and each of them, consisting of three or more counties, is subdivided into three parts, in each of which one judge of the court of common pleas for the district is elected by the electors of said subdivisions. Courts of common pleas are held by one or more of these judges in every county in the district. The probate court of each county is held by a judge elected for three years. Justices of the peace, a competent number, are elected in each township, for three years

A sheriff is elected in each county, and is not eligible for more than four years in any period of six years.

Electors. White males, twenty-one years of age, having resided in the state one year, and in the county, township, or ward, such time as the law shall prescribe.

Education. The principals of all funds for educational and religious purposes are to be preserved inviolate and undiminished; and the income is to be faithfully applied to these specific objects. The general assembly is required to make such further provision, by taxation or otherwise, as will secure a thorough and efficient school system throughout the state.

State Debts. The state may contract debts to supply casual deficits or failures in revenues, or to meet expenses not otherwise provided for, to the amount of $750,000, and no more ; also debts to repel invasion, suppress insurrection, defend the state in war, or to pay present indebtedness ; but no other debt may hereafter be created by the state. Nor may the state loan its credit ; nor assume the debts of any county, city, town, or township, or of any corporation ; nor become a joint owner or stockholder in any company or association. Nor may any county, city, town, or township, be authorized, by vote of its citizens, to become such stockholder, or to loan its credit to any company or association.

Amendments to the constitution are proposed by three-fifths of all the members elected to each house, and ratified by a majority of the voters voting thereon at an election. Or the question of calling a convention may be submitted to the electors, whenever two-thirds of all the members of each house shall think it necessary ; and if a majority of the electors voting shall vote for a convention, the legislature shall provide for calling the same. Every twentieth year, the question of calling a convention is required to be submitted to the electors.

LOUISIANA.

This state was admitted into the union in 1812, with a constitution formed the same year. In 1845, a second constitution was adopted ; and in 1852, the present one.

Legislature. A senate and a house of representatives, together, styled the *general assembly.* Representatives are elected for two years, in the several parishes, (corresponding to counties in other states ;) each parish to have at least one representative ; and are apportioned according to population. The number is not to exceed one hundred, nor to be less than seventy. Senators are chosen in districts, for four years, one-half every two years, and apportioned among the districts according to population. The number of senators is thirty-two ; and no parish is to be allowed more than five senators. Every duly qualified elector is eligible to a seat in either house.

Legislature meets annually. Bills negatived by the governor must, to become laws, be passed by majorities of two-thirds of all the members elected to each house. Also, if not returned by the governor within ten days, they become laws, unless their return is prevented by adjournment ; in which case they will be laws, if not sent back within three days after the commencement of the next session.

Executive. The governor is elected for four years, and is ineligible the next four years. His qualifications are, age, twenty-eight years ; citizenship and residence in the state, four years. A lieutenant-governor.

A secretary of state and a treasurer are elected by the electors ; the former for four years, the latter for two years.

Judiciary. A supreme court and such inferior courts as the legislature may establish, and justices of the peace. The supreme court is composed of a chief-justice and four associate justices ; the former elected by the electors of the state at large ; the latter in their respective districts. The judges are elected for ten years ; one of the five every two years. Judges of the inferior courts are elected in their respective parishes or districts. Justices of the peace are elected for two years by the electors in each parish, district, or ward.

An attorney-general and a requisite number of district-attorneys, are elected for four years ; the former by the electors of the whole state ; the latter in their respective districts.

A sheriff and a coroner are elected in each parish, for two years.

Electors. Free white males twenty-one years of age, citizens of the United States two years, and residents of the state one year, and in the parish six months. An elector removing from one parish to another, may vote in the former until he shall have become a voter in the latter.

Amendments are proposed by two-thirds of all the members of each house, and ratified by a majority of the electors voting thereon at the next general election.

Miscellaneous Provisions. The state may not subscribe for

the stock of, nor make a loan to, nor pledge its faith for the benefit of, any corporation or joint stock company, except to aid companies or associations formed for the purpose of internal improvement, wholly or partially within the state; but debts and liabilities incurred for these purposes may not at any one time exceed eight millions of dollars. Banks must give ample security for the redemption of their bills; and bill-holders of insolvent banks have preference in payment over other creditors. A board of public works, consisting of four commissioners, one in each district, are elected for four years; two every two years. A superintendent of public education is elected for two years. The general assembly is required to establish free public schools throughout the state, and to provide for their support by general taxation or otherwise. The proceeds of the lands granted by the United States, or which may hereafter be granted or bequeathed to the state, and of the United States deposit fund, are to be a perpetual fund, the interest of which is to go to the support of schools.

INDIANA.

This state formed a constitution, and was admitted into the union, in 1816. The present constitution was adopted in 1851.

Electors. White male citizens, twenty-one years of age, having resided in the state six months, may vote in the township or precinct in which they reside. Also foreigners who have resided in the United States one year, and in the state six months, and have declared their intention to become citizens.

Legislature. A *general assembly*, consisting of a senate and a house of representatives. The number of senators may not exceed fifty; the number of representatives may not exceed one hundred; both to be chosen in their respective counties or districts, and apportioned according to the number of white male inhabitants twenty-one years of age in each. A new enumeration and apportionment are to be made every six years. Qualifications: citizens of the state two years; of the county or district, one year. Senators are elected for four years, one-half every two years, and must be twenty-five years of age. Representatives are chosen for two years, and are eligible at twenty-one.

Sessions of the legislature held biennially, commencing on Thursday next after the first Monday of January. Quorum, two-thirds. Bills are passed by a majority of all the members elected to each house; and if not approved by the governor, they become laws by being again passed by the same majorities. If a bill is not returned by the governor within three days, it is a law, unless its return is prevented by adjournment; in which case it will be a law, unless the governor, within five days after the adjournment, shall file the bill, with his objections, in the office of the secretary of state, who shall lay the same before the general assembly at the next session, in like manner as if it had been returned by the governor. But bills may not be presented to the governor within two days previous to the adjournment.

Executive. The governor is elected for four years; is eligible only four in any period of eight years. Qualifications: age, thirty years; citizenship, five years; and residence in the state, five years. A lieutenant-governor.

A secretary of state, an auditor, and a treasurer, are elected for two years, and are eligible four years in any period of six.

Judiciary. A supreme court, circuit courts, and such inferior courts as the general assembly may establish. Judges of the supreme court, not less than three nor more than five, one in each district, are elected by the electors of the state at large, for six years. Circuit courts consist of a judge for each judicial circuit, chosen by the electors thereof, for six years. A prosecuting attorney also is elected in each judicial circuit, for two years. Justices of the peace are elected for four years, in the townships.

There are elected in each county, a clerk of the circuit court, an auditor, a recorder, a treasurer, a sheriff, a coroner, and a surveyor. The first three hold for four years, and are eligible eight years in twelve; the others hold two years; and the sheriff and treasurer are eligible only four years in any period of eight years.

Amendments must be agreed to by two successive legislatures, a majority of all the members of each house concurring, and ratified by the electors of the state.

Education. The school fund is derived from many sources; mainly, however, from the congressional township fund and lands belonging thereto, and the surplus revenue fund, both of which have been mentioned. (Chap. XXII.) The school fund may be increased, but may never be diminished. The general assembly is required to provide by law for a general and uniform system of common schools, open to all, and without charge for tuition. Institutions for the education of the deaf and dumb, and treatment of the insane, are also enjoined; and houses of refuge for the reformation of juvenile offenders.

Miscellaneous Provisions. State debts may be contracted only to meet casual deficits in the revenue, to pay interest on the state debt, to repel invasion, suppress insurrection, and to provide for the public defense. Counties may not subscribe for stock in any incorporated company, unless the same is paid for at the time of subscribing; nor loan their credit to incorporated companies; nor may the legislature assume the debts of any county, city, town, or township, or corporation. Banks may be established under a general banking law, the payment of their bills to be amply secured. A bank with branches may also be established, without collateral security, the branches to be mutually responsible for each other's liabilities upon all paper credit issued as money. Stockholders are to be individually responsible to the amount of their stock. No law may sanction the suspension of specie payments. Corporations other than banking may be created only by general laws. Negroes and mulattoes may not hereafter come into or settle in the state.

MISSISSIPPI.

In 1817, this state was admitted into the union, with a constitution adopted the same year. The present constitution was formed in 1832.

Electors. Free white males, twenty-one years of age; citizens of the United States; residents of the state one year, and of the county four months. An elector who may happen to be in any county, city, or town, other than that of his residence, or who may have removed to any such place within four months preceding an election, may vote for such officers as he could have voted for in the county of his residence, or from which he so removed.

Legislature. A senate and a house of representatives, together styled *the legislature.* Representatives are elected for two years in the several counties, among which they are apportioned according to the number of free white inhabitants; the number to be not less than thirty-six, nor more than one hundred. They must be twenty-one years of age, citizens of the United States, residents of the state two years, and one year of the counties for which they are chosen. Senators are elected by districts for four years, one-half every two years; the number to be not less than one-fourth, nor more than one-third of the number of representatives. They must be thirty years of age, citizens of the United States, inhabitants of the state four years, and of the districts they represent, one year.

The legislature meets biennially. Bills are passed against the governor's veto, by two-thirds majorities. Bills must be returned within six days, or they become laws, unless their return is prevented by adjournment.

Judiciary. A high court of errors and appeals, consisting of three judges, one in each district, elected for six years, and to be thirty years of age; a circuit court, to be held in each county at least twice a year, the judges to be elected in their respective judicial districts for four years, and to be twenty-six years of age; a superior court of chancery, the chancellor to be elected by the electors of the whole state, for six years; a court of probate in each county, the judge to be elected for two years; a competent number of justices of the peace and constables chosen in each county for two years. Other inferior courts may be established by the legislature.

An attorney-general is chosen by the electors of the state, and a competent number of district-attorneys in their respective districts. A sheriff and one or more coroners are elected in each county for two years.

Executive. The governor is elected for two years; must

be thirty years of age; have been a citizen of the United States twenty years, and a resident of the state five years; and may not hold the office more than four years in any term of six years. No lieutenant-governor.

A secretary of state, a treasurer, and an auditor of public accounts, are elected for two years.

Amendments are proposed by two-thirds of both branches of the legislature, and ratified by the people at the next election.

Miscellaneous Provisions. Persons denying the being of a God, or a future state of rewards and punishments, are disqualified for civil office. Laws for borrowing money on the credit of the state, or pledging the faith of the state for the payment of a loan or debt, must be agreed to by two successive legislatures: provided, however, that a million and a half of dollars may be borrowed and vested in stock reserved to the state by the charter of the Planters' Bank. No act for emancipating slaves without consent of owners may be passed, nor for preventing immigrants from bringing their slaves into the state; but slaves may not be introduced into the state as merchandise, or for sale; and actual settlers may purchase them in other states and bring them into this state. Owners of slaves may be permitted by law to emancipate them, saving the rights of creditors, and preventing the slaves from becoming a public charge. Schools and the means of education are forever to be encouraged.

ILLINOIS.

This state was admitted into the union in 1818. A new constitution, the present one, was formed in 1847.

Legislature. General assembly, consisting of a senate and a house of representatives. Representatives are elected for two years; must be twenty-five years of age; inhabitants of the state three years, and of the county or district one year; and must have paid a state or county tax. Senators are elected for four years, one-half every two years; must be thirty years of age, citizens of the United States; five years inhabitants of the state, and one year in the county or district; and must have paid a state or county tax. The senate is to consist of twenty-five members; the house of seventy-five. When the population of the state shall amount to 1,000,000, five members may be added to the house, and five additional members for every 500,000 inhabitants thereafter; but the number is never to exceed one hundred. One senator only is allowed to each senatorial district, and not more than three representatives to any representative district. Cities and towns having the requisite population, may be erected into separate districts. Apportionments are made after each census, taken in 1855, and every ten years thereafter.

Legislature meets biennially on the first Monday of January. Bills are passed against the veto by a majority of all the members elected to each house. If not returned within ten days, they become laws, unless their return is prevented by adjournment; in which case they must be returned on the first day of the meeting of the legislature after the expiration of the said ten days, or be laws.

Executive. The governor is elected for four years, and is eligible only four in eight years. He must be thirty-five years of age, and have been a citizen of the United States fourteen years, and ten years a resident of the state. A lieutenant-governor.

A secretary of state, and an auditor of public accounts are elected for four years, and a treasurer for two years.

Judiciary. A supreme court, circuit courts, county courts, and justices of the peace. Also inferior local courts may be established in the cities by the legislature. The supreme court consists of three judges, one in each of the three grand divisions, elected by the voters thereof, for the term of nine years, one judge to be elected every three years; and the judge having the oldest commission, to be chief-justice. The legislature may provide for their election by the whole state. Circuit judges are elected for six years, one in each of the nine judicial districts, the number of which may be increased, if necessary. A circuit court is to be held two or more terms annually in each county. A judge of the county court is elected in each county for four years. He has also probate jurisdiction. All judges must be citizens of the United States; must have resided in the state five years, and in the district or county two years. Judges of the supreme court must be thirty-five years of age ; circuit judges thirty years.

Justices of the peace are elected in each county, by districts, for four years.

A state's attorney is elected in each judicial circuit, for four years ; or, if the legislature shall so direct, in each county, for such term as may be prescribed by law. In each county a clerk of the circuit court is elected for four years, and a sheriff for two years, who is eligible only once in four years ; supreme court clerks by the electors in each division, for six years.

Electors. White male citizens, twenty-one years of age, having resided in the state one year. The legislature may, in case of necessity, levy upon every legal voter under sixty years of age, a poll or capitation tax of not less than fifty cents, nor more than one dollar.

Amendments. The question of calling a convention is to be submitted to the people by previous recommendation of the legislature, concurred in by two-thirds of all the members of both houses. If a majority of the electors voting for representatives shall vote for a convention, an act shall be passed for calling the same. Amendments made without calling a convention, must be proposed by one legislature, two-thirds of all the members of both houses concurring, and approved by the next legislature, a majority of all the members of each of the two houses agreeing to the same, and ratified by the electors of the state at the next general election.

Miscellaneous Provisions. Corporations not possessing banking powers, may be formed under general laws ; but not by special acts, except for municipal purposes, and when the objects of the corporation can not be attained under general laws. No state bank may hereafter be created ; nor may the state own stock in any banking concern. Stockholders in banking associations are individually liable to the amount of their respective shares. Acts authorizing such associations shall not go into effect, unless they have been submitted to the electors of the state, and approved by them at an election. A tax of two mills on the dollar shall be collected annually, and kept as a separate fund, for the payment of state indebtedness, other than canal and school indebtedness. The corporate authorities of counties, townships, school districts, cities, towns, and villages, may be vested with power to assess and collect taxes for corporate purposes.

ALABAMA.

This state was admitted into the union in 1819, with its present constitution.

Legislature, called the *general assembly*, consisting of a senate and a house of representatives. Representatives are apportioned among the counties according to the number of free white inhabitants. Cities or towns having a representative population equal to the ratio, may have a separate representation. Representatives are chosen biennially; and must be twenty-one years of age, residents of the state two years, and of the county, city, or town for which they are chosen, one year. Senators are chosen in districts, (one in each district,) for four years, one-half of them every two years; must be twenty-seven years age; residence the same as representatives. The number of representatives may not be more than one hundred; the number of senators not more than thirty-three.

Sessions are held annually. Bills are passed against the veto, by majorities of all the members elected to each house. If a bill is not returned by the governor within five days, it is a law, unless its return is prevented by adjournment.

Electors. White male citizens, twenty-one years of age, having resided in the state one year, and in the county, city, or town, three months.

Executive. The governor is elected for two years, and is eligible four years in any term of six years. He must be thirty years of age, a native citizen of the United States, and a resident of the state four years. No lieutenant-governor.

A secretary of state biennially, and a treasurer and a controller of public accounts annually, are chosen by joint vote of both houses.

Judiciary. A supreme court ; circuit courts, to be held in each county ; and inferior courts of law and equity to be established by the general assembly. Judges of the supreme court and chancellors are chosen by the legislature for six years ; judges of the circuit and inferior courts by the people, for the same term. A competent number of justices of the peace, and a sheriff, are elected in each county.

An attorney-general for the state, and the requisite number of solicitors, are elected by joint vote of the general assembly, for four years.

Education. The funds which are raised from the lands granted by the United States for the use of schools within each township, and from the lands granted for the support of a state university, are to be strictly applied to these objects.

Banks. One state bank with branches is authorized. After the establishment of a state bank, existing banks may be admitted as branches thereof. At least two-fifths of the capital stock of the state bank must be reserved for the state. The state is also to have a proportion of power in the direction of the bank, at least equal to its proportion of stock therein. The state and the individual stockholders are liable, respectively, for the debts of the bank, in proportion to their stock. Banks may not commence operations, until half of the capital stock subscribed for is paid in gold and silver, which amount is in no case to be less than $100,000.

Slaves. No law may be passed for emancipating slaves without the consent of their owners, or without paying their owners. Emigrants to the state shall not be prohibited from bringing their slaves with them ; but the bringing of slaves into the state as merchandise may be prohibited. And laws may be passed to permit owners to emancipate, saving the rights of creditors, and preventing their becoming a public charge.

Amendments are proposed by one legislature, approved by the electors at the next election for representatives, and ratified by the next legislature ; majorities of two-thirds of each house being in both cases required.

MISSOURI.

This state was admitted into the union in 1821. The present constitution was adopted in 1820. It has been several times amended.

Legislature. A senate and a house of representative, together styled the *general assembly.* Representatives are chosen for two years, and are apportioned among the counties according to a ratio ascertained by dividing the number of free white inhabitants of the state by one hundred and forty. A county having said ratio, or less, has one representative; having said ratio and a fraction of three-fourths, two representatives. The more populous counties have less representatives than one for each such ratio. Representatives are to be citizens, twenty-four years of age, residents of the state two years, and of the counties or districts they represent, one year, and to have paid a state or county tax within the year. Senators, not to be less than twenty-five nor more than thirty-three, are chosen in single districts, for four years, one-half every two years. Qualifications: age, thirty years; residence in the state, four years; in the district, one year; payment of a state or county tax.

Sessions of the legislature are held biennially, and limited to sixty days. Bills, to become laws against the executive veto, must be passed by majorities of all the members elected. General elections biennially, the first Monday in August.

Electors. Free white male citizens, twenty-one years of age, having resided in the state one year, and in the county or district three months.

Executive—a governor elected for four years, who is ineligible the next four; must be thirty years; have been a citizen of the United States ten years, and of the state five years. A lieutenant governor.

A secretary of state, an auditor of public accounts, a treasurer, an attorney-general, and a register of lands, are chosen by the electors of the state for four years.

Judiciary. The judicial power is vested in a supreme court, circuit courts, county courts, justices of the peace, and such other tribunals inferior to the circuit courts, as the general assembly shall establish. The supreme court consists of three judges, elected for six years by the qualified voters of the state. In each of the ten circuits, (the number of which might not be increased until after ten years,) is a circuit judge, chosen by the electors of the circuit, for six years. Judges of the supreme and circuit courts must be thirty years of age, and have resided in the state five years. In each county is a county court. Justices of the peace are elected in the several townships. Clerks of the circuit and county courts are chosen by the electors of the counties, for six years.

Education. The proceeds of all the lands granted by congress for the support of schools, the income of the United States deposit fund, and of all other sources of revenue designed for this object, are to be strictly appropriated. The legislature is enjoined to provide means for the support of free public schools throughout the state, by taxation on property, and by capitation tax, or otherwise.

State Debts. The entire indebtedness of the state contracted under this constitution, may not at any time exceed $25,000, except in cases of war, insurrection, and invasion, unless the creation of a debt proposed by the legislature, for a specified purpose, shall be approved by the electors of the state, nor unless means shall be provided by taxation for the payment of the debt within twenty years.

Slaves. The legislature may not pass laws for emancipating slaves without the consent of their owners, and without compensation, and removing them out of the state; nor to prevent immigrants and actual settlers from bringing slaves into the state from other states and territories. Laws may be passed to prohibit the introduction of slaves as merchandise, and to permit owners to emancipate their slaves, saving the rights of creditors, and security being given for the immediate removal of the emancipated slaves out of the state. And the legislatur is enjoined to pass laws, as soon as may be, to prevent free negroes from coming to and settling in the state; provided that such measure shall not be construed to conflict with the 1st clause, 2d section, 4th article of the constitution of the United States.

Amendments may be proposed in 1850, and every fourth year thereafter, by a majority of the whole of each house; and they take effect when ratified by the electors of the state.

ARKANSAS.

In 1836, this state was admitted into the union with its present constitution, which was slightly amended in 1845.

Electors. All free white male citizens, twenty-one years of age, who have been citizens of the state six months, and actual residents of the counties in which they offer to vote.

Legislature. General assembly, consisting of a senate and a house of representatives. Representatives are elected for two years; must be twenty-five years of age, and residents of the counties they represent. Their number may not be less than fifty-four, nor more than one hundred. They are apportioned among the counties, according to the number of free white male inhabitants, taking 500 as the ratio; and when the number of representatives shall amount to seventy-five, there is to be no further increase until the population of the state shall amount to 500,000 souls.—Senators are chosen in single districts for four years, one-half, as near as may be, every two years; the number never to be less than seventeen, nor more than thirty-three, apportioned upon the basis of the free white male inhabitants, the ratio being 1,500 until the number is twenty-five; after which the ratio is to be such as not to increase the number of senators until the population of the state shall amount to 500,000. Senators must be thirty years, inhabitants of the state one year, and actual residents of the districts they represent.

Legislature meets biennially. General elections are *viva voce,* until otherwise directed by law, and are held every two years on the 1st Monday of October, until altered by law. Bills are passed against the veto by a majority of the whole of each house. They are to be returned within three days, or they become laws, unless their return is prevented by adjournment.

Executive. A governor is elected for four years, and is ineligible more than eight in any term of twelve years. Qualifications: age, thirty years: residence in the state four years; a native born citizen of Arkansas, or a native born citizen of the United States, or a resident of Arkansas ten years previous to the adoption of the constitution, if not a native of the United States. No lieutenant-governor.

A secretary of state for four years, and an auditor and a treasurer for two years, are elected by a joint vote of both houses.

Judiciary. A supreme court, circuit courts, county courts, and justices of the peace. Corporation courts and courts of chancery may be established by the legislature. The supreme court is composed of three judges, elected by joint vote of the assembly for eight years; one to be elected every four years, one every six, and one every eight years. They are to be thirty years of age. Each circuit is to contain not less than five nor more than seven counties, for which a judge is elected by the general assembly, for four years, who must be twenty-five years of age. There is in each county a county court held by the justices of the peace, who elect a presiding judge, for two years. This court has jurisdiction in matters relating to county taxes, disbursements of money for county purposes, and other local concerns of the county. The presiding judge is also judge of probate. Justices of the peace are elected in the townships for two years. They have civil jurisdiction in actions when the sum claimed is $100 or under, and in penal offenses less than felony.

An attorney of state is elected in each judicial circuit for two years.

A sheriff, a coroner, a treasurer, and a county surveyor, are elected in each county, for two years.

Education. The legislature is required to provide for improving the lands granted to the state by the United States for the use of schools, and to apply the proceeds to the intended object; also to pass laws to encourage intellectual, scientific, and agricultural improvements.

Slaves. Laws shall not be passed for emancipating slaves without consent of the owners; nor to prevent immigrants from bringing their slaves with them. Laws may be passed to permit owners to emancipate, saving the rights of creditors, and preventing the freed slaves from becoming a public charge; and laws may be passed to prevent slaves from being brought into the state as merchandise.

Banks. The constitution authorized a state bank with branches, which was to be the repository of the state funds, and was to loan out the funds to the people of the counties in proportion to representation ; and another banking institution designed to aid the agricultural interests ; and the credit of the state might be pledged to raise the funds of these banks, provided the individual stockholders should guaranty the state against loss. One of the amendments adopted in 1846, prohibits the incorporation, thereafter, of any banking institution in the state.

Amendments may be made by two successive legislatures, two-thirds of each of the two houses concurring in the same.

Other Provisions. Persons who deny the being of a God may not hold civil offices, nor be witnesses in courts. No poll-tax may be assessed for any other than county purposes. All revenue is to be raised by taxation.

MICHIGAN.

This state was admitted into the union in 1836. The present constitution was adopted in 1850.

Legislature. Senate and house of representatives. The senate has thirty-two members, who are elected for two years in senate districts ; that is, a single senator in each district. Representatives, not less than sixty-four, nor more than one hundred, are also elected in single districts, for two years. Apportionments of members are made after each enumeration, taken in 1854, and every ten years thereafter. Any qualified elector holding no other office, is eligible to either house.

Sessions of the legislature are biennial, commencing the 1st Wednesday of January. Members receive ten cents for every mile traveled to and from the place of meeting, and three dollars a day for the first forty days of each regular session, and nothing thereafter ; and the same for twenty days of each extra session. No pay but for actual attendance, except when absent on account of sickness.—Newspapers and stationery, not exceeding five dollars in value, are allowed to each member. The passage of bills requires a majority of all the members elected to each house. Majorities of two-thirds of all the members elected are necessary to pass bills against the veto. Bills not returned by the governor within ten days, become laws, unless their return is prevented by adjournment. Acts passed within the last five days of a session, may be signed by the governor and filed by him in the office of the secretary of state within five days after the adjournment; and the same become laws.

Executive. The governor is elected for two years. He must be thirty years of age; have been a citizen of the United States five years, and a resident of the state two years. A lieutenant-governor.

Judiciary. One supreme court, circuit courts, a probate court, and justices of the peace. For six years, and until the legislature otherwise provide, the circuit judges are to be judges of the supreme court. After six years, a supreme court may be organized, consisting of a chief-justice and three associate justices, to be chosen by the electors of the state for eight years, and to be so classed that only one of them shall go out of office at a time. The supreme court holds four terms annually. A circuit judge is elected in each of the eight judicial circuits for six years. The number of circuits may be increased. A circuit court is to be held at least twice in every county annually; in counties containing 10,000 inhabitants, four times. The judge of the probate court of each county is elected for four years. Justices of the peace, not exceeding four in each township, are elected in the several townships for four years.

Electors. White male citizens, twenty-one years of age, who have resided in the state three months, and in the township or ward ten days. Also foreigners after a residence of two and a half years in the state, and a declaration of their intention to become citizens; and civilized male inhabitants of Indian descent, are electors. General elections are held biennially on the Tuesday succeeding the first Monday of November.

A secretary of state, a superintendent of public instruction, a treasurer, a commissioner of the land-office, an auditor-general, and an attorney-general, are elected for two years.

There are chosen in each county, a sheriff, a county clerk, a county treasurer, a register of deeds, and a prosecuting attorney, all for two years. The sheriff can hold the office no longer than four in a period of six years. The board of supervisors may unite the offices of county clerk and register of deeds in one office.

Education. The constitution pledges to the support of schools, the proceeds of the lands granted by the United States, and of all the lands and other property given by individuals or appropriated by the state for like purposes. The legislature is required to provide for keeping a school, without charge for tuition, at least three months in each year in every district. Three members of a state board of education are elected for six years, one every two years. The superintendent of public instruction is ex-officio a member and secretary of the board. The state normal school is placed under the supervision of this board. Institutions for instructing the deaf and dumb are also to be supported. An agricultural school also is provided for.

State Debts, &c. The state may contract debts not exceeding, at any one time, $50,000, to meet deficits in revenue. The credit of the state may not be granted to, or in aid of, any person or corporation. No scrip, certificate, or other evidence of state indebtedness, shall be issued, except to redeem stock previously issued, or for debts authorized in the constitution. The state shall not hold stock in any company, nor be interested in any work of internal improvement, except in the expenditure of grants to the state of land or other property.

Corporations, except for municipal purposes, shall not be created by special acts, but may be formed under general laws. Banking laws shall not take effect until approved by the electors at an election. Stockholders of banking corporations are individually liable for all debts contracted during the time they were stockholders. Security must be given by banks for all their bills issued; and in case of insolvency, billholders have preference in payment. The suspension of specie payments shall not be sanctioned by law.

Amendments are proposed by two-thirds of all the members of each branch, and ratified by a majority of the electors voting thereon at the next general election. In 1866, and every sixteenth year thereafter, and at such other times as the legislature shall provide, the question of a general revision of the constitution by a convention shall be submitted to the electors of the state.

Other Provisions. No law may be passed authorizing the

granting of license for the sale of intoxicating liquors. No person shall be rendered incompetent as a witness on account of his religious belief.

FLORIDA.

This state was admitted into the union with its present constitution, by act of congress of March 3, 1845.

Executive. The governor is elected for four years, and is ineligible for the next term. Age, thirty years; citizen of the United States; resident of the state five years. No lieutenant-governor.

A secretary of state is elected by the people for four years; a treasurer and a controller of public accounts, for two years.

Legislature. A senate and a house of representatives, styled the *general assembly.* Representatives are apportioned among the counties according to the number of free white inhabitants, and three-fifths of the slaves; the number not to exceed sixty. They are elected biennially. Qualifications: age, twenty-one years; citizenship; residence in the state two years, and in the county one year. Senators are elected in districts, at least one in each district; the number to be not less than one-fourth, nor greater than one-half of the number of representatives. They are chosen for four years,—one half every two years. Age, twenty-five years; other qualifications the same as those of representatives.

The legislature meets biennially on the 4th Monday in November; the time alterable by law. Bills become laws against the veto by majorities of all the members elected to both houses.

Judiciary. A supreme court, courts of chancery, circuit courts. and justices of the peace. The supreme court consists of three judges, elected by the people, for six years; and holds four sessions annually. The state is divided into four circuits, eastern, middle, western, and southern; and a judge is elected in each judicial circuit for six years, who presides in the courts held in his circuit. Justices of the peace for each county are appointed or elected as the general assembly may direct.

An attorney-general is elected by joint vote of the two houses, for four years. The clerk of the supreme court, the clerks of the courts of chancery, and a solicitor for each circuit, are elected by the general assembly; the clerks of the circuit courts, by the electors of the circuits.

Electors. White male citizens, twenty-one years of age; residents of the state two years, and of the county six months; who are enrolled in the militia, unless by law exempted from serving. The general assembly is required to provide for registering the qualified electors of each county.

Education. The proceeds of all lands granted by the United States for the use of schools, are to be a perpetual fund, the interest of which is to be appropriated exclusively to that object.

Banks, &c. No bank charter may be granted for more than twenty years; nor may it be extended or renewed. The capital of a bank shall not exceed $100,000; and dividends shall not be made exceeding ten per cent. a year; stockholders are individually liable; and no note may be issued for less than five dollars. The credit of the state may not be pledged in aid of any corporation.

Slaves. No laws shall be passed to emancipate slaves, nor to prevent immigrants from bringing their slaves with them. Laws may be passed to prevent free negroes from immigrating to the state, or from being discharged from any vessel in any of the ports of Florida.

Amendments. A convention may be called by the general assembly, two-thirds of each house concurring. Alterations may be made by the assent of two successive legislatures, two-thirds of each house concurring.

Other Provisions. No minister of the gospel is eligible to the office of governor, or to a seat in the legislature. All bank officers also are thus disqualified while holding such offices, and for a year after they cease to hold the same.

TEXAS.

Texas, formerly a part of Mexico, declared itself independent in 1835. By a joint resolution of congress, approved December 29, 1845, this independent republic was admitted as a state into the union.

Electors. Free white male citizens over twenty-one years of age, who were at the time of the adoption of the constitution by congress citizens of the republic of Texas, and who have resided in the state one year, and the last six months within the district, city, or town, in which they offer to vote. And if an elector happens to be in any other county within his district, he may there vote for any district officer; and he may vote any where in the state for state officers.

Legislature. A senate and a house of representatives. Representatives, the number of whom shall not be less than forty-five, nor greater than ninety, are apportioned among the counties according to the free population, and elected for two years. They must be twenty-one years of age, and have been inhabitants of the state two years, and the last year of the county, city, or town they represent. Senators, not less than nineteen nor more than thirty-three, are elected in districts, for four years, one-half every two years; must be thirty years of age; inhabitants of the state three years, and of the district one year.

The legislature meets biennially. Bills negatived by the governor, become laws when passed by two-thirds of both houses; or if bills are not returned within five days, they become laws. Ministers of the gospel are ineligible to the legislature. Quorum, two-thirds.

Judiciary. A supreme court, district courts, and such inferior courts as the legislature may establish. The supreme court consists of a chief-justice and two associates, and has appellate jurisdiction chiefly. It holds sessions once a year in not more than three places in the state. District courts are held by the judge of each judicial district, at one place in each county, at least twice a year. The judges of both the supreme and district courts are elected by the people for six years.

There are elected in each county a convenient number of justices of the peace, one sheriff, one coroner, and a sufficient number of constables, all for two years. The sheriff is eligible only four years in six. Also a clerk of the district court for each county is elected for four years.

Executive. The governor is elected for two years ; is eligible four years in every six. Qualifications : age, thirty years ; state residence, three years ; a citizen of the United States, or a citizen of the state of Texas at the time of the adoption of the constitution. A lieutenant-governor.

A treasurer, a controller of public accounts, and an attorney-general, are elected by the qualified electors of the state for two years. A secretary of state is appointed by the govenor and senate, to hold during the official term of the govenor.

Amendments of the constitution are proposed by two-thirds majorities of the legislature, approved by the electors at the next general election, and ratified by majorities of two-thirds of both houses of the next legislature.

Slaves. The legislature may not pass laws for the emancipation of slaves without consent of their owners, nor without compensation ; nor laws to prevent immigrants from bringing their slaves with them. Laws may be passed permitting owners to emancipate, saving the rights of creditors, and preventing the freed slaves from becoming a public charge ; also laws prohibiting their introduction as merchandise only.

Education. The legislature is required to establish, as early as practicable, free schools throughout the state, to be supported by taxation ; one-tenth of the annual revenue derivable from taxation, and the proceeds of all public lands granted for public schools, to be a permanent fund for the support of free public schools.

IOWA.

The state of Iowa was admitted into the union by an act of congress approved December 28, 1846.

Electors. White male citizens of the age of twenty-one

years, who have resided in the state six months, and in the county twenty days, are entitled to the right of suffrage.

Legislature. The two houses are called the *general assembly*. Members of the house of representatives are elected in their respective districts, for two years ; and their number (since the population of the state amounted to 175,000) may not be less than thirty-nine, nor exceed seventy-two. A representative must be twenty-one years of age, a free white male citizen of the United States, an inhabitant of the state one year, and an actual resident for thirty days in the county or district which he is chosen to represent. Senators, in number not less than one-third nor more than one-half of the number of representatives, are elected for four years, one-half every two years. They are to be twenty-four years of age ; in other respects qualified as representatives. Election, 1st Monday in August.

Sessions are held biennially, commencing the first Monday of December next after the election. Bills negatived by the governor, must be repassed by two-thirds majorities of the members present in each house, to become laws. If bills are not returned within three days, they are laws though not signed by the governor, unless their return is prevented by adjournment.

Executive. The governor is elected for four years. To be eligible, he must have been a citizen of the United States, and a resident of the state, two years, and must be thirty years of age. No lieutenant-governor. In case of vacancy in the office of governor, the office devolves upon the secretary of state, until the vacancy shall be filled.

A secretary of state, an auditor of public accounts, and a treasurer, are elected by the electors of the state for two years.

Judiciary. A supreme court, district courts, and such inferior courts as the legislature may establish. The supreme court consists of a chief-justice and two associates, elected by joint vote of the two branches, and hold for six years. This court has appellate jurisdiction only in all cases of chancery, and constitutes a court for the correction of errors at law. Each district court consists of a judge, elected by the voters of the district, for five years. District judges are chosen at the township elections. A prosecuting attorney and a clerk of the district court, are elected in each county at the general election, for two years.

State Debts. The debts of the state shall at no time exceed $100,000, except in case of war, invasion, or insurrection, unless authorized by some law for a single object, which law is to provide for the payment of the debt without loans within twenty years; and before it takes effect, must be approved by the electors at a general election.

Corporations. No bank or moneyed corporation is to be hereafter authorized. Other corporations are to be created only by general laws, except for municipal or political purposes. The state may not be a stockholder in any corporation.

Education. A superintendent of public instruction is elected by the people for three years. The proceeds of all lands granted to the state by the United States for the support of schools, and such other property as has been or may be granted for this purpose, are pledged as a perpetual fund, the interest of which is to be strictly appropriated to the support of common schools. The general assembly is enjoined to provide for keeping up a school in each district for at least three months in every year.

Amendments of the constitution are provided for only by a convention. When the legislature thinks it necessary to revise or amend the constitution, provision shall be made by law for a vote of the people for or against a convention, at the next ensuing election for members of the legislature. If a majority of the votes are in favor of a convention, an election of delegates is to be held within six months.

WISCONSIN.

This state was admitted into the union by act of congress, May 29, 1848.

Electors. White male citizens, or foreigners who have declared their intention to become citizens, having resided in the state one year; also civilized persons of Indian descent, not members of any tribe.

Legislature. A senate and an assembly. The number of members of the assembly is not to be less than fifty-four, nor greater than one hundred. They are elected annually. The number of senators may not be less than one-fourth, nor greater than one-third, of the number of members of assembly. They are chosen for two years, one-half every year. The qualifications of members of both houses are the same, a resident of the state one year, and a qualified elector in the district. Both are chosen in single districts, and are to be apportioned every five years, namely, after each decennial census of the United States, and after each intervening state census. Election, the Tuesday next after the 1st Monday of November.

Annual sessions commence at a time fixed by law. Bills are passed over the governor's veto by majorities of two-thirds of both branches. Compensation of members is $2,50 for each day's attendance, and ten cents for every mile traveled going and returning by the usual route.

Executive. The executive power is in a governor elected for two years. To be eligible to the office of governor or lieutenant-governor, a person must be a citizen of the United States, and a qualified elector of the state.

A secretary of state, a treasurer, and an attorney-general, are elected for two years.

Sheriffs, coroners, registers of deeds, and district attorneys, are elected in their respective counties, once in two years. Sheriffs are ineligible for the next two years.

Judiciary. A supreme court, circuit courts, courts of probate, and justices of the peace. Inferior courts, with limited civil and criminal jurisdiction, may be established by the legislature in the several counties. The supreme court, except in certain cases, has appellate jurisdiction only. By the constitution, the judges of the circuit courts were to be judges of the supreme court, for five years, and until the legislature should otherwise provide ; and authority is given to the legislature to organize a separate supreme court, to consist of a chief-justice and two associate justices, elected by the electors of the state for six years ; one only to be elected at a time. The circuit judges also, one in each judicial circuit, are elected for six years. Judges are to be twenty-five years of age, and qualified electors. The supreme court shall hold at least one term annually at the seat of government, and at such other places as the legislature may provide. A circuit court is to be held at least twice a year in each county.

A judge of probate is chosen in each county for two years; but the legislature may abolish the office, and confer probate powers on inferior county courts. Justices of the peace are elected in the several towns, cities and villages, for two years.

Education. A superintendent of public instruction is elected by the electors of the state. The proceeds of the lands granted by the United States, the proceeds of fines and forfeitures, and moneys arising from grants to the state for no specified purpose, are to be a school fund, the interest of which is to be applied to the support of common schools in each school district, and of academies and normal schools. The legislature is required to provide for establishing district schools, free of charge for tuition, to all children between the ages of four and twenty years. Each town and city shall raise by tax, annually, for school purposes, at least half as much as it receives from the school fund.

Corporations without banking powers may be formed only under general laws, except for municipal purposes, and when the objects of the corporation can not be attained under general laws. The power of cities and villages to assess taxes and to contract debts, is to be restricted. The legislature may not incorporate any bank corporation, until the question of "bank or no bank" shall have been submitted to the voters of the state, and a majority of those voting shall have voted in favor of banks; in which case a general banking law may be passed.

State Debts, &c. The credit of the state may not be loaned in aid of an individual or corporation. The state may not contract any public debt, except for extraordinary expenditures; but such debt may not exceed $100,000; and the law authorizing it shall provide for paying the same by taxation within five years. Money may also be borrowed to repel invasion, suppress insurrection, and defend the state in time of war.

Amendments are to be approved by majorities of the whole of each house of two successive legislatures, and ratified by the electors of the state. Also if the legislature shall deem it necessary to revise or change the constitution, it may recommend to the electors the question of calling a convention; and if a majority shall vote in favor of a convention, the legislature shall at the next session provide for calling the same.

CALIFORNIA.

THE constitution of this state was adopted November 13, 1849; and the state was admitted into the union by act of congress, dated September 9, 1850.

Electors. White male citizens of the United States, and white male citizens of Mexico having elected to become citizens of the United States under the treaty of peace, of the age of twenty-one years, who have resided in the state six months, and in the county or district thirty days. Also Indians, or the descendants of Indians, may be admitted to the right of suffrage, in special cases, by a concurrent vote of two-thirds of the legislature.

Legislature. Senate and assembly. Members of assembly, the number to be not less than thirty nor greater than eighty, are chosen annually by districts. Senators, not less than one-third nor more than one-half of the number of members of assembly, are elected by districts for two years, one-half every year. Members of both houses must have resided in the state two years, and in their respective districts one year, and be qualified electors. They are apportioned under the census taken by the United States every ten years, and the state census taken five years thereafter. Election the Tuesday next after the 1st Monday of November.

Sessions of the legislature are held annually, commencing the 1st Monday of January. Bills are passed against the veto by a majority of two-thirds of each house. Bills become laws if not returned by the governor within ten days, unless the legislature shall sooner adjourn.

Executive. A governor and lieutenant-governor are elected for two years. They must be twenty-five years of age, and have resided in the state two years.

A secretary of state, a controller, a treasurer, an attorney-general, and a surveyor-general, are elected for two years by joint vote of both houses.

Judiciary. The judicial power is in a supreme court, district courts, county courts, justices of the peace, and such municipal and other inferior courts as the legislature may establish. The supreme court consists of three judges, elected by the electors of the state for six years, one every two years ; the senior justice in commission to be chief-justice. The district judges are elected by the electors of their respective districts for six years. A judge of the county court is elected in each county for four years, and performs also the duties of judge of probate. The number of justices of the peace elected in each county, city, town, or village, is fixed by law.

The legislature is required to provide for election by the people, of a clerk of the supreme court, county clerks, district attorneys, sheriffs, coroners, and other necessary officers.

State Debts. The legislature shall not create debts exceeding, in the aggregate, $300,000, except in cases of war, invasion, or insurrection, unless authorized by a law for some single object or work distinctly specified ; which law shall provide means, without loans, for paying the debt within twenty years, and, before taking effect, shall be submitted to the people at a general election, and shall have received the votes of a majority of those voting on the question.

Corporations may be formed under general laws, but may not be created by special act, except for municipal purposes. No banking institution issuing paper to circulate as money shall be chartered. Each stockholder of a corporation or a joint stock company, shall be individually liable for his proportion of its liabilities.

Education. [The constitutional provisions on this subject appear to have been copied from the constitution of Iowa, which see.]

Amendments must be agreed to by majorities of all the members of each house of two successive legislatures, and ratified by the people. If, in pursuance of a previous recommendation of two-thirds of the two houses, the people shall vote in favor of a convention for a general revision of the constitution, the legislature shall accordingly provide for calling such convention.

MINNESOTA.

This state was admitted into the union in 1858.

Electors. White male citizens of the United States, twenty-one years of age, having resided in the United States one year, and in the state four months next preceding any election, are voters. Also white persons of foreign birth, having like qualifications as to age and residence, who shall have legally declared their intention to become citizens; and persons of mixed white and Indian blood, and of Indian blood, under certain regulations.

Legislature. A senate and a house of representatives. The first legislature is to consist of thirty-seven senators and eighty representatives.

Executive. A governor and a lieutenant governor are elected for two years.

A secretary of state, a treasurer, and an attorney-general, are elected for two years, and a state auditor for three years.

Judiciary. The judicial power is vested in a supreme court, district courts, courts of probate, justices of the peace, and such other courts inferior to the supreme court, as the legislature may establish by a two-thirds vote. All judges and justices are elected by the people.

Other Provisions. Slavery is prohibited. A general banking law may be passed by majorities of two-thirds of both houses. The compensation of members is fixed at $3 a day. St. Paul is to be the seat of government, until elsewhere located by the legislature.

REMARKS.

A comparison of the present with the early state constitutions, shows a material change of sentiment on many subjects since the first establishment of state governments.

One of these subjects is the *right of suffrage.* In many of the states, in the election of members of the legislature or of the governor, and in some states of both, none but freeholders were allowed to vote. In some states the lower house was elected by unrestricted suffrage, while the senate, which was considered rather as representing the aristocracy or wealth of the state, was elected by freeholders. At present, no property qualification is required, except in North Carolina, in the election of senators ; in Rhode Island, where naturalized citizens are required to own real estate worth $134, or that rents for $7 a year, and in New York, where colored citizens must possess real estate of the value of $250 to be voters. In several of the states, the payment of a trifling tax is made a necessary qualification.

The difference in the constitution of the two houses of the legislature has been diminished. The senatorial term, in many states, is shorter than it was generally under the old constitutions, except in the New England states, where short terms always existed. In states where formerly the official term of senators was three or four years, it has been reduced to two ; and the term of members of the popular branch has in many states been changed from one year to two years, making the terms of both houses equal. The classification of senators, too, with a view to having portions of them going out and coming into office at different times, has been dispensed with in some states in which it was formerly required.

The property qualification of members of the legislature and governor, is less common than formerly. In most of the states, the necessary qualifications of age, citizenship and residence, are sufficient. No state admitted since the organization of the general government, has, we believe, ever required a property qualification for governor or representative.

The plan which prevailed in the old colonial governments of a council instead of a senate, was continued in some states to a comparatively late period, but it has been entirely superseded by a senate. There is still, however, in the states of Maine, New Hampshire and Massachusetts, an executive council, which acts with the governor in the granting of pardons, in the appointment of officers, &c.

The veto power also has, in many states, been essentially modified. Most of the old constitutions required two-thirds majorities of both houses, (meaning, of course, two-thirds of a quorum,) to pass bills against the objections of the governor. In most of the states, either bills may be passed against the veto by majorities of all the members elected to each house, or they do not require the governor's approval.

In some states, as will appear by reference to the constitutions, a majority of all the members elected is necessary to pass bills in the first instance. There is a manifest propriety in this provision. When only a majority of a quorum is required, a law may be passed by one vote more than one-fourth of the number of the members of each house.

An essential change has also taken place in the appointment and tenure of office of judges. To secure the independence of the judges, and a wise selection, their appointment was devolved upon the executive, by and with the advice and consent of the senate, or some advisory council; or, as in some states, the appointment was given to the legislature. And with a further view to their independence, they were to hold their offices during good behavior. Even justices of the peace were in many, perhaps most of the states, thus appointed, though for specified terms. But for many years the elective principle has been gaining ground. In a majority of the states, all the judges are now elected by the people for specified terms The expediency of the change is doubted by many, but no state, it is believed, has ever restored the old practice; and it is by no means certain that the character and efficiency of the judiciary has suffered by the change.

Restraint upon the power to contract state debts is a comparatively new feature in state constitutions. So deeply have some states involved themselves in debt by borrowing money for state enterprises, and by loaning their credit to insolvent corporations, that the people of many of the states have thought it expedient, in their new and amended constitutions, to limit the power of the legislature to contract debts to a specified amount, except for certain purposes; and such amount of indebtedness shall not be exceeded, unless the consent of the people shall be obtained at an election, or in some other way prescribed by the constitution. This restriction has proved highly salutary in many states. In a few instances, however, it has subjected the people to the inconvenience of an election, and even of amending the constitution, to give the legislature the necessary power to raise money for needful purposes.

LIMITATION OF ACTIONS.

WHILE the courts of justice are open to every citizen who may have occasion to resort to them for the enforcement of his just rights and for the redress of injuries, the states have by statute limited the time within which persons may avail themselves of this privilege. Hence, a statute of this kind is called a *statute of limitations*. As actions can not be maintained unless they are commenced within the prescribed periods, the effect of these laws is the *limitation of actions*. The propriety of such laws will appear upon a little reflection. The failure of the memory of material witnesses in the lapse of time, or their death or removal, or other causes, may render it impossible for a party to defend himself against the unjust claims of another. It is proper, therefore, that certain periods should be prescribed within which suits at law should be commenced, and that after the expiration of these periods, the demands of claimants shall be *presumed* to have been paid. Such demands are commonly said to be *outlawed*.

Actions are variously termed. They are *real*, when a title to real estate is claimed; *personal*, when a man demands a debt, a personal service or duty, or damages for its non-performance, or satisfaction for an injury to property. An action of *assumpsit* is an action founded on a promise. Assumpsit is from the Latin, and, in law, signifies a promise or undertaking founded on a consideration. It is express, when made in words or writing; *implied*, when, for some benefit or consideration accruing to one person from the acts of another, the law presumes that person has promised to make compensation. An action *on the case* is an action in which the whole cause of complaint is set out in the writ.

Different periods of time are prescribed in which the different kinds of actions may be commenced. Nor have all the states fixed the same periods for commencing the same kinds of actions. So numerous are these actions, and so various the periods of limitation in the different states, that only a part of them, those relating to the more common cases of indebtedness and of personal injury will be given in this note. The times limited for commencing actions for the recovery of a title to land in the different states, have been stated in a preceding note. (See Note on Chap. XLIX, § 7, 18, 19.

In Maine, actions of debt founded upon any contract or liability not under seal; actions of assumpsit, or upon the case, founded upon any contract or liability, express or implied; actions for arrears of rent, for waste, of trespass, of replevin, and other actions for taking, detaining, or injuring goods or chattels; and actions upon judgments rendered in courts not being courts of record, except justices' courts, must be commenced within *six* years after the cause of action shall have accrued. Promissory notes signed in the presence of an attesting witness, are in this state excepted from the cases above mentioned. In cases of mutual and open account, the cause of action is deemed to have accrued at the date of the last item proved. This is the rule in most of the states. Actions for assault and battery, false imprisonment, slander and libel, must be commenced within *two* years.

In New Hampshire, the periods of limitation in the cases above mentioned are the same as in Maine. Actions of debt founded upon a judgment or recognizance, or upon a contract under seal, may be brought within *twenty* years.

In Vermont, the actions limited to *six* years in Maine, including judgments in any courts not of record, are limited to the same period, *six* years. Assault and battery and false imprisonment, *three* years. Slander and libel, *two* years. Debts on judgment, and debts on specialties, (contracts under seal,) *eight* years.

In Massachusetts, the cases limited to *six* years, are the same as those of Maine above stated, including all judgments of any court but a court of record. Assault and battery, false imprisonment, slander and libel, *two* years.

In Rhode Island, actions of account and upon the case, actions of debt on contracts without specialty; for arrearages of rent; and of detinue, or replevin, *six* years. Actions of trespass, and trespass and ejectment, *four* years. Actions upon the case for words, (slander,) *two* years.

In Connecticut, actions of account, debt on book, on simple contract, assumpsit founded upon implied contracts, or upon contracts in writing not sealed, and actions of trespass on the case, *six* years. Actions on bonds, contracts under seal, or promissory notes not negotiable, *seventeen* years. Actions on express contracts not in writing, of trespass, and for words, *three* years.

In New York, actions upon contracts or liabilities, express or implied, and liabilities created by statute, (except for penalties and forfeitures ;) for trespass upon real property ; for taking, detaining or injuring goods or chattels ; for relief on the ground of fraud, *six* years. Actions for libel, slander, assault, battery, and false imprisonment ; upon a statute for a forfeiture or penalty to the people of the state, *two* years. Actions upon sealed instruments, *twenty* years.

In New Jersey, actions of trespass, detinue, (which is a *detaining* of property,) trover and replevin ; for taking away goods and chattels ; actions of debt founded upon any lending or contract without specialty ; for arrearages of rent on a parol lease ; actions of account and upon the case, *six* years. Actions for assault, menace, battery, false imprisonment, *four* years. Actions for words, *two* years. Actions upon written contracts under seal, *sixteen* years.

In Pennsylvania, the cases limited to *six* years, are without any material exception, the same as those in New Jersey. Actions for assault, menace, battery, wounding, and imprisonment, *two* years. For words, *one* year.

In Delaware, actions of trespass, replevin, detinue, of account, of assumpsit, upon the case, of debt not founded upon a record or specialty, *three* years. [In these are probably included, actions for assault, imprisonment, and for words, all of which are actions on the case.] On promissory notes, bills of exchange, or written acknowledgments of subsisting demands, *six* years.

In Maryland, actions for trespass, detinue, replevin ; for taking away property ; actions of account, debt, book-debt, or upon the case ; debt for lending ; on contract without specialty ; and for arrearages of rent, are limited to *three* years. Actions for words, assault, battery, wounding, and imprisonment, *one* year.

In Virginia, actions on contracts by writing, signed by the party to be charged or by his agent, and upon other contracts, except for goods charged in store account, *five* years; for articles charged in store account, *two* years. Personal actions for which no limitation is otherwise prescribed, *five* years. Actions on contracts under seal, *twenty* years.

In North Carolina, actions of account rendered; upon the case; for arrearages of rent; of debt upon simple contract; of detinue, replevin, and trespass, *three* years. Assault and battery, wounding, imprisonment, *one* year. For words, *six months.*

In South Carolina, actions of trespass, detinue, trover, replevin, debt, covenant, and upon the case, *four* years. Assault and battery, and imprisonment, *one* year: for slander, *six months.*

In Georgia, actions upon the case, for account, for trespass, for debt, for detinue, replevin, and on open accounts, *four* years. Assault, battery, wounding, and false imprisonment, *two* years. For words, *six months.* Notes, and written instruments not under seal, *six* years; if sealed, *twenty* years.

In Florida, actions upon the case, of account, for trespass, debt, detinue and replevin, for goods and chattels, *five* years. For goods sold and delivered, and for any articles charged in book-account, *two* years: if either party dies within the two years, then the further time of two years. Assault and battery, wounding, and imprisonment, *three* years. For words, *one* year.

In Alabama, actions on contracts under seal, and real actions, *ten* years. On detinue; for trespass to property; on written promises not under seal; on stated account; for rent due on parol lease, and other contracts not specified, *six* years. On open accounts, *three* years. For assault and battery, false imprisonment, slander, libel, penalties, and *qui tam* actions, *one* year. [A *qui tam* action is one in which a man prosecutes for a penalty in behalf of the state, as well as of himself as informer.]

In Mississippi, actions of trespass, detinue, and trover; actions for taking goods and chattels; actions of debt, on contracts not under seal; or for arrearages of rent on parol lease; actions upon the case, and of account, for the recovery of money, except promissory notes, *three* years. On promissory notes and bills of exchange, *six* years. For assault, imprisonment, &c., slander and libel, *one* year.

In Louisiana, actions for labor performed, for provisions retailed, and for board, supplies for vessels, freight charges, &c., *one* year. For arrearages of rent, hire of property, money lent, services of physicians, and of teachers by the year or quarter, *three* years. On promissory notes and bills of exchange, *five* years.

In Texas, actions of trespass for injury to property; of trover and conversion; for taking away goods and chattels; and upon open account, *two* years. For assault and battery, slander, and libel, *one* year. Real actions in three, five, or ten years, according to the grade of title.

In Arkansas, actions upon judgments, decrees, and sealed instruments, *ten* years. Upon promissory notes, and other instruments not under seal, *five* years. Actions of account, assumpsit, or case, founded on any other contract or liability, *three* years.

In Tennessee, actions of account, and upon the case; of debt for arrearages of rent; of detinue, replevin, and trespass upon land, *three* years. On a contract or lending, without specialty, (which includes promissory notes, &c.,) *six* years. Assault, battery, wounding, and imprisonment, *one* year. Slander, *six* months.

In Kentucky, actions upon account for goods, or for articles charged in store account, within *one* year from the first of January next after the times of the delivery. Actions upon ordinary contracts; upon liabilities created by statute other than penalties or forfeitures; for trespass upon real property; for taking, detaining, or injuring personal property; for relief on the ground of fraud; on promissory notes, bills of exchange, &c., *five* years. Assault, &c., libel, and slander, *one* year.

In Ohio, actions on promissory notes, or other obligations or contracts in writing, *fifteen* years. Upon contracts not in writing, book accounts, liabilities created by statute, other than forfeitures and penalties, *six* years. For trespass upon real property; for taking, detaining, or injuring personal property; for injury to the rights of the plaintiff not arising on contract; for relief on the ground of fraud, *four* years. For libel, slander, assault and battery, false imprisonment, and upon a statute for a penalty or forfeiture, *one* year.

In Michigan, actions of debt founded on contract or liability not under seal; for arrears of rent; of assumpsit, or upon the case, founded on any contract or liability express or implied; of waste, of replevin, trover, and other actions for taking, detaining, or injuring goods or chattels; and other actions on the case, *six* years. For trespass upon land, assault and battery, false imprisonment, slander, and libel, *two* years. Personal actions upon other contracts, *ten* years.

In Indiana, actions on accounts and contracts not in writing; for rents of real property; for detaining and injuring property; and for relief against frauds, *six* years. For injuries to person or character, and for a penalty or forfeiture given by statute, *two* years.

In Illinois, actions of trespass, detinue, trover, and replevin; for taking away goods and chattels; for arrearages of rent due on a parol lease; actions of account, and upon the case, *five* years. For assault, battery, wounding, and imprisonment, *two* years. For words, *one* year. Actions of debt on contracts under seal, and promissory notes, *sixteen* years.

In Missouri, actions upon any writing, sealed or unsealed, for the direct payment of money or property, *ten* years. Upon contracts, express or implied; upon a liability created by statute other than a penalty or forfeiture; for trespass upon real estate; for taking, detaining, or injuring goods and chattels, or for the recovery of specific personal property; for injuries to the rights of persons, and for relief on the ground of frauds, *five* years. For penalty or forfeiture, where it is given to the party aggrieved, or to him or to the state, *three* years. *Qui tam* actions, *one* year after the commission of the offense; if commenced by a state's attorney, *two* years. For libel, assault, imprisonment, &c., *two* years.

In Iowa, actions of debt for rent; upon promissory notes or writings for the direct payment of money, or delivery of property; and actions of assumpsit, *six* years. Actions for trespass, detinue, trover, and replevin; for taking away goods, &c.; for arrearages of rent due on parol lease; actions of account, and upon the case, *five* years. For assault, &c., and imprisonment, *two* years; for slanderous words, *one* year.

In Wisconsin, actions of debt founded on contract or liability not under seal; upon judgments in courts not of record; for arrears of rent; of assumpsit, or on the case, founded on a contract or liability, express or implied; for waste, and trespass on land; of replevin, and other actions for taking, detaining, or injuring goods or chattels; and other actions on the case, *six* years. For assault, &c., false imprisonment, slander, and libel, *two* years.

In Minnesota, actions upon contracts; upon liabilities created by statute, other than those for penalties or forfeitures; for trespass upon real property; for taking, detaining, or injuring personal property, and for the specific recovery thereof; for injuries to the persons or rights of another not arising on obligation; and for relief on the ground of fraud, *six* years. An action for libel, slander, assault, battery, and false imprisonment; and for a penalty to the state, *two* years. An action upon a statute for a penalty given in whole or in part to the prosecutor, *one* year; if not commenced by a private party, *two* years. For a penalty where the action is given to the party aggrieved, *three* years.

In California, actions upon contracts, obligations, or liabilities, founded on instruments of writing generally, *four* years. Upon liabilities created by statute, other than penalties or forfeitures; for trespass upon real property; for taking, detaining, or injuring goods and chattels, and for the specific recovery of personal property; and for relief on the ground of fraud, *three* years. Upon a contract or liability not founded on an instrument of writing, except an open account, and articles charged in a store account, *two* years. For libel, slander, assault, battery, and false imprisonment; on an open account for goods, sold and delivered, and for any article charged in a store account, *one* year.

It is provided in most of the states, if not in all of them, that if a debtor departs from and resides without the state during any part of the time limited for commencing an action, the time of his absence is not to be taken as any part of that time; and if a debtor so leaves the state *before* the cause of action accrues, the period of limitation is to be computed from the time of his return to the state.

DECLARATION OF INDEPENDENCE.

July 4th, 1776.

A DECLARATION BY THE REPRESENTATIVES OF THE UNITED STATES OF AMERICA, IN [*general*] CONGRESS ASSEMBLED.*

WHEN, in the course of human events, it becomes necessary for one people to dissolve the political bands which have connected them with another, and to assume, among the powers of the earth, the separate and equal station to which the laws of nature and of nature's God entitle them, a decent respect to the opinions of mankind, requires that they should declare the causes which impel them to the separation.

We hold these truths to be self-evident: that all men are created equal; that they are endowed by their Creator with [*inherent and*] unalienable rights; that among these are life, liberty, and the pursuit of happiness; that to secure these rights, governments are instituted among men, deriving their just powers from the consent of the governed; that whenever any form of government becomes destructive of these ends, it is the right of the people to alter or abolish it, and to institute a new government, laying its foundation on such principles, and organizing its powers in such form, as to them shall seem most likely to effect their safety and happiness. Prudence, indeed, will dictate, that governments long established should not be changed for light and transient causes; and accordingly all experience hath

certain

* This is a copy of the original draft of Jefferson, as reported to congress. The parts struck out by congress are printed in italics, and enclosed in brackets; and the parts added are placed in the margin, or in a concurrent column.

shown that mankind are more disposed to suffer while evils are sufferable, than to right themselves, by abolishing the forms to which they are accustomed. But when a long train of abuses and usurpations [*begun at a distinguished period and*] pursuing invariably the same object, evinces a design to reduce them under absolute despotism, it is their right, it is their duty, to throw off such government, and to provide new guards for their future security. Such has been the patient sufferance of these colonies; and such is now the
alter — necessity which constrains them to [*expunge*]
their former systems of government. The history of the present king of Great Britain, is a
repeated — history of [*unremitting*] injuries and usurpations,
all having — [*among which appears no solitary fact to contradict the uniform tenor of the rest, but all have*] in direct object the establishment of an absolute tyranny over these states. To prove this, let facts be submitted to a candid world, [*for the truth of which we pledge a faith yet unsullied by falsehood.*]

He has refused his assent to laws the most wholesome, and necessary for the public good.

He has forbidden his governors to pass laws of immediate and pressing importance, unless suspended in their operation, till his assent should be obtained; and when so suspended, he has utterly neglected to attend to them.

He has refused to pass other laws for the accommodation of large districts of people, unless those people would relinquish the right of representation in the legislature, a right inestimable to them, and formidable to tyrants only.

He has called together legislative bodies at places unusual, uncomfortable, and distant from the depository of their public records, for the sole purpose of fatiguing them into compliance with his measures.

He has dissolved representative houses repeatedly [*and continually*] for opposing, with manly firmness, his invasions on the rights of the people.

He has refused, for a long time after such dissolutions, to cause others to be elected, whereby the legislative powers, incapable of annihilation, have returned to the people at large for their exercise, the state remaining, in the mean time, exposed to all the dangers of invasion from without, and convulsions within.

He has endeavored to prevent the population of these states; for that purpose obstructing the laws for naturalization of foreigners, refusing to pass others to encourage their migration hither, and raising the conditions of new appropriations of lands.

He has [*suffered*] the administration of justice, obstructed
[*totally to cease in some of these states*,] refusing by
his assent to laws for establishing judiciary powers.

He has made [*our*] judges dependent on his will alone for the tenure of their offices, and the amount and payment of their salaries.

He has erected a multitude of new offices, [*by a self-assumed power*] and sent hither swarms of new officers, to harass our people, and eat out their substance.

He has kept among us in times of peace, standing armies [*and ships of war*] without the consent of our legislatures.

He has affected to render the military independent of, and superior to, the civil power.

He has combined with others, to subject us to a jurisdiction foreign to our constitutions, and unacknowledged by our laws, giving his assent to their acts of pretended legislation, for quartering large bodies of armed troops among us; for protecting them by a mock trial from punishment for any murders which they should commit on the inhabitants of these states; for cutting off our trade with all parts of the world; for imposing taxes on us without our consent; for depriving
us [ ] of the benefits of trial by jury; for trans- in many cases
porting us beyond seas, to be tried for pretended offenses; for abolishing the free system of Eng-

lish laws, in a neighboring province; establishing therein an arbitrary government, and enlarging its boundaries, so as to render it at once an example and fit instrument for introducing the same absolute rule into these [*states;*] for taking away our charters, abolishing our most valuable laws, and altering fundamentally the forms of our governments; for suspending our own legislatures, and declaring themselves invested with power to legislate for us, in all cases whatsoever.

colonies

He has abdicated government here, [*withdrawing his governors, and declaring us out of his allegiance and protection.*]

by declaring us out of his protection, and waging war against us.

He has plundered our seas, ravaged our coasts, burnt our towns, and destroyed the lives of our people.

He is at this time transporting large armies of foreign mercenaries, to complete the works of death, desolation, and tyranny, already begun with circumstances of cruelty and perfidy, [ ] unworthy the head of a civilized nation.

scarcely paralleled in the most barbarous ages, and totally

He has constrained our fellow-citizens, taken captive on the high seas, to bear arms against their country, to become the executioners of their friends and brethren, or to fall themselves by their hands.

He has [ ] endeavored to bring on the inhabitants of our frontiers, the merciless Indian savages, whose known rule of warfare, is an undistinguished destruction of all ages, sexes, and conditions [*of existence.*]

excited domestic insurrections among us, and has

[*He has incited treasonable insurrections of our fellow-citizens, with the allurements of forfeiture, and confiscation of our property.*

He has waged cruel war against human nature itself, violating its most sacred rights of life and liberty, in the persons of a distant people, who never offended him, captivating and carrying them into slavery in another hemisphere, or to incur miserable death in their transportation thither. This piratical warfare, the opprobrium of infidel *powers, is the warfare of the* Christian *king of Great Britain. Determined to keep open a market, where* men *should be bought and sold, he has prostituted his negative for suppressing every legislative attempt to prohibit or to restrain this execrable commerce. And that this assemblage of horrors might want no fact of distinguished die, he is now exciting those very people to rise in arms among us, and to purchase that liberty of which he has deprived them, by murdering the people on whom he also obtruded them: thus paying off former crimes committed against the* liberties *of one people, with crimes which he urges them to commit against the* lives *of another.*]

In every stage of these oppressions, we have petitioned for redress, in the most humble terms; our repeated petitions have been answered only by repeated injuries.

A prince whose character is thus marked by every act which may define a tyrant, is unfit to be the ruler of a [ ] people, [*who mean to be* free
free. Future ages will scarcely believe, that the hardiness of one man adventured, within the short compass of twelve years only, to lay a foundation so broad and so undisguised for tyranny, over a people fostered and fixed in principles of freedom.

Nor have we been wanting in attentions to our British brethren. We have warned them from time to time of attempts by their legislature, to extend [*a*] jurisdiction over [*these our states.*] an unwar-
We have reminded them of the circumstances of rantable
our emigration and settlement here, [*no one of* us
which could warrant so strange a pretension: that these were effected at the expense of our own blood and treasure, unassisted by the wealth or the strength of Great Britain: that in constituting indeed our several forms of government, we had adopted one common king, thereby laying a foundation for perpetual league and amity with them, but that submission to their parliament, was no part of our constitution, nor

ever in idea, if history may be credited, and] we [ ] appealed to their native justice and magnanimity, [*as well as to*] the ties of our common kindred to disavow these usurpations which [*were likely to*] interrupt our connection and correspondence. They too have been deaf to the voice of justice and of consanguinity, [*and when occasions have been given them, by the regular course of their laws, of removing from their councils the disturbers of our harmony, they have by their free election reëstablished them in power. At this very time, too, they are permitting their chief magistrate to send over not only soldiers of our common blood, but Scotch and foreign mercenaries, to invade and destroy us. These facts have given the last stab to agonizing affection, and manly spirit bids us to renounce forever these unfeeling brethren. We must endeavor to forget our former love for them, and hold them as we hold the rest of mankind, enemies in war, in peace friends. We might have been a free and a great people together; but a communication of grandeur and of freedom, it seems, is below their dignity. Be it so, since they will have it. The road to happiness and to glory is open to us too. We will tread it apart from them, and*] acquiesce in the necessity which denounces our [*eternal*] separation [ ]!

have
and we have conjured them by
would inevitably

We must therefore

and hold them as we hold the rest of mankind, enemies in war, in peace friends.

We therefore, the representatives of the United States of America, in general congress assembled, do in the name, and by the authority of the good people of these [*states reject and renounce all allegiance and subjection to the kings of*

We therefore, the representatives of the United States of America, in general congress assembled, appealing to the Supreme Judge of the world for the rectitude of our intentions, do in the name, and by the authority of the good peo-

Great Britain, and all others, who may hereafter claim by, through, or under them; we utterly dissolve all political connection which may heretofore have subsisted between us and the people or parliament of Great Britain; and finally we do assert and declare these colonies to be free and independent states] and that, as free and independent states, they have full power to levy war, conclude peace, contract alliances, establish commerce, and to do all other acts and things which independent states may of right do. And for the support of this declaration, we mutually pledge to each other our lives, our fortunes, and our sacred honor.

ple of these colonies, solemnly publish and declare, that these united colonies are, and of right ought to be, free and independent states; that they are absolved from all allegiance to the British crown, and that all political connection between them and the state of Great Britain is, and ought to be, totally dissolved; and that, as free and independent states, they have full power to levy war, conclude peace, contract alliances, establish commerce, and to do all other acts and things, which independent states may of right do.

And for the support of this declaration, with a firm reliance on the protection of Divine Providence, we mutually pledge to each other our lives, our fortunes, and our sacred honor.

The foregoing declaration was, by order of congress, engrossed and signed by the following members:

JOHN HANCOCK.

New Hampshire.—Josiah Bartlett, William Whipple, Matthew Thornton.

Massachusetts Bay.—Samuel Adams, John Adams, Robert Treat Paine, Elbridge Gerry.

Rhode Island.—Stephen Hopkins, William Ellery.

Connecticut.—Roger Sherman, Samuel Huntington, William Williams, Oliver Wolcott.

New York.—William Floyd, Philip Livingston, Francis Lewis, Lewis Morris.

New Jersey.—Richard Stockton, John Witherspoon, Francis Hopkinson, John Hart, Abraham Clark.

Pennsylvania.—Robert Morris, Benjamin Rush, Benjamin Franklin, John Morton, George Clymer, James Smith, George Taylor, James Wilson, George Ross.

Delaware.—Cæsar Rodney, George Read, Thomas M'Kean.

Maryland.—Samuel Chase, William Paca, Thomas Stone, Charles Carroll, of Carrollton.

Virginia.—George Wythe, Richard Henry Lee, Thomas Jefferson, Benjamin Harrison, Thomas Nelson, Jr., Francis Lightfoot Lee, Carter Braxton.

North Carolina.—William Hooper, Joseph Hewes; John Penn.

South Carolina.—Edward Rutledge, Thomas Heyward, Jr., Thomas Lynch, Jr., Arthur Middleton.

Georgia.—Button Gwinnett, Lyman Hall, George Walton.

CONSTITUTION OF THE UNITED STATES.

We, the people of the United States, in order to form a more perfect union, establish justice, insure domestic tranquillity, provide for the common defense, promote the general welfare, and secure the blessings of liberty to ourselves and our posterity, do ordain and establish this Constitution for the United States of America.

ARTICLE I.

Section 1. All legislative powers herein granted shall be vested in a congress of the United States, which shall consist of a senate and house of representatives.

Sec. 2. The house of representatives shall be composed of members chosen every second year, by the people of the several states ; and the electors in each state shall have the qualifications requisite for electors of the most numerous branch of the state legislature.

No person shall be a representative who shall not have attained to the age of twenty-five years, and been seven years a citizen of the United States, and who shall not, when elected, be an inhabitant of that state in which he shall be chosen.

Representatives and direct taxes shall be apportioned among the several states which may be included within this union, according to their respective numbers, which shall be determined by adding to the whole number of free persons, including those bound to service for a term of years, and excluding Indians not taxed, three-fifths of all other persons. The actual enumeration shall be made within three years after the first meeting of the congress of the United States, and within every subsequent term of ten years, in such manner as they shall by law direct. The number of representatives shall not exceed one for every thirty thousand, but each state shall have at least one representative ; and until such enumeration shall be made, the state of New Hampshire shall be entitled to choose *three*, Massachusetts, *eight*; Rhode Island and Providence Plantations, *one*; Connecticut, *five*; New York, *six*; New Jersey, *four*; Pennsylvania, *eight*; Delaware, *one*; Maryland, *six*, Virginia, *ten*; North Carolina, *five*; South Carolina, *five*, and Georgia, *three*.

When vacancies happen in the representation from any state, the executive authority thereof shall issue writs of election to fill such vacancies.

The house of representatives shall choose their speaker and other officers, and shall have the sole power of impeachment.

SEC. 3. The senate of the United States shall be composed of two senators from each state, chosen by the legislature thereof, for six years; and each senator shall have one vote.

Immediately after they shall be assembled in consequence of the first election, they shall be divided as equally as may be, into three clases. The seats of the senators of the first class shall be vacated at the expiration of the second year; of the second class at the expiration of the fourth year; and of the third class at the expiration of the sixth year; so that one-third may be chosen every second year; and if vacancies happen, by resignation or otherwise, during the recess of the legislature of any state, the executive thereof may make temporary appointments, until the next meeting of the legislature, which shall then fill such vacancies.

No person shall be a senator who shall not have attained to the age of thirty years, and been nine years a citizen of the United States, and who shall not, when elected, be an inhabitant of that state for which he shall be chosen.

The vice-president of the United States shall be president of the senate, but shall have no vote, unless they be equally divided.

The senate shall choose their other officers, and also a president pro tempore, in the absence of the vice-president, or when he shall exercise the office of president of the United States.

The senate shall have the sole power to try all impeachments: when sitting for that purpose, they shall be on oath or affirmation. When the president of the United States is tried, the chief-justice shall preside; and nc person shall be convicted without the concurrence of two-thirds of the members present.

Judgment, in cases of impeachment, shall not extend further than to removal from office, and disqualification to hold and enjoy any office of honor, trust, or profit, under the United States ; but the party convicted shall, nevertheless, be liable and subject to indictment, trial, judgment and punishment, according to law.

SEC. 4. The times, places and manner of holding elections for senators and representatives, shall be prescribed in each state by the legislature thereof ; but the congress may at any time, by law, make or alter such regulations, except as to the places of choosing senators.

The congress shall assemble at least once in every year ; and such meeting shall be on the first Monday in December, unless they shall, by law, appoint a different day.

SEC. 5. Each house shall be the judge of the elections, returns and qualifications of its own members ; and a majority of each shall constitute a quorum to do business ; but a smaller number may adjourn from day to day, and may be authorized to compel the attendance of absent members, in such manner, and under such penalties, as each house may provide.

Each house may determine the rules of its proceedings, punish its members for disorderly behavior, and, with the concurrence of two-thirds, expel a member.

Each house shall keep a journal of its proceedings, and from time to time publish the same, excepting such parts as may, in their judgment, require secrecy ; and the yeas and nays of the members of either house, on any question, shall, at the desire of one-fifth of those present, be entered on the journal.

Neither house, during the session of congress, shall, without the consent of the other, adjourn for more than three days, nor to any other place than that in which the two houses shall be sitting.

SEC. 6. The senators and representatives shall receive a compensation for their services, to be ascertained by law, and paid out of the treasury of the United States. They shall, in all cases, except treason, felony, and breach of the peace, be privileged from arrest during their attendance at the session of their respective houses, and in going to and returning from the same: and for any speech or debate in either house, they shall not be questioned in any other place.

No senator or representative shall, during the time for which he was elected, be appointed to any civil office under the authority of the United States, which shall have been created, or the emoluments whereof shall have been increased, during such time; and no person holding any office under the United States, shall be a member of either house during his continuance in office.

Sec. 7. All bills for raising revenue shall originate in the house of representatives; but the senate may propose, or concur with, amendments, as on other bills.

Every bill which shall have passed the house of representatives and the senate, shall, before it become a law, be presented to the president of the United States; if he approve, he shall sign it; but if not, he shall return it, with his objections, to that house in which it shall have originated, who shall enter the objections at large on their journal, and proceed to reconsider it. If, after such reconsideration, two-thirds of that house shall agree to pass the bill, it shall be sent, together with the objections, to the other house, by which it shall likewise be reconsidered, and, if approved by two-thirds of that house, it shall become a law. But, in all such cases, the votes of both houses shall be determined by yeas and nays, and the names of the persons voting for and against the bill shall be entered on the journal of each house respectively. If any bill shall not be returned by the president within ten days (Sundays excepted) after it shall have been presented to him, the same shall be a law, in like manner as if he had signed it, unless the congress, by their adjournment, prevent its return, in which case it shall not be a law.

Every order, resolution or vote, to which the concurrence of the senate and house of representatives may be necessary, (except on a question of adjournment,) shall be presented to the president of the United States, and before the same shall take effect, shall be approved by him, or, being disapproved by him, shall be repassed by two-thirds of the senate and house of representatives, according to the rules and limitations prescribed in the case of a bill.

Sec. 8. The congress shall have power:

To lay and collect taxes, duties, imposts, and excises, to

pay the debts and provide for the common defense and general welfare of the United States; but all duties, imposts, and excises shall be uniform throughout the United States:

To borrow money on the credit of the United States:

To regulate commerce with foreign nations, and among the several states, and with the Indian tribes:

To establish a uniform rule of naturalization, and uniform laws on the subject of bankruptcies throughout the United States:

To coin money; to regulate the value thereof, and of foreign coin; and fix the standard of weights and measures:

To provide for the punishment of counterfeiting the securities and current coin of the United States:

To establish post offices and post roads:

To promote the progress of science and useful arts, by securing for limited times, to authors and inventors, the exclusive right to their respective writings and discoveries:

To constitute tribunals inferior to the supreme court:

To define and punish piracies and felonies committed on the high seas, and offenses against the law of nations:

To declare war; grant letters of marque and reprisal; and make rules concerning captures on land and water:

To raise and support armies; but no appropriation of money to that use shall be for a longer term than two years:

To provide and maintain a navy:

To make rules for the government and regulation of the land and naval forces:

To provide for calling forth the militia to execute the laws of the union, suppress insurrections, and repel invasions:

To provide for organizing, arming and disciplining the militia, and for governing such part of them as may be employed in the service of the United States; reserving to the states respectively, the appointment of the officers, and the authority of training the militia, according to the discipline prescribed by congress:

To exercise exclusive legislation in all cases whatsoever, over such district (not exceeding ten miles square) as may, by cession of particular states, and the acceptance of congress, become the seat of the government of the United

States, and to exercise like authority over all places purchased by the consent of the legislature of the state in which the same shall be, for the erection of forts, magazines, arsenals, dockyards, and other needful buildings: And,

To make all laws which shall be necessary and proper for carrying into execution the foregoing powers, and all other powers vested by this constitution in the government of the United States, or in any department or officer thereof.

Sec. 9. The migration or importation of such persons as any of the states now existing, shall think proper to admit, shall not be prohibited by the congress prior to the year one thousand eight hundred and eight; but a tax or duty may be imposed on such importation, not exceeding ten dollars for such person:

The privilege of the writ of habeas corpus shall not be suspended unless when, in cases of rebellion or invasion, the public safety may require it.

No bill of attainder or ex post facto law shall be passed.

No capitation or other direct tax shall be laid, unless in proportion to the census or enumeration hereinbefore directed to be taken.

No tax or duty shall be laid on articles exported from any state. No preference shall be given, by any regulation of commerce or revenue, to the ports of one state, over those of another; nor shall vessels bound to or from one state be obliged to enter, clear, or pay duties in another.

No money shall be drawn from the treasury, but in consequence of appropriations made by law; and a regular statement and account of the receipts and expenditures of all public money shall be published from time to time.

No title of nobility shall be granted by the United States; and no person holding any office of profit or trust under them shall, without the consent of the congress, accept of any present, emolument, office, or title of any kind whatever, from any king, prince, or foreign state.

Sec. 10. No state shall enter into any treaty, alliance, or confederation; grant letters of marque and reprisal; coin money; emit bills of credit; make anything but gold and silver coin a tender in payment of debts; pass any bill of attainder, ex post facto law, or law impairing the obligation of contracts; or grant any title of nobility.

No state shall, without the consent of the congress, lay

any imposts or duties on imports or exports, except what may be absolutely necessary for executing its inspection laws: and the net produce of all duties and imposts laid by any state on imports or exports, shall be for the use of the treasury of the United States; and all such laws shall be subject to the revision and control of the congress. No state shall, without the consent of congress, lay any duty of tonnage, keep troops or ships of war in time of peace, enter into any agreement or compact with another state, or with a foreign power, or engage in war, unless actually invaded, or in such imminent danger as will not admit of delay.

ARTICLE II.

SECTION 1. The executive power shall be vested in a president of the United States of America. He shall hold his office during the term of four years, and, together with the vice-president, chosen for the same term, be elected as follows:

Each state shall appoint, in such manner as the legislature thereof may direct, a number of electors, equal to the whole number of senators and representatives to which the state may be entitled in the congress; but no senator or representative, or person holding an office of trust or profit under the United States, shall be appointed an elector.

The electors shall meet in their respective states, and vote by ballot for two persons, of whom one at least shall not be an inhabitant of the same state with themselves. And they shall make a list of all the persons voted for, and of the number of votes for each, which list they shall sign and certify, and transmit, sealed, to the seat of the government of the United States, directed to the president of the senate. The president of the senate shall, in the presence of the senate and house of representatives, open all the certificates, and the votes shall then be counted. The person having the greatest number of votes shall be the president, if such number be a majority of the whole number of electors appointed; and if there be more than one who have such majority, and have an equal number of votes, then the house of representatives shall immediately choose by ballot one of them for president; and if no person have a majority, then, from the five highest on the list, the said house shall, in like manner, choose the president. But in choosing the president, the votes shall be taken by states, the representation from each state having one vote: a quorum for this purpose shall consist of a member or members from two-thirds of the states, and a majority of the states shall be necessary to a choice. In every case, after the choice of the president, the person having the greatest number of votes of the electors, shall be the vice-president. But if there should remain two or more who have equal votes, the senate shall choose from them, by ballot, the vice-president.

[By the 12th article of amendment, the above clause has been repealed.]

The congress may determine the time of choosing the electors, and the day on which they shall give their votes, which day shall be the same throughout the United States.

No person, except a natural born citizen, or a citizen of the United States at the time of the adoption of this constitution, shall be eligible to the office of president; neither shall any person be eligible to that office who shall not have attained to the age of thirty-five years, and been fourteen years a resident within the United States.

In case of the removal of the president from office, or of his death, resignation, or inability to discharge the powers and duties of the said office, the same shall devolve on the vice-president, and the congress may, by law, provide for the case of removal, death, resignation, or inability, both of the president and vice-president, declaring what officer shall then act as president; and such officer shall act accordingly, until the disability be removed, or a president shall be elected.

The president shall, at stated times, receive for his servises a compensation, which shall neither be increased nor diminished during the period for which he shall have been elected; and he shall not receive, within that period, any other emolument from the United States, or any of them.

Before he enter on the execution of his office, he shall take the following oath or affirmation:

"I do solemnly swear (or affirm) that I will faithfully execute the office of President of the United States; and will, to the best of my ability, preserve, protect, and defend the constitution of the United States."

SEC. 2. The president shall be commander-in-chief of the army and navy of the United States, and of the militia of the several states, when called into the actual service of the United States; he may require the opinion, in writing, of the principal officer in each of the executive departments, upon any subject relating to the duties of their respective offices; and he shall have power to grant reprieves and pardons for offenses against the United States, except in cases of impeachment.

He shall have power by and with the advice and consent of the senate, to make treaties, provided two-thirds of the senators present concur: and he shall nominate, and by and with the advice and consent of the senate, shall appoint ambassadors, other public ministers and consuls, judges of the supreme court, and all other officers of the United States, whose appointments are not herein otherwise provided for, and which shall be established by law: but the congress may, by law, vest the appointment of such inferior officers as they think proper, in the president alone, in the courts of law, or in the heads of departments.

The president shall have power to fill up all vacancies that may happen during the recess of the senate, by granting commissions which shall expire at the end of their next session.

SEC. 3. He shall from time to time give to the congress information of the state of the union; and recommend to their consideration such measures as he shall judge necessary and expedient. He may, on extraordinary occasions, convene both houses, or either of them; and in case of disagreement between them, with respect to the time of adjournment, he may adjourn them to such time as he shall think proper. He shall receive ambassadors and other public ministers. He shall take care that the laws be faithfully executed; and shall commission all the officers of the United States.

SEC. 4. The president, vice-president, and all civil officers of the United States, shall be removed from office on impeachment for, and conviction of, treason, bribery, or other high crimes and misdemeanors.

ARTICLE III.

SECTION 1. The judicial power of the United States shall be vested in one supreme court, and in such inferior courts as the congress may, from time to time, ordain and establish. The judges both of the supreme and inferior courts, shall hold their offices during good behavior ; and shall, at stated times, receive for their services a compensation, which shall not be diminished during their continuance in office.

Sec. 2. The judicial power shall extend to all cases in law and equity, arising under this constitution, the laws of the United States and treaties made, or which shall be made, under their authority ; to all cases affecting ambassadors, other public ministers, and consuls ; to all cases of admiralty and maritime jurisdiction ; to controversies to which the United States shall be a party, to controversies between two or more states ; between a state and citizens of another state ; between citizens of different states ; between citizens of the same state claiming lands under grants of different states ; and between a state, or the citizens thereof ; and foreign states, citizens or subjects.

In all cases affecting ambassadors, other public ministers and consuls, and those in which a state shall be a party, the supreme court shall have original jurisdiction. In all the other cases before mentioned, the supreme court shall have appellate jurisdiction, both as to law and fact, with such exceptions, and under such regulations, as the congress shall make.

The trial of all crimes, except in cases of impeachment, shall be by jury ; and such trial shall be held in the state where the said crimes shall have been committed ; but when not committed within any state, the trial shall be at such place or places as the congress may by law have directed.

Sec. 3. Treason against the United States shall consist only in levying war against them, or in adhering to their enemies, giving them aid and comfort. No person shall be convicted of treason, unless on the testimony of two witnesses to the same overt act, or on confession in open court.

The congress shall have power to declare the punishment of treason ; but no attainder of treason shall work corruption of blood, or forfeiture, except during the life of the person attainted.

ARTICLE IV.

SECTION 1. Full faith and credit shall be given, in each state, to the public acts, records, and judicial proceedings of every other state. And the congress may, by general laws, prescribe the manner in which such acts, records and proceedings shall be proved, and the effect thereof.

SEC. 2. The citizens of each state shall be entitled to all the privileges and immunities of citizens in the several states.

A person charged in any state with treason, felony, or other crime, who shall flee from justice, and be found in another state, shall, on demand of the executive authority of the state from which he fled, be delivered up, to be removed to the state having jurisdiction of the crime.

No person held to service or labor in one state, under the laws thereof, escaping into another, shall, in consequence of any law or regulation therein, be discharged from such service or labor; but shall be delivered up on claim of the party to whom such service or labor may be due.

SEC. 3. New states may be admitted by the congress into this union; but no new state shall be formed or erected within the jurisdiction of any other state, nor any state be formed by the junction of two or more states, or parts of states, without the consent of the legislatures of the states concerned, as well as of the congress.

The congress shall have power to dispose of, and make all needful rules and regulations respecting the territory or other property belonging to the United States; and nothing in this constitution shall be so construed as to prejudice any claims of the United States, or of any particular state.

SEC. 4. The United States shall guaranty to every state in this union, a republican form of government; and shall protect each of them against invasion, and on application of the legislature, or of the executive (when the legislature cannot be convened) against domestic violence.

ARTICLE V.

The congress, whenever two-thirds of both houses shall deem it necessary, shall propose amendments to this constitution, or on the application of the legislatures of two-thirds of the several states, shall call a convention for proposing amendments; which, in either case shall be valid to all intents and purposes, as part of this constitution, when ratified by the legislatures of three-fourths of the several states, or by conventions in three-fourths thereof, as the one or the other mode of ratification may be proposed by the congress : Provided, that no amendment which may be made prior to the year one thousand eight hundred and eight, shall in any manner affect the first and fourth clauses in the ninth section of the first article ; and that no state, without its consent, shall be deprived of its equal suffrage in the senate.

ARTICLE VI.

All debts contracted, and engagements entered into, before the adoption of this constitution, shall be as valid against the United States under this constitution, as under the confederation.

This constitution, and the laws of the United States which shall be made in pursuance thereof, and all treaties made or which shall be made under the authority of the United States, shall be the supreme law of the land, and the judges in every state shall be bound thereby, any thing in the constitution or laws of any state to the contrary notwithstanding.

The senators and representatives before mentioned, and the members of the several legislatures, and all executive and judicial officers, both of the United States and of the several states, shall be bound, by oath or affirmation, to support this constitution ; but no religious test shall ever be required as a qualification to any office or public trust under the United States.

ARTICLE VII.

The ratification of the conventions of nine states shall be sufficient for the establishment of this constitution between the states so ratifying the same.

Done in convention, by the unanimous consent of the states present, the seventeenth day of September, in the year of our Lord one thousand seven hundred and eighty-seven, and of the Independence of the United States of America, the twelfth. In witness whereof we have hereunto subscribed our names.

GEORGE WASHINGTON,
President, and Deputy from Virginia.

New Hampshire.—John Langdon, Nicholas Gilman.
Massachusetts.—Nathaniel Gorham, Rufus King.
Connecticut.—Wm. Samual Johnson, Roger Sherman.
New York.—Alexander Hamilton.
New Jersey.—William Livingston, David Brearly, William Paterson, Jonathan Dayton.
Pennsylvania.—Benjamin Franklin, Robert Morris, Thomas Fitzsimmons, James Wilson, Thomas Mifflin, George Clymer, Jared Ingersoll, Gouverneur Morris.
Delaware.—George Read, Gunning Bedford, Jr., John Dickinson, Richard Bassett, Jacob Broom.
Maryland.—James M'Henry, Daniel of St. Thomas Jenifer, Daniel Carroll.
Virginia.—John Blair, James Madison, Jr.
North Carolina.—William Blount, Richard Dobbs Spaight, Hugh Williamson.
South Carolina.—John Rutledge, Charles Pinckney, Pierce Butler, Charles Cotesworth Pinckney.
Georgia.—William Few, Abraham Baldwin.
Attest: WILLIAM JACKSON, *Secretary.*

The constitution was signed by all the members present, except Edmund Randolph and George Mason, of Virginia, and Elbridge Gerry, of Massachusetts, who declined giving it the sanction of their names.

Whilst the last members were signing, DR. FRANKLIN, looking towards the president's chair, on the back of which a rising sun happened to be painted, observed to a few members near him, that painters had found it difficult to distinguish, in their art, a rising from a setting sun. "I have," said he, "often and often, in the course of the session, and the vicissitudes of my hopes and fears as to its issue, looked at that behind the president, without being able to tell whether it was rising or setting; but now, at length, I have the happiness to know that it is a rising and not a setting sun."

The following are the names of delegates who were absent. Those whose names are in *Italic* never attended.

New Hampshire.—John Pickering, Benjamin West.
Massachusetts.—Caleb Strong, *Francis Dana.*
Connecticut.—Oliver Ellsworth.
New York.—Robert Yates, John Lansing.

New Jersey.—William C. Houston, *John Nelson, Abraham Clark.*

Maryland.—John Francis Mercer, Luther Martin.

Virginia.—George Wythe, *Patrick Henry,* (declined attending,) James M'Clurg, (in room of P. Henry.)

North Carolina.—Alexander Martin, William R. Davie, *Richard Caswell,* resigned,* *Willie Jones,* declined.*

Georgia.—William Pierce, William Houston, *Nathaniel Pendleton, George Walton.*

AMENDMENTS.

ARTICLE I. Congress shall make no law respecting an establishment of religion, or prohibiting the free exercise thereof; or abridging the freedom of speech or of the press; or the right of the people peaceably to assemble, and to petition the government for a redress of grievances.

ART. II. A well regulated militia being necessary to the security of a free state, the right of the people to keep and bear arms shall not be infringed.

ART. III. No soldier shall, in time of peace, be quartered in any house without the consent of the owner, nor in a time of war, but in a manner to be prescribed by law.

ART. IV. The right of the people to be secure in their persons, houses, papers and effects, against unreasonable searches and seizures, shall not be violated; and no warrant shall issue, but upon probable cause, supported by oath or affirmation, and particularly describing the place to be searched, and the persons or things to be seized.

ART. V. No person shall be held to answer for a capital or otherwise infamous crime, unless on a presentment or indictment of a grand jury, except in cases arising in the land or naval forces, or in the militia when in actual service, in time of war or public danger; nor shall any person be

* William Blount, appointed in the room of Mr. Caswell and Hugh Williamson in the room of Mr. Jones, both signed the constitution.

subject, for the same offense, to be twice put in jeopardy of life or limb, nor shall be compelled, in any criminal case, to be a witness against himself; nor be deprived of life, liberty or property, without due process of law; nor shall private property be taken for public use, without just compensation.

ART. VI. In all criminal prosecutions, the accused shall enjoy the right to a speedy and public trial, by an impartial jury of the state and district wherein the crime shall have been committed, which district shall have been previously ascertained by law, and to be informed of the nature and cause of the accusation; to be confronted with the witnesses against him; to have compulsory process for obtaining witnesses in his favor, and to have the assistance of counsel for his defense.

ART. VII. In suits at common law, where the value in controversy shall exceed twenty dollars, the right of trial by jury shall be preserved, and no fact tried by a jury shall be otherwise reëxamined in any court of the United States, than according to the rules of the common law.

ART. VIII. Excessive bail shall not be required, nor excessive fines imposed, nor cruel and unusual punishments inflicted.

ART. IX. The enumeration in the constitution, of certain rights, shall not be construed to deny or disparage others retained by the people.

ART. X. The powers not delegated to the United States, by the constitution, nor prohibited by it to the states, are reserved to the states respectively, or to the people.

ART. XI. The judicial power of the United States shall not be construed to extend to any suit in law or equity, commenced or prosecuted against one of the United States by citizens of another state, or by citizens or subjects of any foreign state.

ART. XII. The electors shall meet in their respective states, and vote by ballot for president and vice-president, one of whom, at least, shall not be an inhabitant of the same state with themselves; they shall name in their ballots the person voted for as president, and in distinct ballots the person voted for as vice-president, and they shall make distinct lists of all persons voted for as president, and of all persons voted for as vice-president, and of the number of votes for each, which lists they shall sign and certify, and transmit sealed to the seat of the government of the United States, directed to the president of the senate;—the president of the senate shall, in the presence of the senate and house of representatives, open all the certificates, and the votes shall then be counted;—the person having the greatest number of votes for president, shall be the president, if such number be a majority of the whole number of electors appointed; and if no person have such majority, then, from the persons having the highest numbers, not exceeding three, on the list of those voted for as president, the house of representatives shall choose immediately, by ballot, the president. But in choosing the president, the votes shall be taken by states, the representatives from each state having one vote; a quorum for this purpose shall consist of a member or members from two-thirds of the states, and a majority of all the states shall be necessary to a choice. And if the house of representatives shall not choose a president whenever the right of choice shall devolve upon them, before the fourth day of March next following, then the vice-president shall act as president, as in the case of the death or other constitutional disability of the president. The person having the greatest number of votes as vice-president, shall be the vice-president, if such number be a majority of the whole number of electors appointed, and if no person have a majority, then, from the two highest numbers on the list, the senate shall choose the vice-president; a quorum for the purpose shall consist of two-thirds of the whole number of senators, and a majority of the whole number shall be necessary to a choice. But no person constitutionally ineligible to the office of president shall be eligible to that of vice-president of the United States.

POLITICAL PARTIES:

THEIR PRINCIPLES AND MEASURES; WITH PRACTICAL OBSERVATIONS.

FROM THE REVOLUTION TO MONROE'S ADMINISTRATION, INCLUSIVE.

THE earliest parties in this country were the Whigs and Tories of the Revolution. These names had their origin in England about two hundred years ago. Those who supported the king in his high claims to power were called *tories;* and those who contended for the rights of the people were called *whigs.* These names were applied, during the revolution, to the friends and opponents of the independence of the states. Those who supported the principles of the revolution were called whigs, and those who opposed them were called *tories* and *royalists.*

The first parties under the present government had their origin in the convention which framed the constitution. The difference of opinion which prevailed in that convention has been stated in those chapters of this work which treat of the Government of the United States. Some of the members of that body, it will be recollected, were in favor of continuing the government of the confederation, in which the states were equal. They were opposed to the surrender, by the states, of so large a portion of their sovereignty to the general government, which, they feared, would encroach upon the rights of the states. From their attachment to the plan of the *confederation* they were called *federalists*, and the friends of the new plan were called *anti-federalists* But the names of these parties were soon reversed. Whilst the constitution was before the people for consideration, one of the principal reasons urged by its friends in favor of its ratification by the states, was, that the old plan was inadequate to the preservation of the union; that the confederation of the states, or federal union, could be preserved only by adopting the constitution; and its friends assumed the name of *federalists*, and their opponents were called *anti-federalists.*

Among the federalists of that time whose names are most familiar to the American people, were Gen. Washington, John Adams, James Madison, Alexander Hamilton, John Jay, John Marshall, and others. The writings of Madison, Hamilton, and Jay, aided much in determining the votes of several of the states in favor of the constitution. They were published in successive numbers; and though written by three different individuals, all the articles were signed "Publius." They are regarded as a masterly exposition and defense of the constitution. They were afterwards published in a volume, entitled "The Federalist," which continues to be a standard constitutional text-book for American Statesmen.

Notwithstanding the division of sentiment here noticed, Gen. Washington was unanimously chosen president by the electors; and notwithstanding the leading measures of his administration were opposed from its commencement, there seems to have been for several years no organized opposition party. To Washington personally there was never any open opposition to any considerable extent; his second election, like the first, being unanimous.

The earliest measures of his administration which received any opposition, were his financial measures. One of these was the funding of the public debt. That part of the scheme which was deemed most objectionable was the proposition that the general government should assume the debts of the states contracted during the war. Another measure was the incorporation of a national bank, in 1791. Upon this question his cabinet, then consisting of four officers, was equally divided; and the president himself appears to have had doubts as to its constitutionality; but upon mature deliberation he signed the act of incorporation.

Washington's foreign policy also encountered much opposition. France was in the midst of a revolution. In the war of Europe, then existing, Great Britian and France were the principal belligerents. France had, by her aid in the cause of our revolution, justly gained the sympathies of the people of this country; and many were in favor of our taking part with her against Great Britain. The president, though friendly to France, deemed it inexpedient to involve this country in that war, and determined to maintain a strict neutrality. The stand thus taken upon this question subjected his administration to the charge of being partial to Great Britain. This partiality was also inferred from our treaties with the British government. This French and English feeling continued an element in the division of parties during a period of nearly twenty-five years.

The opponents of the federalists at length took the name of the *republican party*, and, at the expiration of the presidential term of John Adams, obtained the control of the government, having elected their leader, Thomas Jefferson, president over Mr. Adams, who was a candidate for reëlection. These parties continued under the distinctive names of federal and republican, until the disbandment of the federal party, which took place soon after the close of the second war with Great Britain.

One of the causes of the unpopularity and decline of the federal party, was the passage of two acts during Mr. Adams' administration, called the *alien and sedition laws.* The alien law, entitled, "An act concerning aliens," authorized the president to order out of the country any alien suspected of any treasonable purpose, or deemed dangerous to the peace and safety of the country, unless satisfactory proof should be given that no injury or danger should arise from his residing here. The other law was entitled, "An act in addition to 'An act for the punishment of certain crimes against the United States;'" but it is universally spoken of as "the sedition law." This law provided for punishing persons for conspiring to oppose any measure of the government, or for hindering any public officer in discharging his duties; and also for punishing any person for slandering or libeling the government, congress, or the president. Although these acts were well-intended, and approved by many wise and good men, among whom were Washington and Patrick Henry, as being necessary to check the influence of numerous meddlesome foreigners then in the country, who were active in exciting opposition to the administration, and were combined in organized associations which were considered dangerous to the peace of the United States, they were nevertheless disapproved by a majority of the people, who regarded them as infringements upon popular rights especially upon the freedom of speech and of the press.

These laws gave rise to the famed Virginia and Kentucky

resolutions of 1798, which were adopted as the creed of the old republican party. Those passed by the Virginia legislature were drawn up by Mr. Madison. They declared that the constitution of the United States was a compact to which the states were parties, granting limited powers. That in case of a deliberate, palpable, and dangerous exercise of other powers not granted, it was the right and duty of the states to *interpose* for arresting the progress of the evils, and for maintaining the rights of the states within their respective limits. And that the alien and sedition laws were palpable and alarming infractions of the constitution.

The resolutions of the Kentucky legislature were drafted by Mr. Jefferson, and went still further in asserting the doctrine of state rights. They declared the union to be a compact between the states *as states*; that as the parties to this compact had no common judge, each party had an equal right to judge for itself of the constitutionality of a law of congress, as well as of the mode and measure of redress; and that where powers were assumed which were not delegated, a nullification of the act was the right remedy. These resolutions were transmitted to the legislatures of the several states, with a request that they should concur in declaring these laws void, and in requesting congress to repeal them. But as many of the states were still under federal influence, these resolutions received no favorable response from any of the states; in several of them they were expressly disapproved. It was to these resolutions that the nullifiers of South Carolina referred in 1832 for authority to sanction their meditated resistance to the collection of duties in that state.

The doctrine of state sovereignty, to the extent asserted by the Kentucky resolutions, probably never received the unanimous assent of the republican statesmen. According to Mr. Madison's own exposition of the constitution, *not* the states, as *states*, but *the people of the several states*, were parties to the compact; and in 1830 he expressly repudiated "nullification as a right remedy." So also President Jackson in his proclamation against South Carolin, (alluded to on a subsequent page,) denied such right, and maintained the doctrine now generally received by American statesmen, that, instead of there being *no common judge*, it is the prerogative of the supreme court of the United States to judge of the constitutionality of the acts of congress. Were each state at liberty to do so, and to disobey any law it might deem unconstitutional, no general government could be maintained, nor the union preserved.

The transfer of power from the federal to the republican party was not, however, followed by any great changes of policy. The principal one was in the plan of the navy. Mr. Jefferson's predecessors had encouraged effective harbor fortifications, and an efficient navy; whereas he recommended a cheaper system of national defense. Accordingly, for the heavy built vesels in use, were substituted a large number of small vessels, called *gun-boats*. The plan, however, proved a failure, and was abandoned by congress. The great measure of this administration was the acquisition, by purchase, from France, of Louisiana, embracing that vast tract of country west of the Mississippi river, from which have been since formed the states of Louisiana, Texas, (most of it,) Arkansas, Missouri, Iowa, part of Minnesota, and others yet to be formed. This, however, does not appear to have been properly a party measure. The acquisition was generally considered a valuable one. The principal objection to it was, that it was unauthorized by the constitution. So Mr. Jefferson himself believed; but the advantage offered was considered too great to be lost for such a reason. In order to procure a constitutional sanction of the measure, he suggested an alteration of the constitution, but no such alteration appears to have been attempted.

During our commercial controversy with France and Great Britian, prior to and during the war between the latter and the United States, the opposite feelings of the two parties were clearly manifest. The federalists were generally opposed to the declaration of war, the causes being regarded by them as insufficient to justify a war. The republicans, on the other hand, maintained the justice and the propriety of the war, and charged their opponents with hostility to their own country and friendship for the enemy.

The trade of this country had been much embarrassed by the retaliatory orders and decrees by which those two foreign powers endeavored to harass each other; and it became necessary for our government to adopt measures to counteract the effects of their injurious policy. One of these measures was the laying of an embargo, during Mr. Jefferson's administration, by which all vessels bound to foreign ports were prohibited from leaving the ports of the United States. Many American vessels with their cargoes had been captured by the privateers and cruisers of France and Great Britain, and condemned as prize; and the object of the embargo was declared to be to prevent our vessels and seamen and merchandise from being exposed to depredations on the seas. This measure of course almost entirely stopped our foreign trade, and was vehemently opposed by those engaged or directly interested in such trade. As the shipping business was the leading interest of some of the New England States, which were also the most strongly federal, the greatest complaints came from that quarter. It was also pronounced unconstitutional. Congress, it was said, could not, under the power to regulate trade, stop trade altogether. A case, however, was tried in the United States district court of Massachusetts, in which the act was decided to be constitutional.

When the crisis of our difficulties with Great Britain came, Mr. Madison being then president, the federalists as a party were opposed to the war. By this opposition, the party became more unpopular; and as the return of peace in this country and Europe removed the principal cause of party division, the federal party organization was soon after abandoned. In 1816, Mr. Monroe, the republican candidate for president, received 183 of the electoral votes, and the federal candidate only 34; and at his second election he received 231 of the 232 electoral votes. There was now but one party; or rather, perhaps, no party; there being no great political questions upon which the people were divided. At any rate, the federal and republican parties, as such, had become extinct, as is evident from the history of the next election.

DURING THE TERMS OF ADAMS AND JACKSON.

From the year 1804, it had been the practice of the republican members of congress, during the session next preceding each presidential election, in order to concentrate the strength of the party, to meet in caucus, at the seat of government, for the purpose of nominating a candidate. These congressional caucus nominations had become unpopular with the party; and as there was now, (1824,) no party necessity of uniting upon any one candidate, a majority of the members refused to go into caucus. The minority, however, persisted, and nominated William H. Crawford. A very large majority of the people, as the result proved, were dissatisfied with the nomination, not so much on account of their dislike to the nominee as of the manner of his nomination. The opposition votes were divided upon three candidates, Adams, Jackson, and Clay. There having been no choice of president by the electors, Mr. Adams was elected by the house of representatives, as has been elsewhere stated. (See Chap. XXXIX, § 10.)

Not long after the election of Mr. Adams parties were again organized. They were not distinguished by the old names; the causes of former divisions had ceased to exist. Opposition to Mr. Adams's administration was declared before his policy had been developed, even before his inauguration. It had been alleged, and was extensively believed, that his election had been effected by a bargain between his friends and those of Mr. Clay, then a member of the house, by which the latter were to vote for Mr. Adams, who, if elected, was to appoint Mr. Clay secretary of state. The belief of the truth of this charge naturally raised opposition in advance, and aided the opponents of Mr. Adams in their endeavors to disparage the measures of his administration The disappointed supporters of the unsuccessful candidates, especially those of Gen. Jackson and Mr. Crawford, very naturally united against the administration, and chose as their leader, Gen. Jackson, as most likely to give strength to their party, and announced him as their candidate for the next president. The two parties were for the time known as the *Adams* or *administration* party, and the *Jackson*, or *opposition* party, which proved successful at the next election.

About this time arose a new party, based upon the principle of opposition to the institution of Free Masonry. William Morgan, a seceding mason, published what he declared to be the secrets of the institution; for which he was abducted by members of the order, and, as was supposed, murdered. Other and similar publications from other seceders soon followed ; and renunciations of masonry and secessions from the institution became frequent. As the oaths and obligations assumed by members of the order were deemed incompatible with their civil obligations and duties, the overthrow of this institution was made an object of political action. This party acquired considerable strength in several states ; in some, the predominance. Gen. Jackson being, as was alleged and generally believed, a free mason, the anti-masons were less hostile to the Adams than to the Jackson party ; and they derived the greater portion of their strength from the former. The anti-masonic organization continued until after the election of 1832, at which they supported candidates of their own, William Wirt, of Maryland, for president, and Amos Ellmaker, of Pennsylvania, for vice-president.

The Adams party, formerly so called, was for a time distinguished as the *national republican* party, until a year or two after the presidential election of 1832, when the anti-masons gave up their organization and formed a union with the national republicans, under the name of *whigs*, in general opposition to the Jackson, or, as it was then called, the *democratic* party.

We have stated that, after the extinction of the federal party, there were no questions of public policy to keep up party distinctions. There was one, however, the tariff question, which had at times, since 1816, engaged the attention of congress, and had become one of general interest. From that year may be dated what is called the *protective* system. The foreign demand for the products of American agriculture had almost entirely ceased on the restoration of peace in Europe, and, with a view to creating a home market for our surplus breadstuffs, an act was passed for the encouragement of domestic manufactures. Several attempts were subsequently made in congress to modify and extend the system, but without success, until 1824, when, after a vigorous and protracted contest, the friends of protection succeeded. This question did not, however, sensibly affect the ensuing election of that year. The four candidates, as is believed, were all friendly to the protective policy. Mr. Clay and Gen Jackson especially were known to be its ardent supporters ; the latter having taken an active part in the senate in favor of the tariff of that year, and the former had been its leading champion in the house. In fact, nearly all the prominent statesmen belonging to the old republican party, were friends of protection ; Mr. Jefferson, Mr. Madison, and Mr. Monroe, having successively made it the subject of recommendation to congress.

It may be proper here to notice the change of position on this subject by different parties and different sections of the union. Even the system of moderate duties imposed during Washington's administration, designed both for revenue and for the encouragement of domestic manufactures, was opposed ; and chiefly by opponents of the federal party. The tariff of 1816 met with its strongest opposition from federal representatives of the New England states ; and among its leading supporters were representatives of southern interests, among whom were Mr. Calhoun, of South Carolina, and his colleagues. Indeed it has by some been called a South Carolina measure. In 1824, three of the eastern states, Maine, Massachusetts and New Hampshire, together with most of the southern states, including South Carolina, were almost unanimously opposed to the tariff. Of the representatives from the three New England states mentioned, 22, (all but 3, one from each state,) voted against the measure. Delaware and Missouri, having each one representative, and Kentucky twelve, were unanimous in its favor. Of the 77 votes from all the other southern and south-western states, all but 7 were against it. In 1828, the eastern states were almost unanimous in support of the protective tariff, and have so remained ; and a large majority of the southern representatives have continued in opposition.

The principal change of sentiment on this question since the year last mentioned, has been in the middle and western states. The union of the southern and eastern states in 1824 shows that the contest was not one between the old parties ; and it is equally evident, from other circumstances, that the question was not involved in the ensuing presidential election. Nor had it yet become a party issue at the first election of Gen. Jackson. Notwithstanding he had, during the canvass, publicly avowed his adherence to the tariff and internal improvement policy, he received the support of the southern states most opposed to that policy. Soon after his election, however, a material change took place on this subject. A large portion of the southern section of the democratic party having become extremely hostile to these measures, it was evident that, without some concession, the unity of the party could not long be maintained; and the greater portion of the tariff section of the party, including the president, became steady and permanent coöperators with the opponents of protection. This defection, however, was so gradual as to prevent an immediate overthrow of the system. As late as 1832, its friends carried a bill favorable to protection.

The act of 1832, produced a strong excitement at the south. So vehement was the opposition in South Carolina, that measures were adopted by the legislature for forcible resistance to its execution. The collection of duties in that state by United States officers, was forbidden; the militia of the state was placed at the command of the governor; and the purchase of arms and ammunition was ordered. In December, president Jackson issued a proclamation, in which he discussed and denied the right claimed by that state to nullify a law of congress and to secede from the union, and declare the purpose of enforcing the collection of the revenue within that state; and a bill for that purpose, called by some "force bill," was introduced, which soon became a law. Several things conspired to prevent a collision between that state and the United States. The state of Virginia interposed as mediator, and sent a commissioner to pacify the public authorities of South Carolina. A bill for the reduction of duties was at the same time pending in congress. This bill had been introduced with the view, at least in part, of conciliating the southern opponents of the tariff. With so powerful a consideration in its favor as the prevention of a civil war, its passage began to be seriously apprehended by the friends of the existing tariff. To prevent the injurious consequences anticipated, from so great and sudden a reduction as the bill contemplated, as well as to allay the southern excitement, a bill was introduced proposing a gradual reduction of duties, within ten years, to a point which would satisfy the nullifiers. This bill, of which Mr. Clay himself was the author, although opposed by many of his party, who were unwilling to make so great a concession to the enemies of protection, and one which they feared would prostrate our rising manufactures, was passed, and the south was pacified.

A number of party issues of great interest arose during the presidency of Gen. Jackson. In his first annual message, December, 1829, he took ground against the renewal of the charter of the bank of the United States. This attack upon that institution, more than six years before the expiration of its charter, and while performing its duties to the public satisfaction, took the people by surprise. The subject was referred, and committees in both houses made reports in favor of the bank; but the opposition to the bank was continued. At the session of 1831–1832, the stockholders of the bank petitioned congress for a renewal of the charter, and favorable reports were again made; and a bill for a renewal was passed, but was vetoed by the president. This act caused much dissatisfaction among his political friends, especially those of the commercial and other classes of the community interested in the bank. The controversy was however continued until opposition to the bank became a popular party measure; and the charter was suffered to expire by its own limitation in March, 1836.

The history of the two national banks shows a change of position of men and parties similar to that witnessed on the tariff question. The incorporation of the first bank, in 1791, was a federal measure, and was opposed in congress by Mr. Madison and others, who were leaders in the republican party. Mr. Madison having taken a conspicuous part not only in the framing but in the defense of the constitution, was properly a federalist; but after the organization of the government, took the side of those who opposed the administration. The charter of that bank expired in 1811. Application for a renewal had been made, but without success. At the session of 1814–1815, national finances being in a bad condition, and most of the banks except those of the New England states having suspended specie payments, the secretary of the treasury proposed a plan of a national bank; a bill in conformity thereto was introduced, and after some material alterations passed, but was vetoed by Mr. Madison. He objected to the bill, not on the ground of unconstitutionality, but on account of its supposed incompetency to render the government and the country the services required of such an institution. At the next session another bill was passed, more acceptable in its provisions, which was approved by the president. Thus we see that the second bank was a republican measure. It received its strongest opposition from the federalists; the parties having been reversed on the question since the establishment of the first bank.

Another material issue between the two parties during president Jackson's administration, was the Indian question. Intimations had been given near the close of Mr. Adams's term, of the intention of the state of Georgia to prohibit the Indians within the territorial limits of that state from establishing governments of their own, and to bring them under state jurisdiction. One of the first acts of the new president was to send a proposition to the principal chief of the Cherokees to discuss the subject of their removal beyond the Mississippi; but the proposition was declined. In his first annual message, the president expressed a determination to effect their removal from Georgia and Alabama, or permit these states to subject them to their laws. The Indians memorialized congress on the subject. They claimed, under a succession of treaties, from an early period after the close of the revolutionary war, made or recognized by every previous administration, the protection of the general government in the peaceable possession of their lands and the right of self-government. In this contest, which lasted several years, the opposition advocated the claims of the Indians, and the administration party maintained the claims of the states. Under the sanction of the general government, Georgia proceeded to extend her jurisdiction over the Indians. By an act of that state, it was made a misdemeanor for a white man to reside within the limits of the Cherokee nation after a certain date. Under this act, a number of the missionaries were indicted and convicted, and two of them were imprisoned. Application was made to the supreme court of the United States; and by a decision of that court the next year, (1832,) the law of Georgia was declared to be contrary to the constitution, treaties, and laws of the United States, and there fore null and void: and the court ordered the discharge of the prisoner who had applied for relief. But the mandate of the court was disobeyed, and the prisoners were kept in confinement; hoping, however, that the court would, at its next annual session, take measures to enforce its mandate But the missionaries, having become weary of the controversy, discontinued the suit, and left the question of the continuance of their confinement to the magnanimity of the state. They were at length discharged by the order of the governor, nearly a year after the decision of the court.

Notwithstanding this decision in favor of the Indians, they continued to be disturbed in the possession of their lands; and the general government refused them protection. After the president's proclamation of December, 1832, against the nullifiers, the Indians for a time indulged some hope of relief. In that proclamation the president had declared the authority of the supreme court to decide questions involving the constitutionality of laws and treaties; and he had promptly recommended the passage of a law to enforce the collection of the revenue in South Carolina; and it was presumed the treaties would now be enforced and the Georgians expelled. In this hope the Indians were disappointed. Unwilling to live under the laws of Georgia, and having given up all expectation of being allowed a government of their own, a treaty was at length concluded with their chiefs and head men, by which they agreed to sell their lands and remove to the west, against the consent, however, of a large portion of the tribe. The ratification of the treaty was objected to in the senate, on the ground that it had not received the assent of the part of the tribe competent to make a treaty; but it was confirmed May, 1836, and the Indians were removed.

Another principle upon which the parties were divided, was that of internal improvements. Although this had never been properly a party question, the subject itself was not a new one. The power of the general government to make internal improvements had been frequently called in question. As the power is not expressly granted, it must, if it exists at all, be an *implied* power; that is, it must be *included* in some express power. (See Chap. XXXVI, § 7, 8, 9.) Hence, in determining whether an internal improvement is authorized by the constitution, the nature and object of the work must be considered. Under the power to "regulate commerce among the several states," congress has appropriated money for improving navigable waters, and for constructing public roads. The difference of opinion between statesmen has been, not so much upon the question whether this power existed, as upon questions whether the particular improvements asked for were of such a *character* as to bring them within such power ; for it is generally admitted, that a work which is wholly within the limits of a single state, especially if its benefits are confined to the people of that state, is not within the power of congress.

Bills for internal improvements had been vetoed by former presidents on constitutional grounds. Mr. Adams had favored a more liberal construction of the constitution. During the first session under Gen. Jackson's administration, three bills for aiding in the construction of roads were negatived by him ; and two others, one authorizing the general government to aid in the construction of a canal, another for appropriating money for constructing light-houses, improving harbors, directing surveys, &c., were retained by him until the next session of congress, when, in his annual message, he stated his objections to these bills and to the system of internal improvements, and again proposed the distribution of the surplus revenues among the states, to be by them used for internal improvements. Having, before his election, publicly declared himself in favor of such improvements by the general government, many of his political friends were disappointed as well as displeased by his vetoes. At the second session, however, bills were passed for improving harbors and rivers, for carrying on certain roads and other improvements, and for providing for surveys, &c., and were approved by the president. Although during his presidential term he made a free use of the veto upon bills of this kind, a considerable number received his approval. He was charged by some with inconsistency for rejecting bills on the ground of their being not of a *national*, but of a *local* or *state* character, which were no more liable to his alleged objections than others to which he gave his sanction. But however he may have erred in applying his rule of interpretation to the different bills presented to him, it may be safely affirmed that the indiscriminate approval of all bills which might have been passed by congress, would have involved an unwarrantable expenditure, and justly have subjected the government to the charge of prodigality.

With this administration originated the practice of a general removal of political opponents from office. As the concurrence of cabinet and certain other high officers of the government in the views of the executive is necessary to the execution of the laws and to an efficient administration, it had been the practice of his predecessors to select such officers from their political friends and supporters. Farther than this, removals had seldom been made. But the inauguration of president Jackson was soon followed by the removal of district marshals and attorneys, surveyors and inspectors of ports, collectors of customs, naval officers, receivers of public moneys, auditors, controllers, and clerks in the executive departments. Of postmasters nearly five hundred were said to have been displaced within the first year. The removal of men for opinions which could not interfere with the faithful discharge of their official duties, was pronounced by his opponents an abuse of executive power, tending to destroy freedom of opinion and to encourage political corruption. But to whatever objections this practice is liable, it was adopted by the opposing party on their coming into power, and appears now to be recognized by all parties.

One case of removal and appointment occurred which, more than any other, subjected the president to the charge of having abused this power. The public moneys were required by law to be deposited in the Bank of the United States; unless the secretary of the treasury should at any time otherwise order or direct, in which case he must lay his reasons for so doing before congress. The president, entertaining doubts of the safety of the deposits in the bank, directed an inquiry as to the solvency of the bank, which was accordingly made by an agent appointed by the secretary of the treasury. He subsequently requested congress to institute another inquiry, which should extend to the branches. Both investigations showed the bank to be in possession of funds to more than double the amount of its liabilities; and by a vote of 109 to 46, the house declared the deposits safe. The president, holding that the deposits might be removed for other reasons, and having made arrangements with certain state banks to receive and disburse the public revenues, directed his secretary of the treasury, William J. Duane, to withdraw the deposits from the bank. The secretary refused, assigning, among other reasons, that the law gave to him alone the discretion to discontinue the deposits in the bank; that their removal was unnecessary, and would be a breach of faith and illegal; and therefore an act which his conscience condemned. Whereupon Mr. Duane was removed, and Roger B. Taney appointed, by whom the direction was obeyed. This act of the president was pronounced by many of his political friends, and some of the leading presses of the party, inexpedient and unnecessary, and an arbitrary exercise of power; and a few ceased to support him; but his popularity suffered no material injury.

At the session of 1834–1835, was proposed a plan for keeping and disbursing the revenue by agents to be appointed by the treasurer of the United States, the money to be collected and paid out in specie. This proposition, however, met with little favor. The mover was opposed to the bank of the United States as unconstitutional and dangerous, and was opposed to the use of both that bank and the state banks as depositories of the public moneys. The plan received the votes of only 33 members, composed, as is believed, of disaffected democrats, of whom the mover was one, and of whigs who voted for it from their extreme hostility to the state bank, or as it was opprobriously termed, the "pet bank" system. No other proposed measure having been successful, the deposits continued to be made in the state banks, until after the close of Gen. Jackson's administration.

DURING THE TERMS OF VAN BUREN, HARRISON, TYLER AND POLK.

Mr. Van Buren, democratic successor to Gen. Jackson, came into office March 4th, 1837, in the midst of a severe pecuniary pressure, and only about two months before a general suspension of specie payment by the banks, the deposit banks as well as others. As the notes of none but specie-paying banks could be lawfully taken and paid out by the government officers, collections and disbursements could only be made in violation of law. In this state of things, the new president called a special session of congress. He recommended the disuse of banks altogether as fiscal agents of the government, and the substitution of the plan which had two years before been so unfavorably received. A bill for that purpose was introduced, passed the senate, but was lost in the house. A similar bill was introduced at the succeeding regular session, and shared the same fate. But in 1840, the independent treasury, as it was called, was established.

With the accession of president Harrison, March, 1841, the whig party for the first time obtained control of the government. The questions at issue between the two great parties were substantially the same as they had been for many years. On the 17th of March, the president issued a proclamation convening congress on the 31st of May. On the 4th of April, just one month from the day of his inauguration, his administration was terminated by his death; and the executive office passed into the hands of John Tyler, who had been elected as vice-president.

As the object of the extra session was to provide a remedy for the disordered state of the currency and finances, a bill was introduced for the repeal of the sub-treasury, as it was generally called, and another for the incorporation of a bank, which was still a favorite measure with a large portion of the whig party. The former subsequently passed both houses, and was signed by the president. The bank bill also passed both houses; but, although it was said to have been framed with a view to avoid the objections of the president, it received his veto. He was consulted by members of his cabinet, and a new bill was prepared with reference to his views, and passed; but this also was negatived. This second unexpected veto was speedily followed by the resignation of all the cabinet officers excepting the secretary of state, (Mr. Webster,) and the adjournment of congress without accomplishing the object for which it had been convened. No attempt has since been made to establish a national bank.

At the ensuing regular session, (1841–1842,) after having encountered two vetoes, the whig congress succeeded in enacting a tariff law superseding the "compromise act" of 1833, before alluded to, by which all duties above 20 per cent. were to be gradually reduced, by the year 1842, to 20 per cent. ad valorem, which point of reduction had now been reached. The reëstablishment of a protective tariff, which was effected by the law of this session, was the principal measure of the contemplated policy of the whigs which they found themselves able to accomplish. The measure which, more than any other, signalized the administration of Mr. Tyler, was carried against the votes of a large majority of the whigs in congress. That measure is the annexation of Texas to the United States.

The project of annexation originated with neither of the two political parties; nor did it become, strictly speaking, a party measure until several years after it had been disclosed. In March, 1836, Texas, then a province of Mexico, and in the midst of a revolution, declared herself independent. On the receipt of the intelligence at Washington, congress being in session, the subject of recognizing the independence of the new republic was immediately introduced, and resolutions were adopted, in the senate unanimously, and in the house with only 22 dissenting voices, in favor of such recognition, whenever it should appear that Texas had a government capable of performing the duties and fulfilling the obligations of an independent power. At the next session, the last under president Jackson's administration, the president, in a special message, advised congress not to acknowledge the independence of Texas, until she should be beyond the danger of being again subjected to Mexico; stating as a reason, that the revolutionists had instituted a government similar to our own, and had resolved, on our recognition of their independence, to ask for admission into the union, and also to ask us to acknowledge their title to the territory. The movement, if too early, might subject us to the imputation of seeking to establish the claims of our neighbors to a territory with a view to its acquisition by ourselves. Notwithstanding this advice of the president, a virtual acknowledgment was adopted by both houses. At the next session, the first under Mr. Van Buren's administration, Texas having applied for admission, numerous remonstrances against annexation were received, and the measure failed; and the proposition submitted by Texas for admission was withdrawn.

A desire was expressed by southern statesmen and southern legislatures for the annexation of Texas, in order to secure "an equipoise of influence in the halls of congress which should furnish a guaranty of protection" to southern institutions; and an intimation to the same effect was made by southern representatives on the floor of congress

In December, 1843, Mr. Tyler suggested the interference of our government, by force, to put an end to the war between Texas and Mexico; and it was subsequently ascertained that a treaty had already been concluded by Mr. Calhoun, secretary of state, and the Texan ministers, and sent to the senate for ratification. The treaty, however, was rejected. The objections to the treaty were, (1.) That it would cause a war with Mexico; (2.) As Texas claimed a large portion of territory beyond her acknowledged boundary, to receive her would compel us to defend the claim against Mexico; (3.) The annexation of a foreign nation was not authorized by the constitution. Although annexation had not been a party question, all, or nearly all, the democratic senators from the free states, but for these objections would have voted for the treaty. Of the ten, six, together with Mr. Benton, of Missouri, a slave state, voted against it.

Pending the presidential election of that year, (1844,) annexation became a party question. Mr. Van Buren and Mr. Clay were, prospectively, the candidates of their respective parties. Having been interrogated as to their views on annexation, both expressed themselves against the measure under existing circumstances. Mr. Clay was subsequently nominated as the whig candidate. In the democratic convention, Mr. Van Buren received a majority of all the votes; but the convention having adopted a rule requiring a majority of two-thirds, and southern delegates insisting on having a candidate favorable to annexation; Mr. Polk of Tennessee was nominated. The project of a national bank having been generally abandoned, the tariff question had been for some time the principal issue between the parties; the democratic party being opposed to the tariff of 1842. To this question two others were now added. A resolution was adopted, by the convention, declaring "that our title to the whole of Oregon was clear and unquestionable; that no portion of it ought to be ceded to England or any other foreign power; and that the reöccupation of Oregon and the reännexation of Texas were great American measures entitled to the cordial support of the democracy of the union."

To some readers the reasons for the use of the words "reöccupation" and "reännexation," which imply a former possession, may need some explanation. The United States,

Russia, and Great Britain, had severally claimed portions of the Oregon country. Great Britain being unwilling to relinquish her claim, though wholly unjust, as our government believed, a treaty arrangement was made in 1818, by which the parties were to occupy it jointly; the portions claimed by them respectively to be free and open, for ten years, to the vessels, citizens, and subjects of both powers. At the expiration of ten years, the agreement was renewed; after which the joint occupancy might be terminated by either party giving to the other twelve months' notice. By a treaty between the United States and Russia, in 1824, a boundary line was established at 54 degrees 40 minutes north latitude. American fur traders had taken possession near the mouth of the Columbia river, and in 1810 built a small town called Astoria. During the war, the British traders, with the aid of the Indians, had driven off our traders, and held possession until it was restored by the treaty of Ghent. On retaking possession, the agent of the United States took possession also of a British post, the English settlers protesting against our right to take it.

Texas is a part of the Louisiana territory purchased of France in 1803, which it is generally admitted, extended to the Rio Grande; but that portion lying west of the Sabine river, the western boundary of the state of Louisiana, was surrendered to Spain by the treaty of 1819, ceding Florida to the United States, and became again a part of Mexico, then subject to Spain. The facts here briefly stated show to what the words reöccupation and reännexation refer.

Although annexation was a southern measure, the great body of the southern whigs concurred in the views of their party candidate. The democrats were largely in the majority in that section of the union; and as the party, north and south, had unanimously adopted annexation as a party measure; and as a considerable portion of the anti-annexationists voted for the anti-slavery, or "third party" candidate, (Mr. Birney,) Mr. Polk was elected—pledged to favor the annexation of Texas, and to maintain our claim to the whole of Oregon.

At the next session, (1844–1845,) the last under Mr Tyler, while a negotiation was pending between our gov ernment and Great Britain on the Oregon question, a bill to establish a government for that territory passed the house, but was not finally acted on in the senate. In 1843, pursuant to a recommendation of Mr. Tyler, a bill to authorize the taking of possession of the territory had passed the senate ; and in 1844 an unsuccessful attempt was made to pass a resolution proposing to notify Great Britain of our intention to terminate the joint occupancy. The negotiation was continued until after Mr. Polk came into office, and was abandoned ; and apprehensions were entertained of a war between the two countries. The difficulty was finally compromised by an agreement to divide the territory ; our government conceding to Great Britain all that portion of it lying north of the 49th degree, a line which the latter had for years proposed as a boundary.

Annexation was completed on the last days of Mr. Tyler's term, March, 1845. There were in both houses majorities in favor of the scheme ; but many hesitated from doubts of the constitutionality of annexing either by joint resolution of the two houses, or by treaty. A resolution, however, for admission passed the house, and was sent to the senate. Some of the senators being of the opinion that if annexation could be effected constitutionally at all, it must be done by the treaty-making power, an amendatory resolution was added to that of the house, (afterwards concurred in by that body,) providing for the renewal of negotiations to agree upon terms of admission and cession either by treaty to be submitted to the senate, or by articles to be submitted to the two houses of congress, as the president should direct. It was said, that two of the senators, without whose votes the resolutions could not have been passed, voted for them from the belief that Mr. Polk, upon whom they supposed the choice of the mode of annexation would devolve, would elect that of annexing by treaty, and would open a new negotiation. But Mr. Tyler, to whom the resolutions were sent, on the last business day (we believe) of the session, approved them, and at once completed the measure by his own act.

Thus were settled the two new questions upon which the parties joined issue in 1844 ; one, before the president elect came into power ; the other by himself nearly a year and a half after his accession, and but a few days before the passage of the reduced tariff act superseding that enacted by the whig congress of 1842.

Before the adjustment of the Oregon difficulty with Great Britian had been consummated, the country was surprised by the announcement of war. As had been expected, Mexico, considering the admission of Texas an act of war on the part of the United States, had declared her intention to resent the injury and resort to arms. Apprehending hostilities, the president had ordered Gen. Taylor with his troops to some place on the gulf of Mexico, from which, if occasion should demand, he could proceed to the defense of the western frontier of Texas. The general took his station at Corpus Christi, on the west side of the Nueces. Having remained there seven months, and no hostile act having been committed by Mexicans, the army in March, 1846, pursuant to orders, proceeded to the Rio Grande, where Gen. Taylor was met by a deputation from the Mexican commander with a message protesting against the invasion of the territory of Mexico. In April hostilities were then commenced; and on the 11th of May the president, in a message to congress, announced a state of war, which, he said had been "commenced on the part of Mexico, by invading our territory, and shedding the blood of our citizens on our own soil;" and asked for the necessary means to prosecute the war. A bill for this purpose was promptly passed, with only 14 dissenting voices in the house, and 2 in the senate.

This war measure, so far as concerned the president, was highly disapproved by the almost entire whig party, both in and out of congress. They denied the statements of the president. Our army, they said, had invaded Mexico. Blood had been shed on soil far beyond any Texan settlements, and over which Texas had never exercised jurisdiction. They also charged the president with having violated the constitution, in baving virtually made war without consulting congress, to whom alone the war power had been confided by the constitution.

Prefixed to the bill was a preamble declaring the war to exist by the act of Mexico. To this the whig members objected; and they moved to have it struck out; but the motion failed. Its authors were accused of a design to compel the whigs to aid in shielding the president, or to bear the odium of having opposed a war sanctioned by the government. Their unwillingness to take the unpopular attitude of hostility to their own country, and the prevalent opinion that any war, however unjust, or however unlawfully made, ought to be supported, induced the opposition so generally to vote for supplies.

During this session was introduced, or rather revived, a principle which proved the occasion of a temporary reverse of fortune in the democratic party. In August, the senate received from the president a confidential message expressing his intention to propose to Mexico the opening of a negotiation ; an overture being already on the way to that country. And as, in negotiating a peace, it might be found necessary to purchase Mexican territory, he asked an appropriation of money. A bill appropriating two millions for that purpose was introduced, to which Mr. Wilmot, of Pennsylvania, a democrat, moved an amendment, providing that slavery should never exist in any part of the territory thus acquired. The bill, with this proviso, passed the house ; and while under consideration in the senate, when the vote was about to be taken, action was arrested by the announcement that the house, whose clock was a few minutes faster than that of the senate, had been adjourned by the speaker. At the next session, a law appropriating three millions for this purpose was passed without the anti-slavery proviso.

DURING THE TERMS OF TAYLOR, FILLMORE, PIERCE AND BUCHANAN.

Although the principle of the "Wilmot proviso," as it was called, was never incorporated into the national whig party, it governed the action of the northern whig members of congress, and was avowed in political whig conventions throughout the free states. Hence the nomination of Gen. Taylor by the national whig convention in 1848, produced great dissatisfaction among northern whigs. Unwilling to declare his political sentiments, and being a slaveholder, he was presumed to be opposed to the anti-slavery proviso, to which the whigs of the free states were considered fully committed. Gen. Cass, the democratic candidate, declared himself opposed to all interference, by congress, with the subject of slavery in the territories ; and it was supposed that, if elected, he would interpose the veto to any bill on this subject, if passed by congress.

The decided opposition of Gen. Cass to the prohibition of slavery in the territories by congress, aided probably by considerations of a personal nature, caused a serious breach in the democratic party. Another national convention, representing the disaffected portions of both the two great parties, and the anti-slavery party, was held at Buffalo, in the state of New York, and a new party formed on the general principle of opposition to the extension of slavery. Their resolutions declared it to be the duty of the federal government to abolish slavery wherever it had the constitutional power to do so; denied the authority of the general government over slavery within the states; and declared congressional action to be the true and safe means of preventing the existence of slavery in territory now free. The convention nominated Martin Van Buren for president, and Charles Francis Adams for vice-president. John P. Hale, who had been previously nominated by the anti-slavery party, consented to the withdrawal of his name from the list of candidates.

The subsequent publication of some of the views of Gen. Taylor, among which was his repugnance to the free use of the veto power, from which it was inferred that he would not interpose it against any law prohibiting slavery in the territories, and fears of the election of a more objectionable candidate, induced the larger portion of the bolting whigs to return to the support of the party, and secured the election of their candidate.

The administration of President Taylor commenced the 4th of March, 1849, and was terminated by his death about fifteen months thereafter. Since the time of his coming into office, few party questions characterized as whig or democratic have arisen. The great subject of political agitation has been the extension of slavery. The general policy of President Taylor was disclosed in his annual message, December, 1849. A bill for the admission of California as a state had been introduced at the preceding session of congress; but involving the disposal of other portions of territory acquired from Mexico, it failed, as did also a bill to establish a territorial government for Upper California. Presuming that any attempt to establish territorial governments in California and New Mexico would be again attended by the proposition to apply the proviso, and revive the excitement of former years, which he wished to prevent, the president recommended that no territorial gove nments should be formed, but that the people should be left to themselves until they should have formed constitutions preparatory to admission as states.

Several plans were proposed in both houses for the government of the new territory. The representatives of the slave interest were opposed to the admission of California as a free state without some equivalent to slavery. At length, with a view to the settlement of the whole slavery controversy, a compromise was proposed by Mr. Clay. The plan was opposed by southern members as not making sufficient concession to the south, and by northern members on account of its conceding too much, or of its making any concession at all.

The discussion was protracted to a late period of a very long session. The several propositions were first contained in one bill. The result was the passage of five different bills: (1.) A bill for organizing the territory of Utah, without any restriction as to slavery. (2.) A similar bill for organizing the territory of New Mexico; to which was united a bill previously passed by the senate for establishing the boundary of Texas, proposing to pay Texas ten millions of dollars for relinquishing her claims to territory in New Mexico. Although this bill did not concede to Texas the full extent of her claims, yet it was contended—and as evidence Mr. Benton referred to a map, the accuracy of which had been acknowledged by Texan authority—that the bill took from New Mexico 70,000 square miles of territory. This rendered the bill the more objectionable to northern members, as the transfer of any territory to Texas would convert it into slave territory. (3.) A bill to admit California. (4.) A bill providing more effectually for the recovery of escaped slaves, called the "fugitive slave bill." (5.) A bill to abolish the slave trade in the District of Columbia.

The slavery question had for years been obscuring party lines, as between the whig and democratic parties. The settlement of this question, which it was supposed had been effectually done by the late compromise, would leave the parties to resume their former attitude. But the issues upon which they had long been divided, were all, or nearly all, disposed of or abandoned. The whigs were dissatisfied with the revenue tariff of 1846; but the prospect of being able to restore the protective policy was too faint to encourage a renewal of the question.

The declarations of principle of the two national conventions in 1852, showed a narrower difference of opinion upon ordinary questions than had formerly existed: upon that of slavery, both took substantially the same ground. The democratic convention declared "that the party would abide by the compromise measures of 1850, the act for reclaiming fugitives included," and pledged the party "to resist all attempts at renewing, in congress or out of it, the agitation of the slavery question, under whatever shape or color the attempt might be made." The whig convention declared that these "acts, the fugitive slave law included, were received and acquiesced in by the whig party of the United States;" and they would "deprecate all further agitation of the question thus settled, and would discourage all efforts to continue or renew such agitation whenever, wherever, or however the attempt might be made."

Some of the acts of 1850, especially the fugitive law, were highly obnoxious to a majority of the northern section of the whig party; and the indorsement of the whole series of acts by the convention produced an extensive lukewarmness in the party. This, with the large accessions to the democratic party from the dissenters of 1848, who believed the altered state of the slavery question rendered a continuance of the free-soil organization no longer necessary, gave to the democratic party an easy victory. Of the 296 electoral votes, Mr. Pierce received 264; General Scott, 42.

Mr. Pierce came into office the 4th of March, 1853, at a time of a comparative political calm. The exciting question of slavery had been settled nearly three years; and there were no apprehensions of its early renewal. The general expectation that it would remain undisturbed, was strengthened by the president, who had, in his inaugural address, declared that the compromise measures of 1850 were constitutional, and were to be carried into effect; and he expressed the fervent hope that the question was at rest. This expectation of continued quiet received additional confirmation from his annual message in December, which contained the following express declaration: "That this repose is to suffer no shock during my official term, if I have power to avert it, those who placed me here may be assured." From these repeated assurances of the executive, the declarations of both of the national conventions that the agitation should, if possible, be repressed, and the general acquiescence of the people in those measures, the revival of the agitation at so early a period as that very session could scarcely have been imagined.

On an early day of the session, a bill was reported to establish a territorial government for Nebraska. This bill also contemplated the repeal of the Missouri compromise. Perhaps some young reader may not know what is meant by this compromise. In 1820, the people of Missouri applied for admission into the union as a state with a constitution allowing slavery. An amendment was moved with a view to the prohibition of slavery in that state, as a condition of its admission. After a long controversy the question was compromised. The southern boundary of the state was on the line of 36 degrees 30 minutes north latitude; and it was agreed that Missouri should be admitted with slavery, but in no other portion of the territory acquired from France under the name of Louisiana, lying north of that line, should slavery ever be permitted to exist.

The bill to organize Nebraska was subsequently amended so as to divide the territory into two, Nebraska and Kansas, with separate governments. The opening of the country to slavery north of the compromise line, produced an intense excitement. The measure was advocated on the ground that the people should be left free to establish such institutions as they pleased, and that congress had no right to enact any prohibitions on the subject. It was also assumed that the compromise ac[illegible] of 1850 had superseded the Missouri compromise.

The opponents of the bill deprecated the violation of a compact which had long been regarded as inviolable, north and south. The right of congress to interdict slavery in the territories had been abundantly recognized. The ordinance of 1787, excluding slavery from the north-western territory, had been sanctioned by congress under the constitution. And since that time, down to a late period, congress had repeatedly exercised the power of prohibiting slavery when establishing territorial governments. The acts of 1850, they said, could not have superseded or repealed the compromise of 1820. No such idea had been expressed in the long debates on these measures in 1850. And southern senators had but at the last session admitted that the Missouri compromise could not be repealed. Nor did the first report of the senator from Illinois, (Mr. Douglas, who reported the bill, not thirty days before,) express the opinion that the acts of 1850 had superseded the Missouri compromise. The democrats of the north uniting with the south on this question, the bill was passed, in the house, 113 to 100 ; in the senate 35 to 13. Of the members of the house, from free states, 44, all democrats, voted in favor of the bill ; against the bill, from free states, 91, of whom nearly all were whigs. Of the 78 southern votes, only 9 were against the bill.

The passage of this bill produced an unprecedented excitement. Its opponents, regarding it as an aggression upon the interests of freedom, and as disclosing the purpose of an indefinite extension of slavery, formed a new political organization, on the general principle of preventing the extension of slavery into free territory. This party took the name of *republican*, and was composed of the great body of the whig party of the free states, and a considerable portion of the democrats. A new party had arisen a year or two before, called the *American* party, and had increased very rapidly. The leading principle of this party was, that "Americans must rule America." To this end, native born citizens should be selected for all government offices in preference to all others. There should also be made a change in the naturalization laws, requiring of foreigners hereafter, to become citizens, a residence of twenty-one years. During the presidential canvass of 1856, a majority of the Americans, in several states, coöperated with the republicans. The party organization, however, was not abandoned. Parties had previously been formed upon similar principles; but they had had a brief existence. The duration and destiny of the present, are yet to be determined.

Local republican organizations were first formed, it is be-

.ieved, in 1855. In 1856 was held a national convention, composed of delegates from all the free states, and two or three of the slave states. In the latter, however, the party can not, at least for many years, expect to acquire any material strength. The presidential candidate of the party was John C. Fremont, who received the electoral votes of all the free states except New Jersey, Penn., Indiana, Illinois, and California. Of the 296 electoral votes, he received 116; Millard Fillmore, the American candidate, received 8, being the votes of the electors of the state of Maryland; and James Buchanan, the democratic candidate, received 172.

Although the chief object of one of the two great parties is to keep the national territory open and free to the entrance of slaveholders with their slaves; and of the other to keep slavery out of it, there is, upon several subjects, a difference of sentiment upon which the parties base their action. It has until recently been the prevailing doctrine, sanctioned by the practice of congress and the decision of the national courts, that slavery, not being recognized by the common law, can exist only where it is permitted or established by positive enactment; and hence, that when a slave, by consent of his master, enters any free state or territory, he is free. It has also been held, in conformity with the like practice, that, under the power of congress "to dispose of, and make all needful rules and regulations respecting the territory or other property belonging to the United States," congress may provide or establish governments for the people of any portions of such territory, and consequently has power over slavery therein. These doctrines are maintained by the republicans. They hold further, that as slavery is against all natural right and the principles upon which we have declared all just governments to be founded; and as its existence in a state is highly detrimental to its prosperity; it is the duty of the general government to exclude it from all the public territory.

The democratic party, on the other hand, maintains the doctrine assumed in 1848, that congress has no constitutional power over slavery in the territories; the power above cited having reference merely to the disposal of territory as public *property*, and neither refers to nor includes the power to govern the *inhabitants*. And in 1854, the party adopted the sentiment expressed in the Kansas and Nebraska act, which declared it to be "the true intent and meaning of this act not to legislate slavery into any territory or state, nor to exclude it therefrom; but to leave the people thereof perfectly free to form and regulate their domestic institutions in their own way, subject only to the constitution of the United States." This declared right of the people of a territory to govern themselves without the interference of congress, was termed "popular sovereignty," a term which was understood and intended to mean that the people of the territory, and they alone, had the right to make their own laws, and to allow or prohibit slavery. Since the expiration of the last administration, this doctrine has been essentially modified, if not actually rejected. It is asserted by the present administration, not only that the power to dispose of the territorial property conveys to congress no power to govern the people; but that the constitution, by recognizing the right of property in slaves, carries with it into the territories the right to hold slaves therein; and the people of the territory have *not* the power to exclude slavery by law, while in a territorial condition. This prohibition must be postponed until they form a state constitution; when congress may admit the state with or without slavery. It has also been declared by the president and others of high authority, and appears to have the assent of the party, that under the constitution, no person of the African race is, or can be made, a citizen of the United States.

In order to a proper understanding of the several points at issue between the two great national parties, reference must be had to the history of the action of congress and the executive on this question, and of the controversy between the pro-slavery and free-state parties in Kansas. But of this our prescribed limits forbid the briefest sketch. Besides, the transactions are of so recent occurrence, as to render an account of them in this place the less necessary. Therefore we here conclude our sketch of parties.*

* The importance of a familiar acquaintance with our political history, must be apparent to every one. It is, in fact, by a knowledge of the practical working of our system of government, that the citizen is enabled to make an intelligent application of the knowledge acquired from the study of constitutional jurisprudence and political economy. The author takes the liberty to refer the reader

PRACTICAL OBSERVATIONS.

There is an opinion that parties are evils upon the body politic. The more popular sentiment, however, is, "that parties in free countries are useful checks upon the administration of the government, and serve to keep alive the spirit of liberty." To whatever weight these opinions may be entitled, we think it may be affirmed of parties that they are unavoidable—that they exist of necessity; and that their good or bad influence depends upon their proper use or their abuse. Unanimity of sentiment is not to be expected in a political community where freedom of thought and of speech is fully enjoyed; and a division of its members into parties, is both natural, inevitable, and proper. Some believe a certain measure or series of measures to be most conducive to the general welfare; others think the end more likely to be attained by measures of a different character. Entertaining these different opinions, each party engages in appropriate efforts to secure the success of its favorite policy. And while the contending parties keep steadily in view the true object of all party organizations—the public good—no great evils are to be apprehended. For, though majorities, acting with due care and deliberation, sometimes misjudge as to the effects of their measures, their mistakes are not necessarily productive of lasting injury, as a change of policy may be speedily effected.

But serious evils do often result from the acts of political parties. The existence of parties is, however, the *occasion* rather than the *cause* of these evils. It is by the perversion of parties—by diverting them from their original and legitimate purpose—that the evil is produced. Parties are often controlled by corrupt and aspiring men with a view to their own aggrandizement. This is sometimes done by maligning their opponents and disparaging their measures. The wisest policy is not unfrequently assailed by sophistical and ingenious arguments; and different measures are

to The American Statesman, a Political History of this country from its first settlement, complete in a single volume, and at a price which renders it accessible to nearly every citizen.

proposed promising benefits which their projectors know full well can never be realized. The people become dissatisfied. These crafty men fan this dissatisfaction into a flame, and turn the excitement to the success of their party and their own elevation. Thus stimulated by irregular passion, and misled by artful misrepresentation, the people sometimes call for measures which afterward they lament and condemn; or they are deceived into acquiescence in these measures by the misrepresentations of these same men as to the real cause of the evils complained of.

It is a lamentable fact, that men of this description control, to a great extent, the legislation of this country. This is done in two ways: First, by outside influence. Our state and national legislatures are at every session beleagured by large numbers of men who have private ends to be answered. Representatives wanting firmness are fatigued into compliance. The integrity of others is assailed, and in too many cases yields to the considerations offered, as has been abundantly proved by late investigations. Secondly, by a direct participation in the enactment of laws. These men wield the machinery of party to lift themselves into power, and take the business of making the laws into their own hands. We would by no means be understood to accuse majorities in our legislative bodies of corrupt legislation. The most mischievous enactments are sometimes effected by the subtlety of a few designing men.

The means by which this latter class of men reach their position is well known. The mass of our citizens are culpably indifferent respecting public affairs. They allow the slightest considerations to interfere with the discharge of their political duties. A majority of them, it is true, cast their suffrages at the elections; but they leave the primary meetings and the conventions to be controlled by the few for the especial benefit of themselves and their friends. This general apathy affords a powerful encouragement to office-seeking, which has become alarmingly prevalent in this country. How few men most eminent for their talents and private worth are elected to the most honorable and responsible offices! Thousands who would never be called from private life, taking advantage of this prevailing indifference, find it an easy matter to secure nominations, which seldom fail of a unanimous ratification of the party at the polls. Allegiance to party is held by some a paramount duty. Others, afraid of the party displeasure, vote for the "regular ticket" against their better judgment. As mistakes made at the primary meetings and nominating conventions are so seldom corrected at the ballot-box, how important that these meetings which give character to the nominations, and, by consequence, to the public administration, should be participated in by the mass of the electors!

We notice a popular error in respect to parties. It is supposed that a party, if its principles are correct, must needs be, or ought to be, perpetual. But parties are formed for the promotion of definite objects. When these objects have been accomplished, why should these hostile organizations be continued? New questions arise, upon which the people naturally divide anew, according to their opinions upon these particular questions. But cases are not rare in which parties have maintained the same division upon new questions bearing not the remotest relation or the least similarity to those which had been effectually disposed of. It is therefore to be presumed, that either a large portion of the members of each party surrendered their independence of opinion, or all *happened* to form the same conclusions. Strange that in politics alone there should occur such remarkable coincidences of opinion! Hence we see how this unnatural continuance of party organizations after their original purposes have been subserved, tends to destroy that political independence without which the elective franchise is of no value.

Nor is it less erroneous to suppose that political consistency requires the indiscriminate support of all party measures, or an undeviating adherence, under all circumstances, to the same political organization. Parties sometimes, from motives of expediency, change their position on public questions. He that follows his party in such cases, justly incurs the charge of inconsistency. Or a man may, for satisfactory reasons, change his political opinions. A continued adherence to the party in that case argues a want of honesty.

Parties are often diverted from their legitimate purposes by the pernicious influence of party spirit. By party spirit is not meant simply a desire, however strong, for the success of one's party. It is a disposition to support a party for the sake of the party, and manifests a deeper solicitude for the triumph of party than for principle or the public good. There are many who seem to imagine, that the overthrow or disorganization of their party would be a public calamity second only to the loss of liberty itself. This overestimate of the value of party gives demagogues great power over the public mind. Appeals to party prejudice are seldom unavailing. Let it but be intimated that the party is in danger, and its devotees hasten to its defense with intense enthusiasm. Party spirit indisposes the mind to investigation, closes it against the clearest evidence, and thus fortifies it against conviction. A man under the dominion of this passion is beyond the reach of reason and argument. He shrinks from a candid examination of his own opinions, lest he should find something to shake or unsettle them. He maintains an obstinate adherence to his crude notions, and prides himself in his fancied political firmness. To him, party is all in all; and believing in the infallibility of its leaders, they find him a fit instrument to subserve their ambitious purposes.

The baneful effects of the spirit of party are seen in every department of the government. In our legislatures, state and national, measures are not unfrequently supported and opposed simply from their supposed effect upon parties. When party and the public interest come into conflict, the claims of the latter are made to yield. In the executive department, the influence of this spirit is most clearly seen in the exercise of the appointing power. Patronage is often bestowed solely as a reward for party services. Fidelity to party is made an indispensable qualification for office, while tried integrity, distinguished abilities, and acknowledged statesmanship, are among the minor recommendations to executive favor.

Nor have our judicial tribunals wholly escaped this contaminating influence. Charges of judicial obliquity should not be made upon slight grounds. The decisions of our courts are entitled to respectful consideration. They are nevertheless proper subjects of criticism, and sometimes of public censure. Our judicial records furnish numerous instances in which benches have been divided in their decisions in strict accordance with their division in politics. There is in this no certain evidence of judicial corruption; yet when six, or eight, or more members of a court divide upon questions of law exactly as they are divided in politics, there is reason to suspect that their judgments are swayed—insensibly perhaps—by the malign spirit of party.

With singular accuracy does the Father of his country, in his Farewell Address, describe the effects of party spirit. He had encountered it in his own administration, and he felt the necessity of cautioning his countrymen against this "worst enemy of popular governments."

The conduct of the political press, too, is more or less affected by this spirit. This remark is not intended for general application. The press has been not inappropriately styled "the palladium of liberty." It has contributed too largely to our national prosperity and fame to be lightly esteemed or traduced. It will not, however, be disputed, that in many instances it is wanting in independence, and aims at no higher object than the interests of party, or perhaps of a few designing men who control it for their own individual benefit. Such presses aggravate the evils of party spirit by inflaming the passions of men, and engendering and keeping alive party animosities. Political questions they seldom discuss with candor. Facts, the knowledge of which is indispensable to the formation of right opinions, are often studiously concealed, and the views of political opponents misrepresented.

Party spirit is intolerant and vindictive. It proscribes men for expressing their honest opinions. It exacts an unfaltering devotion to party as a condition upon which official favors are granted. A man who presumes to dissent from his party upon a single point, loses his party standing, and with it his office, if he has one, as soon as the appointing power or a popular election can displace him. This tends to destroy political independence, and encourages political dishonesty. When the frank avowal of a man's sentiments exposes him to the loss of office, or when entire assent to a party creed is made prerequisite to office, there is a strong temptation to depart from the principles of political rectitude. In other words, when a man's bread depends upon his political opinions, honesty in politics will not always be considered the best policy. This reward and punishment system, though sanctioned by the practice of all modern parties, is liable to sound objections. Changes of political sentiment and of party relations often take place, which cannot reasonably be ascribed to any other motive than that above suggested.

We have noticed some of the evils incident to political parties, and which have found their way into the government itself. These evils, we think, may be justly traced to one grand cause; which cause, and the remedy it is proposed now to consider. That cause is found in a DEFECTIVE POPULAR EDUCATION, the bare mention of which suggests the true remedy; namely, THE EDUCATION OF AMERICAN CITIZENS WITH SPECIAL REFERENCE TO THE GREAT BUSINESS OF SELF-GOVERNMENT.

Notwithstanding the comparative general intelligence of the people of the United States, it must be confessed that the greater portion of them are greatly deficient in political knowledge. They have not been duly instructed in their duties and responsibilities as citizens of a free government. The unhappy consequences of this defect in their education can not have escaped the notice of any person of ordinary observation. That our country has been prosperous beyond all precedent, is readily admitted. Fortunately we live under a government admirably adapted to promote the well-being of its citizens, and any tolerable administration of it, according to established forms, must insure a good degree of prosperity. But, successful as our free institutions have proved, they are doubtless capable of conferring a far greater amount of happiness than has yet fallen to the lot of the American people.

Although our national prosperity has, on the whole, been great and rapid, it has experienced frequent interruptions and reverses, some of them for considerable periods of time. If those entrusted with the public administration had that knowledge of political economy which ought to be possessed by all who aspire to responsible stations in the government, and which may under ordinary circumstances be attained, it is believed these interruptions would rarely if ever occur. But to secure this result, the people themselves must be better instructed in political science. Although it is not to be presumed that the mass of the electors will ever be, or can become, profound political economists, they may acquire such knowledge of the general principles of the science, and of the operation and effect of the laws relating to the various interests of the country, as would enable them effectually to guard against or correct the mistakes of their representatives. This knowledge need not be confined to the few who have the most leisure to devote to its acquisition. Every man possessing ordinary skill in the management of his private affairs, may gain a knowledge of public economy sufficient not only to qualify him for the intelligent discharge of the duties of an elector, but to give him an honorable standing in the national or state councils.

The general diffusion of a knowledge of political science would more fully develop the democratic principle in our government. The fundamental principle of true democracy is political equality. The constitution recognizes no distinction of class. It confers no special privileges. It places all classes on a level at the ballot-box. But to render their power equally effective, all must exercise it with equal discretion.

A wider dissemination of political knowledge would secure to the laboring classes, so called, a more efficient representation in the state and national councils. They have not hitherto had that measure of influence in the government to which their numbers entitle them, or which their interests demand. Of the higher offices, the professional classes have enjoyed almost a monopoly. This is in a measure the result of necessity. A vastly smaller proportion of the former than of the latter have fitted themselves for the more responsible offices. Even where, as in the lower branch of our state legislatures, they are more nearly represented in proportion to their numbers, owing to their more limited knowledge of public affairs, they have not a corresponding influence. Constituting, as they do, the great majority of the electors, they may elect representatives from among themselves at pleasure ; but the election of any number of their own class destitute of the requisite qualifications, would redound neither to their own honor or advantage, nor to that of the state at large. Too much importance may be attached to the proportional representation of the different classes. Yet an increase of representation from the agricultural and mechanical classes of the community would be manifestly proper, and more in accordance with the spirit of our republican institutions.

A thorough knowledge of our constitutional jurisprudence would constitute *an effectual safeguard against the encroachments of power.* Power is ever liable to abuse. To restrain its exercise is the object of a constitution. But men having favorite ends to accomplish, may be induced to exceed their constitutional powers, and to attempt a justification of their unauthorized acts by forced or false constructions of the constitution. Hence, if the people would protect their rights and liberties against usurpation, they must be capable of interpreting the constitution for themselves. Yet it is doubted whether one-fourth of the electors are familiar with its provisions. A large portion of them have never given it a single careful perusal; and thousands in almost every state of this union, are unable to read or understand it. Can constitutional liberty be safe in such hands? How can men, with qualifications so limited, reconcile it with a sense of justice, to take an equal share, with their more intelligent fellow-citizens, in the management of the important affairs of this great government? The exercise of political power by such men is more likely to become the means of impairing or subverting our liberties than of protecting them.

The universal diffusion of sound political information would *restrain and moderate the spirit of party.* This spirit finds its principal aliment in ignorance. None are so much under its control as the uninformed. Their blind party zeal just fits them to become the dupes and tools of designing politicians. Unable to distinguish between right and wrong in politics, they are more likely to take the wrong than the right side. The doctrine imputed to a certain class of religionists, that "ignorance is the mother of devotion," finds a perfect illustration in the conduct of these devotees of party. The intelligent politician, on the other hand, can not be drawn into the interests of demagogues He detects all departures from the true objects and principles of his party. Aiming at the success of principle, he supports party only as a means to that end; and when his party abandons its proper objects or violates its principles, he withdraws his support.

A familiar knowledge of the government would inspire the public with *a more elevated and healthful patriotism.* There is a spurious patriotism which consists mainly in a pride of one's country, and makes little sacrifice for any higher object than the good of party. Genuine patriotism embraces among the objects of its highest regard the integrity of our free institutions as the means of promoting the general welfare. But how can these be appreciated if they are not understood? Hence, true patriotism is intelligent. It is also jealous of the nation's honor. It would regard as a most serious calamity any act of the government which should subject it to the reproach of civilized and christian nations. It is also disinterested. It leads men to make all needful sacrifices for the public good. Nor is its benevolence limited to the present generation, but extends to the latest posterity. It is needless to say that such patriotism is to be found among those whose knowledge of our constitution enables them to discover its remarkable adaptation to the grand purpose of its formation—to preserve and transmit the blessings of civil and religious freedom.

This knowledge would also *promote the purity of our elections.* The ignorant elector cannot duly appreciate his franchise. Hence, thousands annually cast their votes at the solicitation or for the gratification of personal friends, or at the dictation of party leaders, without any apparent concern as to their effect upon the public interest. Many become the victims of deception and fraud; others hold their votes as a merchantable commodity, the subject of bargain and sale. To those unacquainted with modern party tactics, the number of votes annually purchased at stipulated prices, if it could be accurately told, would seem incredible. Nor is this sale of votes confined to the poor whose virtue often yields to pressing necessity. Many who are beyond the reach of want are in the market with their votes, which are at the disposal of the most liberal purchaser! The vendors, unable to trace their votes to their consequences, and therefore ignorant of their value, consider the paltry sum received for them as so much clear gain; whereas their votes, with others controlled in the different ways above mentioned, sometimes determine measures of policy which inflict upon the country a deep and lasting injury, in which these men are themselves sharers to an amount ten times greater than the value received for their votes.

How sad the reflection—how humiliating to the pride of every true American—that the honor as well as the interests of the nation should suffer from the character of our elections—elections in which the will of the honest, enlightened portion of our citizens is defeated by the votes of the ignorant and the vicious! But let not all our censure fall upon the latter. The mass of the electors are neither corrupt nor corruptible. They desire, so far as they feel any concern in the matter, to see the government well administered. But they are criminally indifferent. Some of them are too neglectful of the means of information to vote intelligently, and seem to regard voting mainly as an act of service due to party. Others, better informed, neglect their duty altogether. The rabble rally at the faintest signal, whilst large numbers of the more intelligent and conscientious electors cannot be brought to the polls by the most urgent solicitations, or the strongest appeals to their sense of duty. By this omission of an incumbent duty, they virtually place the reins of government in the hands of those least qualified to conduct its affairs; and not a few make a merit of this neglect, claiming for it the credit of self-denial. The moral and virtuous constitute a large majority of the electors of the United States, and they might, by a union of effort, purify our elections, and make them what they purport—the fair expression of the will of a nation of intelligent freemen.

But the most thorough political education will never effect the desired reform, unless sanctified by moral and religious principle. Let the public mind be duly imbued with a proper sense of religious obligation, and a palpable improvement of our political and social condition would speedily ensue. The right of suffrage would be more conscientiously exercised. A greater number of good men would be elected. More good laws and fewer bad ones would be made; and the laws would be more faithfully executed. Justice would be administered with a more steady hand. Vice and crime would be more effectually restrained. The rights and interests of the community would be more safely guarded, and the great end of civil government—the highest happiness of the people—would be attained.

The conservative influence of religious principle in a body politic is not an idea of recent origin. It appears to have been a cherished doctrine of the fathers of the republic. Said Washington:

"Of all the dispositions and habits which lead to political prosperity, religion and morality are indispensable supports. In vain would that man claim the tribute of patriotism, who should labor to subvert these great pillars of human happiness—these firmest props of the duties of men and citizens. The mere politician, equally with the pious man, ought to respect and cherish them. A volume could not trace all their connection with private and public felicity. Let it be simply asked, where is the security for property, for reputation, for life, if the sense of religious obligation desert the oaths which are the instruments of investigation in courts of justice? And let us with caution indulge the supposition, that morality can be maintained without religion. Whatever may be conceded to the influence of refined education on minds of peculiar structure, reason and experience both forbid us to expect that national morality can prevail in exclusion of religious principle.

"It is substantially true, that virtue or morality is a necessary spring of popular government. The rule indeed extends with more or less force to every species of free government. Who that is a friend to it can look with indifference upon attempts to shake the foundation of the fabric?"

In nothing ever done or written by this wise and good man, are his wisdom and patriotism more conspicuous than in the sentiments here quoted. These sentiments, however, are of still earlier antiquity, as well as of higher authority. They are briefly expressed in the following words: "Righteousness exalteth a nation; but sin is a reproach to any people." "When the righteous are in authority, the people rejoice; but when the wicked bear rule, the people mourn."

But Washington was not the only one of the political fathers who felt the necessity of guarding the public morals. The same high moral sense was manifested by the patriot legislators in the days of the revolution. In the journals of congress, under date of October 12, 1778, we find the following:

"*Whereas* true religion and good morals are the only solid foundations of public liberty: *Resolved*, That it be, and hereby is, earnestly recommended to the several states to take the most effectual measures for the encouragement thereof, and for the suppressing of theatrical entertainments, horse-racing, gaming, and such other diversions as are productive of idleness, dissipation, and a general depravity of manners."

Four days later, they adopted, for their own rule of action, the following:

"*Whereas* frequenting play-houses and theatrical entertainments has a fatal tendency to divert the mind of the people from a due attention to the means necessary for the defense of their country and the preservation of their liberties: *Resolved*, That any person holding an office under the United States, who shall promote or encourage such plays shall be deemed unworthy to hold such office, and shall be accordingly dismissed."

If legislative assemblies represent as correctly the morals as the political opinions of their constituents, we may not congratulate ourselves on the improvement of the standard of national morality since the time of the revolutionary fathers. There has been an increase of the means of moral and religious improvement; but there has also been an increase of counteracting causes. The increase of wealth and of the means of indulgence, has been productive of idleness, dissipation and vice, especially among the dense population of our cities and large villages, where these habits are more readily contracted. It is doubted whether the passage of resolutions similar to those of the old congress could be effected in legislative bodies in these later days of the republic; or, if they could, whether they would be sustained by public sentiment. Every man who attends a theatre may not be unworthy of official trust; yet the rule of 1778 would, it is believed, operate injuriously in far fewer instances than the lax rule of the present day which makes the habitual patronage of theatrical and other kindred institutions no disqualification.

But whether there has been an advance or decline in the public morality, is a question of minor importance. It is sufficient to know and to act upon the truth already known and acknowledged, that popular liberty can be safe only as virtue and religion are duly appreciated and cherished. The present state of public morals calls loudly for reformatory effort. And may we not indulge the hope that this call will receive a cordial response from every Christian patriot?

No class of persons occupy a more influential or a more responsible position than *parents.* Good government can be maintained only where there are good citizens and loyal subjects. Their training begins, and that of many ends, in the family. Here the character is mainly formed ; and it will generally be good or bad as parents are faithful or remiss in discipline. In family education, the first lesson to be taught is *obedience.* If the *child* is taught submission to parental authority, it is to be presumed that the *man* will respect the constituted authorities and laws of the land. But in how many families is the natural order of government reversed! By a too ready compliance with the wishes of children, they gradually acquire control over their parents, and virtually give laws to the household. The effect of this upon the character of the children is easily imagined. Obedience is indispensable to the successful training of youth. Where the spirit of obedience has obtained possession of the mind of a child, the work of moral culture becomes comparatively easy.

But the duty of parents does not end here. The child is to be prepared, not only to become an orderly citizen and obedient subject, but to take an active part in the government ; and every father is bound to see that his sons have the means of acquiring a good political education ; and he can not innocently turn them upon the community unprepared to discharge their political duties.

Scarcely less responsible is the position of *public teachers.* The aid of the schools is needed in this educational reform. The great body of the people will never be duly qualified for their duties as citizens, until the study of political science shall have become incorporated into the course of instruction. Probably nine-tenths of our citizens receive the whole of their public instruction in the common schools.

These must continue to be the nurseries of American statesmen. Many of our future legislators, governors, and judges, are now in the course of training in these institutions. This consideration adds much to the importance and dignity of the teacher's profession. The instructors of our youth are acting an important part in shaping the destiny of the nation; and their labors and responsibility are increased by the delinquency of parents in the training of their children. How this should impress them with a sense of the magnitude of their trust! The state provides for the education of its citizens, with a view to its own safety and prosperity, and all who assume the office of public teacher should be well qualified to serve the state in this capacity. Has the requisite measure of qualification been attained by any considerable portion of the profession? Of all the sciences, which is of greater practical utility to an American citizen than the science of civil government? And yet there are few of which the people generally, or the teachers themselves, have so little knowledge. The question is candidly submitted, whether the honor of the profession and the interest of the state do not equally demand greater attention to this subject than it has hitherto received; and whether it should not be at once placed on the list of studies in all our public schools.

Among the causes that have retarded the introduction of this study into the schools, are the erroneous ideas that the subject of government is too abstruse and difficult for youth, and that the branches taught are already so numerous as not to leave room for any new one. The truth is, however, as experience has proved, that the elementary principles of political science in general, and the nature and structure of our government in particular, are more easily comprehended than some of those sciences which have hitherto crowded it out of the schools; and being more practically useful, there is no good reason why it should not be admitted even to the exclusion of others. Such exclusion, however, is believed to be unnecessary. And the question is submitted to the superintendents of public instruction and others to whom the educational interests of the states are intrusted, whether the value of their public services would not be enhanced by proper efforts to give this study a place in the course of instruction.

In conclusion, may we not appeal with confidence to the pride and patriotism of that class of our citizens for whom this work is more particularly designed—the young men who have completed their school education, and are about to engage in, or have already commenced, the great business of life? In no way can they more effectually prepare themselves for usefulness than by a course of solid reading. We have already spoken of the necessity of religion and morality in the body politic, as a means of permanent political prosperity: and we might have added, that among the most powerful aids to moral improvement is a sound literature. Yet it is to be deeply regretted, that FICTION forms the staple reading of many families and neighborhoods. Its impress upon the public mind is every where seen. Novels and tales constitute nine-tenths of the reading of some young men. Much of this kind of literature is positively pernicious; while the effect of that which is least exceptionable is to dissipate the mind and produce a disrelish for all that is solid or useful, and, consequently, to dwarf the intellect. It can not have escaped the notice of any careful observer, how few, comparatively, of the young men of our country give promise of intellectual greatness or eminent usefulness; how many are likely to attain a bare respectability; and what numbers have already acquired habits of immorality and even of open profligacy!

But, let the puerile tales which occupy so large a space in their libraries be displaced by works of practical utility, and a vast change would soon appear in the character and the pursuits of this interesting class of citizens. Works of no description would contribute more to this happy result, than those which treat of the principles of political science, and make men familiar with the nature and practical working of our admirable system of government. Few subjects involve interests so varied and important. The social and pecuniary interests of every person are affected by the government. The connection that exists between good government and the public prosperity, is itself one of the strongest inducements to the citizen to fit himself for the intelligent exercise of the powers and duties devolved upon him by the constitution.

To the people of the United States is committed an important trust. Their constitution was "ordained to secure the blessings of liberty." An experience of seventy years has proved it adequate to this object. Corrupt ambition and the lust of power may break down the bulwarks it has erected. Through popular ignorance and indifference it may cease to afford its wonted protection. It has been said, "A nation may lose its liberties in a day, and not miss them in a century." Under the forms of constitutional liberty, the people may suffer the evils of a despotism ; and they may unwittingly become their own oppressors.

If "the price of liberty is eternal vigilance," indifference must be dangerous. Demagoguism, party spirit, a corrupt literature, the want of vigilance, and the other evils to which we have alluded, are sufficient to subvert the liberties of any people. Where will these evils find an antidote but in an IMPROVED EDUCATION—one more highly moral, intellectual, and political? The general diffusion of moral and religious principle, and a familiar knowledge of our republican institutions, would make good citizens, true patriots, and enlightened statesmen, and insure a good administration and permanent political prosperity.

GOVERNMENT OF THE UNITED STATES.

SALARIES OF THE PRINCIPAL OFFICERS.

EXECUTIVE.

President,....	$25,000	Vice-President,..........	$6,000

CABINET OFFICERS.

Secretary of State,........	$8,000	Secretary of War,........	$8,000
Secretary of the Treasury,	8,000	Attorney-General, ...	8,000
Secretary of the Interior,	8,000	Postmaster-General,......	8,000
Secretary of the Navy,....	8,000		

JUDICIARY.

Chief Justice Sup. Court,	$6,500	Eight As. Justices, each,	$5,000

The Judges of the district courts of the states of Maine, New Hampshire, Vermont, Rhode Island, Connecticut, Delaware, New Jersey, Iowa, and Wisconsin, each $2,000.

The Judge of the northern district of Florida, $2,250.

The Judges of the western district of Virginia, North Carolina, eastern, western, and middle districts of Tennessee, northern and southern districts of Mississippi, western district of Pennsylvania, western district of Louisiana, Texas, Kentucky, northern and southern districts of Ohio, Indiana, Missouri, eastern and western districts of Arkansas, northern and southern districts of Illinois, and Michigan, each $2,500.

The Judges of the districts of Georgia, South Carolina, eastern district of Virginia, northern district of New York, northern and southern districts of Alabama, each $2,750.

The Judges of the districts of Maryland, Massachusetts, eastern district of Pennsylvania, southern district of Florida, southern district of California, each $3,000.

The Judge of the eastern district of Louisiana, $3,500.

The Judge of the southern district of New York, $3,750.

The Judge of the northern district of California, $5,000.

MEMBERS OF CONGRESS.

Members of Congress received from the 4th of March, 1817, until the year 185–, $8 a day during the session, and $8 for every twenty miles traveled (by the usual route) in going to and returning from the seat of government. By the act of 1856, they receive a salary of $3,000 a year, and mileage at the rate of 40 cents a mile. For each day's absence, unless from the cause of sickness, $8 is deducted from the salary. The president of the Senate, *pro tem.*, receives the same compensation as the Vice-President. The Speaker of the House of Representatives receives double the salary of a member.

SALARIES OF UNITED STATES MINISTERS.

England.

Minister,	$17,500
Secretary,	2,625
Assistant Secretary,	1,500

Russia.

Minister,	$12,000
Secretary,	1,800

France.

Minister,	$17,500
Secretary,	2,625
Assistant Secretary,	1,500

Spain.

Minister,	$12,000
Secretary,	1,800

Portugal.

Minister,	$7,500
Secretary,	1,500

Belgium.

Minister,	$7,500
Secretary,	1,500

Netherlands.

Minister,	$7,500
Secretary,	1,500

Denmark.

Minister,	$7,500
Secretary,	1,500

Sweden and Norway.

Minister,	$7,500
Secretary,	1,500

Prussia.

Minister,	$12,000
Secretary,	1,800

Austria.

Minister,	$9,000
Secretary,	1,800

Switzerland.

Minister,	$7,500
Secretary,	1,500

Sardinia.

Minister,	$7,500
Secretary,	1,500

Rome.

Minister,	$7,500
Secretary,	1,500

Two Sicilies.

Minister,	$7,500
Secretary,	1,500

Turkey.

Minister,	$7,500
Secretary,	2,000

China.

Minister,	$12,000
Secretary,	5,000

Mexico.

Minister,	$12,000
Secretary,	1,800

Nicaragua.

Minister,	$7,500
Secretary,	1,500

Guatemala.

Minister,	$7,500
Secretary,	1,500

New Granada.

Minister,	$7,500
Secretary,	1,500

Venezuela.

Minister,	$7,500
Secretary,	1,500

Ecuador.

Minister,	$7,500
Secretary,	1,500

Brazil.

Minister,	$12,000
Secretary,	1,800

Argentine Confederation.

Minister,	$7,500
Secretary,	1,500

Chili.

Minister,	$10,000
Secretary,	1,500

Peru.

Minister,	$10,000
Secretary,	1,500

Bolivia.

Minister,	$7,500
Secretary,	1,500

NOTE.—By act of 1855, the distinction, as to grade, between ministers and charges d' affaires, was abolished; the latter also being now called ministers. Formerly

STATE GOVERNMENTS.

States.	*Governor's Salary.*	*General Election.*	*Meeting of Legislature.*
Maine,................	$1,500	2d Mon. Sept.	1st Wed. January.
New Hampshire,....	1,000	2d Tu. March.	1st Wed. June.
Massachusetts,.....	3,500	Tu. af. 1st M. Nv.	1st Wed. Jan.
Vermont, ...	1,000	1st Tues. Sept.	2d Thur. Oct.
Rhode Island,......	1,000	1st Wed. April.	—— ——
Connecticut,........	1,100	1st Mon. April.	1st Wed. May.
New York,..........	4,000	Tu. af. 1st M. Nv.	1st Tu. Jan.
New Jersey,.........	1,800	Tu. af. 1st M. Nv.	2d Tu. Jan.
Pennsylvania, ...	3,000	2d Tu. October.	1st Tu. Jan.
Delaware,............	1,333	2d Tu. Novem.	1st T. Jan. *biennially*
Maryland,...........	3,600	1st Wed. Nov.	1st Wed. Jan. *do.*
Virginia,............	5,000	4th Thur. May.	2d Mon. Jan. *do.*
North Carolina,.....	3,000	1st Thur. Aug.	3d Mon. Nov. *do.*
South Carolina,.....	3,500	2d Mon. Oct.	4th Mon. Novem.
Georgia,............	3,000	1st Mon. Oct.	1st Mon. Nov. *bien.*
Florida,..............	1,500	1st Mon. Oct.	4th Mon. Nov. *do.*
Alabama,...........	2,500	1st Mon. Aug.	2d Mon. Nov. *do.*
Mississippi,.........	4,000	1st Mon. Oct	1st Mon. Nov. *do.*
Louisiana,..........	4,000	1st Mon. Nov.	3d Monday January.
Texas,..............	3,000	1st Mon. Aug.	In December. *bien.*
Arkansas,...........	1,800	1st Mon. Aug.	1st Mon. Nov.
Missouri,...........	2,500	1st Mon. Aug.	Last Mon. Dec. *bien.*
Tennessee,..........	3,000	1st Th. Aug.	1st Mon. Oct. *do.*
Kentucky,..........	2,500	1st Mon. Aug.	1st Mon. Dec. *do.*
Ohio,...............	1,800	2d Tu. Oct.	1st Mon. Jan. *do.*
Michigan,..........	1,000	Tu. af. 1 Mon Nv.	1st Wed. Jan. *do.*
Indiana, ...	1,500	2d Tu. Oct.	Th. a. 1 M. Jan. *do.*
Illinois,.............	1,500	Tu. af. 1st M. Nv.	2d Mon. Jan. *do*
Wisconsin,.........	1,250	Tu. af. 1st M. Nv.	1st Mon. January.
Iowa,...............	1,000	1st Mon. Oct.	2d Mon. Jan. *bien.*
Minnesota,.........	2,500	2d Tu. Oct.	
California,.........	6,000	Tu. af. 1st M. Sp.	1st Mon. January.

In some of the states, the times of holding elections and of the meeting of the legislatures, are alterable by law. Hence, the days above designated may sometimes be found to disagree with those mentioned in the constitutions of these states.

ministers received salaries of $9,000, and an *outfit* equal to one year's salary; and charges d' affaires received half as much. The salaries have been materially increased, but the outfits are no longer allowed. Consuls are numerous. Some of them receive salaries, others *fees* of specified amount for the several acts of service performed.

INDEX.

NOTES.

Page 26, § 4. Slavery, or serfdom in Russia, has recently been abolished by the Emperor.

P. 162, § 12. The franking privilege of Postmasters has been discontinued by act of Congress.

P. 274, § 12. Postage on letters throughout the United States and Territories is now 3 cents. Postage on Papers and Periodicals, also, and certain other Post Office regulations, have received some alterations. But as the Post Office laws are subject to frequent changes, and as these alterations cannot be conveniently made in the body of the work, the reader is referred to the acts of Congress on the subject.

From the New York Herald.

"It is refreshing to meet with a book in which the exact color of events is preserved, and the individuality of the author lost. Every page of the work teems with facts gathered from the daily life of the Revolution, and thus, without the intervention of modern speculation, we have brought before us not merely the actors in the great drama of the Revolution, but their actual thoughts, feelings, and emotions."

From the N. Y. Independent.

"There is not—we speak advisedly and deliberately—in the whole range of volumes and libraries upon American history, there is not to be found any *single* contribution toward that history of such value as that contained in these two volumes. The author has REPRODUCED, AS BY THE PHOTOGRAPHIC ART, THE VERY TIMES AND SCENES OF THE AMERICAN REVOLUTION AS THEY WERE TO THE MEN WHO MOVED IN THE MIDST OF THEM. The labor of such a work is immense; its value is incalculable: the reader will find in it much to amuse and instruct him, and a perfect mirror of the Revolutionary era."

From the London Saturday Review.

"The feeling with which most Englishmen will rise from the perusal of this work will be one of sorrowful but profound contempt for the government under which their ancestors flourished in the good old days. Nobody, except perhaps Washington, appears in very noble colors; but the only actors who make a thoroughly despicable figure are the English ministers and their favorite generals. It was not that they committed here and there an isolated mistake—the demon of blundering possessed them from the very first measure to the very last of the twenty years' struggle."

From the Philadelphia Bulletin.

"A really original work on our revolution is, of course, a surprise. The facts are all so well known that it would seem impossible to impart to them an air of novelty. But Mr. Frank Moore has presented a most fresh and vivid picture of the whole course of events, from the beginning of 1775 till the close of the war. The plan adopted has been to take the accounts of newspapers of the time. The skilful execution of this design has given us one of the most readable and impartial narratives of our struggle for independence that has ever been produced. The events seem to pass before the reader's immediate vision, and to be reported by him while the impression they produce on his mind is entirely fresh."

Valuable Books for Agents.

BAYARD TAYLOR'S WRITINGS,

In Ten Elegant Volumes, Price $1.50 Each.

"There is no romance to us quite equal to one of Bayard Taylor's books of travel Fact under his wonderful pen is more charming than fiction."—Hartford Republican.

1.	VIEWS A-FOOT; or, Europe seen with Knapsack and Staff. Illustrated. 12mo, cloth	$1 50
2.	ELDORADO; or, Adventures in the Path of Empire (Mexico and California). Illustrated. 12mo, cloth	1 50
3.	CENTRAL AFRICA; Life and Landscape from Cairo to the White Nile. Illustrated. 12mo, cloth	1 50
4.	LANDS OF THE SARACEN; or, Pictures of Palestine, Asia Minor, Sicily, and Spain. Illustrated. 12mo, cloth.	1 50
5.	NORTHERN TRAVEL; Summer and Winter Pictures of Sweden, Denmark, and Lapland. Illustrated. 12mo, cloth	1 50
6.	GREECE AND RUSSIA; with an Excursion to Crete. Illustrated. 12mo, cloth	1 50
7.	INDIA, CHINA, AND JAPAN. Illustrated. 12mo, cloth	1 50
8.	HOME AND ABROAD; A Sketch Book of Life, Scenery, and Men. Illustrated. 12mo, cloth	1 50
9.	HOME AND ABROAD—(Second Series). Illustrated. 12mo, cloth	1 50
10.	HANNAH THURSTON: A Story of American Life. 12mo, cloth	1 50

The Life and Letters of Washington Irving.

By PIERRE M. IRVING.

*** No epistolary or biographical collection in the English language, or perhaps in any other, is comparable with this in the variety, scope, and interest of the topics and the characters introduced. It may be described as, "The Autobiography of Washington Irving as [unconsciously] related in several hundred familiar letters to friends; with pen-pictures of the times in which he lived."

In order to meet the wishes of the large number of owners of Irving's Works who will require this work, as a companion to their sets, the price, now that the work is complete, is fixed at $1.50 per Volume. Complete in 4 volumes, cloth, extra, $6.

By special arrangement with Mr. Putnam we are able to supply our agents at his lowest prices.

DERBY & MILLER, Commission Booksellers,

New York.

Single Copies Mailed on Receipt of Price.

www.ingramcontent.com/pod-product-compliance
Lightning Source LLC
LaVergne TN
LVHW021124110826
845150LV00005B/943

* 9 7 8 1 4 2 5 5 5 1 2 8 5 *